D0699385

UNIVERSITY OF HOUSTON
MUSIC LIBRARY
106 FINE ARTS BLDG.
HOUSTON, TX 77204-4893

Machine Models of Music

Machine Models of Music

edited by Stephan M. Schwanauer and David A. Levitt

The MIT Press
Cambridge, Massachusetts
London, England

© 1993 Massachusetts Institute of Technology

All rights reserved. No part of this book may be reproduced in any form by any electronic or mechanical means (including photocopying, recording, or information storage and retrieval) without permission in writing from the publisher.

This book was set in Times Roman by Asco Trade Typesetting Ltd., Hong Kong, and was printed and bound in the United States of America.

Library of Congress Cataloging-in-Publication Data

Machine models of music / edited by Stephan M. Schwanauer and David A. Levitt.
   p. cm.
  Includes bibliographical references and index.
  ISBN 0-262-19319-1
  1. Artificial intelligence—Musical applications. I. Schwanauer, Stephan M.
II. Levitt, David A.
  ML74.3.M3 1993
  781.3′4—dc20   92-17179
                                              CIP
                                              MN

For Caroline Sophia Schwanauer, lest you forget.

Contents

Preface

Machine Models of Music has its origins in systematic efforts to model the mind's musical creative process. If it is possible to model thought, it should be possible as well to model creative thought and, in particular, musically creative thought. If there is a process, musically creative or generally creative or otherwise, duplicating the process should be possible with the precision and consistency of symbolic manipulation afforded to us by machine models of mind.

The questions remain. Do we understand music from a general theory of mind? Or do we start with the musical output of mind that allows us to test our models and expand from there to a more comprehensive model—first of musical creativity and then of creativity in general? Does our understanding of creativity in general help our modeling of music in an interactive way? When does creativity in music begin—with the patterned responses of elementary composition or with the departures from form of genius?

The editors of this book share the premise that the small steps required to model the computer solutions to specific musical problems with techniques learned from mathematics, music theory, and artificial intelligence will advance the understanding of musical and general creativity.

UNIVERSITY OF HOUSTON
MUSIC LIBRARY
106 FINE ARTS BLDG.
HOUSTON, TX 77204-4893

Introduction

Machine models of music date from the earliest computers. Ada Augusta—Countess of Lovelace, programmer of the first analytical engine and mistress of its inventor, Sir Charles Babbage—expressed her hopes for such models in 1843.

The operating mechanism [of the analytical engine] ... might act upon other things besides number, were objects found whose mutual fundamental relations could be expressed by those of the abstract science of operations and which should also be susceptible to the action of the operating notation and mechanism of the engine. Supposing, for instance, that the fundamental relations of pitched sounds in the science of harmony and of musical composition were susceptible of such expression and adaptations, the engine might compose elaborate and scientific pieces of music of any degree of complexity or extent.[1]

What did she mean? Did she think that the analytical engine's operating notation and mechanism could act upon musical relationships were they expressed according to a "science of operations"? Did she mean that the analytical engine, with a theory of the way music works, could *engineer* pieces of music in some objective scientific sense—tuning emotions, cloning styles, generating compositions for targeted audiences?

Ada's remarks suggest a science of music, in its cause and its effect, in which the machine can be the vehicle for developing and testing theories.

Machine models of music let us study musical phenomena in the controlled environment of the laboratory. Whether expressed as a specific model for creating a fragment of a composition or as a general model for how compositions evolve from each other, a machine model of music presents an explicit description of music subject to refutation or verification.

While descriptive and predictive theories of music since the Greeks have assumed internal methodological consistency, machines demand it and tirelessly expose systemic incoherencies. From Guido d'Arezzo's lookup chart for generating pitches from syllables (ca. 1000 A.D.) to current learning theories, models have applied variously mathematics, psychology, linquistics, and ad hoc grammars to encapsulate musical composition. Not until machine computing availability, however, could a music model demonstrate its procedural value over meaningfully large spans of musical time.

Music models easily rendered as machine implementations, for example, Samuel Pepys's *Musarithmica Mirafica* (ca. 1670), Wolfgang Amadeus Mozart's *Musikalisches Wuerfelspiel* (Musical Dice Game) [1791], and

Dietrich Winkel's Componium (1821) existed before the introduction of the von Neumann computer. It was the generally programmable machine, however, that began the main confluence of machines and music.

This anthology includes representative models from the beginnings of machine implementations of music to the present. (We apologize for any relevant work excluded for reasons of oversight or lack of sufficient space.) Historical patterns characterize the development of modeling techniques, and the sections of *Machine Models of Music* correspond to these historical patterns.

I   Foundations: Generate-and-Test Composition

The earliest implemented machine models of music required the filtering of randomly or pseudo-randomly generated notes. Markov chains of probabilities and, occasionally, heuristic constraints controlled various orders of note combinations in a generated composition. Modelers derived orders of combination probabilities from sampled music in a given style.

Lejaren Hiller and Leonard Isaacson's pioneering work on the ILLIAC computer (1955), for instance, generates results in four experiments for musical composition based on the pseudo-random generation of notes followed by the satisfaction of constraints for different styles of composition. Unlike Hiller and Isaacson, Frederick Brooks et al. (1958) do not employ heuristic constraints for a desired style of composition; however, their model does constrain its compositional output with Markov note combination probabilities gleaned from an earlier analytic pass. Stanley Gill's model (1963) introduces the same generate-and-test paradigm to nontonal music composition.

II   Foundations: Composition Parsing

With the establishment of machine models for algorithmic composition, modelers began to focus on the reverse process of algorithmic analysis. Such analysis or parsing had the goal of discovering the patterns and structure of extant musical literature. Not surprisingly, modelers began to appreciate the role of heuristics in avoiding search-related combinatorial explosions.

By 1967, Allen Forte had concluded that musical-analytical questions would eventually become questions of artificial intelligence; his model (1966) establishes a paradigm for the analysis of atonal music. Herbert Simon's pattern description language (1968) and Terry Winograd's systemic grammar (1968) mark the formal intersection of AI and music. Both models employ formalisms successfully applied to cognitive disciplines outside of music; both depart from the earlier combinatorially inefficient brute-force search techniques by directing their parsing of music with heuristics.

III AI and Music: Heuristic Composition

The heuristic approach led to success for composition models as well. By constraining the search space of initially generated notes with explicit musical production rules, modelers reduced the subsequent testing required for satisfactory results. The formal production rule system, as developed by Herbert Simon and Allen Newell, became the de facto framework for most models.

John Rothgeb's rule-based implementation (1968) of the bass-harmonization directives of the eighteenth-century theorists Johann David Heinichen and Michel de Saint-Lambert, for instance, departs from the probabilistic constraints of the Markov processes but still produces acceptable harmonizations in most cases. James Moorer's program (1972) generates chords and melodies mixing pseudo-random Markov methods with heuristics for balancing coherency against "boredom." And in Stephen Smoliar's model (1972), an early self-adjusting or "learning" system, heuristics help to debug incremental compositional passes.

IV AI and Music: Generative Grammars

Although ad hoc sets of heuristics generally contributed to models of music, whole generative grammars for music had still eluded modelers. By applying complete generative grammars similar to those developed for linguistics and limiting themselves to simple music, researchers hoped to attain similar successes in music.

For grammatical generality, Otto Laske (1974) seeks a new generative grammar as "an explication of musical competence" for a machine approach; and Gary Rader (1974) describes two successful stochastic grammars, for the generative modeling of rounds, with heuristic constraints for harmony and melody. Johan Sundberg and Bjorn Lindblom (1970, 1976), for example, link "levels of prominence" projected by transformational rules for metrically, harmonically, and melodically important events in a "hierarchical constituent structure" and generate Swedish nursery tunes that pass as human-composed originals. Fred Lerdahl and Ray Jackendoff (1983), on the other hand, translate aspects of an existing grammar, Heinrich Schenker's method for tonal analysis, into a transformational grammar later expounded upon in their treatise.

V AI and Music: Alternative Theories

While generative grammars had some success for the modeling of simple sentences in language and music, it soon became apparent that explicit grammaticality was not sufficient for realistic models of musical behavior. The Schenkerian Analytic method showed that there was a basis for musical grammaticality—that iterative transformations, into smaller and smaller sets of incrementally and structurally more important notes, could reduce surface detail in music to the linguistic equivalent of "deep structure." Natural language modelers began to observe, however, that we understand ungrammatical sentences and that a small set of primitive semantic constructs considerably aids the successful modeling of complicated concepts; similarly, music modelers began to rely less on strictly grammatical models of music and more on the semantic primitives of music.

James Meehan (1980), for example, notes the relative success over formal grammars of Roger Schank's semantic primitives for natural language models and suggests a similar shift in emphasis in music models. And Marvin Minsky (1981) introduces music to his "Society of Mind"; drawing on his stature as the cofounder of AI, Minsky observes that music can no longer remain satisfied with its status as an isolated field of study, that it must resolve its problems in the larger scientific context of theories of mind and its abilities to segment problems into component activities.

VI   AI and Music: Composition Tools

The limitations of abstracted generative grammars led researchers back to the music itself. They began to try to derive more specific nonrandom information directly from individual pieces in a given style. Unlike the probabilistic information used in Markov processes, this analysis sought explicit directives and constraints for the direct composition of music in a given style. Modeling specific musical problems gained sway over the generic modeling of composition.

Charles Ames (1981), for instance, abandons the conventional approach of purely "random selection and rigid determinism" by using the machine as a tool for evaluating a "repertory of alternatives," according to a protocol of tests of harmonic quality, voice leading, and so forth, to create an interactive composition alternately composed manually and automatically. Kemal Ebcioglu (1986), who makes no claims for the cognitive accuracy of his model, renders his model as an expert system with rules culled from Bach expressly for the regeneration of chorales in the original style. David Cope (1990) similarly derives explicit modeling information from specific compositions in a given style; he defines and implements compositional style largely as a composer's adjustments to "inherited material." Christopher Fry (1984) demonstrates the necessity for the "precision of specificity," the recognition that default settings assumed by some composers—their inherited material—may not be used by others who employ the same templates.

VII   AI and Music: New Directions

With the increasing success of models derived explicitly for fixed styles of composition, modelers have begun to consider whether such machine models for specific compositions fit into a larger context. Does Cope's "inherited material" approach work beyond compositions in a single style by the same composer? Can musical materials inherited by composers from other composers fit meaningfully into a machine model of music? Do individual compositions also derive from or evolve according to explicit rules generated or "learned" from a set of musical axioms?

David Levitt (1990) suggests that musical styles do derive or inherit explicitly useful information from one composer to the next, that explicit "knobs" exist that can transform one composer's piece into another's in the same style. Christopher Longuet-Higgins (1987) uses common-sense heuristics to choose the note spellings (sharp versus flat) in a melody and a simple model of rhythm transcription that accounts for gradual variations in tempo. Attempting a concise model of harmony and mind, Jamshed Bharucha (1987) explores the question of harmonic expectations in terms of a neural network that assumes only the constraints for notes clustered to form chords and chords clustered to form keys. In his learning machine for tonal composition, Stephan Schwanauer (1990) also traces from hypothesized first principles the information acquired during the composition of simple musical exercises and either propagated as "chunked" rules in success-based learning or reordered rule agendas in failure-based learning.

Note

1. Ada Augusta, *Scientific Memoirs, iii*, p. 694, as quoted by Hubert Howe and Michael Kassler, "Computers and Music," in *New Grove Dictionary of Music and Musicians* (*Volume 4*), (London: Macmillan Publishers Limited, 1980), p. 613.

I FOUNDATIONS: GENERATE-AND-TEST COMPOSITION

Hiller and Isaacson describe their technique for programming a system to compose music automatically. One result of the program, the *Illiac Suite*, remains one of the best-known compositions of Hiller's pioneering machine model of music.

The discussion outlines four compositional experiments: (1) monody, two-part and four-part writing with a limited set of rules for first-species counterpoint; (2) four-part first-species counterpoint; (3) experimental music, simple chromatic music; and (4) Markoff chain music.

Hiller and Isaacson describe two fundamental compositional methods for the successive experiments. For the first three experiments, rules constrain randomly generated notes to a desired style; for the fourth experiment, Markoff chains of probable note combinations constrain the compositional results.

The generation of the *Illiac Suite* consists of two steps: (1) generating pseudorandom notes and (2) screening the randomly generated notes with arithmetic tests representing compositional rules. The compositional rules include categories for melodic rules, harmonic rules, and combined rules that encode more complicated interactions; a "try again" technique helps for building the total composition.

If no randomly generated note satisfies the compositional rules, the program erases the entire composition to that point and begins the process again. Despite its lack of an adequate backtracking method, Hiller and Isaacson's program nevertheless represents a seminal machine model of music.

1 Musical Composition with a High-Speed Digital Computer

Lejaren Hiller and Leonard Isaacson

A relatively new application of automatic high-speed digital computers involves the treatment of nonnumerical information. The solution by computers of many complex scientific problems and the processing of business routines are becoming more widely accepted practices, but applications to more remote fields are still considered rather exotic enterprises. Programming computers to play games and to effect the machine translation of foreign languages such as Russian may be cited, however, as typical illustrations of this new trend.

Sooner or later the question was bound to arise as to whether digital computers might assume a useful role in the creative arts. Of the various arts, music can be singled out as a practical medium for this type of experimentation since, in music, meaning and coherence are achieved by more purely formal procedures than usually apply in either the graphic or literary arts. Moreover, the process of musical composition itself has been described by many writers as involving a series of choices of musical elements from an essentially limitless variety of musical raw materials. The act of composing, therefore, can be thought of as the extraction of order out of a chaotic environment, and it can be studied at least semi-quantitatively by applying certain general principles of information theory. In this theory, the information contained in a message is characterized as being directly dependent on the number of available choices. These choices usually involve the successive selection of discrete symbols such as letters of the alphabet or musical notes of a melody. In general, the more freedom we have to choose notes or intervals to build up a musical composition, the greater number of possible compositions we might be able to produce in the particular musical medium being utilized. Conversely, if the number of restrictions is great, the number of possible compositions is reduced. As an initial working premise, it is suggested that successful musical compositions as a general rule are either centrally placed between the extremes of order and disorder, and that stylistic differences depend to a considerable extent upon fluctuations relative to these two poles.

With these thoughts in mind, we started in September, 1955, an investigation of techniques to enable the ILLIAC, the computer located at the University of Illinois, to generate various characteristic species of music

Copyright 1958, *Journal of the Audio Engineering Society*, and reproduced by permission.

subject only to general instructions derived either from well-established logical rules of composition or from more arbitrary and experimental speculative procedures based upon a theoretical extension of traditional concepts of musical structure. This latter procedure was explored because the results of our experimentation soon led to the asking of fundamental questions about the essential nature of music and of how important musical concepts might be restated in mathematical terms suitable for translation into computer language. Computers are ideal instruments for a purely abstract and unbiased study of musical concepts since the control over the musical output is limited solely by the input instructions. Because of the way the problem is handled in the computer, factors not specifically accounted for in the input instructions are left entirely to chance.

By April, 1956, we were able to transcribe our results to that date into the first three movements of a suite for string quartet that we entitled the *Illiac Suite*, the choice of a string quartet medium being a practical solution to the problem of obtaining performance for the suite. In August, 1956, this part of the suite was played and recorded at a concert at the University of Illinois. In September, 1956, a first account of this work was given at the 11th National Meeting of the Association for Computing Machinery at Lost Angeles. Not long thereafter, a fourth and final movement was added to the suite to complete a chronological record of experiments carried out during the course of a year and a half. When the experimental results were transcribed as playable music, the movements of the suite were set up to correspond to the four principle sets of experiments described. Moreover, the musical content of each movement was obtained by means of unbiased sampling procedures so that the most representative sets of experimental results were included in the suite. In May, 1957, the score of the *Illiac Suite* was published by *New Music Edition*, New York, thus making the music generally available. This work, to our best knowledge, represents the most extensive investigation to date of methods for generating computer music. Other published experiments in this field relate to the generation of simple melodies only.[1,2,3]

Outline of Experiments

Our first objective was to demonstrate that technical musical concepts could be translated into computer language to produce musical output. We applied certain basic rules of strict counterpoint, a well-known compositional procedure, to set up an initial test situation. By doing so, we were able to proceed rapidly toward the computer generation of reasonably complex musical textures, while utilizing basically musical concepts to produce a computer output immediately recognizable as resulting from the application of these concepts.

It is perhaps desirable to digress momentarily to define strict counterpoint. Historically, a unique and significant development in Western music was the discovery of polyphony, the art of combining independent melodic lines into a closely interwoven musical texture. Polyphony apparently dates back to about 800 A.D. since, as far as we know, the civilizations of antiquity employed only homophonic music, excepting perhaps some elementary parallel octave writing. The great peak of purely contrapuntal writing occurred in the sixteenth century in the works of composers such as Josquin des Pres and Palestrina, who codified the trends of several previous centuries into a highly organized consonant style of writing. This compositional technique has since become a fundamental discipline in the teaching of music theory because it represents a highly logical abstraction of many basic problems of musical composition. If we follow the method of strict counterpoint, we may expect to simulate to a considerable extent the style of Palestrina and his contemporaries.

In strict counterpoint, we first produce a reference melody called the cantus firmus, and against this melody we then write other melodic lines in such a way that the whole cantus firmus setting conforms to a highly restrictive set of rules. The rules applied in our studies are shown in table 1.1 (under Experiment Two). These particular rules apply in the writing of first-species or note-against-note counterpoint.

In our first set of experiments, we selected a limited number of these rules to produce first cantus firmi alone, then two-voiced settings, and finally four-voiced settings. In this way, we progressed from monody to polyphony, meanwhile confining the music to a relatively simple texture of white notes only.

After completing this initial project, we decided to demonstrate that this style of writing could be adapted essentially entirely for programming into a computer. To this end, the remaining rules tabulated in table 1.1 were included in a new program from the computer, which eventually contained more than 1900 separate instructions. To provide additional interest to this second group of experiments, this program was written so that the rules could be added or removed at will. The music so produced was

Table 1.1
"Illiac Suite" Experiments Summarized

Experiment One: Monody, two-part and four-part writing
Only a limited selection of first species counterpoint rules for controlling the musical output.
  (a) Monody: *cantus firmi* 3 to 12 notes in length
  (b) Two-part *cantus firmus* settings
  (c) Four-part *cantus firmus* settings

Experiment Two: Four-part first species counterpoint
Counterpoint rules were added successively to random white-note music as follows:
  (a) Random white-note music
  (b) Skip-stepwise rule; no more than one successive repeat
  (c) Opening C chord; *cantus firmus* begins and ends on C; cadence on C; B-F tritone only in VII. chord; tritone resolves to C-E except leading into cadence
  (d) Octave range rule
  (e) Consonant harmonies only except for $^6_4$ chords
  (f) Dissonant melodic intervals (seconds, sevenths, tritones) forbidden
  (g) No parallel unisons, octaves, fifths
  (h) No parallel fourths; no $^6_4$ chords, no repeat of elimax in highest voice

Experiment Three: Experimental music
Rhythm, dynamics, playing instructions and simple chromatic writing.
  (a) Basic rhythm, dynamics and playing instructions code
  (b) Random chromatic music
  (c) Random chromatic music combined with modified rhythm, dynamics and playing instructions code
  (d) Chromatic music controlled by an octave range rule, a tritone resolution rule and a skip-stepwise rule
  (e) Controlled chromatic music combined with modified rhythm, dynamics and playing instructions code
  (f) Interval rows, tone rows and restricted tone rows

Experiment Four: "Markoff chain" music
  (a) Variation of zeroth-order harmonic probability function from complete tonal restriction to "average" distribution
  (b) Variation of zeroth-order harmonic probability function from random to "average" distribution
  (c) Zeroth-order harmonic and proximity probability functions and functions combined additively
  (d) First-order harmonic and proximity probability functions and functions combined additively
  (e) Zeroth-order harmonic and proximity functions on strong and weak beats, respectively, and vice-versa
  (f) First-order harmonic and proximity functions on strong and weak beats, respectively, and vice-versa
  (g) i^{th}-order harmonic function on strong beats, first-order proximity function on weak beats; extended cadence; simple closed form

arranged to start with random white-note music and then by the successive addition of counterpoint rules was forced to progress gradually to more and more cantus firmus settings. We thought this procedure would provide an example of how order or redundancy might be brought into a musical texture.

The second basic objective of our work was to generate music less imitative and restrictive in scope and, therefore, more illustrative of how computers might be utilized by contemporary composers. In this part of the project, we developed methods for generating rhythms, dynamics, and instructions for playing stringed instruments (arco, pizzicato, sul ponticello, etc.), this last being an elementary sort of orchestration index. In order to break away from the consonant style of strict counterpoint, we wrote a program for the generation of dissonant chromatic music. This chromatic style was first permitted to be completely random as far as note selection was concerned but was later restricted by the imposition of several simple but rather effective compositional devices. This work was concluded with a brief study of how a computer can be used to generate twelve-tone rows and similar materials.

The final set of experiments illustrates the third basic objective of our work, which was to use the computer as an experimental device to synthesize musical textures based upon mathematical models that we feel abstract certain essential elements of musical structure. Certain "transition probability functions" related to the harmonic series and to rules of melodic writing were devised for successive note selection that, to borrow the mathematician's terminology, permit the generation of what might be called Markoff chain music in the zeroth, first, and i^{th} order approximations. These probability functions are shown in table 1.2. Thus, the transition probabilities can be combined in various ways to produce melodic output in which the proportion and character of skips and stepwise motions, the proportion of consonant to dissonant intervals, and the resolution of dissonant to consonant textures, or vice versa, can be controlled rather easily. Moreover, these quantities can be made to apply simply to successive melodic intervals, or more complexly in relation to a "tonal center" or other distantly related reference point. This last procedure provides a technique for introducing tonality into a musical structure, since from the term tonality we infer a long-range relationship—a process requiring memory. This is accomplished in a computer by calculating weighted probabilities for intervals not between successive notes, but

Table 1.2
Functions for the Generation of "Markoff chain music" in Experiment 4

Interval	Stochastic variable, v_j	Harmonic function, x_j	Proximity function, y_j	Combined function, $z_j = x_j + y_j$
Unison	0	18	13	26
Octave	12	12	1	13
Fifth	7	11	6	17
Fourth	5	10	8	18
Major third	4	9	9	18
Minor sixth	8	8	5	13
Minor third	3	7	10	17
Major sixth	9	6	4	10
Major second	2	5	11	16
Minor seventh	10	4	3	7
Minor second	1	3	12	15
Major seventh	11	2	2	4
Tritone	6	1	7	8

$$\sum_{j=0}^{12} x_j = 91 \quad \sum_{j=0}^{12} y_j = 91 \quad \sum_{j=0}^{12} z_j = 182 = 2 \times 91$$

$$[x_j = x(v_j)] \, [y_j = y(v_j)]$$

rather between the note to be chosen and some earlier note arbitrarily selected as the reference point. This last set of experiments terminates with an example of a simple closed musical structure containing simple modulations and a movement toward a final cadence. The work included in the *Illiac Suite* is summarized in table 1.1.

Generation of Music in the ILLIAC

To prepare a set of musical instructions for the ILLIAC, we first indexed the notes of the musical scale in numerical sequence from low C upward. In the earliest and simplest experiments we utilized only the white notes, omitting sharps and flats, but in later experiments a chromatic scale of about two and one-half octaves was employed. Once this was done, the generation of music in a computer was resolved into two basic operations. In the first operation, the computer was instructed to propagate pseudo-random integers equated to notes of the musical scale and also to rhythms, dynamics, and other musical elements. These random integers, having values from zero to $n - 1$, were generated one by one by multiplying a random fraction by n, separating the resulting integer part as the usable random integer, and multiplying the residual fraction once again by n to produce yet another random integer for subsequent use. The sequence of random digits thus generated was the representation of the initial fraction in the base n number system.

Each random integer thus produced was then screened through a series of arithmetic tests representing various rules of composition and either accepted or rejected depending upon the rules in effect. If accepted, an integer was used to build up a "composition" and stored in the computer until the completed composition was ready to be printed. On the other hand, if a random integer was rejected, a new random integer was generated and examined. This process was repeated until a satisfactory note was found or until it became evident that no such note existed, in which case part or all of the composition thus far composed was automatically erased to allow a fresh start.

Setting up the rules in the computer depends upon the transmission of musical concepts into arithmetic operations. To illustrate how this is done, we have reproduced simplified block diagrams for two of our composition programs. In figure 1.1, for example, a condensed version of our routine for strict counterpoint is shown. It should be pointed out in connection with this diagram that it is convenient to group the rules of counterpoint shown in table 1.1 into three basic categories. The first category consists of "melodic rules" governing linear relationships between successive notes in a given melodic line. The second category consists of "harmonic rules" controlling vertical relationships between different melodic lines, while the last category is made up of what we may call "combined rules" that express more complicated interactions. In the block diagram, it is also shown that we used a "try again" technique for building the total composition, not only for efficiency but also because we felt this simulates more closely the normal processes in musical composition.

In figure 1.2 a block diagram for the main routine for the chromatic writing used in the third set of experiments is shown. This operates in principle much as does the code just described except that the musical rules are different. Three principle rules were applied here. The first was a chromatic jump-stepwise rule used in strict counterpoint. The second was a somewhat complex rule for resolving tritones (augmented fourths and diminished fifths) by either inward or outward chromatic progression,

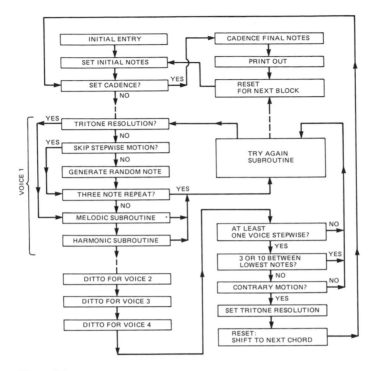

Figure 1.1
Experiment 2: Main routine for strict counterpoint.

while the last was an octave range rule that applied backward for each particular melodic line at least as far as twelve notes. The first page of the Illiac Suite appears in figure 1.3.

In order to program rhythms, we simply generated random binary numbers to simulate rhythms, permitting ones to represent "strikes" and zeros to represent holds or rests depending on the playing instructions produced separately by another part of this particular program. There are sixteen possible quarter-note rhythms in a common-time measure, or eight basic patterns in a ternary rhythm, the other basic metrical pattern. In generating rhythms, we permitted these binary numbers to be applied to all possible combinations of four voices and also for as many measures as desired, depending upon the rules in effect. The coding of simple rhythmic patterns of binary numbers is shown in table 1.3.

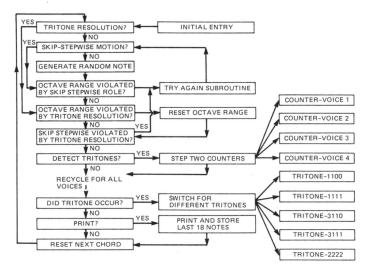

Figure 1.2
Main routine for chromatic music.

Discussion

Q. Has any attempt been made to use computer methods to analyze popular orchestrations to establish what a keen ear will tell, that certain combinations of chords are nonmusical?

A. I think you have asked two questions in one. Number one is, has this analysis been made? It has not been made by me. Also, would it be worthwhile making? I am not sure a computer would be required for this type of analysis of popular music. The properties of this type of music are quite well known already. The second question, which concerns whether certain chords are or are not musical, I think is not quite what you mean—whether a chord is musical or not depends on what styles you are willing to accept. In other words, this is purely a stylistic problem. It depends on what you define as musical. I will accept many chords that perhaps someone else won't. This is a long, involved, difficult question, involving musical esthetics rather than computer techniques. I will say that the analysis with the aid of computers of more complicated music than popular music certainly is an interesting possibility. We are well aware of the possibility of doing this, and as a matter of fact, this is one of our objectives in future work.

III. EXPERIMENT NO. 3

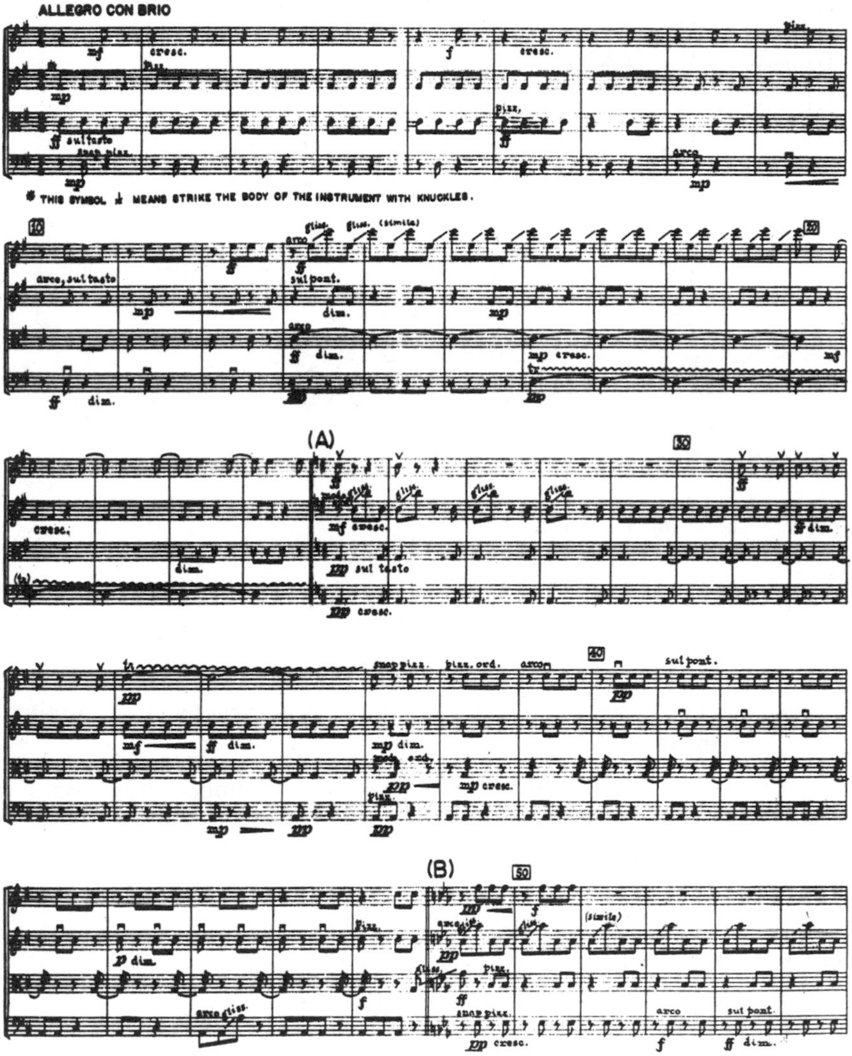

Figure 1.3
First page of Experiment 3 of the ILLIAC Suite. (Copyright 1957 by New Music Edition, and reproduced by permission.)

Table 1.3
Basic Rhythmic Scheme for $\frac{4}{8}$ meter

Decimal number	Binary number	Rhythms	
		Closed	Open

Brooks notes that deduction lends itself readily to computer modeling; induction, in the form of game playing, learning, theorem proving, etc., proves more elusive. Whereas inductive reasoning can be considered separately from deductive reasoning, Brooks observes that the generalization process need not be explicitly formulated as rules but in some form that can be processed deductively.

According to Brooks, the combination constraints of elements in a set, or musical composition, can be procedurally stated in three ways: (1) explicitly as a set of combination rules; (2) exhaustively as a complete enumeration of combinations; (3) probabilistically as a statement of the relative combinations of the elements.

Using Claude Shannon's approach for the "linguistic utterance" problem, Brooks elects the probabilistic method for using analytic results for synthetic purposes in musical composition. Markoff chains of probabilities from two- through eight-element note combinations thus form the basis for random or pseudo-random generation of compositions in a given style.

The sample for the Brooks experiment consists of thirty-seven hymn tune melodies Per hymn, a range of four octaves in the chromatic space and sixty-four rhythmic cells no smaller than an eighth note define the framework for the note digrams, trigrams, etc., to the eighth order.

Results of the experiment include over 600 synthesized hymns for various m-grams. While Brooks includes some of his results, he acknowledges that first- and second-order output results yield unacceptable hymns and that eighth-order results yield original sample members. Further work, he states, should develop better measures of the "structural complexity" of the sample content.

2 An Experiment in Musical Composition

F. P. Brooks, Jr., A. L. Hopkins, Jr., P. G. Neumann, and W. V. Wright

Human thought processes have at least two radically different components, often identified as induction and deduction. Digital computers are readily programmed to perform deductive reasoning, but their ability to draw generalizations from special cases is extremely limited. Many interesting computer experiments in game playing, learning, theorem proving, etc., have been aimed at discovering methods of simulating rudimentary inductive processes with a computing machine.[1,2]

There are often demands for inductive reasoning where the results of the generalization process do not need to be stated explicitly as rules but only need to be in a form suitable for subsequent deductive reasoning. This is the case whenever one attempts to synthesize structures of a certain class, as in the creation of synthetic linguistic utterances or synthetical musical compositions. The simplest way to perform such tasks is for a human to analyze some sample of the type of structure desired, draw up some explicit rules and constraints and allow the machine to operate deductively, although perhaps at random, in the synthesis of new structures. Some workers have performed computer-implemented musical composition in this manner.

It is of considerably more interest to attempt to synthesize musical compositions by having the machine inductively analyze a sample of acceptable compositions and, using its conclusions, deductively synthesize new but original compositions. Such an induction can be performed by determining the probabilities of note sequences. Several theoretical aspects of such a process deserve examination.

Theory of Analysis-Synthesis

The derivation of sufficient information from a sample to permit subsequent deductive synthesis of new and original members of the same class of structure depends not only upon the sophistication of the analysis but also upon the characteristics of the sample analyzed. Suppose one undertakes to analyze a small number of tunes and to use the results in a random process for synthesizing new tunes. One can anticipate three causes of difficulty that can be visualized with the aid of the diagram in figure 2.1.

Copyright 1957, *IRE Transactions on Electronic Computers*, and reproduced by permission.

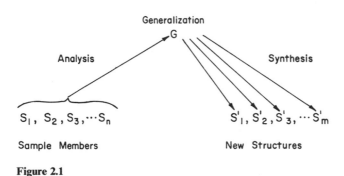

Figure 2.1

This diagram shows that the process of analysis of several members of a sample $S_1, S_2, \ldots, S_n$, belonging to some common class of structure, yields a generalization G. From the generalization, a synthesis is used to derive one or more new structures S', which one hopes will be of the same class as the original sample. The first difficulty is that overly naive analysis may yield a generalization so loose that the resulting S' does not belong to the same class of structure as the sample members. For example, synthetic note sequences may not belong to the class of acceptable melodies from which they were derived. The second difficulty is that the sample may be so small that no generalization may be drawn no matter how sophisticatedly an analysis is performed. The third difficulty is that the sample members may be so alike that when the generalization is formed, it is impossible to create a new structure of the same class that is not identical to one of the structures of the sample.

It appears worthwhile to perform some experiments to verify the existence of these three effects and to learn something about the basic nature of the analysis and synthesis process. For this purpose, two structure classes of interest are the class of linguistic utterances acceptable to human beings as meaningful and the class of musical compositions acceptable to human beings as something a human might have created. The synthetic linguistic utterance problem (which includes the well-known sonnet-writing problem) is more general, more interesting, and more difficult than the musical composition problem. The musical composition problem, interesting in its own right, also serves as a small-scale model of the linguistic utterance problem. For these reasons the experiments described herein were undertaken on the application of the analysis-synthesis process to the musical composition model.

The analysis of any structural system consists of the determination of a set of basic elements and the determination of the combinational relationships among the elements. For the present, we consider that only the second step is sufficiently difficult mechanically to be worth computer mechanization and sufficiently simple conceptually to permit computer mechanization.

The constraints of combination of an element set can be stated in several ways. The first of these is the *explicit* statement of rules as to what combinations may or may not occur. For example, the explicit method of representing linguistic constraints is illustrated by the schoolboy's grammar and spelling books. Here one finds several specific examples of a connective pattern grouped together with the generalization from these to a rule: "*i* before *e*, except after *c*, or when sounded as *a*, as in *neighbor* or *weigh*." From the set of rules on spelling, the explicit method extends to the formulation of rules for the combination of larger elements in formal grammar, syntax, and rhetoric. The expression of all the combinational constraints in a structure by such a method may grow quite complex with many levels of rules, subrules, exception systems, and specific exceptions. Examination of any complete grammar reveals this complexity at which the "*i* before *e*" example only hints.

A second approach is the *exhaustive* one in which all the combinational constraints are listed explicitly. A class can always be completely described by listing its members, and this description is often more useful, more revealing, and less confusing than any set of class characteristics. We do, in fact, learn the constraints of combination for *i* and *e* by long and painful use of spelling book and dictionary which list all the extant combinations. By this means, our description of constraints extends to *seize* and *financier* without any special treatment. While the exhaustive approach has the advantage of conceptual simplicity and guarantees a complete description of any structure, it is tedious and burdensome to apply to any system as complex as language or music.

Both the explicit and the exhaustive methods of constraint description are incomplete; they only indicate which combinations may occur without describing the relative frequency of occurrence. The mere statement that *t* and *e* can each follow an initial *p* is incomplete without the information that *pt-* is much less common than *pe-*. This leads to a third method of constraint description, the probabilistic statement.

The probabilistic description shares the advantages of the exhaustive description; it is simple in concept and uniform in application. Ease and certainty of determining combinational constraints in analysis and following them in synthesis are independent of the complexity or obscurity of the constraints themselves. For computer application these are cardinal virtues and the great magnitude of the task of formulating and applying such a description is a less important problem. The probabilistic method has a further advantage over other methods: the precision and validity of the description are little affected by the inclusion or exclusion of sample members beyond a sample of a certain size. With both the explicit and the exhaustive methods, the existence of an exception not included in the sample analyzed would compromise the accuracy of the analysis. Finally, although analyses for some purposes are required to yield an explicit statement of the common properties of a sample. this is not required for the analysis-synthesis process shown in figure 2.1.

For these reasons, the probabilistic method was chosen for the analysis-synthesis experiments described below. Analysis by probabilities of combinations may be taken to any order. One may use simple probabilities of occurrence, simple transitional probabilities in a sequential, linear structure, or conditional probabilities depending upon any number of preceding or adjacent elements.

The concept of probabilistic analysis as part of an analysis-synthesis procedure is by no means new. Shannon proposed a simple and elegant method of performing an implicit analysis and synthesis of linguistic utterances.[3] Pinkerton and F. and C. Altneave have used simple transitional probabilities for the analysis and synthesis of melodies.[4, 5]

The use of probabilistic descriptions of several orders, however, permits one to apply successively more sophisticated analytic procedures to a given sample in an attempt to determine the existence and behavior of the three hindering effects set forth earlier. This was the primary purpose of the experiments described below. It was an incidental but fervent hope that the sample selected would be sufficiently large and rich to permit some of the more sophisticated analysis-synthesis procedures to yield musical compositions that were both original and musically acceptable.

For structures that are linear or one-dimensional, higher-order transitional probabilities are known as *Markoff chains*, and we shall refer to their determination as a *Markoff analysis* and their use in the construction of new structures as a *Markoff synthesis*. Let us examine in more detail the analytic and synthetic methods used.

Method

A Markoff analysis of order m is the process of determining certain joint probabilities of the occurrences of elements in a sample. Thus, within the sample, a given sequence of $(m - 1)$ elements may be followed by any one of several elements. We wish to find the relative frequency of each of these elements after the given $(m - 1)$ element sequence. A sequence of m elements will be called an *m-gram*. A sample will ordinarily be made of several independent sequences of elements called *utterances*. A step in a Markoff synthesis of order m is performed by choosing an element to follow a given element sequence of length $(m - 1)$ in such a way that, if this process were to be repeated a large number of times, the relative frequencies of the chosen elements would match those found in the sample. Since it is desired that the synthesis be random within these restrictions, the choice is made according to the magnitude of a random or pseudorandom number. It is sufficient for this purpose, then, to construct for each element sequence of length $(m - 1)$, a table of cumulative probabilities which allots to each mth element a segment of the range of numbers between zero and one, the size of the segment being the desired relative frequency of the note. Then a random number between zero and one falls into the range allotted to an element with a probability equal to the relative frequency of the element. This procedure is, in effect, a mapping of a uniform distribution of random numbers into the nonuniform distribution of elements following a given sequence of $(m - 1)$ elements. Consider, for the sake of illustration, the following hypothetical fourth-order analysis and synthesis of musical text. Suppose that the occurrences of a three-note sequence C–E–G in the sample are as shown below:

C–E–G–A

C–E–G–A

C–E–G–C

C–E–G–E

C–E–G–E

C–E–G–G

C–E–G–G

C–E–G–G

C–E–G–G

C–E–G–G

The relative frequencies of notes following the sequence C–E–G are:

A2/10 = 0.2

C1/10 = 0.1

E2/10 = 0.2

G5/10 = 0.5

Synthesis may then be carried out by means of the table of cumulative probabilities which, for any argument, x, between zero and one, will determine the note to be selected. One of the several possible arrangements of such a table is:

A $0 \leq x < 0.2$

C $0.2 \leq x < 0.3$

E $0.3 \leq x < 0.5$

G $0.5 \leq x < 1.0$

If the random numbers x are uniformly distributed between zero and one, the probability of choosing a C is one tenth; and in the course of synthesis, the sequence C–E–G will be followed by C with expectation of occurrence of one tenth. Clearly, the conditional probabilities found by Markoff analysis can be approximated to any desired accuracy by this method.

The three hindering effects considered above can be understood more precisely in terms of the Markoff analysis and synthesis method. The first effect, overly naive analysis, will show itself when only low-order transition probabilities are used, so that the structure of the synthetic composition is insufficiently constrained. This permits the occurrence of note sequences that are not acceptable as legitimate musical structures.

The second effect, insufficient sample size, shows itself at some order m of analysis and synthesis where each distinct m-gram occurs only once. From that order upward, further analysis is useless since the higher-order transition probabilities are completely determined by the analysis to that point. There is no more information to be extracted from the sample. Therefore, if the synthesis at this order fails to yield acceptable and original utterances, nothing can be done, for the sample size is so small that further sophistication of the analysis yields no benefits.

The third effect, insufficient sample diversity, will always show itself before or at the same time as the second effect, and so is of much greater practical importance. Suppose the digrams occurring in the sample have been found, and a trigram analysis is performed yielding one distinct trigram for each distinct digram. Even though there may be many occurrences of each digram and thus of its associated trigrams, an utterance is completely specified by giving the initial digram, for it will specify a trigram whose final two elements uniquely specify another, etc. Further sophistication of the analysis is fruitless beyond this point; all the information in the sample has been extracted. If the analysis to this order is insufficient to yield acceptable and original utterances, nothing can be done; the sample is too redundant to yield more information.

From the theoretical examination of the analysis-synthesis problem, one can see that experiments using Markoff analysis and synthesis will yield any of three results. If too elementary or low-order analysis is used, the results will not resemble the sample members closely enough to be recognized as members of the same class. If too high an order of analysis is attempted for a given sample size and diversity, the synthesized results will degenerate; that is, they will duplicate sample members. Or, if the sample is sufficiently large and diverse, there will be some orders of analysis for which the results are original and still recognizable as members of the class.

For the sample of music selected, each of the three results was found for some order of the Markoff analysis-synthesis.

The Experiments

As indicated, both linguistic utterances and musical compositions are interesting structure classes upon which to perform experiments in Markoff analysis and synthesis; the musical structures were chosen because of the greater simplicity. The selection of music did introduce problems, however. Music has many dimensions, such as pitch, meter, rhythm, key, harmony, dynamics, and quality. Some selection must be made as to which to include as experimental variables and which to ignore. Since quality is not expressed in written music, and difference in key can be grossly compensated by transposition, these were not treated as variables. Harmony introduces a vertical as well as a horizontal structure to the text, and the need for simplicity dictated that the present experiments be confined to the horizontal structure of a single line. The metrical structure was fixed as an experimental variable by using a sample all of whose members had a fixed metrical structure.

After written music was chosen as the structure class to be used in the experiments, a sample was assembled. It consisted of thirty-seven common meter hymn tunes, a choice determined largely by the decision to work within one metrical structure. The common meter hymn is perhaps the most widely used rigid metrical structure and one of the simplest. In fact, several variants are found even within this structure, and the sample was confined to the most common single variant. The common meter hymn tune has the additional advantage of providing a fairly large collection of compositions from different composers and centuries of origin. The hymns in the sample all begin on the last beat of a four-beat measure, and none have any notes shorter than an eighth note.

Several analyses of the sample and syntheses of new hymn melodies were performed with a large-scale computer. The machine has random access storage of 250 sixteen-decimal digit numbers and separate magnetic drum storage of 4,000 numbers and 10,000 instructions. It is synchronous in operation with most instructions requiring 1.3 μsec.

For computer manipulation it was necessary to encode the notes as numbers. A range of four octaves in the chromatic scale was selected, and each tone was assigned a two-digit number. Different time values were represented by dividing the whole hymn into 64 eighth-note cells. The content of each cell was either a tone struck in that cell or one held over from the preceding cell. The even integers from 02 to 98 were used to represent a struck tone while the corresponding odd integers from 03 to 99 were used to represent a continued tone. Henceforth, each of the eighth-note cells will be referred to as a note regardless of whether it represents a struck or a held note. In order to provide a common basis for the analysis, each hymn was transposed upward to the nearest key of C.

As each storage location was capable of holding sixteen decimal digits and hence eight notes, it was convenient to carry out analyses up to the eighth order. As it turned out, this order was the one at which redundancy-caused degeneracy became noticeable.

The first step in the analysis was to isolate all of the eighth-note sequences or octograms occurring in the sample, and then sort them into numerical order.[6]

This sort placed all of the octograms in order within their initial heptagram, all heptagrams in order within their original hexagrams, and so on. Hence, the sorted sequences of lower orders were readily obtainable from the sorted octograms by shifting all the octograms the appropriate number of places to the right, thus eliminating the extraneous notes.

To complete the analysis, cumulative relative frequency tables of the type previously discussed were formed for each value of m for all of the $(m - 1)$-note sequences present in the sample. The relative frequency for each distinct m-gram was calculated directly from the sorted m-grams by counting the number of occurrences of the m-gram. This number; that is, the number of times the mth note followed the initial sequence of $(m - a)$ notes, was divided by the total number of occurrences of all m-grams having the same initial $(m - 1)$-note sequence, thus giving the relative frequency of the mth note with respect to that initial sequence. The entries in the table were calculated by accumulating the relative frequencies pertaining to the same $(m - 1)$-note sequence.

As an illustration of this procedure, consider the hypothetical sequence of sorted octograms shown in table 2.1. The resulting octogram table entries are the distinct octograms (denoted with an asterisk) and their associated cumulative probabilities, shown in the last column. The octogram 3637 2627 3233 2622 corresponds to the eight-note sequence $G\overline{G}C\overline{C}\overline{A}\overline{A}CD$, where a bar over a letter indicates that the note is held.

For each m the number of these tables was equal to the number of distinct $(m - 1)$-grams. Table 2.2 gives the total number of m-grams beginning with struck notes, held notes, and initial rests (00). With 64 octograms in each hymn, the 37 hymns yielded 2368 octograms. As seen from the table, only 1701 of these were distinct. Since the number of distinct heptagrams was 1531, there were exactly that many octogram tables having 1701 entries in all. The 4,000-word drum storage of the computer has sufficed for the storage of both the sorted distinct octograms and their associated cumulative density.

Table 2.1
Sorted Octograms, Illustrating the Formation of the Cumulative Probability Tables

1	2	3	4	5	6	7	8	Octo-gram Count	Hepta-gram Count	Relative Fre-quency	Cumula-tive Probability
				Cell							
36	37	26	27	32	33	26	22	1			
*36	37	26	27	32	33	26	22	2		2/8	2/8
36	37	26	27	32	33	26	27	1			
36	37	26	27	32	33	26	27	2			
36	37	26	27	32	33	26	27	3			
36	37	26	27	32	33	26	27	4			
*36	37	26	27	32	33	26	27	5		5/8	7/8
*36	37	26	27	32	33	26	28	1	8	1/8	8/8
36	37	26	27	32	33	32	33	1			
*36	37	26	27	32	33	32	33	2	2	2/2	2/2
*36	37	32	33	32	33	32	33	1	1	1/1	1/1
36	37	32	33	32	33	36	37	1			
*36	37	32	33	32	33	36	37	2		2/3	2/3
*36	37	32	33	32	33	36	42	1	3	1/3.	3/3

Table 2.2
Distinct M-gram Counts, Beginning with Several Different Notes

Initial Note		Order of Analysis m							
		1	2	3	4	5	6	7	8
12	G	1	3	15	25	57 –	66	99 –	102
13	$\overline{G}$	1	12	30	67 –	84	124 –	131	150
16	F	1	6	14	25	43 –	45	63 –	63
17	$\overline{F}$	1	8	14	32 –	33	51 –	51	66
18	E	1	6	19	32	74 –	83	131 –	131
19	$\overline{E}$	1	11	23	68 –	78	130 –	135	156
22	D	1	4	19	30	66 –	69	104 –	109
23	$\overline{D}$	1	12	21	57 –	64	102 –	106	126
26	C	1	6	18	28	65 –	71	111 –	112
27	$\overline{C}$	1	13	25	65 –	72	112 –	113	136
All Struck Notes		18	47	152	219	444 –	479	698 –	705
All Held Notes		18	110	182	428	–485	717 –	738	869
00 Initial Rest		1	5	10	28	45	70	95	127
Total Distinct m-Grams		37	162	344	675	974	1266	1531	1701

The Synthesis

Syntheses or orders one through eight were then accomplished by the process of Markoff synthesis discussed earlier, using eight-digit pseudo-random numbers obtained from an algorithm known to be nonrepetitive for the first $(10^8 + 1)/17$ numbers.[7] The first note of the hymn was found by entering the probability table for the m-grams whose first $(m - 1)$ notes were rests and choosing at random among these. The second note was selected by choosing an m-gram beginning with $(m - 2)$ rests followed by the first chosen note The procedure of choosing one m-gram, given the preceding $(m - 1)$ notes, was carried on in similar fashion until the 64 notes comprising one hymn had been generated. The encoding of initial rests preceding each hymn thus permitted the synthesis process to operate uniformly, even in starting.

The selection of notes was subject to certain externally applied constraints in addition to those implicit in the frequency tables of the analysis. These explicit constraints, however, were just those permitted by the selection of a sample of uniform metrical structures. In order to force the synthesis to stay within the selected metrical structure, a metric constraint was applied to certain critical notes. For example, the first note of each measure had to be struck rather than held. In addition, the two main phrases both had to end on a dotted half note; hence notes 28 through 32 and 60 through 64 were constrained to be held notes. Each note generated was examined and compared with the metric constraint, if any, for its position in the time basis. If the constraint was not met, the note was rejected and another note was generated by the next random number. If the constraint could not be met after fifteen trials, the hymn was discarded and a new one begun. Using these metrical constraints in this manner can be shown to be equivalent to determining and using separate note combination constraint tables for each time point or for subsets of the time points. The rigid metrical structure represented by the sample permitted the separation of metrical constraints from others with a considerable resultant simplification.

An additional constraint was added in the last measure of the hymn. Since after transposition all of the hymns in the sample ended in C above middle C, every generated hymn was required to end the same way. If, after fifteen trials, no final m-gram was chosen which led into a dotted half note C above middle C, the first 57 notes already generated were used to begin another synthesis. This device distorted the absolute size of the yield percentages (number of acceptable hymns completed over the number of starts). It did not, however, affect the faithfulness with which synthesized hymns obeyed all combination probabilities, nor should it have affected the relative sizes of the yield percentages as metric constraint or analysis order changed. Its use permitted the production of a significant number of acceptable tunes within a reasonable time.

Results and Conclusions

The synthesis just discussed was carried out with various metric constraints for all values of m from one to eight. The constraints were of three types. One of these types was based on even quarter notes throughout the hymn, except during the phrase ends. A second was based on a dotted rhythm in the second and sixth measures. Both of these constraints were varied by the introduction of optional rhythms. The third type was a skeletal constraint requiring only that the first and seventh cells in each measure contain struck notes and that the two main phrases end as usual, leaving the remaining rhythmic structure optional.

In all, over 600 complete hymns were synthesized in some 6000 starts. In cases where the yield was a very low percentage of the number started, more attempts were made than in cases where the yield was high. A summary of the results is shown in table 2.3, which gives the yield for each order m under the various constraints.

The yield is the percentage of the completed hymns out of the total number started. In particular, the similarities between the yields for orders four and five and between the yields for orders six and seven are worthy of

Table 2.3
Percentage of Attempts Yielding Acceptable Hymns

Metric Constraint	Order of Analysis m							
	1	2	3	4	5	6	7	8
Even Quarters	100	40	32	10.8	9.2	3	2.5	8.4
Quarters with Various Options		41	26	15	11	2		10
Dotted	100	13.5	5	2	1	0	0	0
Dotted with Various Options	100	17	4	1.5	0	0	0	0
Skeleton	100			5	4	3	2.4	10

comment since they resemble those between the distinct m-gram counts in table 2.2. As predicted from theoretical considerations, the transition from an odd m to the next higher (even) m introduces more implicit constraints than does going from an even m to the next higher (odd) m because of the basic quarter-note structure. Thus, while the $(2m - 2)$-gram and the $(2m - 1)$-gram extend across at most m quarter notes, the $(2m)$-gram and the $(2m + 1)$-gram each extend across at most $(m = 1)$ quarter notes. Examples of this phenomenon are shown in table 2.4, while the counts of m-grams in table 2.2, having similar extension properties, are joined with dashes.

The synthesis for $m = 1$ is random, obeying the (monogram) probability distribution. Any generated held note was interpreted as a continuation of the preceding struck note. A monogram hymn is given in example 2.1. The particular constraint used for this hymn is shown in table 2.5, along with constraints for the following examples. The low probability of accidentals (sharps and flats) in the sample, less than one per cent, resulted in the presence of only one accidental in example 1: the E flat for the forty-third and forty-fourth notes. Despite this, however, the hymn is not easy to sing and contains unnatural intervals.

The digram hymn given as example 2.2 exhibits several interesting irregularities. The constraint is a dotted constraint with two optional eighths (see table 2.5). Although the trigram G F G exists nowhere in the sample, this combination appears twice in the example as indicated by the brackets. In both cases, the optional cell contains the struck note F even though the held note $\bar{G}$ is much more likely to follow the G. Finally, nowhere in the sample does a G precede a C dotted half at the end of a phrase, nor does a second phrase begin on F after the first phrase ends on C. Indeed, none of these features are in keeping with the usual explicit rules of composition, but they are permitted by the inadequacy of the low order of the analysis-synthesis.

Table 2.4
Example of M-gram Extension Properties

m	Note Brought in	m-Gram, Begun with Struck Note	m-Gram, Begun with Held Note
4	E	$C\ \bar{C}\ D\ \bar{D}$	$\bar{C}\ D\ \bar{D}\ E$
5	E	$C\ \bar{C}\ D\ \bar{D}\ E$	$\bar{C}\ D\ \bar{D}\ E\ \bar{E}$
6	F	$C\ \bar{C}\ D\ \bar{D}\ E\ \bar{E}$	$\bar{C}\ D\ \bar{D}\ E\ \bar{E}\ F$

Table 2.5
Metric Constraints of Examples 1–5

	1	2	3	4	5	6	7	8	9	10	11	12	13	14	15	16	17	18	19	20	21	22	23	24	25	26	27	28	29	30	31	32
Ex. 1	X	—	X	—	O	X	X	X	—	X	X	—	X	X	X	—	X	X	X	X	X	X	X	X	X	X	X	—	—	—	—	—
Ex. 2	X	—	X	—	—	X	—	—	X	X	X	—	X	X	X	—	X	X	X	O	X	X	X	X	X	X	X	—	—	—	—	—
Ex. 3	X	—	X	—	—	X	—	—	X	O	X	—	X	X	X	—	X	X	X	—	X	O	X	X	X	X	X	—	—	—	—	—
Ex. 4	X	—	X	O	O	O	—	O	X	—	O	X	O	O	O	O	X	O	X	O	O	O	O	O	O	X	X	—	—	—	—	—
ℓ; t-32	X	O	X	O	O	O	—	O	X	O	X	O	X	X	X	X	X	O	X	O	O	O	O	O	O	O	X	—	—	—	—	—

Legend: X Struck Note   — Held Note   O Optional: Struck or Held

In the syntheses of orders 4 and 5, there is less roughness of the generated hymn. A tetragram hymn with no options in the metric constraint (table 2.5) is shown as example 2.3. The problem of excessive range is one which was introduced implicitly by the naive method of transposition. Most of the original hymns had melodic lines with a range of about an octave, but the transpositions spread these ranges away from the normal vocal range.

The tetragram hymn illustrates a subtle manifestation of the first synthesis hindering effect, one that was not anticipated. In syntheses or intermediate order, there were long ascending or descending sequences, each made up of a succession of the short ascents or descents so common in the sample. With higher-order procedures, these overlong sequences cannot occur.

In table 2.3 it is seen that the yield with $m = 7$ represents a minimum for each constraint and that the yield with $m = 6$ is quite near this minimum. A hexagram hymn generated with a basic quarter-note constraint is given in example 2.4. This hymn demonstrates the existence of the "middle ground," and nowhere contains more than four consecutive quarter notes of any hymn in the sample. It shows the long-descent effect to some degree.

The yield for $m = 8$ in table 2.3 is appreciably greater than the yield for $m = 7$. An examination of the octogram hymns reveals that a few of them are wholly identical with hymns in the sample. Several others have the entire first phrase of one hymn in the sample and the entire second phrase of another. An output hymn of order eight, which is an interesting composite of three hymns, is given as example 2.5. The constraint is of the skeletal type and is shown in table 2.5. The seven-note section in brackets is common to two hymns at the segments and permits the changing of hymns in midphrase in this otherwise degenerate case. In a large number of output hymns in which such segmentation occurs, the transition preserves the absolute time coordinate of the original hymn. This was not true for orders lower than the eighth. Hence, at the eighth order, the third synthesis-hindering effect originally predicted has appeared. The sample is so redundant that the synthesis will not yield original utterances when carried out beyond the eighth order.

The skeletal constraint managed to produce a greater yield than the quarter-note constraint for $m = 8$. On the lower orders of synthesis ($m = 4$ and 5), the former constraint permitted the hymn to run so astray that it could not meet a subsequent constraint. It hence produced fewer accept-

Example 2.1

able hymns than the quarter-note constraint. For $m = 8$, however, the implicit structures revealed by the octogram analysis were strong enough to keep the synthesis within the framework of the sample, thus producing mostly hymns of which each half was exactly like half of a sample hymn. This is a further result of degeneracy.

Extension

The present experiments have permitted the identification and characterization of the limiting effects that apply to any generalized analysis and synthesis, any induction and subsequent deduction. Since these processes will become more and more important in the application of computing machinery to more delicate and sophisticated tasks, it is desirable to explore their characteristics and properties more fully. It is important to develop some measure of structural complexity in terms of information content, to develop better ways of characterizing the extent of limitation imposed by constraints, and to develop methods of describing the information content of a sample which is sufficient to permit synthesis of original members of some structure class.

Ideally, the present experiments would not have been needed. One would have described the information content of the sample and the extent of the constraints of the musical structure, and from this one could have predicted that first- and second-order Markoff analysis-synthesis would have yielded sequences unacceptable as hymns and that eighth-order analysis-synthesis would have yielded sample members.

The wide discrepancy between the ideal situation and that which currently prevails emphasizes the large amount of theoretical and experimental work that will have to be done before the inductive-deductive processes are well enough understood for general use in computing machine applications.

Acknowledgment

The authors are indebted to their colleagues at the Harvard Computation Laboratory for advice and encouragement. Professors K. E. Iverson, R. C. Minnick, and A. G. Oettinger gave especially valuable assistance. We are also indebted to Professor H. H. Aiken for making available the laboratory facilities for this investigation.

Notes

1. C. E. Shannon, "Computers and automata," *Proc. IRE*, vol. 41, pp. 1234–1241; October, 1953.

2. A. G. Oettinger, "Programming a digital computer to learn," *Phil. Mag.*, vol. 7, pp. 1243–1263; December, 1952.

3. C. E. Shannon and W. Weaver, "The Mathematical Theory of Communication," Univ. of Illinois Press, Urbana, Ill., pp. 11–15; 1949.

4. R. C. Pinkerton, "Information theory and melody," *Sci. Amer.*, vol. 194, p. 77; February, 1956.

5. R. and C. Altneave, unpublished study described by H. Quastler, "London Symposium on Inforrnation Theory," Butterworth, Ltd., London, England, pp., 168–169; September, 1955.

6. The sort was performed by a general purpose digital sorting routine that counts digital occurrences in the $(n + 1)$ column while sorting on the nth column. Rapid and efficient in use

of storage, the routine sorts up to 2000 numbers without requiring any intermediate input or output. The authors are indebted to A. S. Goble III and J. Hines for the programming of the routine.

7. D. H. Lehmer, "Mathematical Methods in Large-Scale Computing Units," *Proceedings of a Second Symposium on Large-Scale Digital Calculating Machinery (1949)*, Harvard University Press, Cambridge, Mass; 1951.

Gill describes a program written to generate music in Schoenberg's twelve-tone style. Coded to produce serial music for the BBC broadcast "Machines like Men," the program produces musical output for three voices in 3/4 time.

The octave series of twelve degrees in a particular sequence, the tone row, forms the basis for Gill's generative algorithm. As dictated by the twelve-tone style, all occurrences of the tone row in his program's output occur as transpositions, inversions, retrogrades, or retrograde inversions of the original.

To constrain his program to "a pleasing pattern of activity in three voices," Gill translates a set of requirements into local rules for determining acceptable sequences as well as avoiding large leaps in the voices, parallel octaves, and so forth. No global rules exist for the determination of structure.

A "tree process" determines the program's approach to music generation. Gill's program maintains eight competitive versions of generated sequences and lets the best version "grow", when an active sequence, that is, the most recently grown branch, fails to satisfy the compositional constraints, the program backtracks to one of the other competitive branches.

Although Gill confesses to being "relatively unmoved" by its output, his program has merit as one of the earliest twelve-tone composing machine models of music. His compositional approach has significance as an alternative to other backtracking methods used in composition models at the time.

3 A Technique for the Composition of Music in a Computer

Stanley Gill

In response to an enquiry from the British Broadcasting Corporation, a program was written for the Pegasus computer to compose music of a particular limited type, and a short passage of the resulting music was broadcast during the program "Machines like Men" on the BBC on Thursday, August 30, 1962. Part of the composition, translated into conventional musical notation and arranged for violin, viola, and bassoon is reproduced in figure 3.1.

Much work has already been done on the subject of musical composition by computer, notable by Hiller and Isaacson (1959). The problem is basically that of producing a detailed score that obeys certain rigid rules, and possesses a number of other desirable features, but that is otherwise arbitrary. The general procedure is to set up a routine that will generate random compositions obeying as many as possible of the rigid rules and then by subsequent scanning to reject those that violate the remaining rules and to select the one having the most desirable features.

It is not practicable to generate entire pieces of music before operating the selection process because that would require far too much material to be scanned, so the work has to be done in stages. Ideally, no doubt, the best procedure would be first to select the thematic material, then a skeleton plan of the work, and then to fill in more and more detail until ultimately the whole composition is expressed in terms of individual notes, rather in the way that a human composer might proceed. This, however, would call for a very sophisticated computer program that would need to deal with suitable representations of incompletely specified passages of music. So far as the author is aware, no work on these lines has yet been published.

For the Pegasus program, the technique of serial composition was adopted, in which at any stage completely specified sequences exist from the beginning up to some point in the middle of the work, the remainder being so far uncomposed. Although many of the details of the program were somewhat arbitrary and not of lasting interest, the overall plan has novel features, which it is the purpose of this chapter to describe.

Copyright 1963, *The Computer Journal*, and reproduced by permission.

Figure 3.1
Part of the composition

The "Tree" Process

The main difficulty with the process of alternate random generation and selection is that the computer may lead itself into a dead end. That is to say, it may find itself in a situation where part of the composition has been completely defined and cannot be altered, but which, if the rules are followed, could only lead to a very unsatisfactory state of affairs in the succeeding stages. It is, therefore, desirable to have some means for allowing the computer to backtrack, so that it can reexamine alternative choices at an earlier point in the composition.

However, to do so brings further complications into the program. Under what conditions should the computer go back, how far back should it go, how should it be prevented from making the same mistake twice, and so on? An alternative technique was, therefore, used in the Pegasus program, and appeared to have certain merits.

The technique adopted was to retain at any moment not one but a small number (actually eight) of competitive versions of the partial composition, each completely specified up to a certain point, but not necessarily all the same length. The generation process took one of these partial compositions, or sequences, at random and extended it a short way according to the rules incorporated in the generating routine, making random choices where allowed. (In fact the extension was always by one quaver period or beat, although in principle the length of the extension could be varied from one step to another. Ideally perhaps one should try to keep constant the amount of *information* introduced by the random choices.) The result was then evaluated according to the remaining rules and criteria, and its value was compared to the values already found for the existing sequences. The sequence that had been chosen for extension was still retained in its unextended form as one of the candidates, so that at this point there was one extra sequence held in the machine. The weakest sequence was then rejected, and the whole process repeated.

The sequences were conveniently represented in the machine in the form of a tree, each sequence being linked backward in time from the end to the beginning. Although eight alternatives were kept these did not all have to be stored independently, because in practice their earlier parts were common, so that they could all be linked back to the same initial passage. When a new sequence was generated it did not have to be copied out completely; it was merely necessary to record a new quaver beat to be added to its "parent" sequence. (Owing to the particular arrangement of block transfers in Pegasus the actual linking procedure was more complicated than this, but the differences are unimportant.) The result of this procedure was that the composition grew like a tree, continually throwing out new branches which grew to a greater or lesser extent depending on how successful they were in meeting the criteria laid down for evaluating sequences. From time to time branches died out, and finally a sufficient length of a single trunk was formed that was taken as the final composition.

Figure 3.2 shows diagrammatically the first hundred steps in the development of a composition by this process. The order in which the various steps were taken is indicated by a serial number attached to each step. For example, the twentieth step extended by one quaver the sequence formed in the eighth step, thus forming a new sequence with a length of three quavers. At any moment, only some of the sequences shown here were actually in the machine. Eight of the nodes in this diagram were current at any one time (except at the very beginning of the process), that is, were available for extension. The only part of the tree existing at any moment

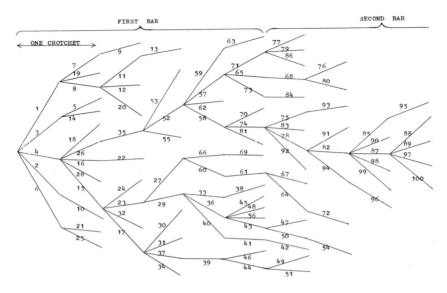

Figure 3.2
The first 100 steps

consisted of these nodes and all the branches leading to them from the starting point. Thus, at one stage the eight current trial sequences were those formed in steps 23, 27, 35, 39, 44, 50, and 52: the storage of these entailed also storing steps 4, 15, 17, 26, 29, 37, and 43. The final composition was actually made up of steps 4, 26, 35, 52, 58, 74, 82, 87, 97 ... (This example was derived from a diagnostic printout obtained during an actual run.)

Arrangement of the Process

The value of a sequnce relates to the characteristics of the whole of that sequence from the beginning of the piece. Therefore, when evaluating a sequence obtained by attaching one further beat to its parent, the value of the parent itself must be incorporated. To this are added several terms expressing the extent to which the new beat satisfies the criteria for good sequences. Some of these terms may be negative so that the new sequence may have a lower value than its parent.

It was felt desirable to add a further feature to the process to discourage more strongly a sequence that, although itself valuable, continually failed to produce successful offspring. To do this a distinction was made between the "intrinsic" value (calculated as described above) of a sequence, and a "comparative" value, which was the one actually used for comparing sequences. The comparative value of a new sequence was initially set equal to its intrinsic value, but every time that the sequence was used as the parent of a new sequence, its comparative value was reduced by a fixed amount. Thus sequences that had already been extended in a number of ways were discouraged so as to give more chance to the newcomers. When calculating the value of a new sequence it was the intrinsic value, not the comparative value, of the parent that was used. Unfortunately there was no time to make controlled experiments to determine the success of this device: it was put in purely as an article of faith.

To start the composition process, all eight trial sequences were initially set to the same state, representing a sentence of zero length. No other special arrangements had to be made before the generating and selecting cycle could be entered. However, an interesting problem arose in ensuring that the process would progress at a satisfactory rate. It is conceivable that if the criteria for evaluating sequences are too severe, the extended sequences or "offspring" will hardly ever succeed in ousting their parents, so that even after many hundreds of attempts the computer will not have gotten beyond the end of the first bar. Alternatively, if the criteria are too lax, almost any extension of a sequence will be accepted and the computer will very rapidly produce a long composition of poor quality.

The distinction between these two extremes lies in one single term contributing to the value of a sequence. The term is one which is contributed solely by the fact that the new sequence is one beat longer than its parent; in fact a single parameter is held in the machine to represent this term and is merely added into the value of every extended sequence. By decreasing this parameter the process is made more selective, and by increasing it the process is made to compose faster.

It was not easy to predict in advance the value of this parameter that would lead to a particular rate of composition, and, therefore, the parameter was adjusted by negative feedback so as to maintain a desirable rate. The observed rate was taken to be the mean rate of increase of the length of all eight trial sequences, smoothed over a period of the order of fifty program cycles. This was subtracted from a number set up on the hand keys, and the difference (suitably sealed) was used as the parameter controlling the composition rate. Thus the speed of composition could be controlled manually according to the amount of computer time available.

Composition Rules

The rules adopted for the Pegasus program were aimed at producing music in the style of Schoenberg (the so-called twelve-tone idiom). The music was (arbitrarily) for three voices in 3/4 time, and no notes shorter than a quaver were allowed. Roughly speaking, each voice was constrained to follow the twelve degrees of the octave in a particular sequence ("tone row"), although the length of each note and the appearance of rests was open to choice. The same series of twelve degrees was repeated throughout the work, although on each appearance it could be transposed up or down by any amount, reversed in sequence, and/or inverted (higher notes being replaced by lower and vice versa); also individual notes could be transposed up or down by complete octaves. Occasional deviations from this were allowed, by which a particular tone row could jump from one voice to another, but by and large the main element of choice lay in the disposition of notes and rests in time.

Some rather complicated evaluating criteria were supplied to endeavor to achieve a pleasing pattern of activity in the three voices. It was desired that each voice should rest for about a bar roughly once in every four or five bars, but preferably no two voices should be resting at the same time. It was also desired that, of the active voices, one should be moving fairly rapidly and another more slowly. These requirements were translated into suitable rules for calculating the value of a sequence, along with a few other terms designed to exercise some control over the length of skips (large changes of pitch) in each voice, avoidance of parallel octaves or near octaves, and so forth.

No serious attempt was made to produce an overall structure to the composition in this instance, since it was intended merely to be used as incidental music in a television program. In particular there was no legislation for producing a satisfactory ending, although there would seem to be no insuperable difficulty in introducing this by making the rules dependent on the point reached in the composition. In this instance Pegasus merely generated a bar or two beyond the required length, and the composition was trimmed to length later.

Storage within the Computer

The storage of the music itself required one computer word per quaver. Thus a complete bar took six Pegasus words, which could be accomodated comfortably within the standard Pegasus block of eight words, leaving two words for linking-information, and so forth. Owing to the characteristics of the Pegasus store the tree was constructed of complete blocks, and no provision was made for linking new sequences to a point in the middle of a bar. This meant that, if a parent sequence did not happen to end at the end of a bar, its last (incomplete) bar had to be copied in order to record the offspring.

The usual device of a "free list" (a simple linked chain of unused blocks) was used to keep track of available storage space. Each block in use contained a counter showing how many later blocks were linked to it, and when this count fell to zero and the block was no longer itself the last block of a trial sequence, the block was abandoned. This meant that it was returned to the free list, and the link-count in the block to which it had been linked was reduced by one (as a result of which this block might also be abandoned).

In addition to the tree comprising these blocks, a special "key block" was maintained for each of the eight trial sequences. Besides a link to the end of the branch representing the sequence, this block contained a fair amount of detailed information concerning the sequence. This included its intrinsic value, the form of the tone row being used by each voice, its current position in that row, and all information about the voice's recent activity required to enable a suitable evaluation of its future activity to be made.

Output

At the end of the composition process, the sequence with highest value was chosen, and the tree was scanned backwards starting from this branch; during this scan all the links were reversed so that the composition was now linked forward starting from the beginning. It was then possible for an output routine to work through the composition in the forward direction converting it to a suitable printed notation.

The output notation was constrained by the teleprinters available, and is illustrated in figure 3.3. Each voice is represented by one of three lines of

```
B.G£F£..0.E.  D.H£J.K.....  L.N.I.O.M£U.  O.O.H.O.J£O.
F£A£C£..F.A.  O.J.K£N...I.  D.E.M£N£H£..  J£..M...H.C.
O.O.O.O.G.L.  J...O.O.O.O.  O.O.O.K£G£..  M.K£M£H£K.F.


O.O.O.O.F...  G£A.F£K.A£..  ..G£L.J.O.O.  A.G.F...K£..
D£G...I.D...  E.F£G£O.G£F£  L.O.O.O.K...  I...N.K£J.H.
G£J.L.N.A.B.  C£B.A.....O.  H.F£D...O.O.  O.O.O.O.O.O.


H.C...L.G£I.  D.F£A£C£K£M.  N.M£G£H£O.J.  D£N...O.O.O.
M...J£....O.  O.O.O.O.O.O.  O.O.O.O.O.O.  H£H£C.D.E.O.
O.O.H£N.L.O.  J.G£F.G.F.D£  C£......A£F£  K.....I.O.O.


O.O.O.O.O.O.  O.I.D.F.O.A.  C£..E.F.N.H.  I.D.F£H£..O.
G...I.K£M£H.  J£M.N£..M£..  E...O.K...O.  O.O.J.A....
O.O.N£..L.O.  J.H.G.A£..D.  O.F£O.H.C...  L...N£I.O.O.
```

Figure 3.3
Output notation

print. The program was such that voices were only allowed a range of two octaves, and pitches were indicated by extending the usual nomenclature (A to G) to cover a second octave (i.e., up to N). Accidentals were indicated by a ♯ sign meaning a sharp (flats were unnecessary since in this style of music no distinction is made between A sharp and B flat). Inside the computer, pitches were represented as the number of semitones above a base pitch. For output, this number was multiplied by 7/12 and a suitable constant added. The integral part of the result gave the letter to be printed, and the size of the fractional part showed whether a sharp should be indicated. Two printed characters were allowed per quaver; the holding of a note for more than one quaver was indicated by a line of dots. Rests were indicated by the letter O.

Conclusion

Although the author was relatively unmoved by it, the resulting music appeared to have some small positive merit to a professional musician. However, this was not achieved without an appreciable amount of experimentation. The miscellaneous parameters appearing in the rules of composition seemed to affect the results in a rather erratic way, and it was not easy to adjust them all by trial and error in order to produce acceptable results. Perhaps, in any future work of this kind, the idea of negative feedback should be used to control some of these parameters as well as the rate of composition. However, there would obviously be a risk of instability if this were carried too far.

The composition of music by means of a computer introduces yet another new complication in the already turbulent world of modern music. The author's experience has convinced him that the computer program is hardly a substitute for the human composer but is rather a new (and somewhat devious) medium of expression. Composers have already faced the challenge of expressing their work in the form of, for example, schedules for the copying of sections of tape recordings through filters (in composing musique concrete), or punched tape to control electronic tone generators. Now they may also express themselves in the form of computer programs (or in the form of controlling parameters to be supplied to music-generating programs).

There is, however, one significant difference between composition by computing and by orthodox methods, namely, that when using a computer a composer is much further removed from the final result (i.e., the music) than he is when writing an ordinary score. Experience will no doubt help a great deal, but it is doubtful whether composers will ever be able to foresee very clearly the result of every choice that they make when feeding the computer.

Perhaps in the end we shall see musical composition taking the form of a cooperative venture between the human composer and the computer, with the computer supplying a number of plausible passages along lines suggested by the composer, who in turn selects the ones he wants and calls for further variations and ornamentations as required. This will, of course, call for suitable designed input and output devices. It would probably be done most effectively by means of a time-sharing program in a very powerful computer, sine it would require spasmodic bursts of rapid computing.

Acknowledgments

The author is indebted to the BBC for their help and encouragement in this project, and in particular to Mr. Lionel Salter who acted as musical adviser, translated and arranged the computer output, and also made valuable comments on this paper. He also wishes to thank Ferranti Limited for the use of Pegasus and for permission to publish this paper.

Reference

Hiller, L. A. and Isaacson, L. M. (1959). *Experimental Music*, New York: McGraw-Hill.

II FOUNDATIONS: COMPOSITION PARSING

Forte describes his score-reading program as part of an overall project to develop a "general structural description of atonal music." An analytic model for the parsing of musical scores, his program applies rules to determine sequence characteristics for music encoded in an input language.

Preprocessing in the program assigns each temporal unit of the analyzed composition to a "block" of musical representations. Association lists link relevant external data, for example, the clef, to each block. Sets of blocks form the analyzed units, the "segments," for a given composition. Forte defines "primary segments" as contiguous musical blocks delimited by musical rests. Parsing of the score scans primary segments for substrings in each intrumental part. Scans occur $(k(k + 1)/2) - k$ times for k substrings in a string of primary segments.

This model for analysis assumes a hierarchy of primary and secondary segments and of block and segmentation parsing. Forte suggests further research to interpret scores with additional levels in these hierarchies.

4 A Program for the Analytic Reading of Scores

Allen Forte

As is well known to most musicians, musical composition underwent a remarkable and revolutionary transformation during the years 1908–1922. This radical change was due almost entirely to the innovations of Arnold Schoenberg and his students, Anton Webern and Alban Berg. The term atonal, commonly used to describe the music of that time, is construed as "not exhibiting any of the structural characteristics of the music of traditional, triadic tonality." However inadequate the term may be, it does indicate that the structural determinants of this complex music are not well understood. The score-reading program described in this paper is part of a larger research project concerned with the development of a general structure description of atonal music.[1]

Certain basic decisions that led to the development of the score-reader are intimately connected with the goal of the larger project. The most fundamental of these decisions, the choice of atonal music as the object of research, brings with it the need for an extensive revision of outlook. For example, conventional descriptive language (melody, harmony, counterpoint) is not very useful, and may even be a significant hindrance to new formulations, since it is oriented toward older music. When, in addition, problems of structural analysis are stated in terms accessible to computer programming, many conventions are set aside and many familiar concepts are rejected after serious scrutiny. These considerations and others, led ultimately to the design of the basic tool described in this paper.

Approach to a Syntax-Based Method

The Score as a System of Graphic Signs

One can obtain information about a particular composition in a number of ways: for example, by reading statements made by the composer that purport to describe his composing techniques or his aesthetic views, or by asking a trained listener to supply a description of some kind. Such information is always incomplete, however, and does not provide an adequate base for an analytic system. The musical score, on the other hand, constitutes a complete system of graphic signs and, properly represented for computer input, may be analyzed by a program as a logical image of the

Copyright 1966, *Journal of Music Theory*, and reproduced by permission.

unfolding musical events that make up the composition. This, then, was the point of departure for the score reading program: the analysis of formal characteristics of sequences of graphic signs in the music input language discussed below.

Advantages of Automatic Data-Structuring

When the trained analyst examines a musical score, he associates certain signs with others to form units and makes a series of basic decisions about the temporal spans of such units and their internal structuring. In a metaphorical sense he places a template over the score to frame patterns and to show how they are interwoven to form local contexts.

Although the decisions the analyst makes may rest upon years of practical experience, they are often unsystematic and are subject to many influences that are not easily identified. Nevertheless, it is apparent that at least part of the time he makes decisions according to rules of some kind. This suggests the possibility that rules could be stated. Such rules, interpreted as algorithms and stated in a programming language, would yield a complete and precise structuring of the data presented by the score. A tool of this kind should produce results at least as good as those produced by the human analyst. It should not give provisional readings that require further hand-editing or interpretation of some kind. Indeed, it would be appropriate to aim for a reader which would produce results superior to those obtained by the human analyst. The use of the expression "human analyst" in this context is not intended to imply that the programmed score-reading process is based upon methods commonly used by human beings. The logical base of the program and its empirical relevance to a fundamental musical parameter, time, will become evident as we proceed.

The Music Representation

Before processing, scores are encoded by hand (keypunched) in a language designed by Stefan Bauer-Mengelberg in connection with a computer-implemented project to print scores automatically.[2] This representation has unique attributes.

1. It is isomorphic to standard music notation.

2. It is highly mnemonic, hence easy to learn.

3. The responsibilities of the encoder are minimal. The encoding rules are unambiguous and do not require the encoder to make arbitrary decisions.

```
WEBERN,FOUR PIECES FOR VIOLIN AND PIANO,OP.7 (1910)
2.101"VIOLIN,/I02"PIANO,/
101 "XG,"XT"$SEHR LANGSAM (E=CA 50)$ "XM2".4 VPP"L1,21-HJ,24-N4J,"AMIT "
$DAEMPFER"A / V"L1"G2,21HJ,24N4J "G2 / "XMR".4 21Q RQ "X3E1".2 RE1,"XVES
PRESS.$ VPP,30""Q1JL+1 / "XM2".4 102 "XG "XM2".4 RW / VPPP,24""H,26""H,3
0"=H"- / "XMR".4 RQ RQ (VPPP,16""E,18""E,22"=EL+1 17""EJ,19"=EJ,23"=EJ)
/ "XM2".4 "+ "XF "XM2".4 RW / 79""H,84""H"- / "XM3".4 RE VPPP"L1,69-EL+1
77""E V"L1"G2,76""Q.L+1 V"G2 / "XM2".4 101 "XG "XM2".4 V"L1,30""E 29""Q
V"L1 27""E / "XM3".4 V"G1,23-E 29""Q.L+1 V"G1 RE,"XVWEICH GEZOGEN$,"XVC
OL LEGNO$ VPPPSEMPRE,26"=EL+1"- / ((28-S"- 26"=S"- 28S"- 26SL+1"-)) ((28
SL+1"- 26S"- 28S"- 26S"-)) ((28S"- 26S"- 28S"- 26S"-)) / "XM2".4 102 "XG
"XM2".4 "X3Q2".2 V"L2,17""H2,19"=H2,23"=H2 V"L2,19""Q2J,21""Q2J,25""Q2J
/ "XM3".4 19Q,1Q,25Q 18""HJ,20""HJ,25-HJ / V"G2,18Q,20Q,25Q V"G2,18-QJ
,21-QJ,24""QJ 18Q1,21Q1,24Q1L+1 VPP,33""E1L+10,"XVAEUSSERST ZART$ / "XM2
".4 "+ "XF "XM2".4 V"L2,69-QL+1 V"L2,77""QJ / "XM3".4 77Q. V"G2 72-E 74"
"QJ V"G2 / 74L+1 RE VPPP,63"=Q.L+1 / "XM2".4 101 "XG "XM2".4 ((28-SL+1"-
26"=S"- 28S"- 26S"-)) ((28S"-,"XTRIT.$ 26S"- 28S"- 26SL+1"-)) / ((V"G1,
28-SL+1"- 26"=S"- 27""SL+1"-)) RS RE ((28S0 V"G1,27S0)) / RW // 102 "XG
"XM2".4 (V"G2,30""E10 24-E10 21""E10) V"G2,17""QJL+1"- / 17Q RQ RE VPPP,
18-Q,21-Q,23""Q RE // "+ "XF "XM2".4 63"=H / RQ2 VPP"G2,76-Q2L+1 V"G2,19
""Q2JL+1 / 19Q. RE //
```

Example 4.1

4. It is economical. The amount of code required for a complete representation is remarkably small. (See example 4.1.)

The representation uses a currently nonstandard character set of 64 graphics, but a set of equivalent codes is available when the expanded set cannot be obtained. Example 4.1 shows a listing made from punched cards that contain the complete code, in Bauer-Mengelberg's music representation, corresponding to a score one page in length.

The Programming Language

The high-level programming language SNOBOL3 designed by Farber, Griswold, and Polonsky, is used for the program.[3] This language handles free-form strings with facility and its generality renders it most appropriate for the kind of experimentation that necessarily accompanies a research project of this kind. The score-reader program itself consists mainly of a number of SNOBOL-encoded functions. A small amount of basic information is stored in lists, but the power of the program resides in the functions. These cope with any eventuality in the input string, including encoding errors.

Output Forms

The current output forms are provisional. An appropriate syntactic structure for output will be developed as the reading process is tested and refined. In all likelihood the output forms will ultimately employ a subset of the input language, since the results of an analysis could then be printed automatically in conventional notation.

In early phases of the processing, the forms of the output (intermediate) strings are constrained by the syntax of the input language because of the relation between input and output strings. The nature of that relation will be made clear in the next section, which begins with a summary of terms, symbols, abbreviations, and conventions used to describe the parsing process carried out by the score-reader.

Description of the Parsing System

Definitions of Terms

Character   One of the 48 standard characters in six bit mode. (The extra character ':' is used in the intermediate strings.)

Space-code   A sequence of characters in the input language which contributes to the specification of pitch.

Accidental-code   A sequence of characters in the input language which, like a space-code, contributes to the specification of pitch.

Pitch-code   A space-code followed by an accidental code.

Time-code   A sequence of characters in the input language that contains information needed to specify the duration of an event.

Element   A sequence of characters in the input language representing a distinct symbol in music notation. For example, '.' represents the dot of music notation.

String   A one-dimensional sequence of characters with markers to delimit beginning and end.

Data string   The original data before processing: a string in the input language.

Input string   A string of characters that is scanned to form a new string. The data string is the first input string.

Intermediate string   A string, constructed by the program from an input string, which represents an intermediate stage in a parsing operation.

Output string   A processed string.

Position-value   An integer in an intermediate or output string that specifies the temporal location of an element or sequence of elements.

Segment   A distinct unit within an output string, delimited by '(' on the left and ')' on the right.

Block   A distinct unit within a segment, delimited in the output string by 'P' on the left and a single blank on the right. The corresponding unit in the input language is delimited by blanks on left and right.

Parsing   The extraction, from an input string, of strings of segments representing classes of event-configurations in the score.

Terminal string   The final output form for a class of segments.

Definitions of Symbols

In the definitions that follow, A and B name arbitrary input, output, or intermediate strings, and the defined affixes denote relations between, or operations upon, pairs of such strings. Variables used as indices, such as I and J, do not imply anything about sequence, but merely indicate distinctness.

$A \to B$	A is replaced by B.
AB	Concatenation of A and B.
$A \cap B$	The set of segments shared by A and B.
$A \equiv B$	A has the same unordered contents as B.
$A \subset B$	A is a substring (proper or improper) of B.
$A \supset B$	A is a superstring (proper or improper) of B.

Abbreviations

1   Special Classes of Strings:

SG	Segment
PSGI	The string of primary segments for input.
PSGT	The terminal string of primary segments.
SSGI	The input string of secondary segments.
SSGT	The terminal string of secondary segments.
RSSGT	A replica of SSGT.
RPSGT	A replica of PSGT.

2   Programmed operations on strings:

BCP	Block-concatenation parsing operation.
SCP	Segment-concatenation parsing operation.

3 Grammatical categories for input, intermediate, or terminal strings.
(The abbreviations that follow will be used for describing the form of
strings according to conventions given below.)

AC	Accidental-code
TC	Time-code
SC	Space-code
PC	Pitch-class, represented by an integer in the set $(0, 1, 2, \ldots, 11)$. The expression pitch-class or the abbreviation PC (after Babbitt[4] is usually used in the sense pitch-class representative. The meaning is clear from the context.
PV	Position-value.
RC	Rest-code, indicating a silence.
♭	A (literal) blank.

Conventions

Names of strings, segments, blocks, functions, function arguments and
indices are in upercase alphabetic characters. Usage conforms to the conventions of the programming language:

Indices are separated from generic names by '.' *Literals* are enclosed
within single quotation marks. *Function* arguments are enclosed within
parentheses, and multiple arguments are separated by commas.

Examples:

A	String name A.
A.I	String name with (variable) index I.
A.'1'	String name A with index 1.
B(X, Y)	Function name B with arguments X and Y.

Grammatical categories listed under 3 of Abbreviations are used in this
chapter to specify the form of a string as follows: If X and Y are grammatical categories, then the expression X Y designates the result of writing, in
the input language, a representative of the grammatical category X followed immediately by a representative of Y, with no intervening space.
Occasionally literals are used where the string-form described contains
invariant items; for example, the expression

PV '$'

displays the form of a string consisting of some PV followed immediately
by the dollar sign.

Example 4.2
Copyright 1924 by Universal Edition and renewed 1952 by Anton Webern's Erben.
Reproduced by permission of Theodore Presser Company.

Preliminary Operations

For the remainder of the chapter a single composition will be used to illustrate the work done by the program. This is shown in example 4.2, together with the corresponding data string encoded in the input language.

Two basic operations are performed on the data string before the main parsing begins. (1) Since the encoding is basically a one-pass procedure, the encoder progressing from left to right across each system on the page for each instrumental part, the characters that belong to a particular instrument are distributed throughout the data string. The program therefore begins by scanning the data string to assemble the complete code-sequence for each instrument. It must deal with such situations as the following: In an orchestral score of 200 measures, the bass clarinet enters on the last beat of bar 75, plays a staccato thirty-second note, and is not heard from again during the remainder of the piece. In this and all such cases where the part is not present either at the beginning or the end of the score, the program

finds the complete instrumental part. (2) The second of the two preliminary operations establishes the basis for the derivation of complex event-
configurations by the application of the parsing rules. This consists of the
assignment of a position-value (PV) to each code, which implies a temporal
position. Two passes through the input string are required. On the first
pass, information relevant to the duration-value of time-codes is accumu-
lated. In particular, a normative or list value is assumed for each time-code.
This value is adjusted if a groupette occurs in the same bar. For example,
if the meter signature is 2/4, an eighth-note triplet is a groupette and
indicates three eighth notes in the normative time of two. For each bar a
number is computed that represents the product of all unique groupette
divisors. The number is 1 if there are no groupettes in any part in a
particular bar. On the second pass a duration-value is assigned to each
time-code by consulting the list of normative values and the number that
represents the product of the groupette divisors. The duration-value DV
for groupette members is then computed by the SNOBOL statement

$$DV = (VL * GP2) * (z / GP1)$$

where VL is the list value of the time-code, GP2 is the normative division
of that value, Z is the groupette product, and GP1 is the groupette divisor.
For all other time-codes in a bar that contains a groupette or groupettes,

$$DV = VL * Z$$

For bars in which groupettes do not occur, the list value is the duration-
value assigned.

Once the position-values have been assigned—and this is straightforward after the duration values have been computed—position value
becomes the main parameter in the parsing since it indicates temporal
position. The string can then be viewed as a succession of blocks within
segments, each block containing the total of codes associated with the
point in time represented by the position value. (To deal with codes that
are relevant to a block but exterior to it—for example, the code for the
current clef sign—the program maintains an association-list.) In this way
it is possible to refer to any moment in a composition and to relate any
event to any other event with respect to a time-continuum. In this regard,
as well as in many others, the analytic technique differs fundamentally
from those employed by researchers in other fields where the string is the
basic data structure. The structural linguists, for example, are not con-

cerned with time-placement in this extended sense, whereas for music research the temporal dimension is always primary.[5]

The association of each event and each event-configuration with a set of position-values has the additional advantage that order characteristics are preserved. Thus, complexities of rhythmic interaction can be deduced from the set of numbers attached to particular configurations. For example, collation functions can be written to search for categories that might be of special interest, such as all segments that have the same first position-value.

Parsing Rules: General Comments

For the description of the parsings, information falls conveniently into these categories:

1. Names of the strings being parsed.

2. An informal description of the parsing technique and a characterization of the event-configurations that it extracts from the input string.

3. A symbolic expression representing the form of the segment in the output string.

4. A formal statement of the parsing rules.

5. A description of the deletion conditions for segments in the output string.

6. Illustrations of program-generated output, music notation, and scanning strategy.

Parsing Rules: Primary Segments

Underlying any segmentation or parsing process, such as the one executed by the score-reader, are certain assumptions regarding the discreteness of events. What conditions determine a unit? Which classes of signs serve as disconnectives? How can one speak with precision of components of larger event-configurations? Questions such as these are in the foreground of the description of parsing rules, and an effort is made to state the answers clearly.

For the first parsing of the input string, each substring representing a complete instrumental part is scanned to extract all primary segments. A primary segment is a continuous unit delimited by the graphic sign denoting silence: a rest in musical notation, RC in the input language. It begins with a PC that has been preceded by a rest (or by an understood (logical) rest if the pitch is the first in a part), contains no internal rests, and ends with a rest. Thus, it is set off from other substrings and is regarded provisionally as a disjunct sequence in a one-dimensional environment. The scan for primary segments in an instrumental part terminates when the input language code '//,' (double bar) is encountered.

In the input language a primary segment has the form

RC ♭ SC AC TC SG ♮ RC ♭   (1)

With respect to sequence in the string, the block SC AC TC is always next. Since there may be more than one RC in a substring of the input string without an intervening SC AC TC—for example,

RC RC RC SC AC TC SG RC RC RC

the first RC in the form given at (1) is always the rightmost with respect to SC, while the second RC shown in the form is always the leftmost with respect to SG.

After parsing, the form of the segment (now in an intermediate string) is

'*' PC 'KA' PV '$' ... 'KZ' PV '$'   (2)

where 'KA' and 'KZ' designate attack and release, respectively, and refer to the position-value that follows. In the case of 'KA', the position-value always refers to the first (attack) PC. In the case of 'KZ', the position-value refers either to the terminal delimiter (some RC) or, if the next code is '//', to some code that is an understood (logical) RC. An example of the latter can be seen in the viola part in example 4.2.

The form given in (2) above is the input form for a primary segment. The terminal form is

'(' 'P' PV '*' PC '*' PC ... '*' PC ')'   (3)

The transformation from input form to terminal form involves two kinds of change deletions and deletions with replacements. Characters deleted (without replacement) are 'A', 'KZ', ♭, PV (when preceded by 'KZ'), groupette definers, and meter signatures. Each pitch-code is replaced by an integer representing a pitch-class PC. The appropriate mapping is executed by a function PCM, that utilizes modulo 7 arithmetic. A number of contextual details require attention here. First, if the instrument is a transposing instrument, the appropriate modulo 12 arithmetic must be

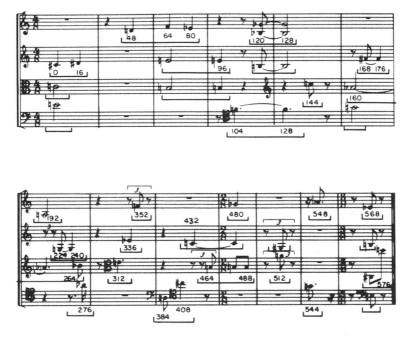

Example 4.3

performed. Second, a scan is made for space-codes that have implicit accidentals, under two familiar conventions of notation, and those accidentals are inserted. Third, the current clef sign must be made available for each pitch-class mapping. Example 4.3 shows the complete string PSGT, together with the music notation, where primary segments (31 in all) are indicated by brackets.

Parsing Rules: Secondary Segments

The string of primary segments is made up of substrings, one for each instrumental part. Every (unordered) pair of these substrings is scanned for secondary segments. This is the first and most important step in the progression from the one-dimensional primary segments to a representation of the analyzed two-dimensional score. At this stage the program is concerned with the ways in which events represented by pairs of primary segments interact in local contexts. Indeed, one of the important consequences of the parsing for secondary segments is to show how the primary segments are affected by motion in other parts of the context. The following combinatory situation provides the basis for a formal description of the parsing.

Given three temporal relations: less than (before), equal to (coinciding), and greater than (after), together with the position-values of the attack (A) and release (R) for each of two primary segments SG.I and SG.J (where SG.I $\subseteq$ PSGT.I and SG.J $\subseteq$ PSGT.J), there are $(3^2 + 4) - 1$ ways in which the two segments interact, excluding the noncontiguous case. Example 4.4 shows the 11 possible interactions reduced to 6 classes by virtue of the symmetry of the defined relations. Each class is assigned a mnemonic name in a quasi-Polish notation; for example, EAR means that the relation equal

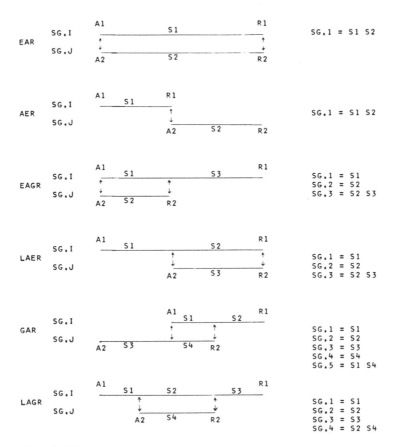

Example 4.4

to obtains between both As and both Rs, while LAER means that the first A is less than (before) the second, while the two Rs coincide. The same name is applied to the second (symmetrical) relation in each class and a subscript is used to distinguish the two.

As indicated above, a given pair of primary segments is scanned (left to right) for A1, R1, A2, and R2. Example 4.5 is a graph of the decision structure that is traversed to determine the particular relation between the pair.

When the relation has been determined, one of four functions is called and secondary segments are formed as shown by the arrows in example 4.4. Observe that the basis of segmentation is attack and release operating reciprocally on the constituent primary segments. Since the disconnectives (attack and release markers) of the original primary segments now themselves point to other disconnectives, it is evident that the parsing is recursive in this limited respect.

The scanning strategy is straightforward: if k is the number of substrings in the string of primary segments, each substring representing an instrumental part, then the number of scans required to find all secondary segments is the same as the number of distinct pairs in the unordered crossproduct of a set of k elements, $(k(k + 1)/2) - k$.

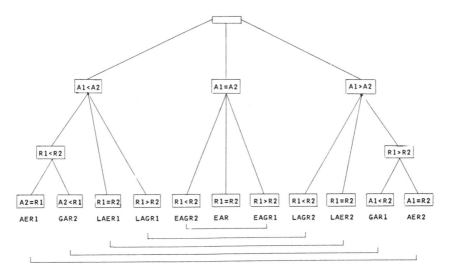

Example 4.5

```
SSGT
(P0#0#1 P16#3 )(P0#1#4 P16#3 )(P0#0#4 )(P48#2 )(P64#5 P80#3 )(P64#4 )(P6
4#4#5 P80#3 )(P64#11 )(P64#5#11 P80#3 )(P64#4#11 P96#4#11 )(P64#4 P96#4
P104#5 )(P64#11 P96#11 P104#5 )(P96#4 )(P96#11 )(P104#5 )(P104#5 P128#5
P144#0 )(P120#6#10#11- P128#6#10#11 )(P120#6#10 P128#6#10 P144#0 )(P120#6
#10 P128#6#10 P160#8 P192#8 P264#10 )(P120#6#10 P128#5#6#10 )(P120#6#10
P128#6#10 P160#7 )(P120#11 P128#11 P144#0 )(P120#11 P128#11 P160#8 P192#
8 P264#10 )(P120#11 P128#5#11 )(P120#11 P128#11 P160#7 )(P128#5 )(P160#8
)(P160#7 P192#9 )(P160#8 P168#6 P176#6 )(P160#8 P192#8 )(P160#7 P168#6
P176#6 )(P160#7#8 )(P160#8 P192#8 P264#10 P276#8 )(P168#6 P176#6 P192#9
)(P192#9 P224#7 P240#7 )(P192#8 P264#10 )(P192#8#9 P264#10 )(P192#9 P276
#8 )(P224#7 P240#7 P264#10 )(P224#7 P240#7 P276#8 )(P264#10 )(P312#4 P35
2#5 )(P312#4 P336#3 )(P312#4 P384#2 P480#1 )(P336#3 P352#5 )(P336#3 P384
#2 P408#1 )(P384#2 P408#1 P432#0 )(P432#0 )(P464#11 )(P464#11 P480#0#11
P488#11 )(P480#0 )(P480#0#6 )(P480#11 P488#11 )(P480#6#11 P488#11 )(P512
#8#9 )(P544#7 P548#8 )(P568#3#11 )(P568#1 )(P568#1#3 )(P568#3#4 )(P568#1
#11 )(P568#4#11 )(P568#1#4 )(P576#2 )
```

Example 4.6

Each scan of a pair of strings of primary segments yields a string (possibly null) of secondary segments. The name of this string is SSGI.J K, where the variable index J is the index of one member of the pair of primary segments, and K is the index of the other. Example 4.6 shows the complete output string SSGT.

The scanning strategy for the deletion of duplicate secondary segments utilizes the fact that for any pair of strings of secondary segments SSGI. J and SSGI. K, where J and K represent catenated indices of primary segments as described above, duplicate segments can occur only if one element of the compound index J is the same as an element of the compound index K. This strategy greatly reduces the number of scans required and permits the operation to be controlled by a nonarithmetic program segment in a fashion idiomatic to SNOBOL. The program segment that performs this operation is shown in example 4.7.

Parsing Rules: BCP(SSGT)

A secondary segment results from the interaction in time of the attacks and releases of two primary segments. Possibly a particular secondary segment is a constituent of a still larger event-configuration; that is, it may be associated with other events in the local context. The parsing function BCP (for block-concatenation parsing) finds such situations and derives a new class of segments.

BCP operates on SSGT and its replica RSSGT as follows. Each block in each segment of SSGT and RSSGT has the form

‘P’ PV ‘*’ PC.‘1’ ‘*’ PC.‘2’ ‘*’ ... PC.N ♭

```
VV    SNM    ꭗN1/'1'ꭗ N2/'1'ꭗ ',' =     /F(WRTE)
      HNM = SNM
V0    HNM    N1 ꭗN3/'1'ꭗ ',' =    /S(V1)
      HNM    N2 ꭗN3/'1'ꭗ ',' =    /S(V2)
      HNM    ꭗN3/'1'ꭗ N2 ',' =    /F(V4)S(V3)
V1    $('SG' N1 N3) = DP2($('SG' N1 N2),$('SG' N1 N3))    /(V0)
V2    $('SG' N2 N3) = DP2($('SG' N1 N2),$('SG' N2 N3))    /(V0)
V3    $('SG' N3 N2) = DP2($('SG' N1 N2),$('SG' N3 N2))    /(V0)
V4    $('SG' N1 N2) = DP2(PSGT,$('SG' N1 N2))
      SSGT = SSGT $('SG' N1 N2)    /(VV)
```

Example 4.7

For every block B.I in a segment SG.I (SG.I $\subseteq$ SSGT), with PV.I, and every block B.J in S $\sim$ .J (SG.J $\subseteq$ RSSGT), with PV.J, if PV.I = PV.J then B.I $\rightarrow$ B.I B.J.

In this way a secondary segment SG.I is expanded by the infixing of all blocks in all other segments that intersect in time with some block in SG. I. Two additional aspects should be noted. First, concatenation is followed by the deletion of duplicate PCs. Second, the process is not recursive, in the sense that only the original blocks in a segment are operated upon; concatenation does not extend to blocks infixed during the parsing.

Possibly some secondary segment does not contain any PV block that intersects with the PV of some other block in the way defined. In this case the segment is complete in itself and does not belong to a larger context. Such residual segments are deleted when the execution of the function has been completed. It is also possible that a segment in the parsed string will have one or more duplicates. These internal duplicates are deleted after BCP has been executed.

Because the concatenation does not take into consideration the order of position-values or the order of pitch-class representatives, it is necessary to call collation functions within BCP. Pitch-classes are placed in ascending order at present. However, the set of indices representing original ordering could be retained, wherever that ordering is significant. Example 4.8 shows the output string BCP(SSGT) and the corresponding notation, with segments delimited by frames.

Parsing Rules: BCP(PSGT)

When BCP operates on PSGT, the result is a string each component of which is anchored to a position-value that occurs in two or more instruments. It should be remarked here that the 'instrumental part' is merely a device. Once the position-values have been assigned, the location of an

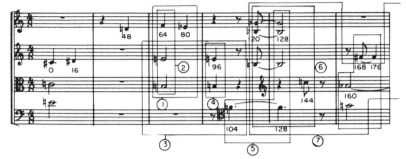

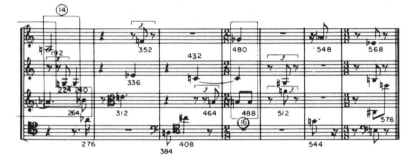

BCP(SSGT)
(P64"4"5"11 P80"3)(P64"4"5"11)(P64"4"5"11 P96"4"11 P104"5)(P96"4"11)
(P104"5 P128"5"6"10"11 P144"0)(P120"6"10"11 P128"5"6"10"11 P144"0)(P12
0"6"10"11 P128"5"6"10"11 P160"7"8 P192"8"9 P264"10)(P120"6"10"11 P128"5
"6"10"11 P160"7"8)(P128"5"6"10"11)(P160"7"8 P192"8"9)(P160"7"8 P168"6
 P176"6)(P160"7"8 P192"8"9 P264"10 P276"8)(P168"6 P176"6 P192"8"9)(P1
92"8"9 P224"7 P240"7)(P192"8"9 P276"8)(P480"0"6"11 P488"11)

Example 4.8

element within a particular part is of no fundamental concern. The reading thus is independent of the notions of "part," "voice," "voice-leading," and other interpretive formulations that belong to a higher analytic level.

Deletion conditions for BCP(PSGT) are as follows. Residual primary segments are deleted. Internal duplicates are deleted. Since the rules for BCP when applied to PSGT may form duplicates of secondary segments, a scan must be made to delete such duplicates. Example 4.9 shows the complete output string BCP(PSGT) and corresponding notation.

Parsing Rules: SCP(SSGT)

The content of segments derived by BCP is limited with respect to span since the concatenation is restricted to units of block form. The function SCP (for segment-concatenation parsing) may extend to event-configurations of greater span since it defines the segment as the concatenation unit. For every PV.I in SG.I (SG.I $\subseteq$ SSGT) and every PV.J in SG.J (SG.J $\subseteq$ RSSGT), if PV.I = PV.J then SG.I $\rightarrow$ SG.I SG.J.

As remarked above, SCP finds event-configurations that are connected by (at least) one common PV. The SCP-derived segments thus represent continuity over longer spans, even though disjunctions may occur in some subparts of the musical context. As a consequence, SCP yields very intricate and subtle readings.

The scanning process for SCP differs significantly from the scan for BCP. In the case of BCP the scan for a new segment always begins at the head of the string. This is not true for SCP. There the first PV in each segment is a potential prime generator of a segment in SCP. If a particular first PV has not previously been a prime generator, it is qualified to become one. Let us assume that some first PV, PV.'1', is a prime generator. The scan to find segments for concatenation begins with the first segment to the right of SG.'1', SG.'2' in RSSGT. If the scan finds a match for PV.'1' in SG.'2', the entire segment is concatenated with SG.'1' after duplicate blocks have been removed. The PV.'2' in SG.'1' then becomes a (secondary) generator; the scan begins again with the first segment to the right of SG.'2' in RSSGT, and so on. Possibly the segment concatenated contains position-values that are not in the original SG.'1'. Such position-values become secondary generators. In this way links are formed to other segments and the new segment in SCP is expanded until there are no position-values for which a complete scan has not been made. Thus, unlike BCP, the scan for SCP is ordered, in the sense that there is more tracing and in the sense that

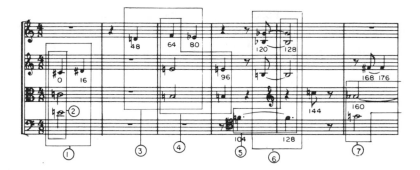

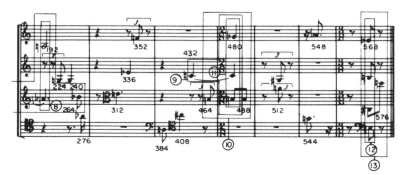

BCP(PSGT)
(P0ᵃ0ᵃ1ᵃ4 P16ᵃ3)(P0ᵃ0ᵃ1ᵃ4)(P48ᵃ2 P64ᵃ4ᵃ5ᵃ11 P80ᵃ3)(P64ᵃ4ᵃ5ᵃ11 P96ᵃ4ᵃ1
1)(P104ᵃ5 P128ᵃ5ᵃ6ᵃ10ᵃ11)(P120ᵃ6ᵃ10ᵃ11 P128ᵃ5ᵃ6ᵃ10ᵃ11)(P160ᵃ7ᵃ8 P192ᵃ
8ᵃ9 P264ᵃ10)(P192ᵃ8ᵃ9)(P432ᵃ0 P480ᵃ0ᵃ6ᵃ11)(P464ᵃ11 P480ᵃ0ᵃ6ᵃ11 P488ᵃ1
1)(P480ᵃ0ᵃ6ᵃ11)(P568ᵃ1ᵃ3ᵃ4ᵃ11)(P568ᵃ1ᵃ3ᵃ4ᵃ11 P576ᵃ2)

Example 4.9

a prime generator heads only one segment. The characteristic nesting of segments generated by SCP is evident in example 4.10, which gives the complete output string and a partial representation of the corresponding notation for SCP(SSGT). This output string contains 11 segments in all. Because of density, however, it is not feasible to give all in notation. example 4.11, gives SCP(PSGT) in its entirety.

Summary: Structure of the Parsing System

From the preceding descriptions of the parsings that make up the system, it should be evident that the system is hierarchic, in the initial sense that primary segments are formed before secondary segments. Further, from the definitions of block and segment and the rules for BCP and SCP, it follows that there is also a hierarchic relation between the function BCP and the function SCP. Specifically, if we regard the function calls as string names: (1) Every SG in BCP(PSGT) is a subsegment (possibly improper) of some segment in SCP(PSGT); (2) Every SG in BCP(SSGT) is a subsegment (possibly improper) of some SG in SCP(SSGT). Moreover, the nesting of BCP and SCP does not produce additional distinct strings of segments. For example:

$$SCP(PSGT) \supseteq SCP(BCP(PSGT))$$
$$SCP(SSGT) \supseteq SCP(SCP(SSGT))$$
$$BCP(PSGT) \supseteq BCP(SCP(PSGT))$$
$$BCP(SSGT) \supseteq BCP(SCP(SSGT))$$

Also,

$$BCP(SSGT, PSGT) \supseteq BCP(PSGT) \cap BCP(SSGT)$$

and

$$SCP(SSGT, PSGT) \supseteq BCP(SSGT) \cap SCP(SSGT)$$

Finally, every SG in BCP(SSGT, PSGT) is a segment in BCP(PSGT) $\cup$ BCP(SSGT), and every SG in SCP(SSGT, PSGT) is a segment in BCP(SSGT) $\cap$ SCP(SSGT). Thus, the most efficient (in the sense of shortest scan) and the complete set of distinct parsings possible within the system is represented by the following 6 names:

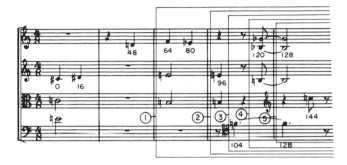

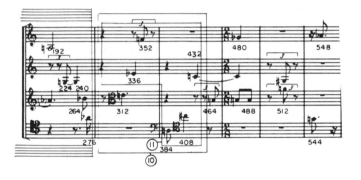

SCP(SSGT)

(P64"4"5"11 P80"3 P96"4"11 P104"5 P120"6"10"11 P128"5"6"10"11
0"7"8 P168"6 P176"6 P192"8"9 P224"7 P240"7 P264"10 P276"8)(P9
4"5 P120"6"10"11 P128"5"6"10"11 P144"0 P160"7"8 P168"6 P176"6
224"7 P240"7 P264"10 P276"8)(P104"5 P120"6"10"11 P128"5"6"10"
P160"7"8 P168"6 P176"6 P192"8"9 P224"7 P240"7 P264"10 P276"8)
 P128"5"6"10"11 P144"0 P160"7"8 P168"6 P176"6 P192"8"9 P224"7
4"10 P276"8)(P128"5"6"10"11 P160"7"8 P168"7 P176"6 P192"8"9 P
"7 P264"10 P276"8)(P160"7"8 P168"6 P176"6 P192"8"9 P224"7 P24
0 P276"8)(P168"6 P176"6 P192"8"9 P224"7 P240"7 P264"10 P276"8
9 P224"7 P240"7 P264"10 P276"8)(P224"7 P240"7 P264"10 P276"8
336"3 P352"5 P384"2 P408"1 P432"0)(P336"3 P352"5 P384"2 P408"

Example 4.10

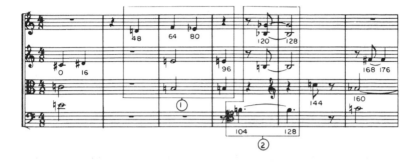

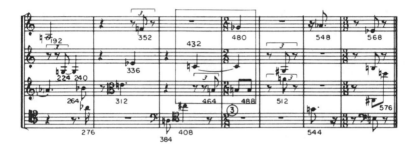

```
SCP(PSGT)
(P48ᴴ2 P64ᴴ4ᴴ5ᴴ11 P80ᴴ3 P96ᴴ4ᴴ11 )(P104ᴴ5 P120ᴴ6ᴴ10ᴴ11 P128ᴴ5ᴴ6ᴴ10ᴴ11 )(
P432ᴴ0 P464ᴴ11 P480ᴴ0ᴴ6ᴴ11 P488ᴴ11 )
```

Example 4.11

PSGT	SCP(PSGT)
SSGT	BCP(SSGT)
BCP(PSGT)	SCP(SSGT)

The output strings are generated in the above order. Accordingly, the schema of string relations for the deletion of all duplicate segments is as follows:

IN:	DELETE DUPLICATE SEGMENTS OF:
PSGT	PSGT
SSGT	SSGT PSGT
BCP(PSGT)	BCP(PSGT) SSGT PSGT
SCP(PSGT)	SCP(PSGT) BCP(PSGT) SSGT PSGT

BCP(SSGT)   BCP(SSGT) SCP(PSGT) BCP(PSGT) SSGT PSGT
SCP(SSGT)   SCP(SSGT) BCP(SSGT) SCP(PSGT) BCP(PSGT)
                SSGT(PSGT)

From Score Reading to Higher Analytic Levels

After a reading has been obtained, the question arises: How is the output
to be interpreted at a higher level? A comprehensive answer to this question would exceed the scope of this chapter. Nevertheless, some indication
of the nature of further analytic operations can be given. A sequence of
linked programs in the MAD programming language has been written to
process the output from the score reading program in order to yield
increasingly higher representations of structural relations. If the collection
of pitch-class representatives in each segment of the output strings from
the reading program is scanned to remove duplicates, the resulting collection may be called a compositional set. Then, from a listing of all the
compositional sets, the analysis programs (1) determine the class to which
each set belongs; (2) list and count all occurrences of each set-class represented; (3) compute, for each pair of set-class representatives, an index of
order-similarity; (4) determine the transposition-inversion relation for each
pair of set-class representatives, 65) list, for each set-class represented,
those classes that are in one of three defined similarity relations to it and
which occur in the work being examined; (6) summarize in matrix format
the set-complex structure of classes represented in the work; (7) accumulate
and retrieve historical and other informal comments in natural language.

These programs thus permit environments to be examined for similarities and differences and for distributional characteristics that might
suggest generalizations about the structure of the particular work or about
the structural determinants of the entire class of compositions to which the
work belongs. To illustrate this, let us consider certain aspects of the
pitch-structure of two contiguous contexts in the Webern work that was
parsed by the score-reading program.

The first context, extending from PV = 160 to PV = 276, is represented
in example 4.12. The position-values are arranged from left to right at the
top of the illustration. Each row below then gives the pitch-class representatives for one segment. The name of the string from which the segment
derives is indicated by the headings at the left margin. The name of the

PV	160	168	176	192	224	240	264	276	CLASS
PSGT									
1	8			8			10		2-2
2	7								
3		6	6						
4				9					
5					7	7			
6									
SSGT								8	
7	8								
8	7			9					2-2
9	8	6	6						2-2
10	8			8					
11	7	6	6						2-1
12	7,8								2-1
13	8			8			10	8	2-2
14		6	6	9					2-3
15				9	7	7			2-2
16				8			10		2-2
17				8,9			10		3-1
18				9				8	2-1
19					7	7	10		2-3
20					7	7		8	2-1
21							10		
BCP(PSGT)									
22	7,8			8,9			10		4-1
23				8,9					2-1
BCP(SSGT)									
24	7,8			8,9			10	8	4-1
25		6	6	8,9					3-2
26				8,9	7	7			3-1
27				8,9				8	2-1
SCP(SSGT)									
28	7,8	6	6	8,9	7	7	10	8	5-1
29		6	6	8,9	7	7	10	8	4-1
30				8,9	7	7	10	8	4-1
31					7	7	10	8	3-2

Example 4.12

set-class to which the corresponding compositional set belongs is given in the rightmost column. The first integer in the name gives the cardinality of the set; the second gives the ordinal position of the class on a stored list. Criteria of class-membership are based upon interval content and will not be explained here.[1] (Since a set containing one element does not form an interval, it is not distinctive with respect to interval content.)

The largest set in example 4.12 is the set numbered 28: class 5-1. It is evident by inspection that all the other sets are subsets of this one and therefore that all components of the context belong to a single set-complex. It should be said that in other cases the determination of set-complex structure is not as easy as this. In all, 7 of the 15 set-classes in the complex are represented: 5-1, 4-1, 3-1, 3-2, 2-1, 2-2, and 2-3.

The second context is displayed in example 4.13. There the largest set is numbered 26: set class 6-1. The number of set-classes represented is 9: 6-1, 5-1, 3-1, 3-2, 3-5, 2-1, 2-2, 2-5, and 2-6. All but two of these belong to the

	PV 312	336	352	384	408	432	464	480	488	CLASS
PSGT										
1	4									
2		3								
3			5							
4				2	1					2-1
5						0		0		
6							11	11	11	
7								6		
SSGT										
8	4		5							2-1
9	4	3								2-1
10	4			2	1					3-2
11		3	5							2-2
12		3		2	1					3-1
13				2	1	0				3-1
14						0				
15							11			
16							11	0,11	11	2-1
17								0		
18								0,6		2-6
19								11	11	
20								6,11	11	2-5
BCP(PSGT)										
21						0		0,6,11		3-5
22								0,6,11	11	3-5
23							11	0,6,11		3-5
SCP(PSGT)										
24						0	11	0,6,11	11	3-5
BCP(SSGT)										
25								0,6,11	11	3-5
SCP(SSGT)										
26	4	3	5	2	1	0				6-1
27		3	5	2	1	0				5-1

Example 4.13

set-complex about class 6-1. The two referred to are: 3-5 and 2-6. The set
2-6 is a subset of 3-5, which first occurs in the output string BCP(PSGT)
and can be seen in the score as the simultaneity at bar 10. Thus, within the
context there is a distinct division into two parts on the basis of set-
complex structure, a division that is signalled by an entrance of pitch-name
C at PV = 432.

A comparison of the two environments shown in examples 4.12 and 4.13
reveals that all the sets in the first are transformed subsets of set number
26 in the second, set class 6-1. This provides a basic and audible measure
of change since the event-configuration that begins at PV = 312 is a continuation of the intervallic complex of the preceding context. The next
distinctive event, from the standpoint of pitch-relations, is the formation
discussed above: the pitch-class collection 0, 6, 11, which is a member of
class 3-5.

Many detailed contextual associations are revealed by interpretation
beyond the score reading stage. To illustrate, example 4.14a shows a
secondary segment distributed between viola and cello. When this is com-

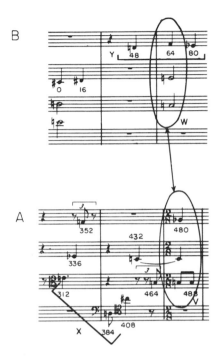

Example 4.14

pared with the primary segment at B, the two are seen to be related: They
are representatives of the same set-class. The first (X) is a transposition of
the second (Y) at the interval of 11 half-steps. The relation is nontrivial, for
the two notes F and E E♭ that sound with the E in X are elements of Y.
The association of the two contexts is further strengthened by the simul-
taneities V and W. Again, these are members of the same class: V is a
transposition of W at the interval of 7 half-steps.

It is hoped that this necessarily incomplete treatment demonstrates the
way in which a basis for a still higher level of analysis can be constructed
in terms of a system of pitch and interval relations interpreted with the aid
of theoretical concepts.

Extensions and Implications

A simplified input string was used in order to facilitate development of the
parsing program. This limitation in no way affects the generality of the

15

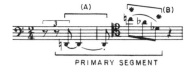

Example 4.15

system. Any syntactic class of interest to the analyst can be associated with a position-value, and an appropriate output format can be designed to accomodate as many properties of event-configurations as desired.

Since the parsing rules are based on the occurrence of syntactic structures in the input language (which is capable of representing every syntactic class), it is possible to extend the system in many ways. It could be extended, for example, with respect to depth of detail, as explained below.

In example 4.15 the primary segment, delimited by the bracket below the staff, contains two subsegments of interest: (A) and (B). In particular, (B) is delimited by the slur, with endpoints marked by ' − '. In the corresponding input language statement given below, these endpoints are represented by 'L + 1'. It would not be difficult to write a parsing function to isolate all subsegments marked by slurs within primary segments. Any syntactic class or combination of classes could be defined as delimiters in a similar way, thus creating new analytic strata. It might be pointed out in this connection that aspects of an individual composer's "style" can be investigated to any depth, provided, of course, that the researcher can specify the syntactic conditions with sufficient precision.

The second possibility for extending the program is more sophisticated and correspondingly more difficult: that of providing an inductive capability such that scans would be modified under certain conditions to consider other possible parsings or to scan for certain structures conditionally. This heuristic facility would greatly increase the power of the program and would make it possible to investigate context-sensitivity in greater depth.

In conclusion it should be recorded that the score-reading program suggests a feasible long-range project: the development of a precise descriptive language for event-configurations. Such a language would be valuable for the study of musical-statements In general and would be especially accessible to computer-implemented studies. Much work remains to be done.

Notes and References

1. Forte, Allen. "A Theory of Set Complexes for Music," *Journal of Music Theory*, 8/2(1964).

2. An abstract of the project is published in Bowles, Edmund, Comp., "Computerized Research in the Humanities," *ACLS Newsletter*, in Special Supplement (June, 1966), p. 38.

3. Farber, D. J., R. E. Griswold, and I. P. Polonsky. "The SNOBOL3 Programming Language," *Bell System Technical Journal* (July-August, 1966), pp. 875–944.

4. Babbitt, Milton. "Set Structure as a Compositional Determinant," *Journal of Music Theory*, 5/1(1961).

5. Babbitt, Milton. "Twelve-Tone Rhythmic Structure and the Electronic Medium," *Perspectives of New Music*, 1/1(1962).

"Pattern in Music" presents a formal pattern language for music. An "extension of a formalism" developed by Simon and Kotovsky (1963) to describe series items in general with "alphabets" and "sequences," Simon and Sumner's pattern language introduces a method for the reduction of music to its simplest components with a shorthand series notation for representative patterns of *music in extenso*.

For the sake of convenience, Simon and Sumner address the multi-dimensionality of music by regarding only rhythm, harmony, melody, and form as individual and simultaneous dimensions of music. Their notation allows the authors to include patterns, variations of patterns, and patterns of patterns (compound patterns) among their defined dimensions of music.

"Pattern in Music" describes the *pattern induction* and *sequence extrapolation* tasks used by Simon and Kotovsky in programs to simulate human pattern recognition of a letter series; it suggests that pattern induction can be thought of as a listener and sequence extrapolation, as a performer.

The distinct tasks of pattern induction and sequence extrapolation, however, also describe a learner and a composer. Simon and Sumner's musical score → pattern inductor → musical pattern → score writer → musical score loop might just as well substitute learner for pattern inductor and composer for score writer. In fact, they write that "the real score writer is the composer ... who first composes the pattern, then produces the score from it."

Although Simon and Sumner had not completed the two programs described as a score writer and a pattern inductor by the time of this chapter's publication, their pioneering exposition of a pattern language for music broaches both the commonality of pattern recognition for music and series in general and the modeling of music for machine representation.

5 Pattern in Music

Herbert A. Simon and Richard K. Sumner

One of the purposes of analyzing musical structure and form is to discover the patterns that are explicit or implicit in musical works. Pattern in music is generally described in ordinary language, supplemented by technical musical terms: for example, "the movement is in sonata form," "the opening section is in the key of C major, it is followed by a section in the dominant, then a return to the original key," "the chord is a G seventh," "the slow movement is written in 3/4 time." No complete formalism has existed for describing a musical pattern precisely; its exact nature can be communicated only by writing out the music *in extenso*—the actual notes in musical notation. Although some abbreviation is achieved by such notation as figured bass, all established notations set forth the notes essentially in the order of their temporal occurrence. This, as we shall see, is not at all the same as describing the pattern contained in the notes.

1 Sequential Patterns

Patterns, temporal as well as spatial, occur in many spheres of life besides music. People appear to have strong propensities, whether innate or learned, to discover patterns in temporal sequences presented by the environment and to use these evidences of pattern for prediction. The ability and desire to discover temporal patterns undoubtedly has had great value for the survival of humankind: in predicting the seasons, for example, or the weather. The urge to find pattern extends even to phenomena where one may well doubt whether pattern exists (e.g., in the movements of the stock market).

Because pattern discovery is a common, and sometimes practically important, cognitive activity, it has attracted some attention in psychology. J. Feldman, investigating ways in which people make predictions of the rise and fall in the level of business activity on the basis of data from previous time periods, observed that this predictive task is formally identical with the task of predicting a series of symbols ("check" or "plus") in the so-called binary choice or partial reinforcement experiment (Feldman 1963). When these tasks are carried out in the laboratory, subjects behave as though the

Copyright 1968, John Wiley & Sons, and reproduced by permission.

stimuli (although they are in fact random) were temporally patterned; that is, they predict "runs" of a symbol, or "alternations."

In research that began independently of Feldman's, Laughery and Gregg (1962) found similar behavior among subjects confronted with a switch-setting task (set each of four switches in a left (L) or right (R) position to turn on a single light) in which the successive correct settings formed a sequential pattern (e.g., RRRR, RRRL, RRLR, RRLL, RLRR, etc.). Subjects used notions of "same," "opposite," "change next column," and so on, to predict the next correct setting (Gregg 1967).

Several types of items in standard intelligence tests call for the discovery and extrapolation of sequential patterns. For example, the Thurstone Letter Series Completion Test contains items like: ABM CDM＿ ＿ where the blanks are to be filled with letters that "reasonably" continue the sequence. Even older than letter-series completion items in intelligence tests are items calling for the extrapolation of number sequences, for example: 1 4 7 10＿ ＿.

Simon and Kotovsky (1963), examining the behavior of subjects performing the letter-series completion test, have again found that their extrapolations are based on notions of simple periodic patterns.

When human behavior in these three rather different classes of tasks is compared, some striking similarities appear. First, in all three cases, subjects view the problem as one of finding simple temporal patterns. This seems as true of the situations where the stimuli are in fact random (the binary choice experiment; see Feldman 1963, 339) as it is of those where a genuine pattern is present. With random stimuli, subjects are prepared to treat certain elements as "exceptional" if they violate what appears otherwise to be an orderly sequence. Thus, people appear to persist strongly in seeking pattern even in the presence of noise. This attitude is no doubt reinforced by the fact that most of the patterns encountered in nature must be extracted from surrounding clutter or disturbance or irregularity of one kind or another.

The second striking similarity lies in the pattern hypotheses used in the three different tasks studied by Feldman, Laughery and Gregg, and Simon and Kotovsky. The patterns in all three tasks can be attributed to a very small number of types, involving a limited range of simple relations. Thus, for the binary choice experiment, Feldman, Tonge, and Kanter (1963, 56) constructed a fairly successful explanation involving only the idea of "run" patterns and "alternation" patterns. Gregg (1967) has shown that notions of "same" and "next" are fundamental to the patterns used in the switch-setting experiment. Simon and Kotovsky (1963) constructed a simple formalism that allows all the letter series items, and others, to be described exactly. Their formalism is based on the notions of "alphabet," and "sequence," and the relations of "same" and "next" between pairs of alphabetic or sequential symbols. If the scheme is supplemented by arithmetic operations of subtraction and division ("differencing"), it handles the number series as well. With a little change in nomenclature, the pattern description schemes used by Feldman, Tonge, and Kanter and by Gregg and Laughery can be equated with that used by Simon and Kotovsky.

We are led by these studies to conclude that pattern-seeking is a common activity of people faced with temporal sequences; the vocabulary, or stock of basic concepts they have available for describing patterns is parsimonious, involving only a few elementary notions together with rules for combining them, and is relatively independent of the specific stimulus material. Trying to outguess a roulette wheel appears to call on the same cognitive skills as taking an intelligence test. And what about listening to music?

In this chapter we explore the possibility that the pattern-description formalism previously applied to business-prediction, binary-choice, switch-setting, and series-completion stimuli may also be applied to musical patterns. More specifically, we wish to show that only a slight elaboration and extension of the scheme employed for these other, apparently simpler, stimuli enables us to describe with precision the pattern in musical works and their parts. Our hypothesis is that musical patterns, even when quite complex and sophisticated, involve only repeated use of the few simple components mentioned in the previous paragraphs, in particular: "alphabet," "same," "next," and rules of combination.

We shall say little here about the psychological processes that enable a listener to detect pattern in a piece of music or the processes that enable a composer to assemble a pattern. If the language of musical pattern we shall propose is adequate, it has strong implications for the nature of these processes. The theory of Simon and Kotovsky (1963), for example, includes not only a formalism for pattern description but also a set of processes for inducting the pattern from a segment of a letter series. The musical counterpart of these processes would be a listener who would induct the musical pattern from the temporal sequence of sounds (or from the sheet music). In the final section of this paper, we outline a set of processes for a listener, but without any pretense of detailed simulation of the human processes. We will make only a few brief comments about the processes for a composer.

Nor will we have anything to say about the reasons why certain patterns are regarded, by composers or listeners, as beautiful or interesting, or why they produce particular emotional reactions in listeners. (In general, we subscribe to Leonard B. Meyer's [1956] views on these matters.) All of these are important questions of musical esthetics. Understanding musical pattern is a prerequisite to answering them, but not, in itself, a sufficient basis for the answer. We will limit ourselves in this paper to proposing a formalism for describing musical pattern, and to demonstrating its adequacy for describing works of music.

Our undertaking, although independent in its genesis, has an affinity with other attempts that have been made in recent years to provide formal language for the descriptions of music. In particular it bears a close relation to the work of Babbitt, Forte, and their students and colleagues.[1] That work, however, has focused primarily on contemporary music; and has been much preoccupied with arriving at axiomatic formulations from which theorems can be derived. Since our own interest is in description and our viewpoint pragmatic, we can get along with relatively simple mathematical underpinnings and with less formalism that is now the fashion.

In some respects our work is less general than other contemporary formal approaches since it postulates a few specific relations (SAME, NEXT), derived from the psychological research on serial patterns, as the basis for its pattern descriptions. In other respects it is more general, since it claims applicability to music of any style. This latter claim remains to be evaluated—particularly with respect to the whole gamut of contemporary atonal music—but it results in our work being rather more empirical than formal. That is, we are interested in the extent to which the extant literature of music can be described by particular formalisms, not with providing formal definitions of particular classes of music or examining the consequences of such definitions.

In the next section, we give some simple illustrations of our notions of pattern as applied to music. In section 3 we introduce the several elements of the formalism, illustrating them again with musical examples. In section 4, we discuss the processes needed for inducting the pattern from a musical score.

2 Musical Pattern—Introduction

Unlike the sequential patterns introduced above, pattern in music is almost always multidimensional. Among the dimensions of pattern that are usually distinguished in works on music are melody, harmony, rhythm, and form. Each of these may actually have several dimensions. For example, in music with a number of voices, each voice may carry melodic and rhythmic patterns simultaneously with the others. There are additional dimensions we have not included—dynamics and orchestration, for example. For simplicity of exposition, we omit these and focus on melody, harmony, rhythm, and form. If we consider each dimension (and each voice, where appropriate) separately, we can often describe the patterns contained in it in terms not more complicated than those we have used to describe letter series. (But, as we shall see, the melodic and harmonic dimensions are not usually entirely distinct.)

For example, a very simple melodic fragment is the descending sequence of notes shown in figure 5.1. Interpreted in the key of C Major, it is a progression by single-scale degrees from the fifth of the scale down to the tonic.

A simple harmonic pattern is shown in figure 5.2. The notes C–E–G are repeated twice. These notes constitute the major triad on the tonic note (C) of the key of C major. They are played in order of ascending pitch, then repeated once.

In both examples, the similarity to the letter series is made particularly evident by use of the usual literal names for the notes. Successive notes in the melodic fragment of figure 5.1 are connected by the relation of NEXT

Figure 5.1

Figure 5.2

Figure 5.3

Figure 5.4

in the alphabet taken backward. In the harmonic pattern of figure 5.2, the members of the triad are related NEXT OF NEXT in the alphabet, forward; and the second triad is related to the first by SAME.

To describe a rhythmic pattern (figure 5.3) we must introduce notation for note durations and stresses. Let us use the term *accent* (following Meyer) to denote any means of singling a note out for attention. Then long duration and heavy stress are two means commonly used to accent a note. Note durations may be indicated by selecting a particular duration (in the example, the quarter note) as the unit, and measuring other durations relative to it. In figure 5.3, the rhythmic pattern, in terms of durations (with a quarter note as unit), is 1–1–2. We will use an alphabet of three symbols to indicate stress: (') for main stress, (") for secondary stress, and *u* for an unstressed note. The unit stress pattern in figure 8.3 is "-u-'. The rhythmic pattern of the example consists of the simultaneous duration and stress patterns, repeated three times.

Finally, a form like the rondo is commonly represented by naming the individual parts, a, b, and so on, and writing:

abacada ...

Combining melodic, harmonic, and rhythmic elements, we show in figure 5.4 the score of the first four measures of Bach's Gavotte from French Suite no. 5. The music is in 2/2 time—that is, there are two half-notes to a measure.[2]

Analysis will show that the basic rhythm is that given in figure 5.3, 1–1–2, with the three-note motive beginning on the third quarter of each measure (as shown by the square braces below the score).[3] Thus the bar-line separating the measures does not mark the beginning of the rhythmic motive but just precedes the note with the primary stress. (The latter is the usual function of the bar—to mark stress, not to divide motives—when the two functions diverge.) Hence, the stresses as well as the durations of the rhythm conform to the pattern of figure 8.3.

If we consider only the top (soprano) and bottom (bass) lines, ignoring the middle one (alto), and separate the motives, we can rewrite these measures in the following recoded form (the sharp in F♯ is omitted):

Rhythm[4]	"u'	"u'	"u"u	'u"u
Soprano	BGD	GEB	ECA	DCCG
Bass (pitch)	GGFF	EEDD	CCDA	FDGD
Bass (octave)	1221	1221	1222	1111
Harmony (α)	G D	e b	C D	D G
Harymong (β)	G	e	C D	G

Several points need explanation here. First, we have simplified the soprano line, omitting the unaccented eighth notes. Second we have indicated separately for the bass voice, but not for the soprano, the scale degree of each note and the octave in which it is sounded. Third, we have inducted two harmonic schemes that are implicit in the notes, and which we will now proceed to explain.

If we consider the three notes of the first chord (figure 5.3), we observe that they are G–D–B. These constitute the major triad on the tonic G (the key is G Major). On the next accented beat—the third chord—the notes are F♯–A–D, the major triad on D. In the second motive, the corresponding chords are the E Minor (e) and B Minor (b) triads; in the third motive, C and D; in the fourth, D and G. This sequence of triads is shown as Harmony (a). The distances in scale steps from one triad to the next follow the pattern − 3 + 1 − 3 + 1 for the first five triads, from G through C.

An even subtler, but simpler underlying pattern, employing so-called figured bass, can also be used to account for the first five chords of harmony (a). The bass begins with downward progression of the diatonic scale (compare figure 5.1), G–F♯–E–D–C, with each note repeated twice. (The notes also move periodically between two octaves with the pattern 1221.) A standard figured bass technique is to erect triads (do–mi—sol) on a sequence of bass notes, the bass notes serving alternately as the tonics (do) and thirds (mi) of their respective triads. Thus the initial G is the tonic of the G triad in harmony (a), F♯ the third of D, and so on.[5] There is a dear break in the pattern in the middle of the third motive. On the main accent of that motive, the bass goes up to D, instead of down to B, then continues A–F♯–D–G–D. Similarly, the sixth chord in Harmony (a) is D (followed by D–G), instead of G (3 steps below C), followed by A–E. The actual harmony in this last segment will be recognized by the musically trained as a *cadence* —usually a sequence from the dominant (here D) of the key to the tonic (here G). The cadence serves to mark a phrase ending; it is, so to speak, a punctuation mark.

Persons trained in harmony would also notice a broader structure underlying the sequence of chords (Harmony b). We will not undertake to explain this sequence G–e–C–D–G except to observe that it occurs frequently in tonal music, hence is familiar to musicians.

The point of all this recoding is that it reveals various elements of pattern based on relations of SAME and NEXT on a few tonal sequences or "alphabets" incorporated in these four measures. The bass employs the alphabet of the diatonic scale, the chords, the triadic (do–mi–sol–do) alphabet, the Harmony b, the conventional sequence G–E–C–D–G. There is a rhythmic pattern of stresses "u' and durations 1–1–2. Using these alphabets we can redescribe the music in terms of underlying patterns.

Our task in the remainder of this chapter is to provide a formal parsimonious way of representing patterns like this and to show that our formalism requires no essentially larger stock of primitive concepts than those already employed in representing the simple letter series.

3   A Formal Language for Pattern Description

Patterns involve periodicity—repetition (in a generalized sense) at intervals that occur periodically (in a generalized sense). Patterns make use of alphabets—sets of symbols ordered in a definite sequence. Patterns can be compound—made up of subpatterns that can themselves be represented as arrangements of symbols. Patterns generally possess phrase structure, which may be explicitly indicated by various forms of punctuation. Patterns, as we have already seen, may be multidimensional. Repetition in pattern generally involves variation. In the following paragraphs we will explain each of these elements and show how the pattern-description language handles it.

Periodicity

The string "ABABABA ..." can be described by the phrase, "Alternation of 'A' and 'B'." In general, to say that a string is patterned implies that there is some way of describing it more parsimoniously than by listing its symbols *in extenso*. Even the use of "...", to indicate the indefinite continuation of the string is an example of such parsimony, for the notation is applicable only to a patterned string that can be extrapolated by rule. The notation would be inadequate to describe the continuation of random string "101 10010 ...".

The simplest patterns have a fixed period, repeating with systematic variation the sequence that constitutes the first period. We have already cited the example ABM CDM EFM__ __.

Even without the spacing, the regular repetition of the letter "M" in this sequence suggests a period of three. With the "Ms" removed, the rest of the sequence simply consists of the letters of the Roman alphabet, in their usual order. Thus, the sequence can be characterized in terms of two relations between pairs of symbols: (1) the relation of SAME, or identity, and (2) the relation of NEXT on some specified alphabet. These relations may hold among the symbols within a single period of the string: for example, the relation of NEXT between "A" and "B," and between "C" and "D." On the other hand, the relations may hold between symbols in successive periods: for examples, the relation of SAME between the "Ms" of each period, and the relation of NEXT between "B" and "C," and between "D" and "E."

These relations serve to define the pattern of the example ABM CDM ..., which can be represented in algebraic notation as follows: Let us designate the symbols in the sequence by x_{ij} where the first subscript, i, names the period in which the symbol occurs; the second subscript, j, the position in that period. Thus we may rewrite the above sequence:

$$x_{11} x_{12} x_{13} x_{21} x_{22} x_{23} \cdots$$

where $x_{11} = A$, $x_{12} = B$, $x_{13} = M$, and so on.

Then:

for $j = 1, 2, 3$	There are three positions in each period).
$x_{11} = $ 'A'	(The first symbol in the first period is 'A'.)

$x_{i1} = \text{NEXT(ENG; } x_{(i-1)2}$
for $i = 2, \ldots$

(For all periods beyond the first ($i = 2, \ldots$), the first symbol in the ith period (x_{i1}) is NEXT in the English alphabet (ENG) to the second symbol in the preceding, or ($i - 1$)st, period ($x_{(i-1)2}$). Thus, $x_{21} = $ 'C' is next in the English alphabet to $x_{12} = $ 'B'.)

$x_{i2} = \text{NEXT(ENG; } x_{i1})$
for $i = 1, \ldots$

(For all periods ($i = 1, \ldots$) the second symbol in the ith period (x_{i2}) is NEXT in the English alphabet (ENG) to the symbol in the same (ith) period (x_{i1}). Thus $x_{22} = $ 'D' is next to $x_{21} = $ 'C'.)

$x_{i3} = $ 'M'
for $i = 1, \ldots$

(For all periods ($i = 1, \ldots$), the third symbol (x_{i3}) is an 'M'. Thus, $x_{13} = $ 'M'.)

The four preceding equations provide a precise formal definition of the pattern.

If the pattern of the example is extrapolated, we eventually reach the end of the alphabet and cannot continue unless we define "the letter NEXT to 'Z'." In the following discussion, we will treat all of our finite alphabets as circulars—as beginning over again when the end is reached. Thus, "the letter NEXT TO 'Z' is 'A'." This convention has great convenience for music.

The convention of circularity of alphabets permits a simple representation of the alternation of two symbols. We simply define the sequence of two symbols, '+' and '−', say, as an "alphabet," which we will call SIGN: SIGN = +, −. Then we can define the simple alternation: + − + − + ... by the relations:

$j = 1$

(There is one position ($j = 1$) in each period.)

$x_{11} = $ '+'

(The first symbol (x_{11}) is '+'.)

$x_{i1} = \text{NEXT(SIGN; } x_{(i-1)1})$
for $i = 2, \ldots$

(The second and subsequent symbols (x_{i1}, $i = 2, \ldots$) are each NEXT on the alphabet consisting of '+' and '−' to the symbols that precede them ($x_{(i-1)1}$).)

Since we will subsequently need notation for relations like "NEXT of NEXT" and "NEXT of NEXT of NEXT," we will abbreviate NEXT by N. We also wish to refer to strings that do not continue indefinitely, but terminate after a specified number of periods. Consider the diatonic "alphabet, C D ... A B, which we will call DIAT. In order to represent the diatonic cycle of fifths, starting with C and returning to that note, we might write:

$j = 1$ (There is one position in each period).

$x_{11} = $ 'C' (The first note is 'C'.)

$x_{i1} = N^4(\text{DIAT}; x_{(i-1)1})$ for $i = 2, \ldots, 8$. (Each subsequent note is four steps—that is, a "fifth" in musical terminology—above its predecessor on the diatonic scale.)

where $N^4(s) = N(N(N(N(S))))$, or, more generally, $N^k(s) = N(N^{k-1}(s))$, for $k = 2, \ldots$. Thus N^2 means "NEXT of NEXT," N^3, "NEXT of NEXT of NEXT," and so on.

We will also need notation to specify the repetition of a symbol or subpattern a specified number of times. We will denote the pattern AAA, for example, by A.[3] This will enable us to describe a pattern like A BB CCC DDDD ... as: $j = 1$, $x_{i1} = (z_i)^i$, $z_1 = $ 'A', $z_i = N(\text{ENG}; z_{(i-1)})$ for $i = 2, \ldots$. In this notation we have introduced the concept of subpattern (Z_i), which we will discuss further.

The final bit of notation we shall introduce at this point is an operator, CARRY, or C for short, to denote the carrying operation familiar in adding and multiplying numbers. Something like this is required to describe a "counting" pattern like: 1, 2, ..., 9, 10, ..., 99, 100, 101, ... The number of symbols in each period grows indefinitely. We use the alphabet DIG = 0, 1, ..., 9. Then, $x_{11} = 1$; $x_{i1} = N(x_{(i-1)1})$ for $i = 2, \ldots$; $x_{1j} = $ blank, for $j = 2, \ldots$; $x_{ij} = C(x_{i(j-1)}, x_{(i-1)j})$ for $i, j = 2, \ldots$, where $C(x, y)$ means performing NEXT in the column of Y, whenever we step past the end of the alphabet in the column of X. (Columns are numbered from right to left.)

Now if we denote the notes of the diatonic scale by letters, as before, and the successive octaves by integers, then the sequence of notes running up the scale can also be described by such a counting pattern: OC, OD, ..., OB, 1C, ..., 1B, 2C, and so on, where the first symbol denotes the octave, the second the note. Here $j = 2$, $x_{11} = O$, $x_{12} = C$; $x_{i2} = N(x_{(i-1)2})$; $x_{i1} = C(x_{i2}, x_{(i-1)})$.

Alphabets

An alphabet is an ordered set of symbols. The alphabets used in patterns are of two kinds: (1) ordered sets already defined in the culture (the Roman alphabet, the notes of the diatonic scale, the days of the week, the Arabic numerals, and so on), and (2) ordered sets that are defined ad hoc for the purpose of pattern construction. Thus, we defined above the ad hoc alphabet SIGN $= +, -$, and, in general, to represent the simple alternation of any pair of symbols, we define the alphabet consisting of just that pair of symbols. When we have occasion to distinguish alphabets of the two major kinds, we will refer to them as "common" and "ad hoc," respectively.

In music, the diatonic scales, including the major, minor, and modal, are important common alphabets. Another such alphabet is the chromatic scale.[6] Each triad, (e.g., (C, E, G)) can also be used as an alphabet in a musical pattern, as can its various inversions (e.g., (E, C, G)). The major and minor diatonic scales and their associated triads are, of course, the most widely used musical alphabets of the tonal period. Contemporary twelve-tone music makes use of ad hoc alphabets so-called tone rows, which are in their simplest forms permutations of the chromatic scale. However, we can think of any sequence of notes employed in a melodic motive or a vertical chord as an ad hoc alphabet. From a musical standpoint the difference between a common and an ad hoc alphabet is that the listener may be assumed to have the former already stored in memory, while he must induct the latter from the music itself. Consider the sequence:

EQDFRMEQDFRMEQDFRM ...

This can be interpreted as a periodic repetition of the ad hoc alphabet (E, Q, D, F, R, M). At least one repetition (or a substantial portion of one) is necessary for the reader to induct that this pattern may be intended. On the other hand, the initial segment Monday, Tuesday, ... may already suggest that the common alphabet of days of the week is intended.

An ad hoc alphabet can be generated from a common alphabet by a selection operator, which defines a new sequence by designating the order numbers in the alphabet of the successive members of the sequence. Thus (E, Q, D, F, R, M) can be generated from the ordinary Roman alphabet by the selection operator (5, 17, 4, 6,18,13). The ad hoc sequence may contain repetitions of symbols. Thus the operator (1, 2, 1, 3) generates (A, B, A, C) from the Roman alphabet.

Compound Symbols

As another important direction of generalization, an entire pattern can be designated, or named, by a single symbol, and this name used as a component in a larger pattern. Consider the pattern:

CQD CQD CQD ...

This pattern can be described simply as

$j = 1.$ (The period is 1.)

x_{i1} = A, for all i, where   ($<---X_i$ is the compound symbol CQD, to
A = 'CQD'   which we give the name A.)

This notation becomes especially convenient when there are several subpatterns, as in:

ABC 123 DEF 123 GHI ...

This is equivalent to:

X_1 Y X_2 Y X_3 Y ... = $(X_i$ Y$)$

where Y = '123', and

$X_i = (x_{i1} x_{i2} x_{i3})$,   (Y is the compound symbol '123'.)

$x_{i1} = N(\text{ALPH}; x_{(i-1)3})$;   ($X_i$ is a compound symbol, whose elements
$x_{ij} = N(\text{ALPH}; x_{i(j-1)})$,   proceed in sequence down the alphabet.)
$j = 2, 3; x_{11} = $ 'A'

The ability to replace subpatterns with names will be important to us in describing musical patterns. For example when we say that a rondeau has the form abaca ..., we mean that it is a sequence involving the subpatterns which may be as complex as we please 'a', 'b', 'c', and so on.

A more specific example can be constructed from the fragment of the Bach Gavotte in figure 5.4, considering only the first ten notes in the bass voice. We can here represent the pattern simply by

$K_i, i = 1, 2, 3,$

where K_i is defined by

$$K_i = \left\{ \begin{array}{ll} \text{Duration:} & 1^4 \\ \text{Stress:} & "u'u \\ \text{Notes:} & X^2_{(2i-1)} X^2_{(2i-1)} X^2_{2i} \\ \text{Octave:} & 1221 \end{array} \right\} i = 1, 2, 3$$

Where $X_1 = $ 'G', $X_i = N(\text{BDIAT}: X_{i-1})$, and BDIAT means the diatonic alphabet taken backwards (i.e., *down* the scale). The formula would predict $\left\{\dfrac{BB}{21}\right\}$ for the 11th and 12th notes, while the actual notes are $\left\{\dfrac{DA}{22}\right\}$, showing that the initial pattern has been interrupted and replaced by a new one (the cadence).

Phrase Structure

In oral and written prose the listener or reader is given clues to the boundaries of periodic and aperiodic subpatterns. In English speech, these clues take the form of changes in pitch (fall in inflection at the ends of words, phrases, and sentences), pauses, and accents. In written prose, they take the form of spaces and punctuation marks.

Music also contains such clues, including among them harmonic cadences, note durations, and dynamics (stress, loudness, attack). In order to have a name for all devices that can be used to mark boundaries, we will refer to them as "punctuation."

Punctuation is an aid to boundary detection, but seldom is essential for that purpose. For example, the subgroups in the following pattern are readily detected without punctuation:

ABC 123 DEF 456 GHI ...

They would be more easily visible, however, if punctuated by spaces:

ABC 123 DEF 456 GHI ...

or by commas:

ABC, 123, DEF, 456, GHI, ...,

or by parentheses:

(ABC)(123)(DEF)(456)(GHI)(...)

Hierarchies of groups, groups within groups, can be marked by punctuation of graduated strength:

ABC123DEF456GHI ...
ABC, 123; DEF, 456; GHI ...;
((ABC)(123))((DEF)(456))((GHI)(...

In the musical example of figure 5.4, several modes of punctuation are in evidence. Half notes, of longer duration than the other notes, are used to terminate the rhythmic motive in its first two occurrences. The bar line is one of several conventional phrase markers. The D chord followed by G (dominant followed by tonic) that interrupts the third and replaces the fourth occurrence of the rhythmic motive is a conventional cadence that would provide a sense of completion to any ear accustomed to music of the tonal period (eighteenth and nineteenth centuries). The finality of the cadence is softened, however, by the use of eighth notes to weaken the rhythm. The cadence serves as a semicolon, so to speak, rather than a full stop.

Multidimensionality

Most of the patterns we have considered thus far consist of single sequences of symbols. As the Bach example shows, however, musical pattern is multidimensional. Not only may several notes sound simultaneously, but we must also be prepared to encode the relations that hold among such simultaneous notes (harmonic or chordal relations) as well as to describe the rhythmic and dynamic patterns that accompany the patterns of pitch. In orchestrated works, we may also be concerned with patterns of tone coloration, and there are other dimensions as well.

Our language for pattern description must be general enough, then, to accommodate all of these complexities, including: (1) parallel melodic patterns, (2) the warp and weft of melodic and harmonic pattern, and (3) rhythmic pattern. In particular, we need a representation that will handle conveniently certain subtle but fundamental interactions among melody, harmony, and rhythm.

Let us designate each note by four numbers: its octave, its scale degree, its time of onset, and its duration. We will assign the number 0 to the octave below middle C. Lower octaves will be assigned negative integers; octaves from middle C (inclusive) up, positive integers. Instead of using the conventional letters or roman numerals for scale degrees, we will also designate these by integers ranging from 0 (for C) for 11 (for B) for the 12 steps of the chromatic scale.

The first note of a piece (or of any segment we are considering) will be assigned onset 0, and the onset of each subsequent note will be the onset of its predecessor (including rests) plus the duration of that predecessor. Durations will be measured as multiples of some unit—the quarter note or eighth note, say, as convenient. Thus if the unit is the quarter note, and we consider three notes of duration 1–1–2. respectively (as the first three notes of figure 5.3), their onsets will be 0, 1 = (0 + 1), and 2 = (1 + 1), respectively, and the note that follows them will have onset 4 = (2 + 2).

For some purposes, it will be convenient to designate scale degrees relative to some note other than C—relative to the tonic associated with the key signature, for example. To designate degrees relative to D (= 2), we simply subtract 2 from the degree relative to C. Likewise, we will sometimes want to talk about degrees in the diatonic major scale (numbered 0 to 6), or some other scale, instead of the chromatic scale. This conversion is also straightforward. (Chromatic degrees 0, 2, 4, 5, 7, 9, 11 become diatonic degrees 0 through 6, respectively.) Unless there is an indication to the contrary, however, scale degrees are given in the chromatic scale relative to C taken as 0. Note that the tonic, or other base of the scale is always taken as zero rather than one. This greatly simplifies the arithmetic as compared with the conventional roman numeral notation.

With these conventions, in a piece in C Major in 4/4 time, a quarter-note C above middle C struck on the third beat of the first four-beat phrase can be denoted: (1, 0; 2, 1). The first 1 designates the octave; the 0, the C in that octave; the 2, the onset at the end of the second beat, beginning of the third; the final 1, the one-beat duration. The gavotte of Fig. 5.4 is in the key of G major. If we shift the origin of the system to the G below middle C, then the third soprano note in the gavotte (D) would be denoted: (1, 7; 2, 1).

Having settled these conventions, let us return to the matter of the interaction of harmony with melody. We can use the Bach gavotte to illustrate how a harmonic pattern can be combined with a rhythmic pattern to generate a melodic phrase. Figure 5.5 shows a succession of chords, G–e–a (or chromatic 0–9–2, relative to G). For reasons we will not try to explain here, the first two chords are in "second inversion"—that is, are written with their respective fifths (chromatic scale degree 7 relative to the tonic) as roots.

Suppose now that we impose on these chords the rhythmic pattern of figure 5.3, striking the highest note (a) of each chord first, the middle note (b) second, and the lowest note (c) third. The pattern may be represented:

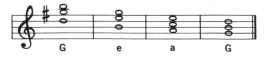

G   e   a   G

Figure 5.5

Note	(α)	(β)	(γ)
Onset	0	1	2
Duration	1	1	2
Stress	''	u	'

The notes themselves are

Motive	I	II	III
Chord	0	9	2
(a)	4	0	9
(b)	0	9	5
(c)	7	4	2
Onset	0	4	8
Duration	4	4	4

The superposition of rhythm on chords generates the following series of nine notes:

Note	1	2	3	4	5	6	7	8	9
Onset	0	1	2	4	5	6	8	9	10
Duration	1	1	2	1	1	2	1	1	2
Degree	4	0	7	0	9	4	9	5	2

But these nine notes are identical with the first nine notes (ignoring the eighth notes of the second measure) in the soprano line of the gavotte. (The cadence causes a modification of the subsequent notes as we have noted previously.) We have thus generated from the harmonic pattern the melody that appears as the soprano line of the illustration. This does not prove, of course, that this is the manner in which Bach created this melodic line. (Indeed it is likely that he created it in a somewhat different way, as we mentioned earlier.) It does show that the melodies that have an underlying harmonic structure can be described parsimoniously by superimposing a rhythmic pattern on an underlying chordal structure.

Using the conventions introduced previously, and one new one ($I_2(x)$) means the second inversion of chord x), the pattern of the nine soprano notes shown above can be described briefly thus:

KEY: G(MAJ)   The key is G Major.

HARM: $(I_2(0), I_2(9), 2, 0)$ The harmony is a list of four chords:

                                G (2nd inver.), e (2nd inver.), a, and G.

SOPR: α_i^4 The soprano notes follow the pattern α_i, $i = 1, \ldots, 4$.

$\alpha_i \begin{cases} \text{DEGR: } N(\text{DTRI: } (H_i))^3 \\ \text{DURN: } (1, 1, 2) \end{cases}$ Three notes are chosen from the chord H_i, in succession down the tread (DTRI); their durations are

$H_i = N \,(\text{HARM: } H_{i-1})$ The chords are chosen in succession from the list HARM.

A second example, drawn this time from Bach's *Passacaglia and Fugue in C minor*, will illustrate further this scheme for factoring harmonic and rhythmic aspects of pattern. The *Passacaglia* is in 3/4 time. The opening statement of the theme (measures 1–8, see figure 5.6) is eight 3-beat motives in length, each motive being, rhythmically:

The opening statement consists simply of a single melodic line, thus of 16 (actually 15, because of the dotted half note in the seventh motive) independent notes. The melodic structure is very simple, for each quarter note, save the first, is on diatonic degree lower than the half note that follows it. Therefore, we can describe the pattern as follows:

KEY: C(MIN)   The key is C minor.

BASS (4 3 5 4 2 0 4 0)   The bass accented notes consist of these scale degrees (diatonic).

STRESS: (u') An unstressed quarter note is followed by a
DURN: (1, 2)   stressed half note; each pair is a tone preceded by
DEGR: $((x_i)x_i)^8$ the next lower tone. The tones are selected in
                          order from BASS.

$x_i = N(\text{BASS; } X_{i-1})$
EXCEPTIONS: $N(x_i) < --0)$;
$N(X_8) < --\text{TIE}$.

	Stress	u	'
	Duration	1	2

Figure 5.6

In Variation I (measures 9–16), there are four voices, constructed from fifteen chords whose bass tones, played in succession, play the *passacaglia* theme we have just described. The first motive of Variation I is shown in figure 5.7. Each two-note motive has essentially the same iambic structure as before, each note serving as lowest member of an entire chord. However, a rhythmic variation is also introduced. The prevailing rhythmic units in this variation are eighth notes instead of quarter notes, so that, for convenience, we will regard the motive structure as 6 eighth notes instead of 3 quarter notes. This motive consists of two subparts of 2 and 4 eighth notes duration, respectively. We can now describe the rhythmic pattern by specifying the onset of the notes belonging to each of the two chords in each of the voices:

Chord	1	2
Chord onset	0	2
Chord duration	2	4
Sopr. onset*	1	2
Alto onset*	1	2
Ten. onset*	1	1
Bass onset*	0	0

Figure 5.7

The rhythmic pattern described above is shown in ordinary musical notation in figure 5.8 (β). The onsets (relative to the motive) are written below the notes. We have simplified the actual rhythmic pattern of the

---

* In describing the pattern, the onset of the individual voices is indicated *relative* to the onset of the chord to which they belong. Hence, to determine their onset relative to the *motive*, the two numbers must be added. Thus, the second tenor note has an onset of 3 = (2 + 1) eighth notes relative to the motive. It is therefore sounded at the *end* of the third, or *beginning* of the fourth beat of the six-beat motive.

Passacaglia in one respect that is easily corrected. The soprano note in the
second chord is embellished by a decoration (échappée) that is a diatonic
third above the chordal tone and occurs one sixteenth note earlier. (See
Figure 5.8 (γ).) Hence, we must replace the soprano note with a subpattern
that designates both pitches and onsets relative to the embedding pattern:

	Soprano	Decoration
Degree (diat.)	0	+2
Onset	0	-1/2
Duration	2	1/2

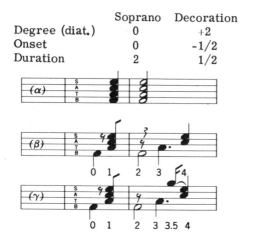

Figure 5.8

Now the whole first variation, eight measures, is defined by the combination of the chordal sequence (based, in turn, on the 15-note melodic line)
with the rhythmic pattern we have just described. (The first motive of the
variation is shown in detail in figure 5.7).

In the next eight measures, the third variation—the melodic and rhythmic patterns—remain unchanged, while a slightly different sequence of
chords is constructed on the melodic line.

Variation

The pattern description scheme needs provision for flexibility in accommo-
dating patterns that repeat with small variations.

First, by allowing names to be attached not only to complete subpatterns but also to particular aspects of a subpattern (e.g., its harmony or
its rhythm), we can construct variations, as in the *Passacaglia*, that make
rhythmic changes while the harmony remains constant, or make harmonic
changes over a constant melody and rhythmic pattern.

Second, by defining intervals and time relations relative to points of origin (of pitch and time), modulations of pitch and syncopations of melodic phrase are handled readily. This coincides, of course, with the standard procedure in music whereby roman numerals denote chords relative to the currently prevailing tonic.

Various forms of inversion and retrograde motion involve merely reversing, in direction or time, respectively, the NEXT relation that is being applied. Different inversions will arise depending on whether the tonic alphabet being used is chromatic, diatonic, or some other.

Ever freer variation can be obtained by regarding the tonal alphabet as one of the parameters that can be changed while retaining intact all or some of the other elements of a pattern. This flexibility even suggests possibilities for musical pattern that we have not yet seen exhibited in the examples of music that we have examined.

If the pattern-description scheme is to be complete, it must also provide for transformations that stretch out patterns (augmentation) or condense them (diminution) by change of rhythmic values (e.g., they may be doubled or halved). In certain cases, particular notes or groups of notes may belong to more than one pattern element. For example, in modulating from one key to another, a pivot chord may be used that can be interpreted as belonging either to the original key or to the new key.

We cannot consider all these elaborations in detail, or even present enough examples to evaluate our claim that music of a wide variety of styles can be represented formally in the notation we have introduced. Instead, we will propose in the next section a *procedure*—for constructing, systematically, the pattern corresponding to a musical score.

4   Induction and Interpretation of Patterns

Let us return for a moment to the letter-series completion task. To perform successfully on a letter-series test, a person must do two things: (1) examine the partial sequence presented to him, and induct from it a pattern consistent with it; and (2) use the pattern to extrapolate the sequence, generating the successive symbols that belong to it. Faced with ABM CDM .., he must discover the pattern we described earlier, or another one that fits the sequence, and then determine that the next letters determined by the pattern are EFM .... We will call the first task *pattern induction*, the second task *sequence extrapolation*.

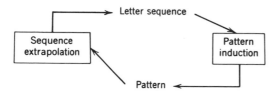

Figure 5.9

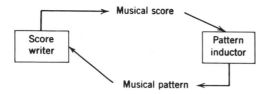

Figure 5.10

Simon and Kotovsky (1963) simulated human performance in the letter-series task by constructing a pattern induction program and a sequence extrapolation program capable of handling sequences of the kinds commonly encountered in such tests. The relation between the two programs is depicted in fig. 5.9.

An almost exact analogue can be constructed for the task of music analysis. The "letter sequence" becomes the musical score; the "pattern" the musical pattern; the "pattern inductor" a program for constructing the musical pattern from the score; and the "sequence extrapolator," a program for reconstructing the score from the musical pattern. (See figure 5.10.)

The pattern inductor may be thought of as a "listener," since it accepts the music (or the score) as input and detects the melodic, harmonic, and rhythmic relations implicit in it. The score writer may be thought of, less accurately, as a "performer." In actual fact, of course, performers are given scores that they translate from written to aural form, rather than patterns, so this analogy is really not precise. The real score writer is the composer who (we would hypothesize) first composes the pattern, then produces the score from it.

The adequacy of the description scheme we have outlined in this chapter may be tested by undertaking to construct such pattern-inducing and score-writing programs. The score writer, while the less interesting of the two, is the simpler to construct and can be used to test whether proposed descriptions of specific pieces of music are accurate and complete. The score produced by the score writer, when it is given the pattern as input, can be compared directly and note for note with the actual score. Inadequacies in the description will show up as discrepancies between the two. We are currently constructing such a score writer, but it is not yet completely debugged. It consists of two parts. One (still under construction) transforms the pattern into all internal representation of the score; the other (now complete) prints the score from the internal representation.

Rhythm as Cue to Pattern

Some aspects of the performance of the pattern-inducting program for music have been hand simulated, but construction of the actual computer program has not yet begun. We can sketch here the approach that is being taken.

First, the larger segments of a piece of music can often be delimited by the presence of conventional punctuation: double bars, key signatures, changes in tempo, and so on. By this means, sections, each four to sixteen measures long, say, are identified.

Second, experiments with a variety of musical styles indicate that rhythmic variations are the simplest cues for delimiting the smaller motives and phrases. Consider, as a simple example, a Beethoven dance, of 16 measures. (The first eight measures are shown in figure 5.11. A double bar occurs at the end of the eighth measure, dividing the piece into two parts. The durations of the soprano notes in the first eight measures are as follows (the eight note is taken as a unit):

$$1 + 1 + 4 + 1 + 1 + 4 + 1 + 1 + 1 + 1 + 1 + 1 + 1 + 1 + 1 + 1 + 1 + 1$$

$$+ 1 + 1 + 1 + 4 + 1 + 1 + 4 + 1 + 1 + 1 + 1 + 1 + 1 + 2 + 4$$

Scanning this sequence from left to right, we find the first occurrence of the longest note (4), then continue to scan to find the next occurrence of the same duration. We now match for identity the patterns from these starting points, first moving left from the longest note (4). In this way we find two groups of $(1 + 1 + 4)$, with total duration of six each.

Continuing to scan, we find two more patterns of the same kind $(1 + 1 + 4)$, whose origins are separated from the earlier patterns by a duration of 12, a multiple of six. We might now rewrite the sequence thus:

Figure 5.11

$$(1 + 1 + 4)^2(1 + 1 + 1 + 1 + 1 + 1)(1 + 1 + 1 + 1 + 1 + 1)(1 + 1 + 4)^2$$

$$(1 + 1 + 1 + 1 + 1 + 1)(2 + 4)$$

But two of the remaining segments are made up of sequences of 6 eighth notes each, so we can rewrite again:

$$(1 + 1 + 4)^2((1)^6)^2(1 + 1 + 4)^2(1)^6 (2 + 4)$$

It is now not difficult to see that this section has the rhythmic form ABAC, where: A = $(1 + 1 + 4)^2$, B = $((1)^6)^2$, C = $((1)^6(2 + 4))$.

In the second half of the dance (not shown here), all notes in the soprano, except in the final measure, are eighth notes, hence they do not help us to find the pattern. In the bass, however, we find $((\underline{2} + 2 + 2)^3(2 + \underline{2} + \underline{2})^2$ where the underlining denotes rests.

In this example, as in many others, the alphabets of durations are ad hoc, that is, $(1 + 1 + 4)$ or $(2 + 2 + 2)$—but stress and duration alphabets are commonly drawn from a small pool of familiar patterns used in both music and poetry—for example, the iambic ($u'/12$) of waltz time, in its simplest form.

Harmonic Cues to Pattern

The dance of figure 5.11 also provides simple examples of how the pattern inductor could discover harmonic elements of pattern. The key signature, final notes, and absence of accidentals allow the inference that the music is written in the key of D major—that is, that the primary relevant alphabet of scale degree is the diatonic scale with D as 0.

If the pattern inductor examines the soprano notes in the groups we called A above, it finds that the first three all constitute the same sequence (with shift of octave): $(0 + 2 + 4)$. But this is a familiar subsequence, the major triad on the tonic. Thus, these notes can be generated by the NEXT operator on the common triadic alphabet, starting from the tonic. The fourth sequence is a simple permutation of the same notes: $(2 + 4 + 0)$. In a similar manner, the groups in B can be generated by NEXT downward on the diatonic alphabet, starting from G (3). The soprano notes in C require a little more subtle interpretation, for they do not form a major triad. We will return to them presently.

If the pattern inductor now examines the eight segments of bass notes corresponding to the pattern elements in the soprano, it finds comparable simplicity. To interpret these patterns, let us consider the triadic alphabet on the diatonic scale as not stopping with 4 (the "fifth" in usual musical terminology), but continuing upward by diatonic thirds: 0, 2, 4, 6, 1, 3, 5. In this way we obtain the major seventh chord, ninths, elevenths, and thirteenths. In each pattern of 6 eighth notes in the dance, exactly three scale degrees appear. In the first two measures, and in the fifth, sixth, and eighth, they are (from low to high) 0, 2, 4, that is, the tones of the major triad on D. In the three remaining measures they are 4, 1, 3, that is, 0, 4, 6 *relative* to A.

We recall that a selection operator generates a sequence from an alphabet by designating the order numbers in the alphabet of the successive members of the sequence. Thus, from the alphabet (1, 4), the selection operator $(1 + 1 + 2)$ generates the sequence $(1 + 1 + 4)$. Consider now the selection operator $(1 + 3 + 2 + 3 + 1 + 3)$ on the alphabets (0, 2, 4), and (0, 4, 6), respectively. In the first case, it generates the sequence $(0 + 4 + 2 + 4 + 0 + 4)$; in the second case, the sequence $(0 + 6 + 4 + 6 + 0 + 6)$. But these are precisely the sequences of notes that occur in the bass voice of the dance (the two patterns taken relative to D and A, respectively). The pattern produced by this particular selection operator is well known in music of the late eighteenth and early nineteenth century; it is the so-called Alberti bass.

If we review the analyses to this point, we find that all the notes of both soprano and bass in measures 1, 2, 5, 6 and 8 belong to the major triad on D, while the bass notes of measures 3 and 4, and soprano and bass of measure 7 belong to the triadic alphabet of A. We can therefore associate a scale degree, or "chord," with each subpattern, obtaining the harmonic pattern: $0 + 0 + 4 + 4 + 0 + 0 + 4 + 0$. Again this is a simple (and common) musical pattern in which the harmony moves from tonic to fifth, then from tonic to fifth and back.

The induction strategy outlined here parallels closely the one used for letter series, where the pattern induction program first detected the periodicity of the pattern (which corresponds to detection of motive boundaries), then proceeded to describe the relations that defined the pattern.

The pattern thus inducted from the musical example of figure 5.11 is shown in figure 5.12. The smallest pattern elements are designated by the Greek letters ρ (for rhythmic patterns) and π (for melodic patterns). There are three of the former and six of the latter in the soprano and bass lines, taken together, of the eight measures. (Thus, considering rhythm and melody of both voices, this part of the notation achieves a compression from 32 to 9 independent elements.) The Greek letters, β name two combinations of rhythm and melody that are repeated several times in the bass voice. The pattern named M is a combination of soprano and bass patterns

$$\binom{M_i^2}{(i=0)} \begin{bmatrix} \text{Degree: 4} \\ S\begin{bmatrix} (\rho_2, \pi_3(i))^2 \\ (i=6,0) \end{bmatrix} \\ B: \beta_2 \end{bmatrix} \binom{M_i^2}{(i=0,2)} \begin{bmatrix} \text{Degree: 4} \\ S: \rho_2, \pi_5 \\ B: \beta_2 \end{bmatrix} \begin{bmatrix} \text{Degree: 0} \\ S: \rho_2, \pi_6 \\ B: \beta_1 \end{bmatrix}$$

where

$$M_i = \begin{bmatrix} \text{Degree: 0} \\ S: \rho_1, \pi_1(i) \\ B: \beta_1 \end{bmatrix}$$

$$\pi_1 = \text{Degree: } (i, (N(\text{DIAT}))^2)$$

$\rho_1 = \text{Duration: } (1, 1, 4) \qquad \pi_3 = \text{Degree: } (i, (N(\text{BDIAT}))^5)$

$\rho_2 = \text{Duration: } (1)^6 \qquad\quad Q = \text{Select: } (1, 3, 2, 3, 1, 3)$

$\rho_3 = \text{Duration: } (2, 4) \qquad \pi_2 = \text{Degree: } Q(0, 2, 4)$

$\beta_1 = \pi_2, \rho_2 \qquad\qquad\quad \pi_4 = \text{Degree: } Q(0, 4, 6)$

$\beta_2 = \pi_4, \rho_2 \qquad\qquad\quad \pi_5 = \text{Degree: } Q(2, 6, 4)$

$\qquad\qquad\qquad\qquad\qquad \pi_6 = \text{Degree: } (0, 0)$

Figure 5.12

that occurs, with parameterized variation, in measure 1, 2, 5, and 6. The top part of figure 5.12 shows the pattern for the entire eight measures described in terms of these more elementary components.

Conclusion

In this chapter we have presented a scheme for describing music in terms of underlying pattern. A pattern language was introduced that is a slight extension of a formalism that has been used previously to describe patterns in certain intellectual aptitude tests and psychological laboratory tasks. Examples were presented to show how language would be used for the description of tonal music.

A program is under construction that will translate pattern descriptions into printed music in order to test the accuracy and adequacy of the formal language. A second program was described in outline that will induct the pattern description from the printed score. The pattern description language we have described may prove useful both in psychology and in music theory. As a tool in psychology, it can be used to try to arrive at an understanding of the cognitive activity of the music listener. As a tool of music theory, it may be used to provide rigorous descriptions of musical pattern as a prerequisite for the characterization and comparison of style. In the more distant future, it may provide an interesting basis, different from those employed heretofore, for experiments in musical composition by computer.

Acknowledgment

Ellis B. Kohs, composer and professor of music at the University of Southern California, has served as consultant on this project. He has helped us avoid numerous musical blunders but should not be held responsible for those that remain. His *Music Theory* and forthcoming book on musical form have been major sources of insight to us, as has been also Leonard B. Meyer's *Emotion and Music*. Professors Meyer, Allen Forte, and Allen Newell have also supplied valuable comments on an early draft of this paper. They, too, must be held blameless for errors that remain. This research has been supported by Public Health Service Research Grant MH-07722, from the National Institutes of Mental Health.

Notes

1. For a recent survey of formal approaches to music with a bibliography. see Rothgeb (1966).
2. To avoid fractions in analyzing this music we will take the quarter note as the unit, although in the music as written the half-note is the basic pulse.

3. The term *motive* is usually used in music to refer to a short pattern. Lacking a better term, we will use motive both for the pattern and for its individual occurrence, even though the latter usage may appear strange to a musically trained reader.

4. It might be debated whether the rhythm is 'u" or "u', but the distinction is not important for our analysis.

5. This pattern was pointed out to us by Allen Forte (personal communication). There is good historical reason for believing that Bach used figured-bass techniques to generate patterns. Our present concern, however, is not with how the pattern was represented to the composer, but with the different elements of pattern that might be detected by a listener. The pattern description of a piece of music is not necessarily unique, nor will all listeners hear the same relations.

6. The seven white notes on the piano, from C through B, constitute a major diatonic scale. The same notes, with some other note than C as starting point, yield other minor and modal scales. The chromatic scale consists of all twelve white and black notes.

References

Feldman, J. Simulation of behavior in the binary choice experiment. In Feigenbaum, E. A., and Feldman, J. (Eds.) *Computers and Thought*, New York: McGraw-Hill, 1963, p. 329–346.

Feldman, J., F. Tonge, and H. Kanter. Empirical explorations of a hypothesis-testing model of binary choice behavior. In Hoggatt, A. C., and Balderston, F. E. (Eds.) *Symposium on Simulation Models*, Cincinnati: South-Western Publishing Company, 1963.

Gregg, L. W. Internal representations of sequential concepts. In B. Kleinmuntz (Ed.) *Concepts and the Structure of Memory*, John Wiley & Sons, 1967, p. 107–142.

Laughery, K. R., and L. W. Gregg. Simulation of human problem-solving behavior. *Psychometrika*, 1962, 27, 265–282.

Meyer, L. B. *Emotion and Meaning in Music*. Chicago: University of Chicago Press, 1956.

Rothgeb, J. Some uses of mathematical concepts in theories of music. *Journal of Music Theory*, 1966, 10, 200–215.

Simon, H. A., and K. Kotovsky. Human acquisition of concepts for sequential patterns. *Psychological Review*, 1963, 70, 534–546.

Winograd sets a forth a systemic grammar for the parsing of tonal harmony. His accompanying program realizes the grammar for the harmonic "reading" of simple tonal exercises and compositions.

To arrive at his choice for a type of grammar, Winograd chooses among three "natural language" grammars: immediate-constituent, transformational, and systemic. He assumes that the parsing of harmonic structure "is closely related to the parsing of tonal music as a language."

Ultimately, Winograd chooses the systemic grammar because it allows the interpretation of harmony in terms of "inversion" as well as "completeness." This systemic grammar consists of five ranks: composition, tonality, chord group, chord, and note.

The process of parsing structures produced by systemic grammars is complex, and because Winograd's goal is a best parsing rather than all possible parsings, the semantic measures selected depend on harmonic progression and tonal hierarchies. Winograd's model of his grammar, implemented in LISP, applies semantic heuristics to produce a parsing tree for the composition.

Despite the program's inability to explain particular contextually determined harmonies, for example, passing 6/4, and its focus on harmony exclusive of melody and rhythm, it achieves some "quite sophisticated parsings." Winograd recommends further application of semantic-directed parsing to other types of music.

6 Linguistics and the Computer Analysis of Tonal Harmony

Terry Winograd

I Introduction

I.1 Linguistics and Music Theory

Fifteen years ago, linguistics was the private preserve of a small number of anthropologists and philosophers, along with an occasional language teacher or intrepid psychologist. Today it has become a home for not only a large number of specialized linguists but also of mathematicians, engineers, and the loosely defined group in the computer sciences. This migration has resulted both in new insight into language and the application of this insight to a variety of phenomena.

What used to be simply "language" is now "natural language" and is seen as a particularly well developed example of a much more general class of abstract languages. In one of the key early works in this new linguistics, Noam Chomsky defined all language as a set (finite or infinite) of sentences, each of a finite length and constructed out of a finite set of elements (Chomsky 1957). The term "sentence" of course covers a much broader range than its popular meaning and can be generally interpreted as any "well-formed string of a language, which can stand independently." A large body of theory has been developed concerning the possible grammars for abstract languages and the properties of the languages they produce.

The strongest motivations for much of the research have been the desire to understand the structure of natural languages and the use of special artificial languages in the building, programming, and understanding of computing machines. However, Chomsky's definition is not limited to these areas. A wide variety of structures can be viewed as abstract languages, and from this vantage point we can see more clearly both the objects being studied and the linguistic methods being used.

One particularly attractive area for exploration is music. The similarity of music to language at many levels has long been a subject of discussion, and studies are now beginning that use some of the basic ideas of linguistics in order to better express the structure of music (see Forte(3)). No major attempt has been made to apply large bodies of linguistic techniques

Copyright 1968, *Journal of Music Theory*, and reproduced by permission.

to music, but there are several reasons why this seems to be a profitable undertaking.

First, as the great body of scholarship on music theory shows, there is a set of quite specific structural (syntactic) rules governing most types of music, and a generative grammar (see Chomsky 1963) would provide a neat and useful way of expressing them. It is possible to separate various aspects of music into partially independent areas, and the number and complexity of the rules operating in any such subset are quite small compared to those that must be used in any reasonable theory of a natural language. At the same time, music is a natural language, having evolved independently rather than being constructed with regard to linguistic theory. Thus it has many of the quirks and foibles that make natural language processing so difficult a task. It may then be possible to experiment with linguistic techniques on this more manageable language while still getting a good indication of their wider applicability.

I.2   The Application of Linguistics to Tonal Harmony

One aspect of music highly amenable to this treatment is the harmonic structure of tonal music. First of all, it is not trivial. It takes a rather sophisticated understanding of music to perform harmonic analysis (as opposed to simple chord identification). One program has been written, (Jackson 1967) which is said to match the performance of a college sophomore, clearly lacks this sophistication. Further, even experienced theorists can disagree on the "reading" (parsing) to be assigned to a particular composition. This poses interesting problems of performance, since no absolute standard can be set by which to judge the performance of a parsing program. There is of course close agreement on all but the most detailed points, and a program should strive for an "intelligent" reading. This makes the problem interesting as a problem in artificial intelligence not only for its own sake but also because of its clear relationship to the problem of parsing and understanding structures in other languages with a semantic component.[1] Finally, along with this complexity there is a rather simple syntactic structure. The theory used, although not yet adopted by all music theorists, is quite explicit and highly successful in explaining the harmonic structures found in tonal music. Thus there is a firm base on which to build a program.

In this chapter the problems are viewed from all three directions—music, linguistics, and artificial intelligence. It is assumed that the reader is familiar with the theory of tonal harmony. This work is based on the principles explained in Forte's *Tonal Harmony in Concept and Practice*, simplified as necessary to meet the goal of writing an effective grammar and parsing program.

Section II deals with the linguistic concepts applied to the problem. Due to both the nature of the subject and the considerations of heuristic programming, a relatively new form of grammar, systemic grammar, was applied. That grammar is being developed by a group at University College, London, and has previously been applied only to natural languages, primarily English. However its properties make it highly adaptable to other types of languages and it is particularly well suited to music. Since this theory is not widely known, I have attempted to explain its basic ideas and notations. It is sheer folly to try to explain an entire linguistic theory in a few pages, and the reader is assured that it is much more fully developed than this explanation demonstrates. I have not tried to justify the theoretical assumptions or methods or discuss their validity. For a discussion of this sort, see Halliday (1967), Huddleston (1965), or Hudson (1967). A number of modifications were made in adapting the theory to music, but a larger number of features (not all of which appear in the explanation) have been used directly as formulated. The main advantage of this type of grammar is the extremely close connection between the syntax and the semantics. This connection does not show fully in this case since a radically simple semantic system is used, but it could be developed in relation to other languages in the future, as it is closely related to the parsing methods developed.

Section III deals with these parsing methods and is actually a proposal for a very general algorithm, applicable to any natural language with a defined semantic structure. It is derived from the method of "predictive analysis" (Kuno and Oettinger 1963), but incorporates a number of features that greatly increase its practicability. Of these, two syntactic features and two semantic features are most important. Syntactically, it employs a preliminary local analysis that first eliminates the context-sensitive aspects of the grammar and second greatly reduces the number of paths in the parsing. In addition the algorithm employs what I will call (by gross liberty with both words) "semantic heuristics," both to resolve ambiguity and to direct the parsing. In addition to its grammar or syntactic rules, the program has a set of semantic rules, assigning a level of "meaningfulness" to any possible parsing. It is here that the intelligence of the program resides, choosing between various parsings all of which are consistent with the grammar, and, more significantly, using these evaluations to direct its search. This is done by eliminating paths that seem least meaningful, even if they are grammatically feasible, in order to reduce the search.

Section IV describes the LISP program written to perform the parsing, discussing some of the techniques and data structures used. A complete documentation and listing of the program is available on request. Section V discusses the results of this program when applied to examples selected from music literature and suggests some possible improvements to the program. Several actual inputs and outputs are included for comparison. Section VI discusses more general conclusions and the applicability of the techniques used here to other problems.

II   A Systemic Grammar for Tonal Harmony

II.1   Types of Grammar

The problem of explaining a composition in terms of its harmonic structure is closely related to the parsing of a sentence in a language. If we express the structure in terms of a grammar, this can then serve as the basis for the parsing of tonal music as a language.

Since the usual concepts of language were designed to deal with simple strings of symbols, we must adapt them somewhat for the special requirements of music. In order to have explicit information, we would like a generative grammar (see Chomsky 1963) and we can choose among a number of models that have been devised by linguists. The simplest is an immediate-constituent or phrase-structure grammar, expressed in the form of a series of productions. Each of these gives a possible expansion of a nonterminal symbol into a string of other (terminal or nonterminal) symbols. For example, a simplified grammar of tonal harmony might include productions of the sort:

harmonic phrase → opening cadence

cadence → plagal

cadence → authentic

authentic -→ dominant (linear) tonic

dominant → V

dominant → VII

$V \rightarrow V_{triad}$

$V \rightarrow V_{seventh}$

$V_{seventh} \rightarrow V_7$

$V_{seventh} \rightarrow V_6 \atop 5$

...

A derivation in such a grammar begins with a starting symbol (in this case "harmonic phrase") and replaces it with the right side of a production for which it is the left side. It then continues, sucessively replacing each symbol in the string with the right side of a production of which it is in turn the left. The process continues until all symbols remaining are terminal symbols (those which do not appear on the left of any production), which in the case of music would be individual notes. The result of a derivation in such a grammar is a linear string, and this must be modified to produce the essentially two-dimensional structure of harmony (vertical concatenations of notes into chords and horizontal concatenation of chords into a composition). However much deeper problems arise in this type of grammar.

We should have a single symbol "dominant," which would then be expanded into the actual notes of a particular chord functioning as a dominant. However the notes in the chord will depend on its place in the tonality hierarchy of the composition. In order to decide what notes to expand it to, we must consider the context in which it is embedded. We could maintain the simple form of the rules by adding separate symbols such as dominant $_{C major}$, dominant $_{C\sharp major}$, and so forth through the keys. This would involve multiplying the number of rules in the grammar by the total number of possible tonalities, and the resulting totally unwieldy system would ignore all of the regularities that form the heart of the tempered tonal system.

A second problem is exemplified by the place of chord inversions in the grammar. In classifying chords by function, we would most probably have at some point in the grammar the usual roman numeral labels. In order to expand these into all possibilities, we would have to take into account all the possible inversions. Thus we would have rules such as

$I \rightarrow I_{5 \atop 3}$ $II \rightarrow II_{5 \atop 3}$

$I \rightarrow I_6$ $II \rightarrow II_6$

$I \rightarrow I_{6 \atop 4}$

This kind of multiple-dimension structure occurs at a number of places in music and would make any simple phrase-structure grammar impractical. These defects could be remedied by adding the concept of transformations, which act on strings produced by a simpler phrase-structure grammar. Thus, for example, the phrase-structure component could have a production expanding the symbol I to the vertical grouping of notes "c♮ e♮ g" and expanding V to "g♮ b♮ d♮", and so forth. There would then be transposition transformations that could act on any chord, depending on place in the tonality structure, transposing all of its notes to the proper pitches for that tonality. In a complex tonal structure several such transformations might operate on a single chord. Similarly, other transformations could modify the note order to produce different inversions, could delete various notes to form incomplete chords, and could add the other parts of chord structure. These mechanisms would involve a number of changes to transformational grammar as it has been developed for natural language. First, transformations must act on individual constituents (chords and notes) rather than whole sentences. More important, there would have to be ways in which the tonality structure could be introduced to control the transformations that are actually carried out. The methods used for natural language are not directly applicable, but it seems possible that others could be devised.

Another possibility that seems more profitable is systemic grammar, a somewhat newer system but one that has a flexibility lending itself to such applications. This generality is gained by untying the structure of the grammar from the structure of the sentences it produces. Transformational grammar makes a step-in this direction but still ties "deep structure" to the form of a "kernel sentence," while allowing no structuring of the transformation rules except through their effect on the transformed sentences.

II.2 Systemic Grammar

Systemic grammar is based on the fact that any sentence in a language will exhibit a number of features that the speaker has selected from a limited and tightly organized set available in that language. What is important in the understanding of a language is the way in which these features are dependent on each other, rather than the particular details of the exact form of the sentences they produce. Thus we will first deal rather abstractly with features, without dwelling on the form of their realization or mapping onto the output structures. Since all of the previous work in systemic grammar has concerned natural language, we will use the terminology and examples from its application to English. In particular we will refer to the systems of the English clause.

A feature T1 may be conditional on a feature T2, in that the presence of T1 implies the presence of T2. For example the feature "wh-question" is conditional on the feature "interrogative." In our grammar, the feature "major" for a chord is conditional on the feature "harmonic." A feature T1 may on the other hand preclude the possibility of T2. Thus, "interrogative" and "declarative", or "triad" and "7th," are incompatible pairs. Indeed, a feature may be conditional on any Boolean combination of other features. Further, a set of mutually exclusive features may exhaust the possibilities for an obligatory property of the sentence. Every sentence meeting certain entry conditions (Boolean conditions on the presence of other features) must exhibit exactly one feature from this set. Such sets are called systems and form a key part of he theory.[2] A system may be given a name for reference. Thus, the voice system in English has two features, or terms; active and passive. The diatonic note system in music has seven terms (A, B, ..., G) while the linearity system used in this grammar has six: (passing, anticipation, suspension, auxiliary, contained in adjacent chord, and nil). This last example illustrates the presence of a default term, which does not represent simply the lack of a choice in the system but a definite denial that any of the other features can be present. We can express the dependencies among the entire set of features in the form of a system network. This is closely related to a decision tree, but is not actually a tree due to the possibility of the complex Boolean conditions relating features. Even though the framework is extremely general, most natural languages (including tonal harmony) make limited use of complex interrelations, and with a few notational tricks, the networks can be displayed in a treelike form.

The greatest power of systemic grammar comes from its recognition that the form of a sentence may be the result of several systems operating simultaneously. Thus the final form of a chord depends on the choices of terms in a system of "inversions" and one of "completeness" as well as the more obvious systems of harmonic structure. This allows it to avoid the problems described in section II.1.

II.3 Realization Rules

Notice that so far no mention has been made of the form of the sentence except to say that it in some way "realizes" the features. This is central to the theory. The "deep structure" of a sentence is not the same type of object as the "surface structure." It is not a string of words or a labeled constituent tree. The deep structure of a particular sentence is simply a set of features selected in accordance with the system network of its grammar. Of course if grammar is to have any meaning, these must be mapped in some reasonable (and observable!) way onto the apparent structure of the sentence. This realization of features is not a simple one-dimensional concatenation of constituents but can operate on a number of simultaneous dimensions. Every sentence has a number of types of structure, including the grouping of its members into syntactic units, into informational units, into intonational units, and so forth. In addition it has prosodies such as intonation (or for written language, punctuation).

The realization of any feature is a set of partial specifications of some of these structures of prosodies. We will be concerned primarily with the syntactic constituent structure, but one of the strong points of the theory is that it can handle a number of other aspects, often ignored and actually of great importance to the functioning of language. A unit (e.g., a sentence, clause, tonality, chord, ...) can then be viewed as a structure containing a set of constituents each of which has a certain function in relation to that unit. One type of realization partially specifies the constituents. Since constituent structure is based on multary, not binary, branching, it may take a number of features together to completely specify the constituent structure of a unit. For example in the clause, the feature "indicative" is realized by the presence of a constituent with the function "subject," and the feature "operative" is realized by the presence of a constituent functioning as "extensive complement" (direct object in more traditional terms). These operate independently, producing different possibilities for the constituent structure (e.g. Come here. Watch the birdie! The nation slept. Yastrzemski hit the ball.).

Other realization rules can specify the order of constituents. The feature "yes-no question" is realized by the ordering first word of predicate, subject, rest of predicate. Still others may limit the type of unit that can fill that function in the structure. The feature "middle" in the transitivity system thus limits the unit serving as predicate to a verbal group containing one of a small number of implicitly reflexive verbs, such as wash, as in, "She washed (herself)." We cannot explain as realizations of clause features the particular structure of the nominal group serving as its subject. The features of a clause determine only the type and ordering of its constituents and any clause prosodies. Each constituent is then an entry to a separate system network and may itself be a structure of still other constituents. In this way, the infinite variety and recursion of natural languages are easily introduced.

The usual notion of constituency (as used in phrase-structure grammars) is clearly inadequate for these purposes, since the number of different types of constituents (non-terminal symbols) is far too large to speak of separate system networks for each. However it is clear from the types of realization rules described that this is neither necessary nor desirable. It is an observable fact of natural language that there is a definite hierarchy of ranks of units and that the options open to a speaker are organized around a very small number of these. Thus in English syntax there are only three basic ranks: clause, group, and word. Rather than view two types of noun-phrase as different types of constituents (for example determined vs. nondetermined) we see that they both originate as realizations of nominal groups that have selected different features. The constituents of unit can be either units of the immediately lower rank, or units of the same or higher rank that have been rank shifted. The basic pattern in English is a clause made up of groups (either nominal, verbal, or adverbial), in turn made up of words (perhaps morpheme would be a better term for this, but the independence of morphemes is not as clear as many theories suppose). However, rank shifted clauses (relative clauses, nominalizations) can operate as constituents at both the clause rank and the group rank, while rank shifted groups are a major source of constituents for groups. At the lowest level, the networks are actually choices between large numbers of individual items (words), and the structure of the system network is more closely related to semantic than syntactic considerations, although there is a close interrelation. As mentioned above, the choice of features at any rank may be partially determined by the features of the unit in whose structure the unit being considered functions.

Any sentence can then be described as a sequence (related by other structures not discussed here) of clauses each of which can be specified by a listing of its features, along with the features of each of the constituents implied in its realization, the features and constituents of these subunits, and so forth to the depth of recursion. In general there is a close mapping from semantics onto the features in the system networks, and a systemic description of a sentence is a highly "meaningful" representation.

II.4 A Grammar of Tonal Harmony

For the purposes of music I have made a rather free adaptation of the grammar described, in order to fit the peculiarities of harmonic structure. The modification is, as should be expected, almost entirely in the form of the realization rules. All of the basic principles and elements of "deep structure" are applicable directly as employed for English (or for a number of other types of languages). It is only the particular features, their interrelations, and the way they map onto the output structures that are peculiar to a particular language.

The principles of harmonic structure can be succinctly expressed in terms of a grammar with five ranks: composition, tonality, chord group, chord, and note.[3] By making further use of special structures, this could well be reduced to three: tonality, chord, and note. The resulting economy would be accompanied by an undesirable complication of the systems, and the larger but simpler form was chosen for this project.

A composition (network 6.1.) is a simple paratactic structure (a simple concatenation: A and B and ...) whose constituents are tonalities. One feature of the composition as a whole is its key, represented by the two systems of "mode" and "root," where "root" is in turn a pair of systems, representing the diatonic and chromatic level. The realizations of these features are primarily restrictions on the tonalities which function as constituents. The restrictions are primarily of root and mode, but there is the additional restriction to "simple" tonalities (those ending with a cadence).

The rank of tonality (network 6.2.) includes most of the features that give tonal harmony its characteristic structure. It is through the use of rank shifted tonalities as constituents of other tonalities that the recursive structure, or hierarchy of tonalities, is built up. The realizations of the features include both the specification of constituent structure and the specification of the particular constituents, particularly as to mode and root. The basic types of structure are: complete (containing a cadence) and implied (containing a sequence "dominant preparation → dominant"). Complete tonalities are further classified as simple (ending with a cadence) or modulating. These features are of central importance in determining the way a tonality can function in the tonality hierarchy. It is interesting to note that often in languages there are similar but not identical systems of features at different ranks, and this is particularly apparent in comparing the system network for tonality to that of chord group.

The chord group (network 6.3.) is a unit formed by local methods. It has a single root and type and thus functions as a unit within the harmonic structure. It may contain a number of different inversions and linear chords, or may consist of a single harmonic chord.

The chord (network 6.4.) is an obvious unit, and the features are those commonly assigned in music theory: root, type, inversion, and linear function. Note that this last feature is context sensitive. The other parts of the grammar are context dependendent in the way described in section II.1, but this distinction is not as clearcut (or necessary) for a systemic grammar, since the realization rules can depend on terms selected at any rank above the unit under consideration. Linear function is, on the other hand, truly context dependent, with the realization of features depending on features of other units functioning as constituents of the same structure. This poses interesting theoretical problems, but since it is strictly local, there is no practical difficulty in parsing. It seems that many context dependencies in

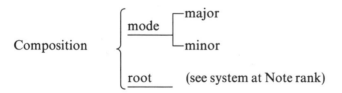

Realizations:
    Composition :: T⁀ (T) ⁀ ... ⁀ (T)
    mode, root :: These features are realized through the *K* system
                described above.
Constituents
    T :: Tonality$_{simple, I}$

Network 6.1

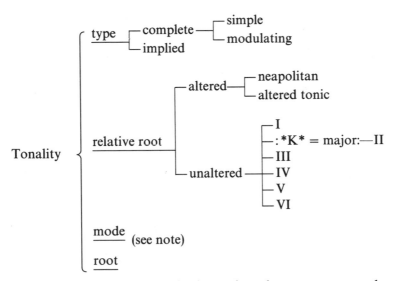

Note: The choice of features in the mode and root systems are dependent in a complex way on the choice of relative root and on *K*. This dependence is most easily expressed in the form of a table, table 6.1, but the status in the grammar is the same as dependencies indicated with lines and brackets.

Realizations:

Tonality :: +dominant; +(sec)...(sec); (sec)⌒dominant

complete :: +tonic; dominant⌒tonic

simple :: tonic⌒♯

modulating : +sec$_2$⌒(sec$_2$)⌒...⌒(sec$_2$); tonic⌒sec$_2$

implied :: +domprep; domprep dominant; dominant ≡ Chord Group
        direct relative root, The realizations of the relative root system
        act through

mode, root :: the connections with the mode and root systems to
        produce *K* as indicated in table 6.1.

Constituents:

dominant :: Tonality$_{simple, v}$ or Chord Group$_{V or VII}$

sec :: Tonality or Chord Group

tonic :: Chord Group$_{I, direct}$

sec$_2$ :: Tonality$_{simple or implied}$ or Chord Group

domprep :: Chord Group$_{II or IV or VI}$

Network 6.2

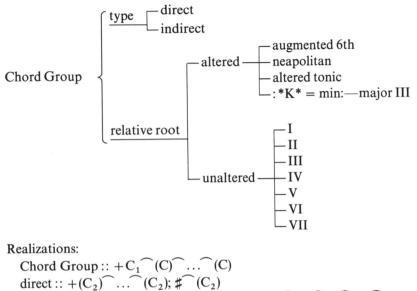

Realizations:

Chord Group :: $+C_1 \frown (C) \frown \ldots \frown (C)$

direct :: $+(C_2) \frown \ldots \frown (C_2); \sharp \frown (C_2)$

indirect :: $+(C) \frown \ldots \frown (C) \frown C_3 \frown (C) \ldots (C); C_3 \frown (C) \frown \ldots \frown (C) \frown C_1$

relative root :: All features in the relative root system are realized by determining the root and type of constituent chords (i.e., by selecting features at the next lower rank). The details are expressed in table 6.2.

Constituents:

C_1 :: Chord$_{\text{harmonic, *X*}}$

C :: Chord$_{\text{harmonic, *X*}}$ or Chord$_{\text{linear}}$

C_2 :: Chord$_{\text{harmonic, *X*}}$ or Chord$_{\text{linear, nonharmonic}}$

C_3 :: Chord$_{\text{harmonic, not *X*, linear}}$ where *X* is the combination of type and root determined by the realization of relative root.

Network 6.3

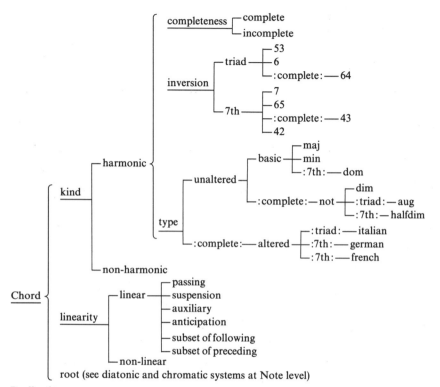

Realizations:

completeness, inversion, type :: These three systems are realized jointly in the specification of notes which serve in the constituent structure. Completeness and inversion function together to determine the diatonic values of these notes. The realization is a list of diatonic intervals above the bass, where each note must form one of these intervals, and there must be at least one representative for each interval. This pair of systems also specifies which note has the subscript root, by specifying its interval above the bass. The details of these facts are included in table 6.3. All three systems jointly determine the set of chromatic intervals in the chord in the same way. The facts are included in table 6.4, where empty entries appear whether the particular combination of features is precluded by the system network.

non-harmonic :: This is a default term, realized by the presence of a structure which cannot be produced by any combination of features depending on harmonic.

linear :: This is a context-sensitive realization, which limits the notes according to the notes of the following (FOL) and preceding (PREC) chords. Details are in table 6.5.

non-linear :: A default term.

root :: The selection of features is passed down to the constituent $Note_{root}$ as a restriction.

Constituents:

   N :: Note

Network 6.4

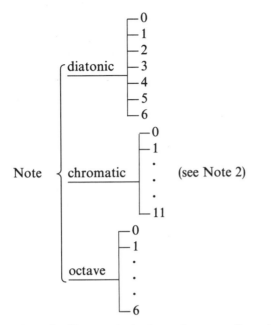

Note 2: Chromatic is dependent on diatonic as expressed in table 6.6. Chromatic must be within the range of two more or less of f(diatonic).

Realizations:

   Note :: name · modification · octave

   diatonic :: Specifies name: $0 = c$, $1 = d$, ... $6 = b$

   chromatic :: Operates with diatonic to specify name, according to the difference between chromatic and f(diatonic).

     $+2$ = doublesharp, $+1$ = sharp, 0 = natural, -1 = flat, -2 = double flat.

   octave :: Specifies octave of note.

Network 6.5

Table 6.1

	Major	Minor
I	maj(0.0)	min(0.0)
II	min(1.2)	– – –
III	min(2.4)	maj(2.3)
IV	maj(3.5)	min(3.5)
V	maj(4.7)	maj(4.7)
VI	min(6.9)	maj(6.8)
Neapolitan	maj(1.1)	maj(1.1)
Altered Tonic	min(0.0)	maj(0.0)

Columns indicate the mode of *K*. Rows indicate relative root. The entry in each position contains the mode selected, and an interval (a.b) from *K* to the selected root. The notation for intervals is the same as that for notes discussed in section IV.2. Thus, for example, (2.4) is a major third.

Table 6.2

	Major	Minor
I	maj(0.0)	min(0.0)
II	min(1.2)	dim(1.2)
III	min(2.4)	aug(2.3)
IV	maj(3.5)	min(3.5)
V	dom or maj(4.7)	dom or maj(4.7)
VI	min(5.9)	maj(5.8)
VII	dim or halfdim(6.11)	dim(6.11)
Neapolitan	maj(1.1)	maj(1.1)
Altered tonic	min(0.0)	maj(0.0)
Major III	– – –	maj(2.3)
Augmented 6th	french, german, or italian(3.6)	french, german or italian(3.6)

This is the same as table 6.1, except that the choice is of type, rather than mode.

natural language may be of this local nature, thus presenting less of a problem in practice than in theory.

Finally, the note (network 6.5) is the obvious basic unit, and the features are obvious. For reasons of computer application I have chosen to represent notes primarily in a numerical form and to consider the traditional names as realizations. This is a highly convenient but not logically necessary step.

The complete grammar used in this project is included in the five networks with their accompanying notes and tables. The use has somewhat determined the form in which the realization rules are stated. A more

Table 6.3

	Complete	Incomplete
53	(0 2 4) 0	(0 2) 0
6	(0 2 5) 5	(0 5) 5
64	(0 3 5) 3	– – –
7	(0 2 4 6) 0	(0 4 6) 0
65	(0 2 4 5) 5	(0 4 5) 5
43	(0 2 3 5) 3	– – –
42	(0 1 3 5) 1	(0 1 3) 1

Rows are terms in the inversion system, columns are choices in the completeness system. Each entry contains a list of intervals for the note specification, followed by the interval of the root above the bass.

Table 6.4

	Complete		Incomplete	
	triad	7th	triad	7th
major	(0 4 7)	(0 4 7 11)	(0 4)	(0 4 11)
minor	(0 3 7)	(0 3 7 10)	(0 3)	(0 3 10)
dim	(0 3 6)	(0 3 6 9)	– –	– – –
halfdim	– – –	(0 3 6 10)	– –	– – –
dominant	– – –	(0 4 7 10)	– –	(0 4 10)
augmented	(0 4 8)	– – –	– –	– – –
italian	(0 2 6)	– – –	– –	– – –
french	– –	(0 2 6 10)	– –	– – –
german	– –	(0 2 6 9)	– –	– – –

Rows are terms in the type system, columns are terms in the completeness system and the inversion system. Entries are lists of intervals as explained in table 6.3.

theoretical grammar would make deeper use of the structure of the major and minor scales and their relation to chord types. In this version a number of simple tables were used to express this dependence, and each table resides intact at some point in the program. The tables do not represent any theoretical addition to the form of the grammar but represent information that could have been included (rather tediously and confusingly) in the networks and in simple realization rules. Rather than add much notation, a Father conversational style was used in some realization rules. This, of course, does not affect their status in the grammar, and the fact that they were implemented in a computer program shows that they are fully formal and unambiguous, as is demanded for a valid grammar.

Table 6.5

The relation of a note to the notes of another chord will be represented by one of the following codes:

MEMBER   actually contained in that chord
OMEMB   the same note class appears in the chord
ADJ 2   within a whole step of a note in the chord
ADJ NIL   with a whole step of a note in the chord, but not a member
ADJ O   either a half or whole step above a chord member
ADJ 1   either a half or whole step below a chord member

PREC is the preceding chord, FOL the following chord.

The realizations are:

passing::   Every N is ADJ NIL PREC or ADJ NIL FOL
auxiliary::   Every N is OMEMB FOL or both ADJ O PREC and ADJ O FOL or both
            ADJ 1 PREC and ADJ 1 FOL
suspension::   Every N is OMEMB FOL or both OMEMB PREC and ADJ NIL PREC
anticipation::   Every N is either OMEMB PREC or MEMBER FOL
subset::   Every N is MEMBER of PREC or FOL, respectively.

In addition, each realization includes the implication that no possibilities further down on the list can possibly apply.

Table 6.6

diatonic	0	1	2	3	4	5	6
f(diatonic)	0	2	4	5	7	9	11

One very useful notation that was adopted is the relative key. The problem of relative realization was discussed in section II.1, and through this simple notation it can be handled directly. The units Composition and tonality have as features a "key", consisting of a mode (major or minor) and a root. Whenever the symbol *K* appears at any rank, it refers to the key of the tonality (or at the top level, composition) nearest above it in constituent structure. This allows the rules to be formulated generally while creating no problems in the design of a parsing algorithm.

II.5   Semantics of Tonal Harmony

Working within the grammar described, we see that tonal harmony is a highly ambiguous language. The meaning of a chord is not determined by its structure but rather by its function in a tonality. The identical chord in terms of notes could appear at different place in the same composition with entirely different functions, some linear, others harmonic. The structures

Figure 6.1

are ambiguous at every level. Consider for example the progression of figure 6.1, taken out of context. If we consider C major as the tonality of the segment, it can be interpreted in many ways. It might be a normal VI → V → I sequence in C major. It might be part of a secondary tonality in G major, with the sequence II → I → IV. Or, in either case, the middle chord could be a passing chord, leaving progressions of VI → I in C or II → IV in G respectively. Or, in this case, it may be I → III in a minor with a passing chord. These do not even begin to account for the possibility of recursion in secondary tonalities—the possibility that either of the end chords may be a linear chord leading to something else, and so forth. The only way to decide which of these structures is actually functional is to place the progression in the context of the entire composition. Even if we accept a particular choice, such as V → V → I in C major, this may still be a secondary tonality serving any function in the larger progression, and without this the full function of the chords is not known.

Even with the full context of the composition, a good deal of ambiguity remains, and a second type of consideration must be used to explain the structure. We must consider the logic of a progression in terms of the principles of tonal harmony. The basic relationship concerns an interval of a fifth. The dominant → tonic cadence is its primary expression, but wherever it occurs it gives direction to the progression. Therefore a progression such as III → VI → II → V → I is in good accordance with this logic, and although IV → II → VI → V → I is possible, it is less likely, since there is no meaningful harmonic reason we can give to explain the particular order of the harmonies. This applies as well to the decision as to whether a chord is structural or linear. Given the choice of analysis V → II → I, or an analysis V → passing → I, the second is more reasonable since the entire progression can then be explained. On the other hand, given the choice of VI → V → I or VI → passing → I, the first is clearly more in accord with the principles.

These considerations are not as sharply delineated as those expressed above, and they form only one part of a whole range of semantic considerations. These are the concepts that guide a theoretician in giving a composition a "reading" he believes expresses its basic logic. The factors are complex and concern larger context in such things as melodic patterns, sequences, and the repetition of structures at different levels. An intelligent parsing of a composition must take into account many of the semantic factors, and it is a matter of experiment to determine which factors are significant and to what degree. Clearly this is different for different people as they may dispute particular parsings for a given composition. For our purpose, we will consider only the most basic principles: sequence of progression, clarity of function, and complexity of the parsing.

The first of these has been explained immediately above. Some progressions such as V → I or II → V have a clear function, while others such as VII → II or III → I may occur, but do so at the cost of confusion of the tonal structure and can thus considered less likely, or less "meaningful." This is vague territory, and for this project only very rough guides were used, as described in the next section. Second, if a chord is interpreted at a higher level in the tonality structure while it could be interpreted instead at a lower level (e.g., interpreting C major as IV of V of C major), it will tend to weaken the structure by confusing for the hearer the levels of tonality. Of course, this can happen if the surrounding tonalities are clearly enough defined to prevent confusion, but again we can consider analyses of this type "less meaningful." Finally, if a simpler parsing can explain a composition as well as a more complex one, it is clearly better. As a rough measure of complexity we can consider the maximum depth of nesting of secondary tonalities and the average depth through the composition.

For use in a parsing program, these factors can be combined in simple linear fashion to produce a single "plausibility value" for any parsing of a sentence (composition). Of course, a given composition may have as its best parsing one with a bad plausibility value. This would reflect its lack of adherence to the principles of tonal harmony. The two main factors discussed above are sequence of progression and clarity of function, and these two have been combined to produce the main parameter of the plausibility value. The rules for progression assign an integer value to each possible sequence of two harmonies operating in adjacent positions in the same tonality as follows:

authentic cadence (dom. → tonic)
opening (tonic → anything)

0   dominant preparation (dom. prep. → dom_1)
dominant substitution (dom_1 → dom)
substitution (anything → itself)

fifth progression (e.g., VI → II)
plagal cadence (IV → tonic)
deceptive cadence (dom → VI)
triad outline (III → V)

5   confusion of tonal structure (anything → I)

4   anything not covered above

Where dom = V, VII; dom_1 = V, VII, I_6^4; dom. prep. = II, IV, VI

The rules are ordered, so if anything higher in the list applies, the others are ignored. The presence of a linear chord between two structural chords is ignored by this part of the semantic evaluation but must be accounted for as an element of structural weakening. If a chord could be interpreted as serving a clear structural function (those with plausibility values 0 and 1), its linear possibilities should be ignored as less revealing of the actual structure. Thus a value of 3 is added for any linear chord (clearly, lower numbers represent more plausible parsings). The confusion caused by a chord that could be interpreted as a tonic at some level of its tonality hierarchy is accounted for by adding 1 for each chord in this state. The establishment of a secondary tonality that is "held up" on the tonality hierarchy in this way further muddles the tonality structure and results in a value of 3 being added. The sum of these two sets of values for the part of the composition already parsed is then the main plausibility value for that parsing. If in comparing two parsings these are identical, then information as to the complexity of the analysis is used to decide.

Due to the slant of the process, the plausibility values have been dealt with in terms of parsing. It would be as easy to set them out in terms of a generative grammar, relating them more closely to the representation of the grammar. The important point is that they present information of an entirely different type from the syntax. They are not rules in the sense of prescriptions that must be followed. A composition could be structured in such a way as to make their application meaningless. They are based instead on the idea that a sentence in a language can be expected to be meaningful—not only to conform in grammar but also to have an inner logic. The semantic rules represent a way of searching for this logic.

III Parsing

III.1 Basic Parsing Methods

The process of parsing a structure produced by a systemic grammar involves both the delineation of units, including their place in the constituent structure, and the determination of the features selected for each unit. Due to both the nature of the grammar and the highly ambiguous, context-sensitive syntax of the language, most of the standard parsing techniques (such as those used for artificial languages) are not applicable. No other research has been done on the parsing of systemic grammars in general, and the freedom implicit in the use of realization rules makes useful generalization difficult. However there is an obvious relation between a system network and a decision tree, and between realization rules and programmed operations on various data structures. This makes it a reasonable task to write programs that handle a great deal of the parsing. It may be a characteristic of natural languages that in most places, the theoretical freedom of realization is actually constrained by the fact that simple decision procedures for parsing must be possible or the language would be unintelligible. As an example, a routine that examines a chord and determines its inversion, root, and type can be easily written using the information in the system network and realization rules. The resulting parsing of the chord is a list of its features. These of course imply a number of facts about it, including its constituent structure. For more complex structures that allow rank shift, the problem is much more difficult since the boundaries of the unit are not marked and must be determined as part of the process. It is often not possible to determine the extent of a unit without some reference to its features, so the process must allow constant interaction between these two aspects.

One successful technique that has been used on context-free languages is predictive analysis (see Kuno and Oettinger 1963). The basic algorithm is a one-directional scan of the string. As each element is reached, a separate "path" is established for each of the different possible parsings of the string encountered up to that point, taking into account all possible continuations of the string. At each point, the new parsings will be based on the paths "passed along" by the previous stage, possibly terminating some of them as the new content is considered, and possibly branching into several new paths from one of the previous paths. When the end of the string is reached, any paths leading through the entire string represent syntactically possible parsings for the sentence. If there are none, it is ungrammatical. If there is more than one, it is ambiguous.

The obvious defect of this method is that the tree of paths produced can grow exponentially with the length of the string. For any reasonably complex or ambiguous system, this will always occur with a high branching number. Let us consider the case of tonal harmony. Since the presence of modulatory progressions is rare compared to complete tonalities, a parse from right to left will reduce the number of actual ambiguities encountered, even though the theoretical characteristics are the same. Therefore the scan is in the reverse order of the music. The current list of parsings (paths) at a point will give for each chord (or chord group) so far encountered both its structural function within the tonality of which it is a constituent and the nested structure of tonalities in which it operates. The chord to be analyzed then has the following possibilities:

1. It can function directly in the same tonality as the chord following it (i.e., previously analyzed). This is the simplest case, as in local progression.

2. It can be the tonic of a new secondary tonality, which as a whole will function directly in the same tonality as the following chord.

3. It can function in some tonality present in the tonality hierarchy of the following chord, but at a higher level. This will occur, for example, where a chord is followed by a secondary dominant. (Remember that the parsing proceeds backwards.)

4. It can be the tonic of a new secondary tonality that operates as in (3).

5. It may be the final secondary harmony following the tonic in a modulatory tonality.

6. It may be the dominant of an implied tonality.

7. It may be the dominant of an implied tonality which is in turn the final secondary harmony in a modulating tonality.

8. It may be a linear chord with no harmonic function.

Actually, there are other possibilities implied by these. In cases 5, 6, and 7 the secondary or implied tonality can in turn function either as in (1) and 2, or as in 3 and 4. This additional complexity was avoided by allowing the simple type of function 1 and 2 only. The more complex possibilities occur rarely enough that this causes few problems (see section V). In addition, several of these do not represent single choices. In 5 and 7, for example, the analysis depends on the key of the modulatory tonality in which the chord is interpreted, and since this will not have been encountered in a right-to-left scan, separate paths must be set up for each possible tonality in which the chord could serve. Possibilities 3 and 4 are multiple choices as well, since they allow reference to any depth in the tonality structure. Of course, not all possibilities will be open to every chord, but following all of the rules of harmony, the branching rate remains unbearably high (10 is a conservative estimate).

Clearly the method must be augmented with look-ahead capabilities, which can prevent the formation of paths that will lead obviously to nought. By making a first pass through the string, a number of simple but effective devices can be added. On this pass, the chords can be analyzed (i.e., the features of each chord can be determined). The linear capabilities of a chord depend on the context of the preceding and following chord, but since this context is strictly local, the determination is straightforward. Further, the potentiality of serving as a cadence (dominant → tonic) or an implied cadence (dominant preparation → dominant) is also a local property. We can decide without larger context whether a local progression can possibly be one of these, but the larger context is necessary to decide its actual function. These local checks allow the possibilities listed above to be cut as follows:

Possibilities 2 and 4 can function only if the chord is a potential tonic.

Possibilities 6 and 7 can be true only if the chord is a potential tonic .

Possibility 8 can function only if the chord has a potential linear function.

Possibilities 5 and 7 can function with a given tonality only if that tonality is established at an earlier point in the composition (i.e., there is a potential cadence in that tonality).

The last of these is the most important, since it eliminates much of the branching caused by the relativeness of structures. Out of at least forty-two possible tonalities (seven diatonic notes with three possible accidentals in both major and minor), a small number (generally less than five) are established in a short composition.

These reductions keep the number of paths reasonably close to the number of actually possible ambiguous parsings, but, since the language is so deeply ambiguous (due to the relative nature of most realizations), this is still an unreasonable number. This first improvement must be a path elimination technique (see Kuno and Oettinger 1963) that avoids redundant paths. This is possible because constituents can be independent. If one constituent has three possible parsings, and another has four, the result will be separate paths. However, only seven are necessary to include all of the possibilities, if they are properly recombined at the end. In our case, the only material relevant to the parsing of a string at any point is the set of possible functions and tonality structures for the most recently analyzed chord. The way in which that was reached is irrelevant to the continued parsing. Thus if two parsings of a section of the string lead via different paths to the same analysis for the final chord, we want to consider only one continuation.

III.2   The Use of Semantics

Since our goal is to produce a best parsing rather than all possible parsings, this is particularly easy. The semantic measures chosen depend only on the progression of harmonies and the tonality hierarchy, so they can be evaluated at any point of the parsing without reference to the yet-unparsed section. This allows us to simply eliminate the path or paths that are worse, knowing that whatever the continuation, they will remain worse than the one selected. This completely reduces the path elimination problem to one of semantic evaluation, and the result at the end of the parsing process will be a single "best" parsing (i.e., most in accord with the logic of tonal harmony) . This reduces the number of separate paths at a point to the number of actually distinct possibilities for the continuation of the parsing, but this is still generally a large number.

The second use of semantics is the most crucial, and is the one best dignified as a "heuristic." At any point in the parsing we can assign a plausibility value to each of the parsings (paths) of the string up to that point. Instead of carrying all of these forward, we can select only the most promising—those that are most likely to lead to good parsings. We thus give up a path that seems to be doing badly, and at times this may result in discontinuing a path only to see all the others become much worse (or even impossible) as the parsing continues, as the eliminated path accounted for context not yet encountered. This can be largely avoided by care in the semantic measure, but the possibility remains and is the price paid for the efficiency gained by this type of heuristic search. Of course there is a great deal of control over just how bad a path must be before it is eliminated. A balance must be found between clogging the machinery by keeping too many paths and throwing away too many, including possibly the right one.

Since we have used a simple integer value for the primary semantic evaluation, the elimination involves only the setting of a limit for the difference between the value for a path and the value for the best path found to that point. For other languages this would need to be much more complex, and it might be best to change from a width-first search with semantic-directed pruning (as used in this project) to a depth-first semantic-directed search. In this case some sort of acceptability criteria would be set, and if an entire parsing passed this criteria it would be accepted without trying any others. This would make relatively great demands on the semantic component, in order to direct the search accurately. One case would be natural language, where we interpret a sentence in the first way that occurs to us that makes sense, checking the possibility of ambiguities only if this first interpretation is for some reason unacceptable.

IV Computer Implementation

IV.I Programming Methods

The applicability of a computer language to this parsing algorithm depends on the presence of several important properties. First, it must be able to handle the wide variety of complex data structures, in the form of lists, trees, and networks. Second, it must be able to deal with the recursive structure of harmony efficiently. Finally, it must be able to communicate information easily from one part of the program to another, as the algorithm demands constant interaction between the semantics and several different aspects of parsing. LISP was chosen because it has all of these features, and particularly heavy use was made of free variables for inter-function communication.

A number of special tricks were used to make the program more efficient than the algorithm would be if implemented directly. Two of these are important enough for special mention. The first is the use of possibility lists in building the parsing tree. In analyzing the function of a chord, each of the many possibilities explained in Section III.1 must be checked. The various heuristics cut down the number of actually successful paths, but they do not necessarily reduce the number to be examined at a point. Each check involves seeing whether a particular chord or tonality can be interpreted in some other particular tonality. This is a straightforward but time-consuming procedure and may occur several hundred times for each chord. However, every tonality must be established at some point in the composition, and as was pointed out above a local check can find all of the possible established tonalities in the first scan of the string. A list (TONALIST) of these is made, and as each chord is reached in the parsing, the checking procedure is carried out with each member of this list (usually less than five), to produce a list (POSSLIST) of all the possible interpretations it could have at any point in the composition. Then for each further check, it is only necessary to look through this list. In order to handle modulating tonalities, a second list (POSSPOSS) is made of all of the possibilities for each member of POSSLIST. A similar pair of lists is used for implied tonalities. The use of these produces a major reduction in the amount of computation, and further efficiency is gained by attaching an atomic symbol (produced during the first scan by the LISP function (GENSYM) to each possible tonality, so all of the searches can be done with SASSOC, the fast LISP search function. The second method is the preliminary grouping of the chords. The algorithm is essentially a two-pass operation, but by including a third pass between these two, a further improvement is obtained. A sequence of chords that are different inversions of the same harmony, or a sequence that contains nonharmonic linear chords (i.e., chords that must be interpreted as serving a linear function) must form part of a single chord group. The grouping into chord groups may include other chords, but by making this preliminary grouping, we reduce the number of separate harmonies to be considered. The output form (see below) reflects this preliminary grouping, but its importance lies only in the internal functioning of the algorithm, not the resulting analysis.

IV.2   Computer Representation of Music

Since we are dealing only with the harmonic aspects of music, a particularly simple form of representation for music is possible. The program accepts a list of chords, each of which is a list of notes. (See Section V.1 for a description of how nonharmonic tones can be accounted for in this scheme.) A note is designated by a note class and an octave. The note class designates both the pitch class and the enharmonic spelling since this is vital to harmony. The internal representation of a note class is simply a dotted pair (the LISP form of an ordered pair) of integers, the first of which gives the diatonic class ($c = 0, \ldots, b = 6$) and the second gives the chromatic pitch class ($c = b\sharp = d\,\flat\flat = 0, \ldots, b = a\,\sharp\sharp = c\,\flat = 11$). A note is represented by dotting this pair with an integer representing the octave. Thus (3 . (4. 8)) is a g $\sharp$ in the third octave. This numerical representation is convenient for manipulations but not for input. Therefore conversion is made from a simpler form used by the person reading the score. The input includes a key signature in the form ($x\ n_1, \ldots, n_i$) where x is either "fl" or "sh," and each n_i is a note name. Thus the key signature of either c minor E flat major would be "(fl b e a)". Each chord is a sequence of note names; either atoms ("a," "b," etc.) or dotted pairs (n.p) where n is a note name, and p is the accidental ("fl," "sh," "n," "flfl," "shsh"). The atom "o" represents the jump of an octave, and the notes are listed in order from the bottom up. Thus O C O E G C is a chord containing a C in the second octave, and E and a G in the third octave, and a C in the fourth. The key signature is assumed to apply to any note not explicitly represented as a dotted pair. See figure 6.2 for some sample inputs.

The output of the program is a single best reading for the composition. It gives for each chord its function within the tonality of which it is a constituent, its inversion, and the tonality hierarchy in which it operates. Thus, "(II (6) (IV I))" represents a II6 in a secondary tonality, which in turn serves as IV of the main tonality. Instead of a roman numeral, the function can be as an altered chord (e.g., Neapolitan), or linear chord (e.g., Passing). As was explained above, a preliminary scan of the string reduces it to preliminary chord groups, and the output is grouped in the same way. Thus, "(IV (53 passing 65) (I))" represents a sequence $IV_5^3 \rightarrow$ passing $\rightarrow IV_6^5$ operating in the primary tonality of the composition.

IV.3   Description of the LISP Program

A program in LISP is made up of a number of individual functions. Each function accepts a number of arguments (inputs) and from them computes a value (result). These arguments and values may be numbers, symbols, or complex data structures. A number of basic functions for handling data structures and numbers form the LISP system. To these the programmer

Sample Inputs

EXPLAIN((
(BACH CHORALE 12)(N)
(A O C E A)(O A C E A)(O G C E A)(O(F. SH)D A)(O G D G B)(O D D G B)
(O F D G B)(O E C G C)(O C O E G B)(O F C F A)(O C C E G)
(O C O E G C)(O O C E G C)(O B E(G. SH)D)(O A E A C)(O(F. SH)D A C)
(O G D G B)(O C O E G C)(O O C E G C)(O A E A C)(O(F. SH)D A C)(O D D(F. SH)C)
(O G D G B)(O E E G B)(O(C. SH)O E G A)(O D D G A)(O(D. SH)B(F. SH)B)(O E B E(G. SH))
(A O C E A)(O F A D A)(O F B D G)(O E C E G)(O(F. SH)A D A)(O G D B)(O(F. SH)B D B)
(O(G. SH)D F B)(O A C E C)(O D D F)C)(O E D G B)(O F C G A)(O(D. SH)C(F. SH)A)
(O E B E(G. SH))(A O(C. SH)E A)))

EXPLAIN((
(SCHUBERT OP 33 NO 7)(FL B E)
(O O F B D)(F O F B D)(O F E F A C)(F O F A C)(O F E F B D)
(O F E F C E)(B O F D F)(O F D F B D)(B O F D F)(O F D F B D)
(F O F B D)(O F E F A C)(F O F A C)(O F E F G B)(O F E F A C)
(B O F B D)(O F B D F B)(B O D F B)(O O (A. FL) B D)
(B O (A. FL) B F)(O B F (A. FL)B D)(B O (A. FL)B F)(O B F(A. FL)B D)
(E E O (A. FL) B F)(E B E G B E)(O C G C G E)(O D G (B. N)F G D)
(O E G C E G C)(F O D F C)(O F B D F B)(F O D F)
(O F B D F B)(O F B D F C)(F O E F D)(O F A E F C)
(B F B D F B)))

EXPLAIN((
(BACH NO 57)
(N)
(O E B(G. SH)E)(O A E C)(O (G. SH) A E B)(A (F. SH) E C)(A(F. SH)(D. SH)C)
(O E(G. SH)E B)(O D B E(G. SH))(O C C E A)(O F B D A)(O F A D A)
(O E B E(G. SH))(O E B(G. SH)E)(O A C A E)(O(G. SH)B B E)(O A C A F)
(O B D A F)(O O C E G C)(O O C G D)(O(F. SH)C A D)(O G B G D)
(O G B F D)(O C C E C)(G O D G B)(A O C F C)(A O C E C)
(B O G D D)(B O G O D)(O C G O C E)(O C A O C E)(O(G. SH)B B D)
(O E(G. SH) O B D)(O A E A C)(O E E(G. SH)B)
(O(F. SH)E E A)(O(F. SH)D E A)(O(G. SH)D E B)(O(G. SH)C E B)
(O A C E F)(O G B E C)(O F A A D)(O E A G E)(O D A F B)
(O E(G. SH)E B)(O E(G. SH)D B)(A E C A)))

Figure 6.2

adds a set of special functions (subroutines) to perform the desired computation. The complexity of a program arises from the ability of a function to call as a part of its computation either some other function or itself. Many LISP programs are therefore highly recursive.

Below are summaries of the major functions written for the parsing described above. A number of smaller functions were also written to carry out the details of the computation. The names of functions, arguments, and variables are completely arbitrary and were intended to have some mnemonic value. The basic functional notation is used: A(B C) implies that the function named A is to be applied to the arguments B and C.

EXPLAIN(INPUT) This is the main bookkeeping function that is called to use the system. It accepts an INPUT in the form described in section IV.2, asks for LIMIT to be typed in at the console, initiates a timer, then calls the working functions. It ends by printing the final parsing as returned by GIVE and returns the execution time as its value.

IDENTIFY(CHORDS, KEY) The first pass operates on the INPUT to produce a parsing of each chord. The value is a string of lists of features, giving all of the chord rank information for each chord. The function LIN(CHORD) is called to determine the LINEARITY term, accounting for context. IDENTIFY has the one additional function of setting a flag if the final chord contains a Picardy third.

SIMPLIFY(CHORDS) The second pass performs a number of tasks. It outputs statistics (number of chords, and number of preliminary chord groups), does the grouping into preliminary chord groups, sets up the TONALIST of established tonalities, and flags possible cadences and implied tonalities. TONALIST is set as a free variable, and the value returned is a list of preliminary chord groups with their features.

ANALYZE(INPUT) The main parsing algorithm is carried out by ANALYZE operating on the result of SIMPLIFY and producing the parsing tree by using a set of nested PROG loops. It loops through INPUT, producing a list NEWLIST of nodes at each layer as it is encountered. Generation of the tree is width-first. For each preliminary chord group it first generates the possibility lists POSSLIST and POSSPOSS, using the function SCAN (TLIST CHORD). It then loops through the nodes (CU) of the previous layer (CURLIST), checking for possible branches. When a possibility is found, BUILD(P) is called to decide whether the new path is eliminated by one of the semantic heuristics, and if not, to add it to the tree. At each layer it outputs the number of nodes, and before returning its value it prints the total number of nodes in the tree and the number it attempted to build before use of the semantic heuristics. The value returned is the set of terminal nodes of the tree.

BUILD(P) The argument of BUILD is an indicator of the point in the program from which it was called. The nine choices correspond roughly to those described in Section III.1. All of the other data used is from free variables, and the result, if any, is the modification of a free variable

(NEWLIST, the new layer of the tree) with a RPLACD. The information for the new node is gathered, and the functions PLAUS(FROM TO) and HOLDUP(CHORD PDLIST) are called to determine the plausibility value. If this exceeds the best at this level by more than LIMIT, no action is taken and BUILD returns. Otherwise,

COMPARE(READING TLIST)   This checks to see if the node is a candidate for path elimination, using COMP2(READING TLIST) for the actual semantic computation. If the new path is eliminated, no action is taken. If it eliminates a previous path, it is put in its place with RPLACD. If there is no elimination, COMPARE adds it to NEWLIST. COMPARE and BUILD then both return irrelevant values.

REDUCE(TLIST)   The list of nodes produced by ANALYZE is checked for one last syntactic problem. Some may have an unestablished modulatory tonality and are eliminated. The rest are compared semantically, using COMP2(READING TLIST), and the best is returned.

GIVE(READING)   Since each node contains a pointer to the immediately dominating node, GIVE is able to trace the best parsing all the way back through the tree, producing a unique parsing path. The information at each node is converted to the output format and the resulting list is returned as the value to be printed by EXPLAIN.

V   Results

V.1   Program Use

The program was written and debugged using the LISP system of the Compatible Time-Sharing System at Project MAC. It was tested by coding and parsing a number of actual compositions. Due to computer time limitations, no extensive analysis was made of the effects produced by changing various parameters. Since the semantic evaluation scheme was rather ad hoc, it is likely that changes in it will result in some improvement of the program's performance. However, even with this first approximation the program performed excellently on simple compositions and relatively well on more complex works. The goal was to achieve "intelligent" parsings that avoided the simplistic one-dimentional results of other programs. This was achieved, and the outputs included some quite sophisticated parsings, including the recognition of implied tonalities, modulations, and complex tonality structures.

Due to the difficulty of coding the harmonies present in complex music, the works selected had simple rhythmic and voice structure, so they could be input relatively directly to the program. For simple structures some Schubert dances were chosen, and more complex structures were chosen from textbook examples (Forte 1962, Hardy and Fish 1964) and from a collection of Bach chorales.

A chorale presents a direct sequence of harmonies, yet has a rather complex harmonic structure. Submetrical notes were entered by giving the entire chord once for each submetrical division that involved a change of notes (see below for a discussion of the problems this raises). Figure 6.2 shows the input to the program for three works. Figure 6.3 contains the corresponding computer outputs, and figure 6.4 displays these results on the score. The results are exactly as returned by the program, including the submetrical analysis.

The program in compiled LISP took around 30 seconds for a typical chorale of 30 to 40 chords. This could be improved through programming tricks, but no effort was made to do so. The form of the program is the result of the interactive experimental nature of its development. A large part of the success of the program is due to the ease with which the interactive system allowed continual experimentation and modification.

V.2   Discussion of Problems in Analysis

In analyzing the difficulties encountered by the program, it is important to separate those problems that could be overcome by minor program challenges and those that are more basic to the approach. The primary limitation is that the program is intended for the analysis of harmony, not the analysis of a musical composition as a whole. This leads to several difficulties. In any but the simplest pieces, a large amount of analysis is needed to determine just which harmonies are present where. Since the input to the program is a series of chords, the results will depend on how the score is broken up by the person providing the input. The examples given followed a simplistic approach and, for example, the repeated 164 chords in the first few measures of the Schubert work would have been better read as part of the surrounding chords. The same problem arises with non-harmonic notes. As was explained above, all pitch changes are represented

Sample Outputs

(477 BUILT 267 KEPT)
((BACH CHORALE 12 (FULL FIRST PART)) (I (53 53 42) (I)) (V
(6) (V III-MAJ I)) (V (53 64) (III-MAJ I)) (V (42) (III-MAJ
I)) (III-MAJ (6) (I)) (III-MAJ (7) (I)) (IV (53) (III-MAJ I))
(I (53 53 53) (III-MAJ I)) (PASSING (43) (III-MAJ I)) (VI (
53) (III-MAJ I)) (V (65) (V III-MAJ I)) (V (53) (III-MAJ I))
(III-MAJ (53 53) (I)) (VI (53) (III-MAJ I)) (V (65 7) (V III-MAJ
I)) (I (53) (V III-MAJ I)) (VI (53) (V III-MAJ I)) (V (65 NIL)
(V V III-MAJ I)) (PASSING (6) (III-MAJ I)) (PASSING (53) (III-MAJ
I)) (VI (53) (III-MAJ I)) (II (6) (III-MAJ I)) (V (42) (III-MAJ
I)) (III-MAJ (6) (I)) (IV (6) ((I . MAJ) I)) (PASSING (53)
((I . MAJ) I)) (II (64) ((I . MAJ) I)) (VII (7) ((I . MAJ)
I)) (I (53) (I)) (IV (7) (I)) ((I . MIN) (7 PASSING) (V I))
(VII (7) (V I)) (V (53) (I)) ((I . MAJ) (53) (I)))
(TIME 351)

(466 BUILT 250 KEPT)
((BACH NO 57) (V (53) (I)) (I (53 PASSING) (I)) (PASSING (65)
(V I)) (VII (43) (V I)) (V (53) (I)) (V (42) (I)) (I (6) (I))
(PASSING (43) (I)) (IV (6) (I)) (V (53 53) (I)) (I (53) (I))
(PASSING (6) (III-MAJ I)) (IV (6) (III-MAJ I)) (VII (7) (III-MAJ
I)) (I (53 PASSING) (III-MAJ I)) (V (65) (V III-MAJ I)) (V
(53) (III-MAJ I)) (V (7) (III-MAJ I)) (III-MAJ (53) (I)) (V
(53) (III-MAJ I)) (PASSING (6) (III-MAJ I)) (VI (53) (III-MAJ
I)) (V (6 6) (III-MAJ I)) (III-MAJ (53) (I)) (I (6) (I)) (VII
(53) (I)) (V (7) (I)) (I)(53) (I)) (V (53) (I)) (VI (7 ANTIC)
((I . MAJ) I)) (V (65 PASSING) ((I . MAJ) I)) (I (53) (I))
(III-MAJ (43) (I)) (IV (6 NIL) (I)) (PASSING (65) (I)) (V (
53) (1)) (V (7) (I)) (I (53) (I)))
(TIME 279)

(134 BUILT 82 KEPT)
((SCHUBERT OP 33 NO 7) (I (64 64) (I)) (V (7) (I)) (V (53 PASSING
PASSING) (I)) (I (53 64 53 64 64) (I)) (V (7) (I)) (V (53 AUX)
(I)) (V (7) (I)) (I (53 64 53) (I)) (V (42 CONT2 7 CONTI 7
ANTIC) (IV I)) (IV (53) (I)) (II (53) (I)) (V (43) (II I))
(II (6) (I)) (SUSP (65) (I)) (I (64) (I)) (III (6) (I)) (I
(64 NIL PASSING) (I)) (V (7) (I)) (I (53) (I)))
(TIME 160)

Figure 6.3

as chord changes. This can work only in simple rhythmic forms like
chorales, and even there can lead to trouble. In the second beat of "O
Traurigkeit," one tone is passing and another an auxiliary, so no simple
label can be attached to this as a chord. Since the program was designed
essentially to analyze harmony and only secondarily to identify linear
relations, an extremely simplified set of definitions was used, as described
in table 6.5. This led to a number of mislabeled linear chords. The important point is that the program decided when a chord functioned as a
structural harmonic chord and when it indicated their specific function.

O Traurigkeit

Figure 6.4

This would also involve writing a less ad hoc grammar for this aspect, but would fit well within the general framework of the grammar.

Another problem arises from the fact that the program deals only with the principles of harmony. Much of the structure of music is based on melodic and contrapuntal ideas, and sometimes the harmonic structure cannot be adequately explained without referring to these. This occasionally prevents the program from finding subtle analyses in harmonically difficult passages, such as in the 13th and 14th measures of "Puer natus in Bethlehem". Once in a while, such a problem may cause the program to distort the entire harmonic structure of a piece in order to find some sort of harmonic explanation for a particular passage. In one case, an entire passage was interpreted as V of III of IV when it should clearly have been III. Adding more weight to the complexity measures would prevent this sort of large-scale distortion but would not solve the problems in the more difficult areas. This problem is basic to the approach of a strictly harmonic analysis and would involve a large-scale broadening of the program to bring melodic and contrapuntal considerations into the semantic evaluation. It might be possible to do this within the framework of the specific grammar given here, but it would be difficult. The problem of analyzing an entire musical composition rather than a series of harmonies would be extremely difficult and probably beyond the range of these specific methods.

Since there was insufficient opportunity to modify the program after seeing its results, it retains a number of small problems that cause mistakes in the output but could be remedied by slight changes. For example the second chord in measure 4 of "O Traurigkeit" is analyzed as serving a linear function rather than a dominant function. This happened because it did not resolve in any normal way, and thus did not seem to function within the semantic rules. The program (and grammar) could be extended to look for simple substitutions of this sort, particularly in the case of the V → I progression. In "Puer natus in Bethlehem" the secondary dominants are recognized (as are almost all in the pieces analyzed), but the structure in measure 11 is missed. This is due to the fact mentioned in section III.1 that the program does not take into account all of the structural possibilities at every point. This problem was encountered only twice in all the parsing and could be eliminated as explained there by considering the extended possibilities. This would involve including only a few more lines of code in the program, and is already implicit in the grammar.

The cost would be an increase in the number of paths traced in the parsing, and it is difficult to calculate the amount of increase. Along with a general program speedup, it would probably not be unacceptable.

The assumption that incomplete chords should always be handled by completing them with a fifth led to the mistaken III6 of measure 15 of the Schubert example. All that is needed here is to let the program take both paths, one assuming the fifth is missing and the other that the tonic is missing. Similarly, the assumption that incomplete chords always have a third led to missing the V7 in measure 3 of the same work. A few additions to table 6.4 would solve these problems for both the program and the grammar.

Overall the program gives sophisticated readings, identical at most points to those of a human analyst. With the minor improvements discussed in the last few paragraphs and with a more elaborate grammar for nonharmonic tones, it would perform nearly perfectly on simple pieces such as the Schubert dances and competently in works such as the Bach chorales. In order to analyze the latter completely, or to handle more difficult rhythmic structure, it would have to be greatly modified. Even so, this might well be done using the same basic approach, a semantic-directed parsing using a systemic grammar.

VI Conclusions

The work described in this chapter has implications for two different fields of study—the structure of music and the use of semantic techniques in parsing arbitrary languages.

We have demonstrated the possibility of writing a plausible systemic grammar for at least one aspect of tonal music, and the form of the grammar seems applicable to many other aspects. Reviewing some of the properties of the grammar discussed above:

1. The structure resulting from realizations is not necessarily a one-dimensional string but can have several independent dimensions (time, pitch, loudness).

2. At any rank in the grammar a number of different systems can operate independently. Thus at note rank, we would have systems of pitch, duration, articulation, and possibly others.

3. The resulting structure is not segmented in a single way but may have several constituent structures, even in the same dimension. This could account for the analysis of music into phrase groupings, melodic groupings, harmonic groupings, and so forth.

4. The syntax is based on the use of systems, containing limited sets of mutually exclusive features. Systems of this sort abound in music, with systems of pitches, durations, chord types, inversions, key, time signature, and numerous others.

We have applied this analysis to tonal music, but it seems applicable in principle to other types. For any type of music, the formulation of semantic rules will be difficult (as for all natural languages). The use of systemic grammar to outline the syntactic choices can provide a clear framework for discussing semantic notions. A complete parsing system for music would be extremely complex and might even be more difficult than a system for natural language, since the semantics (and even the syntax) of music is extremely elusive once we leave simple areas such as harmonic structure. However it is important to realize that the application of linguistic principles to music can be of great value without attempting to achieve this goal. The formalization of its syntax into an explicit grammar (even a partial grammar) can give insight into the way in which the resources of music interact and combine in structures. Of course different styles of music would be different languages and would demand different grammars, but the basic principles and formalism introduced here may be productive for a variety of studies.

The use of semantic-directed parsing seems applicable as well to other natural languages. Through the close relation of systemic features to semantic features, it is feasible to bring semantic considerations into all levels of the grammar. Of course this would imply the existence of a semantic evaluation scheme or model to which the parsing routines could refer. The form of such a model would need to be worked out, but even a simple model would be of use, as shown in this chapter.

Through the use of semantic considerations we can devise algorithms that can efficiently parse even rather unruly ambiguous languages. In addition, the existence of such a system would imply the ability to convert language directly into statements in the semantic model, thus introducing a first step towards the processing of language in terms of meaning and understanding. Clearly this is a distant goal, but it is only through this sort of intimate interaction between syntax and semantics that successful processing of natural languages will be achieved.

Acknowledgments

Work described in this chapter was supported in part by Project MAC, an MIT research project sponsored by the Advanced Research Projects Agency, Department of Defense, under ONR contract Nonr-4102(01). The linguistic research was supported by a Fulbright-Hayes Grant at the University of London. I would like to thank Professor Allen Forte for his advice and encouragement at every stage of the project, and John Rothgeb, A. W. Slawson, Richard Judson, and Afaf Elmenoufy for their helpful comments on both the musical and linguistic ideas.

Appendix: Notations of Systemic Grammar

As implied by their name, the system networks that form the heart of a systemic grammar are best displayed in the form of a treelike network showing their dependencies. The following conventions are standard:

1. Dependencies are represented by lines from left to right. Thus if A is conditional on B, we draw

—A———B

2. Systems are represented by square brackets to the right. Thus if the choice of A implies that we must then choose between B, C, and D, we draw

3. Simultaneous systems, all of which must be considered, are represented by brackets to the right. Thus if the choice of A implies that we must choose one feature from each of the pairs B, C and D, E, we write

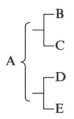

Often it is convenient to give these systems names for reference. These names do not represent features, and are written above the lines, as in

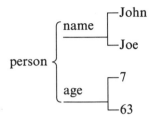

4. If a system is operative if any of a group of features is present, we use a square bracket pointing left. If the presence of either A or B implies the presence of C, we write

If the presence of A or B implies we must choose between C and D, we write

5. If a system is operative only when all of a set of features is present, we use left facing brackets. If in case four we must have A and B, we write, respectively

$$A- \rbrace\, C \quad \text{and} \quad A- \rbrace\!\!\left[\begin{matrix} C \\ D \end{matrix} \right.$$

In addition to these notations, I have adopted one other that reduces the number of lines in the diagram. If a feature is conditional on a feature at some other point in the network, rather than connecting them, we can include a reference using the notation –:A to show the dependency. Thus, if B is conditional on A, we can replace the B node with —A:—B wherever it appears. For example, if the presence of feature A demands a choice between B, C, and D, but the feature B can be present only when some feature E is present (wherever E may appear in the network), we write the system as,

$$
A\left\{\begin{array}{l} \text{—:E:—B} \\ \text{C} \\ \text{D} \end{array}\right.
$$

In addition to this two-dimensional representation, there is a simple linear form for describing system networks. It is rather harder to follow, and is not used here. For a description of this, and a number of other details concerning the formal representation, see Henrici (1966).

Since realizations can be of a number of types, no set notation has been adopted. However, there are some conventions for specifying partial structures, as follows:

1. $+A$ implies that a constituent with the function A is to be added to the structure.

2. A $\bullet$ B is an unordered structure consisting of the two elements A and B. It is the same as B $\bullet$ A.

3. $A \frown B$ implies that A and B are concatenated in that order.

4. (C) represents an optional element of the structure.

5. There are marker symbols used for the ends of the string. I have used $\sharp$. The standard British usage is §.

6. A_B implies a restriction, B, on the unit A that fills that slot in the structure. This is used in two ways. Either B is a subscript whose meaning is described in listing the possible units that serve the designated function, or it is a feature of the system network for that unit, which must be selected. Which convention is being used will always be clear from context.

7. $\triangle A$ implies that some element of the structure has the restriction A, but does not specify which.

8. A $\sim$ B implies that the two functions A and B are to be filled by the same constituent unit. This is used to attach dummy restrictions to particular constituents.

In addition to these, I have adopted two others. $A = N$ implies that the constituent with function A has feature N. It is the same as attaching a subscript N to A. $A \equiv N$ implies that the function A is filled by a unit of rank N. I have also used commas to attach several restrictions, and logical terms are used directly. Thus $A_{B,C}$ implies that the constituent functioning as A has both the restrictions B and C, while $A_{B\,or\,C}$ indicates that it has one or the other (or both, if that is not precluded by the network).

Notes

1. Throughout this paper, the term "semantic" is used in a nonformalized heuristic sense. The usage should become clear through its application in the paper.

2. The name of the grammar derives from this use of "system". In both the theory and this paper this word is used only in its technical sense as described.

3. The word "tonality" is used in two senses in this paper. In addition to its usual sense, as in "the composition is in the tonality of $c^{\sharp}$ minor", it is used to refer to a group of successive chords functioning in the same tonality. In the usual tonal structure one tonality may be embedded within another. Instead of saying that there is "a sequence of chords functioning in the tonality of G major", we say that there is "a tonality with 'root' G and 'mode' minor". This is nonstandard terminology, but makes the grammar clearer, and causes no confusion in context.

References

Chomsky, Noam. *Syntactic Structures* (Mouton, s'-Gravenhage, The Netherlands, 1957).

Chomsky, Noam. "Formal properties of grammars", in *Handbook of Mathematical Psychology*, ed. Luce et al. (Wiley, New York, 1963).

Forte, Allen. *Tonal Harmony in Concept and Practice* (Holt, Rinehart, and Winston, New York, 1962).

Halliday, M. A. K. "Some notes on 'deep' grammar", *Journal of Linguistics* 2, 1967.

Hardy, G., and A. Fish. *Music Literature*, Vol. I (Dodd, Mead, & Co., New York, 1964).

Henrici, A. "Some notes on the systemic generation of a paradigm of the English clause", mimeographed, 1966.

Huddleston, R. D. "Rank and depth", *Language* 41, 1965.

Hudson, R. A. "Constitutency in a systemic description of the English clause", *Lingua* 17, 1967.

Jackson, R. "The computer as a 'student' of harmony", Tenth Congress of the International Musicological Society, 1967.

Kuno, S., and A. G. Oettinger. "Syntactic structure and ambiguity of English", *Proceedings of IFIPS Congress*, 1963.

III AI AND MUSIC: HEURISTIC COMPOSITION

To ascertain the computational soundness of the theories of Johann David Heinichen and Michel de Saint-Lambert, two eighteenth-century music theorists, Rothgeb realizes in code (SNOBOL) their rules for harmonizing the unfigured bass. Thus, for the first General Rule of Heinichen, Rothgeb uses the procedural description in his system for, "If the bass of a triad descends a semitone ... (then) the next bass note has a sixth."

In a diagram to describe its syntax, Rothgeb parses the above rule into terms, functions, one-term, and two-term predicates. The functions take bass notes as their arguments, and the predicates return values as to the applicability of a given rule.

Although it encapsulates the complete bass-realization rule sets of both Heinichen and Saint-Lambert, Rothgeb's program does not always succeed in harmonizing an unfigured bass. When this happens, the program returns an error message.

Rothgeb finds in this study that both Heinichen and Saint-Lambert fail to solve the unfigured bass problem with their rule sets. He conjectures that the "principal source of inadequacy" of these two theories has to do with their failure to consider the "hierarchic, stratified character of the bass."

7 Simulating Musical Skills by Digital Computer

John Rothgeb

It was perhaps inevitable that the digital computer, an instrument of such potential and accomplishment in the study of both natural and social sciences and humanities, should have been applied to the investigation of problems in the fine arts as well. Among the latter, music was predictably the art form most directly accessible to computational study. Painting and the plastic arts do not readily lend themselves to direct computer applications; their analysis and elucidation with the aid of computers will necessarily await the development of highly sophisticated optical scanning devices at the very least. Music, on the other hand, is normally set down and transmitted graphically in the form of a notated score that can be almost completely represented in a code consisting of discrete symbols. It must be said at once, however, that the notated musical score, even of the simplest traditional western art music, is incomplete: The musical work, as conceived by the composer and as produced by the sensitive musical performer, deviates from the precision of the written or printed score in countless ways—most obviously with respect to temporal organization, but also, even, with respect to pitch and timbre.[1] Thus the score is at best an approximation to what can be properly be designated as "the" composition. To appreciate fully what this means, it is instructive to imagine, or actually to experience, if possible, a literal realization by synthesizer of, say, a Bach sonata for unaccompanied violin (to choose a particularly extreme example). The hearer of such a realization finds it almost impossible to "follow the music," to "make sense" of it, and this has far less to do with the timbral inadequacies of the synthesizer's violin tone than with the missing temporal and dynamic nuances. (The same music speaks eloquently on ancient phonorecords, despite their obvious timbral deficiencies.) But the printed score and its representation in an appropriate linear form, incompleteness notwithstanding, present a sufficiently detailed picture of the music's structure to render it accessible to analytical probing in a depth not approachable in many other art forms.

Tonal Music

Music theorists customarily group musical artworks into classes defined on the basis of shared structural characteristics. Tonal music, or the class

Copyright 1969, *IEEE Transactions on Computers*, and reproduced by permission.

of tonal compositions, is one such class; twelve-tone music (ingenuous to the twentieth century) is another. It is convenient, moreover, to distinguish between the compositions belonging to a given class and the language underlying those compositions; this distinction is often compared to that made in linguistics between the corpus of sentences in a language and the grammar according to which those sentenced are produced and interpreted. (The analogy, though useful, is far from perfect; I shall not develop it further here.) Tonal music, comprising most of the music written between about 1650 and 1900, is especially suitable as an object for rigorous and therefore computational) study for several reasons. First, its significance as a pinnacle in the history of art music in general is indisputable. Secondly, it has a highly constrained syntax embodied by many known regularities: for example, the class of interval characterized as dissonant, and the structural obligations incumbent upon such intervals, were firmly established before 1650 and remained constant throughout the period of tonal music.[2] Finally, tonal compositions are structurally organized in terms of a series of strata (each stratum specifiable in its own musical notation) that relate to one another as simple to (more) complex.[3] This means that one can *explain* a tonal composition according to the venerable explanatory model wherein complex phenomena or configurations are related through known operations to simple and familiar ones. (This notion elucidates, among many other things, the basis of the art of musical variation as applied not only in works entitled "Theme and Variations" but also from phrase to phrase and bar to bar in the classical masterworks: variations which contrast markedly in notation and—therefore—in sonic qualities may share a common underlying stratum.) For convenience, I shall speak here occasionally of the simple-to-complex array or simply array of strata associated with a given composition.

Computer-Accessible Problems in Music Theory

In view of the characteristics of music representation and the nature of tonal music as outlined, and the capabilities of the digital computer, a wide range of possible computer applications in music theory comes to mind. Well-trained musicians have a thorough but inexplicit understanding of the elements and operations that make up the language we call classical tonality. It is part of the essence of theoretical studies, however, to render explicit that which has been inexplicit. The familiar result of such work is that new areas of inexplicitness are exposed, and those areas are then subject to study and explication in their turn. By symbolically representing the elements of musical notation and expressing in formal terms those operations believed to form the basis of interstratal relations, the music theorist obtains something comparable to a generative grammar with all of its advantages for the refinement and verification of theories.

There are several avenues through which one may approach such research; they may be characterized in terms of the requirements one might impose on the theory to be tested. In the first place, a theory might be required, in its computational implementation, to compose credible tonal music and only such music, starting from minimal axiomatic bases of some kind and applying the known operations to derive further steps in the simple-to-complex array. In principle, one could require the output of such a machine to include the *Goldberg Variations* and *Hammerklavier Sonata* while excluding such conservative departures from classical tonal syntax as the milder pieces from Hindemith's *Ludus Tonalis*. (The exclusion clause is obviously necessary: trivial theories could be constructed that would generate authentic tonal pieces among countless arbitrary concatenations of notes.) A weaker requirement would be that the theory be capable, given an authentic tonal composition, of constructing the simple-to-complex array associated with it. Or, a theory could be designed to operate as a decision procedure: given an arbitrary musical score, does the composition specified belong to the class of tonal compositions, or not?

Investigations of each of the above types have been proposed, but to my knowledge none has been brought to a satisfactory conclusion. Nor is this surprising, in view of the obvious complexity of the tonal language and of the compositional technique displayed by its greatest "native speakers." One might, therefore, want to consider possibly useful initial limitations of the foregoing experimental designs. For example, work is currently being done toward solution of the following problem: given level n in the simple-to-complex array (or possibly levels 0 through n), compute level $n + 1$ (or $n + m$, for some relatively small value of m).[4] Alternatively, one could start with an extremely restricted corpus of music—initially even a single work—and proceeding from an apparently correct rational reconstruction thereof, supplement the rules of procedure for moving from stratum n to stratum $n + 1$ with rule-constraints appropriate to the particular style of composition under investigation.[5] In either case, the advantages afforded by the computational implementation for verification of the theory and in suggesting new lines of inquiry are both obvious and familiar.

The Unfigured-Bass Problem

I was invited to prepare this chapter as a pioneer in the field of computational studies in music. That characterization can be considered accurate only if it is interpreted as indicating that the project that I undertook several years ago, and that I will now describe to you with merciful brevity, belongs properly to the prehistory of such endeavors.[6]

The unfigured-bass problem can be fitted in a loose way into the schema of simple-to-complex arrays previously outlined in that it involves a progression from a less fully specified pitch structure to a more fully specified one. From the locution unfigured bass, you may correctly infer that there is such a thing as a figured bass; the latter entity is, in an important and interesting sense, more advanced in the array terminating in a tonal composition than the former. A figured bass, that is, a bass line with certain combinations of arabic numbers and musical accidental symbols adjoined either above or below it, specifies not only the bass voice of the composition with which it is associated but also the chords that accompany those bass notes, and, to a considerable extent, the voice leading (horizontal progression) of the (as yet unwritten) voices above that bass.

During the seventeenth and eighteenth centuries, the figured bass (or thorough-bass) was applied as a kind of musical shorthand in notating all music accompanied by a *basso continuo*, normally played by cello, gamba, or bassoon together with a keyboard instrument. The keyboard player was expected to infer and supply chords and voice leading on the basis of the figures given; this was known as realizing the figured bass.[7]

Since a figured-bass realization as performed by a trained accompanist can also be written down in standard musical notation, the art of realizing such a bass is itself a skill that admits of simulation by computer. If the continuo bass was unfigured, as occasionally happened in the thorough-bass period, the accompanist was still required to provide a competent realization. The necessary musical skill in this case involves two distinct steps: (1) infer appropriate figured-bass figures from the structure of the bass itself, and (2) realize the resulting figured bass in accordance with the conventional rules. It was the first step of this process that I endeavored to simulate computationally.

To supply appropriate figures for an unfigured bass is a nontrivial problem; although some latitude exists, an arbitrary assignment of figures would, in general, result in violations of tonal syntax. For example, the penultimate note of a "cadential" configuration must be set with a figure that determines a major triad or a "dominant-seventh" type chord; other combinations of figures such as 6, 6/5, 4/3, etc., although in themselves possible in figured-bass realization, would be incorrect in such a context.

The problem of the unfigured bass was recognized by a number of eighteenth-century thorough-bass theorists and treated in some detail by a few. Among the more extended informal algorithms for solving the unfigured-bass problem—that is, for determining appropriate figures from the organization of the bass itself—were those by Heinichen and Saint-Lambert.[8,9] One of the main computational aspects of my study, then, was the explication and testing, by computer, of the theories set down by those eighteenth-century authors.

It would far exceed time and space limitations to undertake an exhaustive description of the Heinichen and Saint-Lambert procedures for bass harmonization. For our purposes it is sufficient to state briefly the necessary components of a computational implementation of them. First, the computer must have access to an unfigured bass in a symbolic code readable by it. Secondly, computer programs must be defined in a suitable programming language; these programs must have the capability to examine the encoded bass, derive from it information of various kinds, and generate new symbolic code incorporating the computed figured-bass specifications.

The music-representation system adopted for this purpose was the code known as DARMS (Digital Alternate Representation of Musical Scores), developed by Stefan Bauer-Mengelberg and his associates. DARMS is capable of representing all aspects of even very complex conventional music scores, including stem-direction, beaming, dynamics, and expression marks. The unfigured-bass programs accept as input data relatively simple monophonic musical utterances, and it was not necessary to retain all of the information included in the musical notation; for example, stem-direction is irrelevant to the harmonization procedures and therefore was not specified in the code.

The programs were written in the SNOBOL3 programming language, then one of the more sophisticated languages available for problems involving operations on data in the form of free character strings. They comprised a network of variable and constant terms (used for designating individual bass notes and musical-interval constants, respectively) one- and two-termed predicates, and one- and two-termed functions. The relation of these two entities to bass-harmonization rules as formulated by the eighteenth-century theorists under consideration can best be shown with reference to a specific example. The first of Heinichen's General Rules (his theory also includes Special Rules, which will not concern us here) for assigning figures to an unfigured bass is stated as follows: "If the bass of a triad descends a semitone ... (then) the next bass note has sixth." Figure 7.1 illustrates the analysis of this rule into its component parts. The predicates (some of which were regarded as "primitive" and others as "defined") accept as arguments individual bass notes as represented in DARMS and/or musical interval names (with or without specification of interval quality and direction) and return truth values. The functions accept bass notes as arguments and return other bass notes. In general the functions enable the program to look forward and backward in the bass line, while the predicates answer questions about the mode of progression of the bass and about the figures already assigned to specific bass notes. The values returned by predicates determine the applicability or inapplicability of a given rule. The operation of the program, then, follows closely the logical structure of the individual rules.

The bass-harmonization procedures set forth by Heinichen and Saint-Lambert were completely formulated as computer programs and were

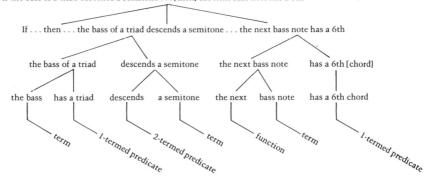

Figure 7.1
Analysis of Heinichen's first "General Rule"

tested for completeness and adequacy on input data derived from several standard figured-bass treatises of the eighteenth century. The programs were allowed to admit failure and print the message "undefined" when necessary; this permitted discrimination between a program's occasional inability to compute a figure (signalling incompleteness of the harmonization procedure under investigation) and the absence of a figure for reasons consistent with figured-bass practice, wherein the assignment of the figure 5/3 was regarded as a "default" situation not requiring any explicit figure specification. The adequacy of a given solution was determined by fiat emanating from the investigator's intuitive grasp of figured-bass lore.

As expected, both of the procedures tested were shown to be partially incomplete and to a certain extent inadequate. The deficiencies revealed in both procedures suggested certain refinements that were incorporated in subsequent versions of the programs and that led to improved results. Nevertheless, it gradually became clear that general solutions to the unfigured-bass problem were probably inaccessible to procedures of the type represented by those of Heinichen and Saint-Lambert. The principal source of inadequacy seemed to be that such procedures did not allow for a sufficiently sophisticated analysis of the structure of the bass line; in particular, they failed to take into account the hierarchic, stratified character of the bass. As a result, they were unable to identify cadential configurations and to cope with the implications of compositional elaborations of a single harmony within the bass line.

The musical skill involved in assigning figures to an unfigured bass has not yet, to my knowledge, been fully explicated and computationally simulated. The study that I have briefly reported constituted an initial step toward such a solution. The computer made a significant and well-defined contribution to the study by exposing deficiencies in the theories under investigation and in suggesting further lines of inquiry. Although I have not elected to follow them up systematically, there is no doubt that the experience of attempting to simulate a musical skill with the digital computer has made its mark on my way of thinking about musical problems of all kinds.

Notes

1. During the past three hundred years or so, the general trend in notating music has been to make the written score more and more explicit. At the same time, the interpretative responsibilities of the performer have increased (at least up until the first decades of the

twentieth century), so that the written score of a Mahler symphony, however fully specified it may appear, is not an appreciably closer approximation to an orchestral performance than is the score of a Brandenburg Concerto by Bach.

2. Indeed, the structural significance of the various intervals is a defining property of tonal music; the departure from established norms of intervallic behavior, thus, became *the* salient feature of pitch organization in the "atonal" music of the early twentieth century.

3. The concept of structural strata was most fully and convincingly expounded by the Austrian music theorist Heinrich Schenker from about 1906–1935.

4. By Stephan Haflich, for a Ph.D. dissertation in progress at Yale University.

5. This is the strategy employed by James L. Snell in his *Design for a Formal System for Deriving Tonal Music* (M.A. thesis, State University of New York, Binghamton, N.Y., 1979).

6. Rothgeb, John, *Harmonizing the Unfigured Bass: A Computational Study* (Ph.D. dissertation, Yale University, 1968).

7. With the demise of the basso continuo, the figured bass disappeared from finished musical scores; but masters such as Mozart, Beethoven, Mendelssohn, and even Brahms continued to use it in sketching their compositions. It provided them with a record, for their own reference, of the basic harmonic and voice-leading content of composition in progress. Figured bass remains loday an indispensable pedagogical aid in the study of tonal harmony and voice leading.

8. Heinichen, Johann David, *Der Generalbass in der Composition* (Dresden, 1728).

9. Saint-Lambert, Michel de, *Nouveau traite de l'accompagnement du clavecin* (Paris, 1707).

Moorer describes one of the most complex tonal melody generators of its day. Because little work had been done by 1971, Moorer includes an overview of the field.

Like Minsky, Moorer attempts a psychological and even a biological framework for why melodies affect us. His frank speculation on the possible influence of sexual biology on music is intuitive and does not appear in other writing on musical modeling.

Moorer quickly summarizes the mathematics of rhythm; musical form (which can to a degree be described in simple BNF-type grammars), and the origins of harmony in the fusing overtone series. Moorer is refreshingly critical of prior Markov chain methods of melody generation. On the other hand, he describes "probability parameters" in his own program that, while operating on a higher level than Markov chains for individual notes, are not justified or explained.

Moorer's program generates harmonic progressions and simple melodies, with simple internal repetition pattern. While quite interesting, the description of the program and the brief example are too sketchy to evaluate fully either technically or musically.

Without flow or control diagrams, or even a description of the development environment, it is difficult to picture Moorer's program or its control structure. Musically, it is hard to tell whether the repetition pattern for any two songs was always very similar to the example shown or differed widely in his experiments.

8 Music and Computer Composition

James Anderson Moorer

Considerable work has been done on the use of the computer as a highly versatile performer of music and as a random number generator to select certain aspects of pieces of music it is playing. An early ILLIAC experiment produced a string quartet that was composed entirely by computer. Very little work, however, seems to have been done on the problem of simulating human composition using heuristic techniques rather than relying on random number generation. The purpose of this chapter is to explain some of the difficulties involved, to give some of the background material for those wishing to pursue the topic independently, and to discuss some of the schemes that have been tried.

The Problem of Style

There are several times as many different styles of composition as there are (or ever have been) composers. This is because style changes as the composer matures, and since Beethoven's expansion of classical forms, there has been less and less tendency to unify compositions. There has been little or no emphasis on self-consistency in music. Indeed, even within a single composition, harmonies and rhythms may vary drastically.

Our appreciation of music has been widening over the past two hundred years. Today, more combinations of sounds are called good music than ever before. With such a profusion of styles, we might begin to wonder what it is that makes a random sequence of notes a "good" or a "bad" melody. Melodies used by such popular idols as the Beatles would have been considered absolutely degenerate a hundred years ago. Why is it, then, that many of these "degenerate" melodies can attract our attention? To answer this, we should spend some time researching musical taste and why people like the music they do.

Taste or Lack of It

If without any explanation a musician were to play for an American audience a composition from India's master musician, Ravi Shankar, the

Copyright 1972, Association for Computing Machinery, Inc., and reproduced by permission.

audience would most likely find the droning quite boring, being unable to appreciate the subtleties of the music. Similarly, Greek and Slavic 5-, 7-, and 11-beat rhythms sound quite strange to us. My observation of dance hall behavior and study of folk music lead me to believe that American audiences have a very hard time dancing to prime rhythms, whereas the Greeks find it quite natural.

Anthropologists tell us that there has never been a culture that has not had music of some form. Even pre–Stone Age tribes had something that could at least be called sounds to dance to.

Obviously, there is a great deal of cultural influence in musical taste. This may lead us to wonder exactly what, if any, are the fundamental sounds that bridge the gaps between cultures. The only things that all these "musics" have in common are rhythm and the mimicking of human noises like laughing, crying, and screaming.

For the sake of this discussion of the common traits of musics shared by different cultures, we must temporarily exclude the recent atonal and aperiodic musics practiced by, among others, John Cage fans. However, Stockhausen, Webern, the pointillists, and many other modern composers, although their music sounds aperiodic at first, still use unifying underlying structures—that is, their music often has underlying mathematical patterns—and because of this they can be included in my discussion.

Fundamentals

Let me discuss rhythm and why I believe it to be of such importance. When man first appeared on this bail of rock, there was periodicity staring at him from every direction–the seasons, day and night, and even the beat of his own heart. Periodicity is very deeply impressed on people of all cultures. We may imagine, then, that there has grown in men's minds a relation between periodicity and quality. The most primitive forms of "music" occurring in tribal situations are nothing but rhythms. There is, for example, a Stone Age culture in New Zealand whose entire musical repertoire consists of stomping twice with one foot and once with the other foot and a stick, simultaneously. There has been no culture whose music has begun with aperiodicity. Although many Oriental rhythms are "rhapsodic" in nature, that is, for emotional value the melody is broken at odd times rather than at regularly spaced intervals, much of this music is still quite periodic, and its origins are firmly rooted in periodicity.

It should be pointed out that this is only my own plausibility argument for belief in the fundamental nature of periodicity; I certainly know of no way to verify this.

An excellent but brief treatment of the periodic aspects of music is given by Simon and Sumner (1968). They show that periodicity is present simultaneously in many different dimensions of music. For example, the melody itself may be organized into sections that repeat in exact or altered form. The chord structure may repeat either exactly or in transposed form. The periods of repetition of the chords and melody may not even be the same, but often they are integral multiples.

Other attributes that are not so global are human noises. It is generally considered that high-pitched or loud utterances convey anxiety or tension of some sort, although it is difficult to say whether this tension comes from joy, anguish, or sorrow, but we can say merely that they express more tension than low-pitched or soft utterances. The distinction between the peculiar diaphragmatic spasms of laughing and crying is sometimes obscure, a feature that has been exploited thoroughly in modern drama and music; but we can be somewhat assured that the occurrence of one or the other sound indicates a height of emotion of some form.

We must also examine the sound perception mechanisms to help us determine why certain timbres and combinations of notes are considered pleasing and others displeasing.

So we start with these few fundamentals, and culture supplies the rest of our musical taste. Nonetheless it is true that even these very fundamentals can be easily trained out, leaving the prospective computer music composer somewhat at a loss for notes.

Speech or Music

It is often said that the speech mechanism has a generalized "generative grammar" scheme that allows a human to produce an infinite number of utterances that are syntactically consistent with a certain grammar. We might assume that this would be a good place to start in melody production, since composers like Mozart, over restricted intervals in their lives, seem to be capable of producing an infinite number of melodies that sound very similar. In Mozart's early years, many of his pieces were formula compositions that might be described by a BNF-type grammar with loss of genius only in the production of the melody itself and in the fluidity of the transitions. Indeed, if we were to compare the early clarinet and bassoon concerti, we might well be struck by the extreme simplicity of the global formulation. This would indicate that the music composition mechanism might be very closely related to the speech production mechanism, but I can demonstrate that it is more complicated than this simple BNF-type grammar by attempting to produce a grammar that would generate a Mozart composition. This argument is not meant to be entirely convincing, but is merely a way to lead into a refutation of the formal grammar approach to music composition.

An example of a BNF-type grammar that might be used in such an attempt may be described as an ordered quadruple $(N, T, :: =, S)$, where N and T are sets of symbols and S is a single symbol, $S \in N$. The elements of N are called the *nonterminal* symbols of the grammar and do not appear in the final sentences. The elements of T are called the *terminal* symbols of the grammar and constitute entirely the symbols found in the final sentences. The symbol ":: =" is a relation on $N \times V^*$, where $V = \{\alpha | \alpha \in N \cup T\}$ and V^* is the set of strings over V, consisting of concatenations of members of V. The grammar is written as a set of "rewriting rules" that have the format "$\alpha ::= S^1 S^2 \ldots S^n$," meaning that α may be replaced by the string "$S^1 S^2 \ldots S^n$," α is called the left part of the rule, and $\alpha \in N$, $S_i \in N \cup T$. Several rules that have the same left part indicate an ambiguity in that a single nonterminal may be replaced by any one of several strings. This is often abbreviated by the use of the symbol | to indicate a nondeterministic choice. For example, the two rules "$\alpha :: = a$" and "$\alpha :: = b$" might be abbreviated "$\alpha + :: = a | b$."

We might start by saying a piece is a sonata, a rondo, or a fugue. We could then proceed by saying that a sonata is an exposition followed by a development followed by a recapitulation. We could even go so far as to say that the exposition consists of either (l) a melody, another melody in the key a major fourth higher, and then the first melody again, or (2) a melody, another melody in the key a major fifth higher; and the first melody again; and in either case, followed by a transition to the development section, which is often in another related key. Some of the rules might be summarized as follows:

PIECE:: = SONATA|RONDO| FUGUE

SONATA:: = EXPOSITION DEVELOPMENT RECAPITULATION

EXPOSITION:: = MELODY__IN__C__MAJOR
            MELODY__IN__F__MAJOR
            MEOLDY__IN__C__MAJOR

Here we have already run into problems: how do we specify in this notation that the recapitulation must involve the same melodies as were used in the exposition; or how do we specify one of the alternative possibilities for the exposition which includes a repeat of the first melody in the third position; or finally, how do we also make the development section use embellishments on the themes used in the exposition?

These problems alone are not grounds for abandoning the generative grammar scheme. Because of the works being done on grammatical inference, this avenue may well prove fruitful in the future in the following manner. The goal of grammatical inference is to take a set of utterances that were produced by some grammar and discover a minimum grammar that will produce this set. Consider taking a restricted set of pieces produced by a single composer over a short period of time and choosing the pieces that exhibit a high degree of self-consistency. In this case, the minimum grammar for these compositions might well be one that would generate many more enjoyable compositions in that same style. The difficulty comes when we mix styles. If the grammatical inference program were given strings of both German and English sentences, it would have to be sophisticated enough to insure that the resulting sentences generated by the grammar would be in one language or the other, not in polyglots, such as many young children in multilingual homes tend to speak. Indeed, we would expect the first statement of the grammar to be something like this

SENTENCE:: = GERMAN-SENTENCE|ENGLISH-SENTENCE

or the equivalent. Likewise, if we were to give a grammatical inference program a Mozart piece and a Beatles piece, unless the program was of the proper degree of sophistication, we might expect some very strange results.

The questions and problems I have raised here are probably quite familiar to those readers who are working on natural-language parsing. Indeed, the BNF-type grammar is unsuitable for the bulk of English sentences for reasons similar to these. There have been developed more complex grammatical schemes that shed more light on the subject. The

MITRE transformational grammars offer considerably more flexibility, but are still not the entire solution.

That is not entirely true, for the MITRE transformational grammar, if we allow deletions, is a Turing machine and is thus quite adequate for generating music. The only difficulties are, again, style and the infinite variety of musics. For a given discipline, the transformational grammar may indeed provide a useful generating algorithm.

A transformational grammar is essentially an augmented BNF-type grammar. The added relations are transformations on the syntactic tree at any position in the expansion. Zwicky et al. (1965) describe completely the transformational grammar.

An interesting aspect of inferring automata, whether by Markov probabilistic methods or grammatical inference methods, is that the results are disappointingly similar. When higher order methods are used, we get back fragments of the pieces that were put in, even entire exact repetitions. When lower orders are used, we get little meaningful information out. When intermediate orders are used, indeed we do get back some new and different pieces that sound like the input sample, but we get back a much larger proportion of "degenerate" melodies consisting of ascending or descending scales. What is needed here is an intermediate-order grammar with a selection mechanism that filters out things that can be represented too simply.

The fact that the problems of representing music by a grammar are similar to the problems of representing speech by a grammar I take to be another indication that the speech mechanism and the music production mechanism are actually closely related. This is a useful point to establish, for instead of having both the problem of speech parsing and generation and the problem of music parsing and generation, we have only one slightly larger problem.

Music as Different from Speech

Now that we have considered the similarities of music and speech, let us discuss their differences. Speech is a tool to communicate, but can we say the same about music? If we can, then we must realize that the subject matter communicated in music is much more elusive than in speech. In most cases, it is very hard to decide what, if anything, a given piece of music is communicating.

Consider from the composer's point of view trying to communicate something by music. Let us attempt to convey a setting, say a brook in the forest. We may mimic brook noises and forest noises, but who is to say that these sounds do not actually represent, say, a vacuum cleaner and a leaky, gurgling faucet? If we are to communicate concepts by music, we must first define "words" and give them "meanings," as Polynesians or Africans have been known to do with their music, and then, using this predefined vocabulary, we can create unambiguous statements. In other words, to communicate by means of music, we must endow music with the traits and constructions of a spoken language; or simpler yet, to make music behave like a comprehensible language, we must make music into a language.

Although speech generation may be quite similar to music generation, it has been shown that speech perception is quite separate from music perception or music generation. There are reported cases of brain-damaged composers who lost the ability to communicate by language but who continued to compose and listen to music. One of the reasons that music perception is so different from speech perception may be found in an analysis of the important elements of music and speech. For example, in speech the pitch is of little consequence except for inflectional value, whereas in music, pitch and rhythm are the essence of the piece. A sentence may be spoken with inverted pitches at one-half the speed and still be understood, but the same transformation makes music into noise. In music, most often a pitch is accompanied by harmonics, which are notes of frequencies that are integral multiples of the pitch of the note. The ear is quite sensitive to changes in the harmonic structure of a sound. So sensitive is it that a person can detect the difference between a violin note plucked in the middle of the string and the same note plucked near the end of the string. There is a difference of a few percent in amplitude in the higher harmonics that causes the sound to appear slightly more "tinny" as the string is plucked closer to the end and more mellow as it is plucked closer to the middle. In the perception of Western speech, vowels are distinguished by the dominant harmonics. Resonances of the vocal tract, called "formants," modify the overtones of the sound source to enhance certain overtones. The distinction between the "ah" sound and the long "o" sound is principally determined by the distance between the fundamental and the first formant. The exact placement of the formant, however, is not the least bit critical. In fact, we may speak with overtones that are inharmonic (nonintegral multiples of the base frequency), as in whispering or rasping voices. In speech the pitch of the formants may vary by as much as twenty percent and still be readily understood. But the precision in music must be within only a very slight percentage of variance or the fundamental and its harmonic are perceived as two different notes.

At this point, we may ask what is conveyed by music. Often music puts the majority of its listeners in a certain mood, so perhaps emotion or feeling is carried, nonverbally, to the listener. To pursue this discussion further will require the extensive use of ill-defined words like "tends to," "tension," "climax," "resting point," "resolution," and many others.

With this in mind, let me attempt to explain another of my theories as to the nature of the musical fundamentals. We have already mentioned periodicity, or rhythm. Let us explore now some emotional elements in music.

Sex and the Single Melody

Have you ever gotten a piece of music stuck in your head? It often seems that when your mind has nothing else to do, it plays this piece, or fragment, over and over again. Why should this be? What is it about music that causes this to happen? It is rare indeed that a piece of prose will stick in one's head like this.

The first answer to this riddle is periodicity. The melody has rhythm, most likely, and in itself is periodic in that the ending of most melodies is a natural lead-in to a repeat of the melody. So the melody is a cycle of some sort that begins and ends in emotionally similar places. For the purpose of this discussion, I am taking as our sample space popular, tonal, periodic melodies, such as those found in songs and ballads and in much classical work.

Let us pursue further the nature of this cycle. Most melodies of this form are said to "come to rest" at the end. There is something about the ending of most melodies that leads us naturally to the conclusion that the melody has terminated. Composers call this the "resolution" of the melody. A melody may be thought of as a sequence of notes that create tension or anxiety of some form in the listener, in such a way that if the melody were terminated abruptly, the listener might be struck with a feeling of frustration. I am tempted at this point to recall the story of Beethoven who, upon trying to fall asleep one night, found himself listening to the piano downstairs. The pianist played the piece through to the end but omitted the final resolving chord. After sitting with this for a number of minutes, Herr Beethoven found himself unable to relax again, and finally he went downstairs and played the resolving chord himself! Having discharged the tension in this manner, he slept well.

The point I am working toward is that melodies might well be sexual in nature. It is very rare indeed for a piece to start loud and become softer and softer until it disappears. Most often, a piece or a melody has one or more places where tension mounts and then resolves. It is even difficult to define what it is that creates tension. A musical climax can, of course, be made by having the music speed up and get louder, but we can also make a tension-building climax with the music getting softer and slower. There is some relation here to speech in that, when we are excited, our voices often get higher in pitch and intensity. And so we may conclude that this is a very natural form of building tension by sounds, but certainly not the only method. Within a melody itself, the composer often uses "leading tones" to maintain tension. These are notes that create a desire in the listener to hear the resolving chord immediately thereafter. Extensive use of leading notes and leading chords often keeps the audience on the edge of their chairs until the music resolves. If no resolution occurs the audience may get bored and cease to pay attention.

There are composers who do not use climaxes and resolving chords, but they have to arrange specifically to destroy resolution. For example, in *Sacre du Printemps* and *L'Histoire d'un Soldat*, Stravinsky chops up melodies and reassembles them out of order so that resolutions do not occur. The effect is that the music is continually tense. He occasionally has symbolic resolutions by juxtaposing several simultaneous resolving chords, but this does not bring the music or the audience to rest. This principle was related to me by Charles Carter, an excellent modern composer, and may receive additional plausibility from a brief comment on Stravinsky's method of composition at that time, which included the frequent use of scissors and paste to help rearrange music fragments. Stockhausen eliminates resolutions by carefully arranging the pitches so that the music does not define a key or a resolving chord. This is difficult to do, for most modern orchestral instruments have the diatonic (tonal) scale deeply embedded in their constructions.

When Western audiences hear Indian or Chinese music, they often get bored, or the melody seems to wander aimlessly for great lengths of time with seemingly no resolution. The quick tension-climax-release sequence in Western music is not present, and this greatly limits the attention span of an audience that is used to being entertained in this manner. In Indian music the time scale is greatly exaggerated so that the sequence of climax and resolution occurs only at the very end of the piece. The Indians place a greater emotional emphasis on the twists and turns of the melody than do Westerners; this, combined with the long time scale, makes the sequence of climax and resolution, when it occurs, quite dramatic for one accustomed to the discipline.

In other words, most composers either use tension, climax, and resolution, or specifically go to lengths to destroy these relations. This led me to wonder if there could be something fundamental about the notion of tension climax, and resolution. One is tempted to say it is essentially sexual in nature.

Perhaps this is stated too strongly. Perhaps it is not that music is sexually derived, but that music and sex have in common a fundamental emotional mechanism. Another explanation that serves the same purpose is to say that the appeal of tension-climax-resolution is muscular in nature, that as musical tension builds, the muscles of the listener also become tense, if the piece is successful. The resolution is then the relaxing of the muscles and the associated comfort. Noticing that during sex the muscles tense and later relax in this same manner, we can say that the above becomes a roughly equivalent description.

Perhaps this relates back to periodicity. When a listener hears the first part of a typical popular melody, the period of the melody is perceived very quickly, and there is such a marked anticipation of the end of the melodic cycle that the periodicity itself creates a climax. This climax can be greatly reinforced by a cyclic nature in the chords of the piece.

It would seem that the brain is quite keen at extrapolating a series from the first few terms. This mechanism may explain how a person hears the first notes of a piece and begins to anticipate the conclusion, or cycling, of the music.

Tonality or Not Tonality

The question of how the ear perceives consonance and dissonance is one that has intrigued composers for many years. For one example, we have

Beethoven's First Symphony, which was criticized by his contemporaries because it began with the dominant seventh chord. This chord, in such an unheard-of position, offended the ears of audiences used to Mozart harmonies in which the dominant seventh was carefully mitigated by more consonant chords. For another example, we have the Greeks, who considered the major third a dissonant interval rather than an interval that is thought to be one of the keys to richness in musical sound and that we have been hearing daily ever since Detroit tuned automobile horns to the interval of the major third. It has been discovered that dissonance is a "one-ear" effect, that is, if two notes that would combine to form a dissonant are played separately so that they are simultaneously heard, one in one ear and one in the other ear, no dissonance is perceived. Even more amazing (to the musician) is the fact that, by using earphones, a piece of music in the key of C can be heard by one ear while the same piece of music in C sharp is being heard by the other ear and there is no perception of dissonance. Furthermore, it is generally conceded that dissonance is a quality attributed to music only by those with uneducated ears—after listening to a great deal of "dissonant" music, a person no longer perceives dissonance at all. This explains why composers of dissonant music can draw such large audiences, whereas a dissonant song played for the general public could never make the top ten. The modern classical composer is writing for a relatively sophisticated audience.

After having claimed that dissonance and consonance may be trained out and are very much a matter of culture and experience, I shall embark on a discussion of exactly those matters on the grounds that the music I am interested in having the computer compose is essentially popular music, which is characterized by complete tonality and a high degree of consonance.

To a common ear, certain combinations of pitches seem to "go together." We might wonder why that should be, and the answer is neither clear nor simple. I can only offer essentially a plausibility argument.

I say a "common" ear rather than an "untrained" ear because most people have received some amount of "training" simply by exposure. It is, in fact, unclear what an "untrained" ear is or what it hears.

Let us start by examining the relations between intervals that are commonly thought to be consonant; the unison is, of course, the most consonant interval, the ratio of the pitches being 1:1. The octave is next with ratio 1:2. The perfect fifth is next with ratio 2:3. The perfect fourth has ratio 3:4; the major third, 4:5; and the minor third, 5:6. The major second is considered consonant only in some contexts and has ratio 6:7 At this point, a pattern may be staring you in the face. The most consonant intervals are the ones with the simplest ratios. As to why this should be, we can only guess. My own theory is not well formed but has to do with the way the ear detects the presence of an instrument and its harmonics. It so happens that the first harmonic of a note is the octave. The second harmonic is a perfect fifth above the first harmonic and is next to the octave in consonance. The third harmonic is a perfect fourth above the second harmonic; the fourth harmonic, a major third above the third harmonic; and the fifth harmonic, a minor third above the fourth harmonic. Thus we see that the order of descending consonance is the same as the order of ascending intervals in the harmonic series.

An excellent summary of research, which includes this theory and many other equally plausible ones, may be found in Lundin (1953). I have been unable to devise or conduct experiments to examine this hypothesis.

As has been mentioned before, the ear is extremely sensitive to the harmonics of a pitch, for that is how, among other things, it distinguishes different musical instruments. This being the case, we can see that the relations between the notes in the harmonics must be well known by the mind's music perception system, such that two notes played simultaneously with a simple relation between their pitches become "fused" in the mind into one note. The fact that the notes do not fuse when played into different ears merely indicates that the mind's decision to fuse notes is done before comparisons are made between the two ears' received sounds. The fact that a person can be trained to hear the individual notes of a chord even though they are "fused" indicates that this is part of the mind's programming and is not indelibly built into the hardware.

At this point, a further revelation may be in order. Studies have been done using as subjects musically untrained people who listen to Western music (as if they could avoid it!). The subjects were played two different notes and asked in which order they should be played to produce an effect of resolution. The results were striking. They led to the formulation of a simple algorithm which allows a person who knows the pitches of the two notes to predict in that order they should be played to produce a resolution effect to most listeners. The rule is something like this: take the ratio of the two pitches and reduce it to a ratio of integers, then if either of the integers in the ratio is nonprime, replace it by its smallest prime factor. The pitch whose integer reduces to the smallest number is the one that should be placed last, that is, the one that is the resolving tone. For example, if a C and a G are played together, the ratio of the pitches is 2:3. Both of those are small prime integers, so the resolution will be on the one represented by the 2—that is, the C. A C and an F have ratio 3:4. We replace the 4 by a 2 and find that the second note, the F, is the resolution tone. The major third tends to resolve to the tonic; the minor third tends to resolve to the third. If the ratio turns out to be 3:5, then the note represented by the 3 will be the resolving tone, although the effect of resolution is not as pronounced as it would have been if the ratio had had a pitch whose integer could have been reduced to 2. Thus we see that the ear tends to hear a resolution when the pitch with the simplest integer representation is played. Again, Lundin (1953) may lead the interested reader to what little basic research has been done in this area.

It is also interesting to note that the relations between lengths of pairs of notes in popular melodies are also generally integral ratios. When notes are played without integral ratios between the lengths of the notes, the mind cannot find the periodicity and simplicity of relations that is present in so much music.

Other Musical Mechanisms

The above discussion has focused on elements that are common to most musics. By far the most important mechanisms are the cultural ones, which are not fundamental. A study of these mechanisms can only be done with respect to a given musical discipline and does not necessarily have any relation to other musics.

The other mechanism to be discussed is the mind's memory system. Each piece of music we hear evokes recall of dozens of associations. The music is called "impressionistic" if it causes a recall of actual physical scenes; it is called "expressionistic" if it causes a recall or reexperience of emotions; it is called "abstract" if it does not cause recall, or if the recall is entirely uncorrelated.

When we hear a piece of music, small details may remind us strongly of a previous piece of music that in gross character might be entirely different. This process of remembering old pieces of music from small details of a piece is very important to popular music, for much of it depends on our having heard the performer's previous works, or on our pleasant associations with similar pieces of music. The Beatles have a talent for producing a melody that violates no copyright law but sounds remarkably like older tunes. In this case, it is because the chord progressions and melodic nuances are often quite standard and have been used by popular composers for years.

This would tie in with the capabilities of extrapolation of the mind since the most likely extrapolation would certainly be the one heard most often. If we hear a particular pattern too often, however, we get bored with it. Successful patterns then are ones that are moderately but not entirely predictable.

Thus, if we are to produce computer music that appeals to the popular audience, it must sound like the kind of music that audience is used to hearing. This provides built-in obsolescence, for as soon as musical tastes change, the computer composer finds itself making antiquated music; the presumption is that there will be continuing work to keep it up-to-date, or perhaps it could be endowed with the ability to listen to the radio and see what kind of music is popular these days.

The random recall of parts of previously heard pieces of music gives a statistical character to the music. If we do a Markov analysis of note or chord sequences in popular music, we find that certain sequences of notes or chords are tremendously more prevalent than others. This is due only in part to the nature of the sound of one chord after the other. It is also due to the fact that people expect certain chords after certain others, due to their previous listening experience. This is one of the reasons for the success of music generation by Markov methods, two examples of which will be discussed.

Previous Computer Compositions

In this section, I shall briefly cover some of the aspects of previous computer compositions. In evaluating these criticisms the reader must be careful to remember the point of view from which they are made. It is meaningless to criticize any piece of music without giving the class of musical taste from which the criticism is given. There is certainly an appreciative audience for every piece of music ever written. We cannot criticize Stockhausen for his atonality or the Beatles for their stock sound on the basis of some mythical standard of musical taste—all we can say is that to people who like tonal music, Stockhausen is not terribly popular, and to those who admire atonal music, the Beatles are somewhat dull. My goal in my exploration of composition by computer is the production of Western tonal music, such as is found in popular music and in classical music from its beginnings through most of the romantic period. My criticisms of the two computer compositions I have chosen to examine must be regarded as differences in a comparison I have made between these pieces and the kind of computer composition I am seeking.

Possibly the most publicized piece of computer composition is the *Illiac Suite*. This is described in detail by Hiller and Isaacson (1959). It is a string quartet produced by a mixture of random choice and the application of some of the rules of classical harmony and counterpoint. The rhythms were chosen entirely at random. The melodies were constructed using a Markov method and the application of some harmony rules.

While we listen to this piece, we may be struck by the unpredictability of the melodies. There are repetitions, but there is no extended use of periodicity. Melodic groups do not return or become transformed. Chord sequences do not repeat. There is no overall AABA (or some such) structure. In short, the piece would certainly not have been accepted by Mozart's contemporaries, but this is not its objective. The piece uses dissonance as many modern composers do; thus the style aimed at was not the one I have directed my studies toward, but rather a much freer type of music.

A very careful and scientific study of the Markov technique was given by Brooks et al. (1957). In this study, church hymns of a certain class were chosen and analyzed by Markov methods. The probabilities resulting from the analysis were used to generate several new hymns with varying degrees of success. Probabilities of orders 1 through 8 were used. This gives one an excellent feel for the possibilities and limitations of the Markov method. The results are quite interesting. Pieces generated with low order methods show considerable randomness. Pieces of high order consist of parts of the original hymns spliced together, such as the first half of one hymn followed by the second half of another hymn. The methods of intermediate order did indeed produce some entirely original hymns, but they also produced many "degenerate" pieces, such as those having long scalar ascending or descending sequences. The pieces had to be filtered out by hand as to which ones sounded good and which ones did not. In other words, the

Markov method produces some reasonable pieces, but it took human judgment to select the final examples. The Markov method is not complete enough by itself to produce high-quality music consistently. Perhaps if more factors were taken into account, a greater percentage of success would be obtained. This, however, remains to be studied.

An Experiment in Composition

In this experiment the pieces are composed in an orderly, sequential manner. The overall form of the piece is chosen first, the chords are chosen second, and the melody last. This ordering may seem strange to human composers who may begin a piece with any of these aspects or often envision a complete melody with chords and structure at once. The choice of chords before melody is to avoid the problem of deciding what chords should go with a given melody. The problem is reversed and simplified to constraining some number of the prospective melody notes to lie in the chord. The overall structure is similarly chosen first, to prevent attempting to derive the structure from the melody. Deriving the chords or the structure from the melody would amount to analyzing the melody, a subject that has not been programmed entirely successfully as yet.

The overall structure is decided upon by first choosing two numbers, the number of major groups and the number of minor groups. Each of these numbers is constrained to be a power of two. The next number chosen was the number of beats per minor group. This is constrained to be a power of two times the number of beats per measure, a parameter supplied by the operator. The total piece length is then the product of the number of major groups times the number of minor groups times the number of beats per minor group. The total piece length is then accepted or rejected according to the limits of the length of the piece supplied by the operator.

In this experiment, many parameters governing the composition of the piece are set by the operator. The ones already mentioned are the beats per measure and the limits on the total piece length. The probabilities of the various decisions described below are also set by the operator. The effect is that the operator tweaks the algorithm for the production of pieces that he likes. The algorithm is actually quite general and could produce a tremendous stylistic variety of music depending on the setting of the parameters. We could also envision learning schemes where pieces are chosen and then graded by a listener, such that the program could "learn" the proper settings of the parameters for that listener.

The structure is built up by repeating some of the groups. At the time each group is chosen, a decision is made, weighted by a probability parameter, to either invert a new group or copy a previous group. This decision is made both at the major group level and at the minor group level. The result is that a form, like ABAC, is generated, and each major group is composed of a subform, like *ab* or *ac*. The total form may well look like *ababacbc* when complete.

The rhythms of each independent minor group are chosen at this point at random, with the only constraints being the maximum and minimum note length. It is done in this manner because in the class of music in which I was interested all possible rhythms had been used. To eliminate some of them would restrict the generality of the program. The rhythms are produced by filling the minor group with notes of the minimum length and then combining groups of them to form longer notes.

The chords are chosen by first generating a hypothesis using first-order probabilities and then accepting or rejecting the hypothesis by application of several heuristics. The probabilities simply state the chances of this or that chord occurring. The heuristics filter out long sequences of nontonic chords or otherwise dull sequences. Sequences of chords that never reach the tonic are immediately discarded. Sequences in ABBA form where the A part was not the tonic are discarded.

The resulting chord sequence is then typed out with one letter typed for every beat in the piece. Minor groups are separated by using a period and major groups by using a space. The sequence

CCCC.FFFF   CCCC.GGGG

indicates that beats 1 through 4 and 9 through 12 are on a C-major chord, and beats 5 through 8 and 13 through 16 are on an F-major and a G-major chord, respectively. The piece in this example is 16 beats long.

Now the hardest part—the choosing of the melody notes. This part of the program takes about three times as long and occupies about three times the space of the remainder of the program. The reason for this is the number of devices built in to preserve repetition and periodicity but deny boredom. To do this properly would require a program many times the size of that used in this experiment, but some preliminary results may be shown in this simplified attempt.

The notes are chosen on a minor group basis. At each point, a decision is made as to whether to invent a new figure or to copy and possibly alter a previous one. New figures are invented by the use of second-order probabilities, that is, probabilities of the use of certain intervals between adjacent notes and probabilities of constraining notes to the chord. There are separate probabilities of chord constraint for stressed notes and unstressed notes. Stressed notes are notes on the stressed beats of the measure, set by the operator, or notes over a certain length.

When a decision is made to copy a figure, it is copied exactly, if the chords allow, or it is transposed to fit the chords, or it is transposed even if the chords are the same and if the melody may be made to fit. If the melody is transposed and parts of it do not really fit, these parts may be altered or recomposed to fall within acceptable tolerances. The result of all of this may be printed out in musical script or may be played over the digital-to-analog converter.

Results of the Experiment

In figure 8.1, five short single-voice examples are presented without the related chord structures. There was no editing or human selection. On the contrary, these were five consecutively composed selections. The parameters had been previously set to simulate Western popular melodies. One can easily see the repetition and pattern that has been built into these pieces.

The interesting point here is that statistical simulation is not used to select the note sequences. This results in note sequences that are undeniably melodies but are strangely alien sounding, indicating that perhaps not all "legal" melodies are interesting melodies. The repetition and structure of the pieces are similar to those used by modern composers but nonetheless do not convey the emotional impact of human-composed pieces. This indicates many things—first, that the structure and the note and chord selection are not independent and second, that the structure is probably not chosen just to provide a low entropy piece, but is chosen for some unknown aesthetic reason. This composing program uses "planning," in that the structure used as a plan for the generation of the note sequences and the chord changes; but the "plan" is apparently not the one that humans use, and any attempts to simulate the compositional abilities of

Figure 8.1

humans will probably not succeed until the musical models and plans that humans use are described and modeled.

In conclusion, the pieces are not yet top-ten material, but they are definitely legal popular melodies. The computer time required to produce these selections was less than 10 seconds, which indicates the shallow nature of the generating heuristics. Considerable work remains to be done in the study and simulation of musical taste.

It is hoped that this experiment may serve as an inspiration and starting point for others wishing to pursue the subject of computer composition. It is also hoped that this experiment may help dispel doubts that musical composition is "sacred" and unreachable by mechanical methods.

References

Brooks, F. P., Hopkins, A. L., Newmann P. G., and Wright W. V. 1957. An experiment in musical composition. *IRE on Trans. Electronic Computers EC-6:1* (Sept. 1957), 175–182.

Hiller, LeJaren A., Isaacson, L. M. 1959. *Experimental Music*. New York: McGraw-Hill.

Lundin, Robert. 1953. *An Objective Psychology of Music*. New York: Ronald Press.

Simon, Herbert A., Sumner, Richard K. 1968. Formal representation of human judgement. In *Pattern in Music*. New York: Wiley.

Zwicky, A. M., Friedman, Joyce, Hall, B. C., and Walker, D. E. 1965. The MITRE syntactic analysis procedure for transformational grammars. *Proc. AFIPS* 1965 FJCC Vol. 27, Pt. 1. New York: Spartan Books.

In "Process Structuring and Music Theory," Smoliar describes his model for music as a metaprocess consisting of two kinds of instructions: note instructions and branching instructions. *Note instructions* describe the acoustic realization of music, such as play middle C for one second starting at time t_i; *branching instructions* control note and other branching instructions; for example, *da Capo al Fine* is a branching instruction.

Music consists of a list of such instructions, and Smoliar illustrates his approach with a description in terms of note and branching instructions of Bach's Two-Part invention in D Minor (normalized to C major in his example). To represent the style of the invention, Smoliar defines a *schema* as an abstraction of the branching or control instructions of a set of musical works said to have a given style.

To represent the theme of the invention, Smoliar describes lists of note instructions respectively as THEME, SEQ, and FIG. The control schema then invokes these subroutines with specific descriptions for how they should be modified: whether they should be inverted, what key they should have, and what parts should appear.

A higher level branching process exists to allow plugged-in modifications of the subroutines to be debugged to satisfy overall stylistic constraints. Thus, when a new permutation of the fixed list of note instructions given in the original Two-Part Invention in D Minor has produced parallel octaves, Smoliar's model then substitutes an acceptable revision of the permutation.

A significant feature of Smoliar's model is its flexibility. Smoliar's paradigm of note and branching instructions can occur at multiple levels in the composition of music. A list of his two kinds of instructions can account for musical phenomena as subtle as the different styles of a mordent or as dramatic as sonata style. Although much of the flexibility of stylistic information described in the above approach could be represented in his earlier special-purpose programming language EUTERPE (1971), Smoliar proposed his new approach as a formalization for how stylistic descriptions (schemata) of music correspond to specific descriptions (metaprocesses) of compositions.

9 Process Structuring and Music Theory

Stephen W. Smoliar

1 Representation of Musical Structures

1.1 Processes and Their Relation to Musical Activity

We would like to establish a framework for the modeling of musical processes. Our notion of "model" follows the definition given by Marvin Minsky in his paper, "Matter, Mind, and Models" (1969): "To an observer B, and object A* is a model for an object A to the extent that B can use A* to answer questions that interest him about A."

In establishing such a definition, we are obliged, at least in part, to characterize those questions which "interest" us. In Smoliar, 1971 we oriented our model about one basic question: What are the processes underlying musical structures? This was based, to some extent, upon arguments brought forth by Jan LaRue in his book, *Guidelines for Style Analysis* (1970), in which he proposed the dismissal of the word "form" in favor of what he called "the growth process":

The style-analytical view of musical form as a resultant and combining element requires a fresh, stimulating term to express the vitality and immediacy of a functional approach as well as to dissolve the rigidities suggested by the unfortunately static word "form." Happily the word "Growth" admirably fulfills these needs, since its connotations include both the feeling of expansive continuation so characteristic of music and also a parallel sense of achieving something permanent.... If the *Guidelines* have accomplished anything thus far, they should have instilled a settled habit of regarding music first as a process of growth, then attempting to understand this growth by an analysis that fully reflects the character of musical flow. (P. 115)

Prior to the development of third-generation computer technology, computer programs tended to be regarded as a formalization of processes. However, these more recent advances provide facilities capable of simultaneously administering several programs running either totally independently or under mutual cooperation and give rise to control structures with far more capabilities than those of, for example, a conventional FORTRAN program. This more general view tends, as we hope to show, to be more amenable to those processes underlying musical structure.

Copyright 1974, *Journal of Music Theory*, and reproduced by permission.

By its very nature a process, in this more general sense, is more difficult to characterize than a computer program. In fact, as was shown in a survey paper by Horning and Randell (1973), this concept has been assigned a wide variety of working definitions which, while they may be compatible at some levels, are sharply distinct in their foundations. For our purposes, it will be most appropriate to regard processes in terms of the behavior of physical objects, which we shall call *processors*, with respect to the element of time.

We shall introduce the notion of an *atomic action*, or *elemental* (this term is due to R. J. DuWors), as a basic, indivisible unit of activity. Such an action must, of necessity, be associated with some physical object that performs the action. If that physical object is the central processing unit of a digital computer, the action may be the transfer of bits from one internal register to another. Alternatively, the physical object may be a musical instrument. In the case of a piano, we may regard the pressing of a key or pedal as an atomic action. (For the sake of simplicity, we shall not concern ourselves with the amount of force with which the action is applied; we shall, rather, regard the action as a binary event that either does or does not happen.)

We may now inquire of two atomic actions whether or not they are "interfering." Informally, we may say, for example, that the atomic actions of pressing two distinct keys on a piano keyboard are noninterfering. On the other hand, in a central processing unit two atomic actions that cause data to be transferred into the same register are definitely interfering. For now, we shall try to make do with this informal characterization.

(Note: While it may seem a trivial observation, we wish to qualify the fact that two distinct atomic actions involving two totally distinct physical processors are obviously noninterfering. Clearly, the incrementing of a program counter does not interfere with playing middle C on a grand piano in the same room. However, as a less absurd example, playing middle C on two pianos in the same room also constitutes two non-interfering atomic actions.)

Having established the property of interference, we now define an *event* to be set of noninterfering atomic actions. The example of playing middle C on two pianos demonstrates a simple event. A linear ordering of a set of events may then be interpreted in terms of time. At the most elementary level, we may discuss whether or not event T_i precedes event T_k. Alternatively, we can be more stringent and define a *schedule* that specifies that event T_i occurs at time t_i. This interpretation, however we choose to characterize it, will be said to constitute a *process*.

A performance of a musical composition is an example of a process according to these definitions. We may establish as our atomic actions the soundings of designated pitches for given durations. We might further specify atomic actions with respect to loudness or timbral characteristics, but for the sake of simplicity, we shall restrict our concerns to pitch and duration. Notice, however, that this characterization of atomic actions is not necessarily unique. It is, by its nature, compatible with the notational concepts underlying a musical score; but, given a processor such as a player piano, atomic actions, at least in terms of their physical realization, would be better regarded in terms of chords on the piano keyboard, that is, rows of holes punched in the piano roll.

In this latter example we must emphasize the fact that the piano roll itself is not a process. The process arises when the roll is mounted on the player piano and the instrument is activated. The piano roll, taken by itself, is a *metaprocess*, that is, a description of a process. It bears the same relation to the player piano that a computer program bears to the computer. Another basic example of a metaprocess is a musical score.

It should also be emphasized that the actions of mounting a piano roll and activating the player piano also constitute a process. In fact, any process can only arise from some external start originating from another process, which may be called the *starting process*. Furthermore, every process is involved in two important relationships: first, to the process which starts it, and second, to any other processes in the system under consideration. The nature of these relationships is an important one; but in order to understand it better, we shall first consider some fundamental aspects of conventional computer programs.

1.2   Computer Programs and Processes

Now let us propose an extension to our piano roll example. First of all, let us assign positive integers to successive rows on the roll, beginning with zero. The integer assigned to a given row will be called the *address* of that row. Second, let us assume that the player piano that reads this roll accommodates one additional column. If there is no hole in this column, then the remaining columns are "played" in the normal manner. However, if there is a hole in this column, then the rest of the column is regarded as a representation of a positive binary integer, and this integer will be interpreted as the address of the next row to be read.

From the point of view of digital computers, the extension we have proposed is a profound one. The piano roll now becomes what is known as a *random-access memory*. This essentially means that any row the piano reads may be followed by any other row conveniently. This means that the remaining columns are subject to more than one interpretation (in this case, two), and the role of the instruction variable is to determine which interpretation is taken.

Notice that we have now introduced a new class of atomic actions. In addition to the atomic actions of depressing sets of keys simultaneously, we now have those atomic actions that involve the positioning of the piano roll for each reading. A single row on a piano roll entails either a single atomic action or a sequence of two atomic actions. If this additional column is punched, then we have the atomic action of repositioning the roll to a new address. If not we have the atomic action of depressing those keys corresponding to the holes punched in the remainder of the roll followed by advancing the roll one row forward, that is, i.e., to the address immediately following the current address.

We shall call such a sequence of events an *instruction*. (Note that an instruction is thus, by our definition, a process; however, it is a special class of process whose properties we shall discuss in greater detail in section 1.3.) Thus, in our piano roll metaprocess, each row of the piano roll is a representation of a single instruction. We may further classify these instructions according to the state of the instruction variable. If the instruction variable is not punched, we shall call the row a *note instruction*. The implication is that the rows are read sequentially (that is, in order of increasing addresses) until one of these instructions is encountered at which time control branches to another address in memory (i.e., on the roll) and continues, again sequentially, from there.

The extended player piano we have described thus far is very similar to a channel for a large-scale computer system. A channel is essentially a special-purpose small computer dedicated to performing time-consuming input-output operations concurrently with the activities of the large computer to which it is attached. It is not too far-fetched to regard our player piano as an output device for a digital computer. (A similar project has been implemented by Willson and Johnson [1973]). In this case, our channel would have two possible commands: OUTPUT (the note instruction) and TRANSFER IN CHANNEL (the branch instruction). A performance would consist of the large computer loading the channel with a program and then activating it (i.e., putting a roll in the piano and turning it on).

1.3 Parallelism

Let us now return to our original notion of regarding the sounding of a single pitch for a specified duration as an atomic action. As we already observed, the musical score is the basic metaprocess for describing processes composed of such atomic actions. For our purposes, the major difference between a musical score and a piano roll is one of parallelism. We may regard a score as a set of disjointed part books, each of which is assigned to a different processor (instrument), The performance arises as each processor executes its respective sequence of events concurrently with the other processors with respect to some basic rules of synchronization.

We must now return to two basic concepts we introduced in previous sections. The first involves the act of assigning different part books to different processors. We have already observed that such activities are performed by a starting process. We now consider starting processes as a special case of a broader class of processes called *switching processes*. Switching processes encompass all those processes whose atomic actions may affect the behavior of other processes.

The second concept is that of the part book as a metaprocess that describes a sequence of events. In section 1.2 we called such a sequence of events an instruction. We now regard an instruction as a special case of a *sequential process*. Observe that if we adhere to the letter of our definitions, then in the last analysis any process is a sequential process. For purposes of discussion, however, we shall regard sequential processes as component subprocesses from which larger processes are composed.

In particular, consider a starting process that starts a sequential process. Two possible relationships may exist between the starting process and the sequential process. These may be called the *subroutine* relationship and the *parallel process* relationship, and both are relevant to our model of musical structures.

A subroutine relationship involves the suspension of the starting process upon activation of the subordinate sequential process. Such a starting activity is usually termed a *call* or *invocation*. After the subroutine is initiated, the invoking process effectively waits for the subroutine to terminate. This termination then involves the dismissal of the subroutine and the resumption of the invoker's activity. Notice that the action of invocation belongs to the invoker while the resumption of the invoker is performed by the subroutine.

Bearing this in mind, let us return to our definition of instruction. We see that an instruction functions as a subroutine with respect to the higher level process (such as the playing of the piano roll). In a converse sense, a sequence of instructions may also serve as a subroutine. This is the computer programmer's conventional view of subroutines. The basic element, however, which all subroutines have in common, from any point of view, is their sequential nature. Whether they are sequences of events, instructions, or entire processes, all subroutines are functionally the same.

The alternative to starting a process as a subroutine is to start it as a parallel process. Dennis and Van Horn (1966) term such a starting activity a *fork*. The distinction is that the starting process does not terminate after it has forked to the parallel process. Rather, the two processes both function concurrently. Under these circumstances, the started process is no longer obliged to effect a resumption of the process which started it, since the starting process was not suspended.

It is important to observe that a finite process with a well-defined beginning and ending may function both as a subroutine and as a parallel process In OS/360 (IBM, 1972) a *load module* is a metaprocess whose execution may be invoked either as a subroutine (by a command called LINK) or as a parallel process (by a command called ATTACH). In fact, the OS/360 programmer can even ATTACH and LINK the same load module at the same time.

Observe also that a subroutine can only relate to its invoker and to subroutines it invokes. However, relationships among parallel processes are not as clearly defined, and this is precisely why switching processes are necessary. Thus far we have only considered the starting and termination of sequential processes, but this is hardly the complete picture. The terms *monitor* and *supervisor* are usually used to describe these more general switching processes, and we shall now consider their role in our model of musical structures.

There is one aspect of starting a process that, until now, we have taken for granted. When we loaded our piano player with its piano roll metaprocess, we could make the assumption that it would begin execution at the beginning of the roll. In a more general sense, the starting of a sequential process may be regarded in terms of two activities. The first consists of loading the process, that is, assigning it to a processor. The second consists of specifying a *starting address*—the designation of the beginning of the sequence of events that constitutes that sequential process. This specification is usually incorporated into the call or fork command.

Let us consider as an example the realization of a performance of Contrapunctus VII of Bach's *Die Kunst Der Fuge*. For this composition we have four metaprocesses that serve as part books. In order to realize a performance, we need a monitor process that will assign these metaprocesses to appropriate voice processors. We may assume that these four voice processors are identical to the extent that they will realize identical note instructions in the metaprocesses in an identical fashion. Thus, after the metaprocesses have been assigned, the monitor process need only make sure that all four processors are started simultaneously. Hence, in this particular example, the four voice processes will function as subroutines of the monitor.

Consider now the violin cadenza towards the end of the first movement of the Brahms *Violin Concerto*. The orchestral score notates this as a grand pause of indefinite length. The only information given is how it ends the trill on the high C-sharp. In musical terms this trill serves as a cue by which the conductor may reinitiate the orchestra for the movement's coda. In programming terms this would be called a *monitor call* or a *supervisor call*. The basic idea is this: One subordinate process (the violin soloist) wishes to pass a message to one or more other subordinate processes (the members of the orchestra). However, the only available path of communication is through the monitor. The monitor call thus constitutes a request to the monitor to pass that particular message on to the other subordinate processes. This need for message-handling implies that our switching processes must be more sophisticated than simple starting processes. Most musical structures do not involve true parallelism but require higher mechaanisms of control.

1.4 Musical Structures as Processes

We may thus regard our voice processes as being founded on two basic classes of atomic actions. One class is based on those instructions in the metaprocess related to the actual performance—the note instructions. The other class must account for the voice process capacity to act as a switching process, and this class consists consists primarily of a set of monitor calls.

Thus far, the only atomic actions we have considered for a monitor are those of loading and initiating processors. A related action is that of scheduling—determining when, over the course of time, individual processes should be loaded, initiated, or perhaps terminated. This latter entails that all processes are effectively subroutines of the monitor and that, if a voice wishes to terminate its performance, it should do so by a monitor call so that at all times the monitor knows the status of all voices.

These actions may be found, in one form or another, in most multi-programming operating systems. However, if we are concerned with the representation of musical structures, there are other considerations that must be taken into account. We have already established that a note is interpreted with respect to parameters of pitch and time. In conventional notation, the position and shape of the note are not sufficient to specify the sounding of a given pitch for a given period of time. The clef sign, key signature, accidentals, and specification of instrument all contribute to determining the exact pitch, while metronome markings are used to determine exact durations. These constitute an environment within which those parameters given by the note instruction are translated into physical specifications for the acoustical voice.

As was demonstrated (in Smoliar 1971), many basic concepts of music theory may be modeled in terms of environmental control. Parallel organum may be represented as a single metaprocess interpreted by different processors with different pitch environments. Thematic augmentation is a similar situation with respect to the duration environment. As a more powerful example we offer in the next section a full analysis of Bach's Two-Part Invention in D Minor, in which the principal subjects are each represented as metaprocesses that are repeatedly invoked by two voice processors, with modification in the pitch environment to account for the harmonic progressions.

We would like to regard environmental control as lying within the domain of the monitor. It is true that, in general, an instrument should be capable of taking care of its own environment; but by letting the monitor control all the environments of all the instruments, we may readily allow one voice to cue a tempo change for an entire ensemble by means of a monitor call. We have even developed an entire composition based on the concept of voices altering each other's environments (Smoliar, 1972).

Thus far we have considered environmental control only with respect to our basic concept of a voice. Clearly, we would like to be able to extend our model to accomodate more general instruments, such as those available through electronic music. In this case the monitor should be capable of implementing a particular instrument design for a given voice, and the voice's program will then be executed within the environment determined by that particular design.

This problem has already been considered by Mathews (1969), and his Music V system poses a viable solution. A Music V program consists of a series of records, of which there are three categories: instrument definition records, function definition records, and note records. A record is a sequence of entries, the first of which always serves to classify the record.

The next three entries of a note record specify the starting time of the note, the instrument playing the note, and the duration of the note. The remaining entries are parameters that relate to the definition of the instrument.

An instrument is defined as a network of modules in a manner similar to the configuring of a Moog synthesizer by means of patch cords. Available modules consist of oscillators, adders, envelope generators, and others. A module has some set of input lines and one output line. An input entry in an instrument definition record may refer to either an output line of a module or an entry of a note record. In addition, oscillators and envelope generators are based on internal functions specified by function definition records. Environmental control is thus within the domain of both the instrument definition records and the function definition records.

This particular example exhibits almost all the relevant aspects of process theory that we have attempted to harness. At the very lowest level, each module effectively constitutes a processor. The metaprocesses that drive these processors are determined in part by the internal functions and in part by the fact that each processor is capable of switching the other processors. We may then pull back our point of view and regard an entire instrument as a processor. Now the metaprocess is defined by the sequence of note records passed to this instrument. Finally, a full Music V run of an entire composition is a process. The atomic actions of this process are defined by the note records as well as by the information within each note record that determines to which processor it is describing the particular activity.

2   Stylistic Schemata

Having developed materials for the representation of musical structures, we may now consider to what end they may be applied. In particular, we claim that our representation is such that we may exploit inherent similarities between musical compositions and computer programs. More specifically, we would like to consider the representation of stylistic information in terms of schemata in our information system.

We define a *schema* to be an abstraction of the control structure from specific data associated with a particular metaprocess. Notice that we have not given a formal characterization of data; however, we would like to be able to say that two distinct metaprocesses are similar by virtue of their having the same schema. We shall not attempt to pin down the degree of abstraction by which the control structure is isolated from the metaprocess, but we have one basic desideratum that we may use to establish a suitable criterion: we would like to develop a schema by which program representations of two musical compositions of the same style will have the same schema. This is understandably a rather vague criterion, but we hope to clarify it by means of an example.

In Smoliar, 1971, we discussed how a wide variety of stylistic information could be represented in EUTERPE, a special-purpose programming system based on the principles presented in the preceding section. For the most part, our arguments consisted in presenting metaprocesses of individual compositions in their entirety and and demonstrating informally how a structural description of the metaprocess corresponds to a structural description of the composition. We would now like to establish a less informal approach.

One of the compositions analyzed in Smoliar, 1971 was Bach's Two-Part Invention in D Minor. Let us consider figure 9.2 as a proposed schema for the metaprocess presented therein. In this schema, THEME, SEQ, and FIG are subroutines that we shall present in a normal form transposed to C Major (figure 9.1):

Figure 9.1

Figure 9.2

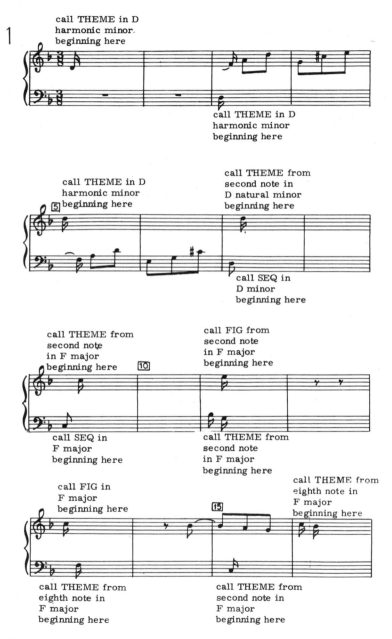

Figure 9.2 (continued)

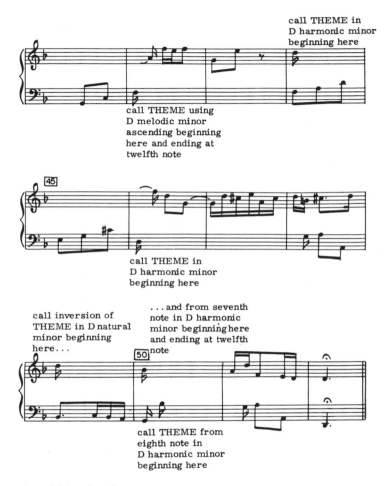

Figure 9.2 (continued)

They are invoked according to the verbal descriptions given in the schema. With these definitions, a knowledge of the basic scale types, and the proper interpretation of the trill function ($\sim$) (also a subroutine), we play now (construct the invention from the schema).

Now let us consider to what extent we may interpret this schema as a basis for an exercise in style based on this particular invention. For example, may we assign arbitrary sequences of notes as our definitions of THEME, SEQ, and FIG? The answer is obviously negative. For one thing, our description is designed in such a fashion that if we alter the rhythmic patterns of these subroutines, we shall be in grave trouble. We also have to be a bit cautious about which pitches these subroutines have for their beginnings and endings, as well as the tonalities they define in their entireties. Finally, we know in advance that SEQ must serve as counterpoint against THEME; and this imposes constraints upon what notes we may choose.

Bearing this in mind, let us propose the following alternative definitions for THEME, SEQ, and FIG (figure 9.3):

Figure 9.3

Admittedly, these do not deviate from the originals very radically. However, it is not our intention to produce a mechanism for composition; we merely wish to explore the possibilities of an exercise of style.

Given these subroutines as inputs, our schema will yield the result given in figure 9.4. A quick glance at this manuscript readily reveals many of its inferiorities to the Bach original. The parallel octaves at measures 16 and 49 are glaring problems, and the passage from m. 30 to m. 36 leaves much to be desired. On the other hand can we readily blame our schema for these shortcomings? Nowhere within the schema, as it is defined, is it specified that parallel octaves are to be avoided, although the passage at m. 30 might well serve as an excellent Luddite argument that computers will never have the taste of human beings.

There are two ways in which we can view our situation. The first is that this schema (and, perhaps, any schema constructed on similar principles) is an inadequate representation of the style of the Bach invention and that our theories are worthless. The second is that the output provided by the schema is a computer program which, like many computer programs when

Figure 9.4

Figure 9.4 (continued)

they are first written, has one or more bugs. This is what Papert (1970) calls
"positive thinking about errors," and we regard it as the healthier point of
view.

   If now we regard our results as a bug-laden program, our next question
is, How do we go about the process of debugging? To formulate an answer,
we may turn to the process-theoretic considerations of the previous section. In the first place, the realization of a schema is a process. In fact, it is
a relatively low-level process involving a basic symbol-manipulation program for an ordinary digital computer. Suppose, however, that we endow
it with the capabilities of a switching process that may invoke a higher-
level process whose duty it will be to debug the lower process. This higher-
level process must, in a sense, maintain a data base on the expertise of the
Bach style. This may include such information as the evils of parallel
octaves and fifths as well as some basic criteria for desirable melodic
construction. From an operating systems point of view, the actual switching of processes is known as a *program interrupt*. In more conventional
facilities, a program interrupt arises from a faulty operation such as divi-

sion by zero, addition resulting in overflow, or an illegal instruction code. The interrupt switches control to a service routine, which takes some form of appropriate remedial action. Depending on the severity of the situation, control may or may not be returned to the lower level. Thus, what is required in our case is a suitable definition of conditions for program interrupt along with a set of service routines for these conditions.

Admittedly, these definitions are not an easy matter, but if we inspect the Bach example, we can find the makings of some useful primitives. For example, at m. 16, the parallel octaves may be overcome by raising the notes in the upper voice by a third. This would then give the entire measure a melodic curve that more closely matches THEME. Likewise, the three notes in the lower voice at m. 49 that form parallel octaves may be lowered a third. Thus, the operation of transposition that was used in formulating the schema may also be employed in debugging its realization.

The case at m. 30 is a bit more drastic. The main problem is that m. 31 does not serve as a suitable consequent to m. 30's antecedent. If we wish to keep m. 30 and still have it bear some basic resemblance to THEME, we might hypothesize a new variation on THEME as follows (figure 9.5):

Figure 9.5

This passage is still built on the ascending version of the A melodic minor scale, as was defined in the schema. However, the notes describe a smoother melodic curve. Furthermore, we may build this pattern in a sequence, transposing it up a third at m. 32 and up another third at m. 34.

Other program interrupts may be attacked by similar techniques. Figure 9.6 is a proposed "debugging" of the original results. The replacement notes have been written above or beside the notes they are replacing. Observe that no rhythmic values have been altered.

This particular example was produced by hand. We are currently implementing a system of programs that will realize these techniques, and it remains to be seen just how far we can go. We do believe, however, that this represents a significant advance over previous work involving com-

Figure 9.6

Figure 9.6 (continued)

puters and music composition and that, in addition, it may provide us with a new approach to the teaching of composition.

3   Conclusions and Applications

At first blush it might appear that we are proposing yet another heartless attempt at mechanizing music theory. However, we feel, quite the contrary, that an approach via process theory will put us in a better position to understand the nature of music theory and thus to appreciate those qualities that make it a distinctly human activity. Laske (1973) has written on "the methodological problems posed by an ... explicit and formal ... theory of music." Process theory provides a basis for such a methodology without distorting traditional notions of music theory.

From an educational point of view, such an explicit and formal approach allows one to express fundamental principles with greater clarity. Furthermore, by founding the theory on the act of computer programming, one establishes a constructive approach. One may regard the study of a given style as a problem in designing the appropriate system to realize schemata based on that style. Initially, a student may use the debugging apparatus to analyze his own work, possibly gaining deeper insight into its structural characteristics.

Such an approach also provides us with an opportunity to consider the natural language concepts of syntax and semantics in terms of how they may relate to music theory. From a programming linguistic point of view, syntax is a matter of well-formedness. We may regard an attempt to realize a schema supplied with a specific set of inputs as an attempt to "parse" a "musical string" with respect to that grammar which is a characterization of the specific style. If the string is not well formed, that is, if it is ungrammatical, then, rather than rejecting the string, the system proposes a "patch" to make it well formed. Such a patch may be said to realize the "semantic intent" of that string. In other words, the semantic aspect involves the search for the appropriate program schema and the proper monitor, while the syntax entails the actual realization of a score.

Finally, there are the creative implications of such a system. Thus far, we have only considered exercises of style as realizations of known schemata. On the other hand, if we can program the monitor to supervise a schema with respect to a traditional theory, why not formulate an original theory for it to enforce? In fact, such a theory need not even have foundations we would be inclined to call musical. "Variations on a Theme of Steve Reich," (discussed in Smoliar 1972), arose from experiments with purely computational phenomena. Nevertheless, the results are undisputedly musical. Composers would do well to consider Dijkstra's (1972) description of LISP as a programming language that "has assisted a number of our most gifted fellow humans in thinking previously impossible thoughts," for is this not the ultimate goal of any creative artist. By influencing the way he thinks about music, the computer can only extend the creative intellect of the composer.

Acknowledgments

This paper would not have been possible were it not for the many hours of conversation and correspondence the author has had with Robert DuWors. The basic ideas concerning the relevance of a multiprogramming operation system originated during a drive through the Negev Desert, to which I am also deeply indebted. Finally, I must thank Allen Forte for providing the necessary impulse to have this material set down on paper.

References

Dennis, J. B., and Van Horn, E. C. "Programming Semantics for Multiprogrammed Computation." *Comm. Acm* 9, 3(1966), 143–155.

Dijkstra, E. W. "The Humble Programmer." *Comm. Acm* 15, 10(1972), 859–866.

DuWors, R. J. "On the Nature of Parallel Processes." Unpublished notes.

Horning, J. J., and Randell, B. "Process Structuring." *Computing Surveys* 5, 1(1973), 5–30.

IBM Systems Reference Library. "IBM System/360 Operating System Supervisor Services and Macro Instructions." GC28-6646-6. International Business Machines Corporation, March, 1972.

La Rue, J. GUIDELINES FOR STYLE ANALYSIS. New York: W. W. Norton, 1970.

Laske, O. E. "Introduction to a Generative Theory of Music." Sonological Reports No. 1. Utrecht: Institute of Sonology, Utrecht State University, 1973.

Mathews, M. V. et al. The Technology of Computer Music. Cambridge, Massachusetts: The MIT Press, 1969.

Minsky, M. "Matter, Mind and Models." Memo 77, Massachusetts Institute of Technology Artificial Intelligence Laboratory, March, 1969.

Papert, S. "A Plan for a Tool-Using Educational System." Unpublished draft, Massachusetts Institute of Technology Artificial Intelligence Laboratory, March, 1970.

Smoliar, S. W. "A Parallel Processing Model of Musical Structures." AI TR-242, Massachusetts Institute of Technology Artificial Intelligence Laboratory, September, 1971.

Smoliar, S. W. "Music Theory—A Programming Linguistic Approach." Proceedings of the 25th Anniversary Conference of the Association for Computing Machinery. New York, 1972, 1001–1014.

Willson, M. J., and Johnson, T. H. "A Computer Assisted Music Facility at the Moore School of Electrical Engineering." Proceedings Spring, 1973 Decus Symposium, 175–179.

IV AI AND MUSIC: GENERATIVE GRAMMARS

Laske seeks a generative grammar for music. Distinguishing between analytic and generative models, he describes a generative grammar as an "explication of musical competence."

Generative grammars for music and the artificial intelligence approach for general problem solving, Laske argues, will converge with clearer formulations of "epistemically adequate" musical cognition problems. Such formulation constitutes "rule-governed creativity obeying (or setting forth) music-grammatical constraints."

The rule order to generate musical structures, according to Laske, must be as flexible as possible. Writing a "programmed grammar" becomes the basis for the statement in full of a generative grammar; it "codifies the rules underlying the generation of musical objects."

Laske suggests a network of connected procedures, each, given a satisfied condition, producing a "choice" and a production. The rule ordering device implicit in this programmed grammar thus forms an "assemblage of black boxes."

Laske's discussion centers on two issues: the music-grammatical and the epistemological importance of compositional programs. He observes the relevance of the distinction between "general problem solving" (weak AI) and "specifically musical processing" (strong AI) and recommends further research in the interaction between cognitive and behavioral compositional determinants.

10 In Search of a Generative Grammar for Music

Otto E. Laske

The idea of a generative grammar for music is the outcome of research geared toward the formulation of a system, or a set of rules, capable of rewriting the sequence of mental representations (of sound structures) that are assumed to underlie the execution of activities called musical. Such a system can be called a (general or particular) competence model for music or, since it is a rewriting system, a grammar for music.[1] The research, undertaken in order to formulate a methodological framework for programmed studies in musical competence, was initially conceived as consisting of two principal kinds of investigation

A That of the internal componential structure of a generative grammar for music, that is, of a general mode of musical competence

B That of the systems theoretic structure of a programmed compositional strategy and, in consequence of these investigations, as

C The formulation of a particular grammar for music that would be both a result of formalizing insights into the strategy investigated (B) and a manifestation of the general competence model outlined (A)

In this chapter, the author proposes to comment on the changes that his conception of the project has undergone through continued work (1971–1972), especially insofar as these changes concern the methodological basis and the means of his research. The development of ideas that occurred essentially affected the conception of the mutual relationship of the three topics of investigation; this development was proposed by a deepened insight into the task proposed under (B).

At the time of the first definition of the project, the author was under the influence of the theory of formal grammars, its natural language interpretation elaborated by N. Chomsky, and of psycholinguistic problem formulations.[2] He can say that he had insufficient knowledge of methods utilized in artificial intelligence studies of systems-theoretic concepts,[3] as well as the discipline of sonology,[4] and thus lacked insight into performance models for music.[5] The publications that have appeared since 1972 hopefully remedy, or at least mitigate, these deficiencies.[6] The project outlined

From *Introduction to a Generative Theory of Music* (*IGTM*), *Sonological Reports*, no. 1, Institute of Sonology, Utrecht, The Netherlands, (January 1973). Copyright 1974, *Perspectives of New Music*, and reproduced by permission.

above is of a metatheoretical nature; a metatheory of music is a theory of musicality. Such a theory can be conceived as a general competence model for music or a generative grammar. A comprehensive musical competence model gives an answer to the following questions:

• What are the minimal universal constraints shared by all particular grammars of music?[7]

• What is the class of possible particular grammars for music?

• What is the internal structure of a general performance model for music?

• What is the format of particular performance models associable with particular grammars for music?

• What is the relationship of counter-grammars (theories of individual compositions) to particular grammars for music?

Already in the first definition of the project it was implied that to cope with the problems stated, a metatheoretical investigation has to unite a formal language approach and a machine (robot) approach to the definition of music, or rather of musicality. Such an investigation was conceived as concerning both the knowledge indispensable for a musical activity and the products of such an activity. The twofold nature of the project was seen as deriving from the dichotomy between two hypothetical kinds of knowledge to be reconstructed: music-grammatical and music-strategical knowledge. Although the methodological fruitfulness of such a distinction is still undisputed, it became clear during further investigations that in order to define the internal componential structure of a general competence model, it is indispensable to specify the task-environment, that is, the strategical framework, in which particular grammars for music function. Further insight into the logical structure of a generative grammar for music presupposes:

1. A clear notion of the strategical preconditions of a performance system incorporating music-grammatical postulates.

2. The elaborations of a unified methodology that unites the formal language and the machine approach to the definition of musicality, leads to a formulation of criteria by which to judge the epistemic and music-theoretical relevance of composition programs, and makes possible the elaboration of composition programs that are methodologically adequate both in the music grammatical and the music-strategical sense.

The latter task (2) led to changes in the conception of the notion of *grammar for music* and to the elaboration of the notion of sonology. Now that he is in the final phase of his methodological preparations the author wants to state the scope and the implications of the methodology to be adopted in greater detail.

Clarification of the Methodology Adopted

Changes in the Concept of a Metatheory of Music

The construct called a generative grammar for music was initially conceived as an autonomous device for reconstructing the components of the competence assumed to underlie all possible musical activities. Such a *general competence model* was thought to be at the center of a metatheory of music clarifying the scope, the method, and the problems of theories of music. In the attempt to work out the internal structure of such a general model, it became evident that a detailed specification of the strategical problems environment of grammars for music is indispensable. To specify the task environment of such grammars, the notion of *performance model for music* was introduced; such a model was defined as a system capable of simulating one or another type of musical activity, especially composition and listening. It was thought that, by way of simulation, models of musical activity would lead to insights into the formal structure of such activities and would make it possible to explicate their strategical differences. The method of research in music activity was conceived as subject to two requirements: first, to also support investigations into physical sound systems; second, to permit inclusion of the vast amount of available psycho-acoustic knowledge into a formal and explicit theory of music. For this reason, the notion of *sonology* was defined as the name of a discipline dealing with the design of sound artifacts and leading, in three stages to the formulation of performance models for music.[8]

1. Sound engineering and sonic representation
2. Pattern recognition and sonological representation
3. Musical representation and definition of intelligent music systems

The investigation carried out was above all concerned with intelligent performance systems, specifically with the conditions such systems have to fulfill in order to incorporate cognitive imperatives of such music-grammatical postulates.

The essential problem one encounters in formally and explicitly analyzing musical performance systems is the fact that such systems seem to incorporate two fundamentally different classes of determinants, strictly cognitive (grammatical) and behavioral (strategical) ones. To investigate in depth the interrelationships of these determinants, one needs precise notions of such terms as *problem, decision, solution, optimality, control,* and *feedback.* Continued work made further evident that the investigation of musical performance systems can be rigorously carried out only if a distinction is made between general problem-solving procedures used by the system and their application to specific, in this case musical, tasks. The subject of an investigation of general, problem-solving procedures is the formal, structural aspect of plans developed in order to solve a problem and of systems necessary to actually realize such plans. A study of musical problem-solving systems can be seen as an application of general systems theory whose theorems can be made fruitful in simulating processes of musical cognition by means of a computer program.

Musical performance can be conceived as based on the application of two very different sets of determinants—first, of music-grammatical rules, second, of general problem-solving operators. The insight in the twofold nature of performance determinants entails that the conception of a grammar for music as an autonomous device, and thus a self-sufficient determinant of music-strategical problem solving, is to be modified. Obviously, a grammar for music is not simply a set of cognitive determinants actualized in performance but is simultaneously a concrete tool in music-strategical processes geared to producing a solution.

As a consequence, grammars for music can be said to exist in two fundamentally different formats, in a task-dependent and in a task-independent format. In its task-independent format, music-grammatical knowledge can be called the *innate program* (W. Jacobs) of a performance system; as such it makes possible the development of problems of an intersubjective nature and the generality of musical problem formulations; moreover, music-grammatical knowledge embodies a set of criteria for judging the descriptive adequacy of problem representations produced by a performance system. In its task-dependent format, on the other hand, music-grammatical knowledge is actively engaged in producing comparison structures, thus mediating the application of general problem-solving procedures to specifically musical tasks.[9]

As a consequence of the introduction of systems-theoretic notions into music-strategical investigations, two aspects of the initial conception of a grammar for music were more clearly distinguished

1. Grammars as tools for problem solving (grammars in a task-dependent format)

2. Grammars as pure manifestations of musical competence (grammars in a task-independent format)

As a result, the conception of a metatheory of music equally underwent changes. Such a theory rests on two fundamental disciplines: a theory of musical activity seen as a problem-solving behavior, and a theory of musical competence, that is, of music-grammatical postulates. A metatheoretical investigation of music is thus an inquiry into the infrastructure of a general performance model as a system incorporating, as an integral part, a general grammar for music.[10] The theory of musical activity proceeds by way of programmed simulation; to explicate an activity, one formulates and tests programs for that activity and attempts to produce the behavior one investigates.[11] The formulation of a performance-detached, task-independent grammar for music presupposes an intermediary type of grammar (or syntax) capable of characterizing the music-grammatical principles of a program for music under a music-strategical aspect. Such a grammar is a *programmed grammar* (Rosenkrantz 1960); the rules of such a grammar, rather than being pure manifestations of musical competence, are approximations of the program's flowchart; in their totality, they characterize music-grammatical knowledge as a tool employed in strategical problem-solving situations.[12] A further clarification of the nature of grammars for music can be derived from the fact that grammars are either generative or analytic models (S. Marcus 1967).[13]

The Twofold Nature of the Approach

General Remarks The generative approach to the definition of musicality and the artificial intelligence approach to music programs have in common that both are investigations of musical cognition and are, more specifically, concerned with an explication of the intrinsic tacit knowledge that forms the basis of any musical activity whatsoever. They differ, however, in the way in which they interpret the relationship of music-grammatical and music-strategical knowledge, and in their means of establishing answers to their problems. While formal grammars are logical axiomatic systems above all dealing with the syntactic structure of languages, the formal study of general problem-solving programs and the design of intelligent problem solvers most often rest on set-theoretic concepts, on notions of control theory and of heuristic programming.[14]

The presence of divergent methodologies does not facilitate research in musical cognition. However, it is to be expected that progressively clearer formulations of musical cognition problems will lead to a unified methodology. The coming into existence of such a methodology depends on the thrust of the insight that problem-solving behavior presupposes the intrinsic capability of producing epistemically adequate problem formulations. In the case of music and other symbolic systems, this capability is competence-determined and cannot be taken for granted; it constitutes a rule-governed creativity obeying (or setting forth) music-grammatical constraints. As long as this essential component of musical intelligence remains unexplicated, the investigation of musical cognition will be unrewarding. Moreover, negation or neglect of the difference between strictly epistemological, grammatical, and more or less behavioral, strategical determinants of musical activity leads to confounding criteria of well-formedness of an infinite set of musical structures with criteria of the acceptability of finite sets of such structures.[15] Positively speaking, this confusion implies the assertion that a reconstruction of elements of musical competence is impossible or meaningless. It would seem, however, that too little is known about musical cognition to support such assertion.

The Formal Language Approach

The Two Kinds of Musical Grammar

While a generative grammar of music is intrinsically programmable, the converse is not true: a programmed approach can also lead to an analytic grammar for music.[16] In methodological terms, the difference between generative and analytic models of musical competence hinges on the problem of well-formedness. The grammaticalness of musical structures is essentially inexhaustible (Marcus); *grammaticalness* is a notion answering to the problem of syntactic ambiguity, namely to the question whether or not a given string is, or is not, the member of well-formed terminal set, that is, of a formal language. In the narrow, music-syntactic sense of the term, a generative grammar is thus a decision procedure for the well-formedness of structures produced by a program for music and, by extension, of any musical structure whatever.[17] Restricted to the consideration of well-formed strings, a generative grammar excludes the investigation of degrees of grammaticalness, and thus more or less deviant strings; for studying degrees of deviance from a defined music-grammatical norm an analytic model is needed.[18] On the basis of such a model one can investigate the types of syntactic structure characterizing a musical corpus, as well as syntagmatic and paradigmatic aspects of a particular set of deviant strings.

In order to state more precisely the difference between a generative and an analytic grammar, we define the following symbols:

Γ = an alphabet

T = the total language over an alphabet

ϕ = the set of well-formed strings defined over an alphabet

T $-$ ϕ = the set of deviant strings on which a partial order with regard to a norm t can be defined

Γ is a finite set called a *vocabulary* whose elements are *words*; the strings in ϕ are *marked strings*; T is a free monoid (semigroup), namely, the set of all finite strings of words which is endowed with an operation of concatenation. While a string of words is a *string over* Γ, the subset ϕ of T is a *language over* Γ. A generative grammar of ϕ is a finite set of rules specifying all and only the strings of the subset ϕ of T and assigning to each such string a structural description. In contrast to such a decision procedure for the well-formedness of strings, an analytic grammar considers ϕ as given and on that assumption studies the universal language T, and thus the set of deviant strings T $-$ ϕ.

Considered from the point of view of the total language over Γ, T, the nature and the size of ϕ depend on the notion of absolute grammaticalness introduced. Grammaticalness in music is, however, not exclusively a syntactic notion; a sequence of sound objects can be considered as well-formed, that is, as *musical* only if it equally fulfills certain semantic and sonological requirements. To begin the study of musical competence with a generative grammar as an autonomous device, independent of the strategical task environment it functions in, would therefore presuppose that one is capable of defining and justifying a notion of absolute well-formedness.

As this chapter points out, the investigation of the strategical task environment of grammars and studies in sonology are, however, indispensable prerequisites of an explication of musical competence. Given this methodological state of affairs, it seems inevitable to abandon the project of formulating a generative grammar a priori, that is, in purely epistemological terms. Accepting this conclusion, one confronts the following alternative: either (1) to adopt an analytic grammar for music, or (2) to choose a type of grammar that by its very nature lends itself to representing insights into the structure of the programmed task environment of musical competence.

To clarify the implications of the first option, some further remarks about the nature of an analytic grammar are in place. Such a grammar is a device with the aid of which one can analyze a given finite corpus of musical objects considered as a total language; in order to arrive at an insight into the internal structure of the corpus the analysis proceeds from lower to higher levels of grammaticalness.[19] Studies in analytic grammars for music are essentially studies in the degrees of grammaticalness manifested by a finite set of musical structures forming the corpus of an investigation.

In contrast to the analytic model, a generative grammar is concerned not with a finite, but with an infinite set of strings, and thus not with an actual given corpus but with the set of all and only the well-formed strings potentially derivable from a number of hypothetical constraints.[20] While the formulation of an analytic model proceeds from a corpus representing some language to the grammar that underlies it, that of a generative model proceeds from a hypothetical grammar to the language that is derivable from it. Consequently an analytic grammar for music is appropriate if the intrinsic interest of the investigation lies in obtaining a description of the more or less well-formed strings constituting a finite corpus and of the relationships between their basic units. However, not only does such an analytic study take for granted the well-formedness (musicality) of the corpus chosen, it also places the major emphasis on the corpus instead of explicating the rule-governed creativity presupposed by its production. The generative approach to musical grammar, on the other hand, places primary emphasis on investigating the structure of musical competence itself, that is, the internal componential structure of a device able to produce an infinite set of syntactically, semantically, and sonologically well-formed musical structures. Thus, while an analytic grammar is an *illustration* of musical competence (taken for granted), a generative grammar is an *explication* of musical competence.[21]

Taking into account this difference in result of the two types of grammar, it becomes evident that a metatheory of music accepting the analytic approach fails to satisfy the indispensible requirements of an explicit theory of musicality. This does not imply, however, that analytic studies are of no importance for a theory of music, nor that the incorporation of analytic elements into generative models is methodologically excluded from consideration. By way of the second option proposed, adoption of an intermediary programmed grammar, one is in fact able to incorporate certain assumptions as to the internal structure of the corpus to be introduced. A programmed grammar is, however, strictly generative in that with its adoption the major emphasis is placed on the study of the structure of musical competence itself (not on the corpus resulting from its actualization) and thus on the task-(in)dependent grammatical knowledge that is necessary to produce an infinite set of musical structures. In a project based on programs for musical composition, moreover, a generative grammar constitutes the most sensible approach. A composition program, whether instrumental or based on sound synthesis, proceeds from a set of music-grammatical and/or music-strategical postulates, to derive a certain (essentially infinite) set of structures.[22]

In the generative approach to the definition of musicality, one starts out with a hypothetical grammar, as incorporated by a program. The production of a corpus of structures is essentially not an end in itself; rather, it is a means for exploring, through systematic changes of instructions, first, the structure of the strategy itself and the nature of the task-dependent knowledge it utilizes and, second, the dependency of the structure of the corpus produced on the strategical structure of the program. The primary object of such a study is the structure of the program and of the grammar implied by it; emphasis is given to the corpus only as the terminal set of a specific hypothetical grammar, by no means to the corpus as such. The decisive problems of a generative study arise in the methodological domain; they are, above all

• What is the appropriate format into which to transcribe the task-dependent grammatical knowledge manifested by the program?

• What is the relationship of such a (strategy-mediated) transcription of grammatical knowledge to a generative model in the strict sense, that is, to the innate program of the performance system?

In the center of attention stands thus always the generative mechanism capable of producing an infinite set of well-formed musical structures.[23]

The limitations of this project in its first stage are due to the fact that the algorithm to be investigated is a program for instrumental composition.[24] The nature of an instrumental program entails acceptance of the conventional sonological representation of some (imagined) sonic repertory needed for the realization of the composed structures. As a consequence, the emphasis of results obtained in the first, instrumental, phase of research will concern the syntactic and, indirectly, the semantic component of musical knowledge. An awareness of this limitation leads to the insight that in order to achieve a comprehensive view of musical competence the consideration of programs for sound synthesis is indispensible. Such programs equally concern the structure of the sonic repertory of composition and its sonological and syntactic-semantic organisation; they are therefore free of instrumental predefinitions of the sonological competence they actualize. In order to explore the sonological component of musical competence, the project outlined will, in its second stage, be concerned with totally computerized composing systems having synthesizing capacity.

The Generative Grammar as Programmed Grammar

A programmed grammar, in the sense of this project, is a construct fulfilling the following requirements:

• To provide insight into the strategical structure of the program investigated, that is, into the problem-solving procedures used by the program and into their mode of cooperation

• To constitute an adequate formalization of the task-dependent music-grammatical knowledge incorporated by the program

• To act as a set of determinants from which to extrapolate the minimal constraints of the task-independent music-grammatical knowledge incorporated by the program

Only a grammar simultaneously satisfying the first two requirements is capable of directly mirroring the procedure actually used by a program to generate musical structures. To fulfill this demand, the grammar has to allow for an order of rules that is as free as possible. Only in the case that rule order is not intrinsically predetermined by the availability of non-terminals of the productions is the grammar flexible enough to render the nature of a particular strategy employed.

A grammar introducing an extrinsic order of production rules either adopts a strict cyclic scheme (*matrix grammars*) or an essentially free order (*programmed grammars*).[25] The latter makes it possible to specify the order of the rules "in a way which corresponds to the way in which humans envision the generation" of structures (Rosenkrantz 1969). Writing a programmed grammar, instead of the ordinary kind of production grammar, is thus similar to writing a program for the generation of a certain set of structures—taking into consideration, of course, that the programmed grammar formulated is not a duplication of the program but its theory. In formulating a programmed grammar as an account of a program for music, be it implied by a subject's strategy or fully automated, one codifies the rules underlying the generation of musical objects. This formulation of a programmed grammar is a prerequisite for stating in full the rules of a generative grammar in the comprehensive sense.

The rule-ordering device inherent in programmed grammars can, in contrast to the program under investigation, be called a programme; the programme is able to make precise a wide variety of orderings of rule applications. Viewed from the normal type of generative grammar, a programmed grammar is a formal system which comprises, next to its two vocabularies (V_{NT}, V_T), an initial symbol (S), and a set of productions (P) also a set of procedures (Q), or a programme.[26] The programme is a set of rule applications or permitted productions that specifies for each rule the next following production, even in the case that the preceding rule does not apply.[27] The programme Q thus permits all imaginable specifications of the order in which productions are used in generating a certain set of structures.

In more formal terms, Q_1 in Q is a procedure where Q is a finite set of quintuples (i, P, S, F, O) for $i = 1, 2, \ldots k$ (k being the cardinality of Q), and where S, F, O are subsets of (1, 2, … k).[28] If r is the r-th procedure (rule application) in Q and $a \in W$ (V_{NT}, V_T), it is said that (a, r) *generates* (b, q) if there is a chain of pairs such that

$$(a, r) = (a_1, r_1) \to (a_2, r_2) \to \cdots \to (a_n, r_n) = (b, q)$$

for some $i = 1, 2, \ldots k$. The subsets of i, S, F, O are sets of production labels indicating whether a procedure *succeeds* (q in S), *fails* (q in F), or does not apply at all (q in 0). The procedures contained in Q, that is, needed for a particular generation, are stated thus:

$(1, P_1(x), (y), (z))$

$(2, P_2(x), (y), (z))$, etc.,

where (x) is in S, (y) in F, and (z) in O. The programme Q in its entirety can be represented as a network of appropriately connected procedures in which each procedure can be thought of as a condition followed by a choice and a production. In the form of a flow diagram, a procedure (r, P, S, F, O) can be depicted as in figure 10.1.

The programme Q is thus an assemblage of *black boxes* Q1, each of which represents a procedure in Q and possesses one input- and three optional output-channels (S, F, O). The network constituted by the connected procedures is the flowchart of the programme Q. Due to the rule ordering device, the flowchart of the entire programme can be rendered as an ordered set of grammatical rules whose order of application mirrors the actual generation process. A set of productions ordered according to a programme embodies a formal statement of the task-dependent music-grammatical knowledge that underlies a specific programmed generation of structures.

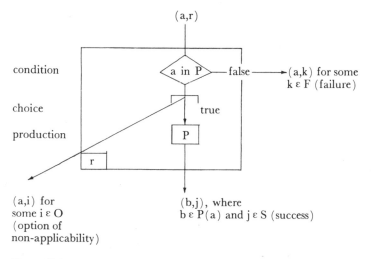

Figure 10.1

The essential question now to be answered is how far the programme, that is, the set of rule applications underlying the production, reflects in fact the generative mechanism that epistemologically must be assumed to underlie compositional activity. Proceeding from a programmed strategy via a programmed grammar to a comprehensive generative grammar for music, one can divide this question into two subproblems: first, what is the associated programmed grammar of a programmed musical strategy and, second, what is the generative grammar associable with the programmed grammar arrived at?

The Machine Approach

The Notions of *Musical Robot* and of *Musical Intelligence* The machine approach to the definition of musicality, if by machine one refers to the theory of automata, is trivially implied by the formal language approach. A new methodological element is introduced, however, if by the term machine one refers to a cybernetic system or robot simulating a certain, for example, a musical, behavior. In this case one is dealing with the problem: what are all the possible acts of behavior a musical system can perform and a suitably defined program can simulate? As a consequence, a theory of programmed musical strategies cannot dispense with insights of a theory of systems, whether living or symbolic, that is, of general systems theory. Simultaneously with being biological systems,[29] music-strategical systems are intelligent systems simulable by robots, that is, by computer-controlled mechanisms that can interact with their real-world environment in an autonomous, reasonably intelligent manner (B. Raphael).

It is important to realize that both the generative grammar and the systems theoretical approach are not restricted to actual phenomena but envisage a set of possibilities much wider than a given corpus of structures or a given activity in fact actualizes; this search for generality is in keeping with the task of exploring all the possible acts a (musical) system is able to perform, irrespective of its actual limitations. It is then a further step in the investigation to ask why the particular system under scrutiny should conform to the restrictions it actually exhibits.[30]

A musical robot is a system composed of three parts.

1. A sensory pattern recognition system

2. A particular grammar for music (acting as a synthesizer of comparison structures)

3. A general problem-solving device

The system produces artifacts that are in interface between an outer, sonic, and an inner, biologically grounded, epistemological environment; the latter is of a perceptual as well as cognitive nature. The sensory pattern recognition system enables the robot to deal with physical sound and, on a more abstract level, to compare its own productions with a music-grammatically defined norm. Its internalized particular grammar enables the robot to design sonological, syntactic, and semantic representations of the sonic repertory it reacts to; these representations are comparison structures more or less satisfying the music-grammatical constraints that determine which of the outputs are indeed cognitively adequate in view of the inputs to the system. The general problem-solving device renders the robot capable of developing general strategies for dealing with problem situations and to adapt these strategies to tasks arising from intelligible sonic inputs. Elements of the sonic environment entering into a musical performance system are already "filtered" by music-grammatical constraints; such environments vary with the specific strategical nature of the performance task.

The music problem-solving activities of the robot fundamentally depend on the internal representations of the outer (sonic) and inner (perceptual-cognitive) environments the robot can design. The strategies developed by a musical robot essentially aim at, first, producing an entire hierarchy or more or less grammatically well-formed representations of a sonic repertory and, second, at inventing a mechanism that will successfully transform some representation—and thus problem formulation—into another that is more adequate for finding a solution. Sonic environments pose problems for the robot only through the agency of internalized music-grammatical constraints. Depending on the set of constraints the system disposes of, its sensory, problem-solving, and motor functions are cognitively more or less adequate for dealing with strictly musical, in contrast to simply sonological, problems.

A programmed strategy is a robot in the sense that it can be said to generate the compositional behavior that is necessary to produce musical artifacts. In terms of musical competence, that is, epistemologically, a musical robot is an open, essentially restricted system, while it is closed in terms of biological energy, information, and control. Research in performance models for music, understood as musical robot research, is concerned with three main problems:

1. The structure of the set of music-grammatical constraints internalized by the performance system

2. The interactions of this set of constraints with the set of general problem-solving constrains available to the performance system

3. The effect of the biological, perceptual, and cybernetic (system-inherent) limitations on the grammatically and strategically open system

The robot is intelligent to the degree that it is capable of replacing a *search-through-all-possibilities* by plans developed on the basis of music-grammatical constraints. In this sense, problem-solving intelligence and music-grammatical determinateness of the robot are inseparable. The more intelligent a musical robot, the less directly does it deal with physical sound environments; instead, it deals with sonic, sonological, and syntactic-semantic representations of such environments. Thus the robot is musical to the same degree that it is intelligent. The intelligence a musical robot disposes of is of two kinds: strategical and grammatical. The first kind of intelligence is concerned with forming plans for arriving at the solution of complex problems through their transformation into problems of a lower order of difficulty (Minsky). The second kind of intelligence is task-independent; it is the very capability of conceiving of musical problems provoked by intelligible sound inputs. The difference between these two kinds of intelligence can be clarified by stating the two different problems they refer to. Strategical intelligence attempts to cope with the problem: how can a certain finite set of sonic objects be made intelligible, that is, transformed into a set of musical objects? Music-grammatical intelligence, on the other hand, deals with the question: what are the minimal universal conditions under which an infinite set of sonic objects is musically well formed? The intelligibility of sound artifacts is thus not merely a music-strategical problem.

Musical Goal Algorithms and Their Problems   The task of testing the two hypothetical kinds of intelligence defined is facilitated by distinguishing (1) general problem-solving heuristics from (2) the problem-oriented factual processing (Minsky). Particular problem-solving procedures can be specified in terms of the objects they deal with, the operators employed to find a solution, and the range of internal representations of an input they are equipped to design.

In terms of the first aspect, a composition program is a (nondeterministic) goal algorithm (Michie), that is, a set of heuristic procedures.[31] As a problem solver, the program is optimizable, that is, the versatility of its knowledge-handling procedures and the kinds of knowledge represented in it can be improved in view of a strategical and/or a cognitive norm. Such a program is an inexplicit theory of problem-solving behavior underlying intelligent human activities. The program takes as input a set of initial objects (constituting the elements of some problem representation); it attempts to arrive at a goal (or a set of terminal objects) through the application of a set of operators whose defined sequence constitutes a solution. In symbolic systems, the solution mostly consists of finding that specific problem representation of an input that makes it optimally intelligible. In strategical terms this means to invent and to realize a set of decisions on the basis of which the performance system acts most efficiently. To the extent that cognitive constraints are available to a performance system, strategical efficiency defines itself in terms of norms of the well-formedness (grammaticality) and the intelligibility (musicality) of sound objects. In a musically intelligent program, therefore, grammatical rules, rather than being approximations of the program's flowchart (Minsky), are the determinants of that flowchart.

A musical performance system essentially deals with a change of mental representations and an ensuing change in problem formulation and in problem-solving efficiency. (The latter, evidently, depends on the former.) While the primary properties of a program are those that characterize its general problem-solving procedure, secondary properties accrue from the specific task environment the program deals with. For instance, a strategy is *compositional* if it deals with the production of artifacts definable on the basis of some symbolic system, whether sonological or other. Programs for musical composition can be differentiated according to the specific initial representation they are supposed to transform. A program is concerned with *instrumental composition* if the sonological representation it acts upon falls outside of the problem domain and thus outside of the search space of its strategy; in this case, the sonological representation is simply taken for granted. The problem is involved with sound synthesis (that is, programmed electronic composition) if the sonological representation it acts on is not predefined but is established by the program itself on the basis of music-grammatical constraints; in this case, the robot has to deal with the entire range of sonological, syntactic, and semantic problems posed by an artificially synthesized sonic repertory.[32]

Strategically speaking, a compositional task consists of defining some elementary repertory as the basis of plan formation and of attaining a finite set of more and more abstract and complex representations of that repertory that are cognitively adequate in view of the initial representation striven for. Grammatically speaking, composition is centered around the goal of producing an infinite set of comparison structures of a definable degree of well-formedness. The theoretical difficulty of exploring composition in the second sense of this term is that the competence determinants guiding a performance system are for the most part not open to introspection or observable; rather, they seem to have to be inferred from strategical procedures which, in intelligent systems, are determined by them. The distinction between general problem-solving heuristics and specifically musical processing is methodologically fruitful in this respect; the distinction suggests that to elucidate the elements of musical competence essentially means explicating the interaction between musical competence constraints and the determinants of general problem-solving procedures (which obviously can interact also with principles of logical, linguistic, visual, etc., competence). It is foreseeable that programmed studies in cognition will be able to explore to what extent strategies called musical have their own specific heuristic structure and to what extent they in fact share their strategic potential with other kinds of activities based on different kinds of competence. More immediately, programmed studies in musical cognition should be able to develop precise formal notions of such terms as *(musical) problem, solution, move (operator), goal, judgment, experience, recognition, and learning.* A clarification of these terms is in fact a precondition for approaching the primary topic of such studies: an explication of the interaction taking place between strictly cognitive (music-grammatical) and behavioral (music-strategical) determinants. Only if the interdependence of these two hypothetical kinds of knowledge becomes open to programmed test can one proceed to questions like the following:

- What is *musical intelligibility*?

- How is a musical problem posed and solved?

- What is an intelligent, cognitively adequate representation of a given input?

• Are intelligent responses possible in the absence of music-grammatical constraints?

• Can different grammars for music be accomodated within the same strategy, etc.?

With a view to programs for musical composition, the most urgent question at present seems to be this: What is the range of problems a specific program can solve, arid what are the conditions under which it solves them?[33] To study the application of heuristic procedures of the program to specifically musical tasks is possible only once this question has been answered.

The Future Task

The methodological discussion contained in this report should have shown that the music-grammatical and epistemological relevance of a program for composition is essentially a function of the task-independence it incorporates. The same can be said of the importance such a program has for artificial intelligence studies. It seems reasonable to assume that music-grammatical constraints equally affect

• The problem formulation
• The internal representation of the input
• The execution of the program's plan
• The format of the output

and thus act as constraints on the objects, the operators, and search space of a given program. The music-grammatical intelligence of a strategy depends on the limitations on the size and complexity of its innate program. Since task independence is a criteria not only of music-grammatical knowledge but is equally characteristic of the general problem-solving (as against music-specific) procedures utilized by the program, any explication of the innate program will lead to a twofold description.

The most immediate problem, of explicating in the format of a programmed grammar, and thus in partially strategical terms, the music-grammatical determinants of a program, poses itself differently in the case of an instrumental and in the case of a sound synthesis program.[34] In the project under discussion, the problems posed by an instrumental program will be attacked first.[35] In order to escape the methodological limitations imposed by the technology of instrumental composition, the investigation will later be extended to sound synthesis programs. Such programs deal with musical composition at the most fundamental level, namely, with establishing a sonic repertory from which sonological and syntactic-semantic representations can be drawn, and further with the formulation of plans for interrelating and transforming these representations. Contrary to methods of classical electronic composition, sound synthesis programs are not committed to any particular hardware configuration since all such configurations are replaced by software operators. Since no predefined sonological representation exists in such programs, the latter are of great importance for studies in the sonological component of musical competence and in the relation of that component to syntactic and semantic aspects of musical competence. Furthermore, investigation of sound synthesis programs enlarges the domain of possible music-strategical insight. From a music-strategical point of view, the relevance of such programs resides in the fact that the basic compositional process involved is perception (listening) and that thus the two basic, conventionally separated, musical strategies can be studied in their interaction.[36] One cannot overestimate the methodological relevance of musical strategies which are, entirely programmed, that is, in which no single operator that is strictly part of the strategy remains outside of its software definitions. While this state of affairs bereaves the composer and the researcher of the many "inbuilt" programs which musical strategies conventionally count on (as those incorporated in conventional instruments, in electronic equipment, and in "performance" conventions), it established, on the other hand, a sonologically neutral basis on which to define and to investigate the various levels of organized music-grammatical knowledge. Although composition programs of a degree of sophistication comparable to certain artificial intelligence programs do not yet exist, it is foreseeable that more and more adequate ways of programming musical thought processes will be found through explorations of the kind here summarized. Moreover, these explorations have opened up a large number of problems that a single investigator, even in a lifetime, cannot possibly begin to work on, such as the problems of

• Musical learning, that is, of an acquisition model for music

• The biological foundations of competence and of performance models for music

• The semantic component of a general competence model for music

• The relationship, in musical thought processes, of strictly cognitive to behavioral determinants

• The relationship of musical competence and cognition to logical, linguistic, visual and, specifically, artistic competence

Among these general topics of investigation, the problem of most immediate relevance to this project is that stated under (4). While the author intends to do further work in musical syntax and semantics, in sonology, modal logic and programming languages, the most urgently needed studies are those in the domain of general systems theory and artificial intelligence. The methodological reorientation discussed in this report (specifically, the necessity of approaching problems of musical competence on the basis of programmed performance models for music) makes the formulation of a comprehensive grammar appear as a late achievement. The fact that, contrary to the state of affairs in linguistics, grammaticalness in music can be investigated only within the realm of performance, forces the reader to set the machine approach over the formal language approach to music. Accepting the construct called a programmed grammar as the intermediary device for explicating the task-dependent music-grammatical knowledge incorporated in a program, the future tasks within this project are the following:

1. Investigation of the strategical structure of programs in terms of general problem-solving heuristics, and in terms of specifically musical problem solving

2. (After an informal characterization of a particular program) formalization of its task-dependent competence in the format of a programmed grammar

3. Investigation of program outputs primarily with regard to their dependency on different substrategies developed within the framework of a program and secondarily with regard to their own intrinsic structure

4. Formulation of a hypothesis as to the task-independent musical competence incorporated in, and perhaps extrapolable on the basis of the programmed grammar associable with, the program[37]

During all these future investigations, the tentative statement of a comprehensive general competence model for music, worked out during 1970–

1971, will be treated as a hypothesis whose final formulation depends on the outcome of research in individual composition programs. It is hoped that the codification of a general competence model for music will lead to the definition of criteria by which to judge the epistemic adequacy of programs for music; such a codification will facilitate the elaboration of compositional strategies that are methodologically adequate form the point of view of music-grammatical competence as well as of insights into general and artistic problem-solving heuristics.

Notes

1. Presently available are two kinds of composition program: that for instrumental composition and that for sound synthesis. Although it has not been demonstrated that the difference between them is more than a technological one, it seems evident that their potential importance for music-theoretical investigation is very different. Instrumental programs, in presupposing a conventional sonological representation of some sonic repertory, are sonologically prejudicial and tend to support insight into the syntactic component of musical competence; sound synthesis programs can serve as a neutral basis for investigating sonological designs of various kinds. Clearly, the semantic conceptions implied by both kinds of programs are quite different.

2. See O. E. Laske, (a) A Methodological Inquiry into Computer Composition (MICC), unpublished manuscript, 1970; (b) "The Logical Structure of a Generative Grammar for Music" (LSGGM), unpublished manuscript, 1971.

3. See M. D. Mesarovic, (1) "Systems Theoretical Approach to Formal Theory of Problem Solving," in R. Banerji and M. D. Mesarovic, eds., Theoretical Approaches to Non-Numerical Problem Solving, Berlin and New York, Springer, 1970, pp 161–178; (2) with D. Macko and Y. Takahara, Theory of Hierarchical, Multilevel Systems, New York, Academic Press, 1970.

4. For details concerning the notion of sonology, see O. E. Laske, On Problems of a Performance Model for Music (PPMM), Utrecht, The Netherlands, Institute of Sonology (February 1972), chapter II.3, pp. 65–90; see also Introduction to Generative Theory of Music (IGTM), Sonological Reports, no 1, Utrecht, The Netherlands, Institute of Sonology (January 1973), chapter 3, pp. 35–52.

5. A performance model for music is a theory of musical activity; for the notion of performance in the linguistic literature, see G. A. Miller, et al., Plans and the Structure of Behavior, New York, Holt Rinehart & Winston, 1960; N. Chomsky, Aspects of the Theory of Syntax, Cambridge, Mass., M.I.T. Press, 1965, pp. 10–15, J. Fodor and M. Garrett, "Some Reflections on Competence and Performance, in J. Lyons, ed., Psycholinguistics Papers, Edinburgh, Scotland, Edinburgh University Press, 1966, pp. 135–154.

6. See no. 6 of the bibliography.

7. Giving an answer to this question is synonymous with determining the internal componential structure of a general competence model.

8. A detailed discussion of this tripartite division can be found in IGTM, source as quoted in note 4 above, chapter 3, pp. 46–47.

9. The notion of generation of comparison structures was developed by G. A. Miller in the work listed under no. 10 of the Bibliography; in that it assumes that communicative activity is essentially generative and cannot be based in a stimulus-response scheme, this motion implies a critique of the conception of communication as nothing else but a kind of informa-

tion processing. For details concerning the notion of "comparison structure in the musical sense, see O. E. Laske, PPMM, source as indicated in note 4, pp. 11–12, 104–109.

10. The interrelatedness of a general competence model for music and particular grammars is one of the most crucial problems in music theory; suggestions concerning a solution to this problem were made by B. Boretz in "Meta-Variations I/II." *Perspectives of New Music*, Fall-Winter 1969, pp. 1–74 and Spring–Summer 1970, pp. 49–111; see also his "Construction of Musical Syntax I/II," *Perspectives of New Music*, Fall–Winter 1970, pp. 23–42 and Double Issue 1971, pp. 232–270.

11. The problem of testing the interdependence of grammar and strategy, i.e., of epistemological and behavioral determinants of music activity, falls into the domain of artificial intelligence studies. In operations terms, the relationship of grammar to strategy in music is that between the internal problem representations a performance system is capable of creating and its problem-solving efficiency.

12. An alternative formal system developed recently is called a "rule-based grammar," see J. van Leeuwen, *Rule-Labeled Programs*, Ph.D. thesis, Utrecht, The Netherlands, Utrecht State University, Summer 1972. While a programmed grammar imposes restrictions on the order of productions to be applied, the restriction defined by a rule-labeled program concern the selection of the symbol to be rewritten.

13. Concerning the notion of "analytic grammar," see S. Marcus, *Algebraic Linguistics; Analytic Models*, New York, Academic Press, 1961.

14. Concerning the concept of formal system as applied to grammars, see M. Gross and A. Lentin, *Introduction to Formal Grammars*, Berlin and New York, Springer, 1970, pp. 22–43 (56); see also note 19.

15. For a detailed discussion of the difference between grammaticalness and acceptability, see J. Lyons, *Introduction to Theoretical Linguistics*, Cambridge, England, Cambridge University Press, 1968, pp. 137–142, 154–155, 421–423.

16. The generative (procedural) approach to the study of musical competence has been elaborated in the following essays by this author: (1) "On the Understanding and Design of Aesthetic Artifacts" (UDAA), 1968, revised version published in *Musikalisches Verstehen*, Staatliches Institut für Musikforschung, ed., Cologne, Arno Volk Verlag, 1974, pp. 190–217; (2) PPMM, source as stated in note 4; (3) *IGTM*, source as stated ibid; (4) "Toward a Science of Musical Problem Solving," unpublished manuscript (Spring 1973).

17. According to the broader notion of *generative grammar for music*, such a construct contains three components: a syntactic, a semantic, and a sonological component. For details see O. E. Laske, *PPMM*, pp. 22–27, 33–38; see also, *IGTM*, chapter 1, pp. 1–20.

18. This is a problem of utmost importance for the definition of *counter-grammars for music*, i.e., of theories of individual composition viewed as products of a rule-governed artistic creativity.

19. Note that the notion of *language* as used in this context refers to the theory of formal languages; the term has thus a strictly methodological meaning and implies no reference to, or analogy with, natural language.

20. In the terminology of the theory of generative grammar, a set of such hypothetical constraints is called nonterminal vocabulary of the grammar; for details concerning the derivation procedure in generative grammars, see Lyons, op cit., pp. 215–227.

21. The syntactic notion developed for twelve-tone music by M. Babbitt and atonal music by A. Forte form part of a particular analytic grammar for music. (Babbitt's distinction of *precompositional* and *compositional* operations is analogous to, but by no means identical with, that between musical competence and musical performance in the framework of the present theory.) Although due to their generality the two theorists mentioned imply meta-theoretical elements, they are essentially concerned with an infinite set of well-formed musical

structures but with elucidating the structure of a corpus of individual compositions. The fact that the theories seem to advance the twofold claim of being a grammar (or at least a syntax) and—potentially—the theory of a class of individual compositions further emphasizes their analytic character; this fact suggests that the line of demarcation to be drawn between grammatical and strategical constraints of musical activity not strictly maintained throughout these theories (although this is more clearly in evidence in Forte's than Babbitt's theory). Finally, these theories are essentially and exclusively a syntactic systems; they do not account for the music-grammatically crucial relationship between syntax and sonology, nor do they conceive of music semantics as a grammatical discipline. (In the understanding of these theories, semantics is a theory of musical context, thus a performance discipline.) To the degree that sonology (in the grammatical sense) is considered at all by these theories as, for example, in Babbitt's "Twelve-Tone Rhythmic Structure and the Electronic Medium" Perspective of New Music, 1962), it is conceived as an extension rather than an interpretation of a (particular) music syntax.

In contrast to the theories of Babbitt and Forte, the notion developed by Boretz (op. cit. in note 10) are clearly of a metatheoretical character in that they lead from an *all-musical system* to particular syntaxcs for music. In contrast to the present theory, however, B. Boretz does not postulate three distinct, interrelated factors of musical competence (i.e., a syntactic, a semantic, and a sonological component of music-grammatical knowledge); moreover, the distinction between musical competence and musical performance is only implied, not maintained or made a subject of inquiry in his writings. Finally, B. Boretz's theory is geared toward a finite corpus of individual compositions and thus implicitely claims to be an (analytical) metatheory of music as well as the immediate basis of a musical poietics or theory of individual compositions.

According to the conception of musical competence developed by the author of this essay, a grammar for music, whether general or particular, is to be distinguished from a musical poietics; the latter is concerned with individual compositions as products of a musical creativity systematically deviating from a grammatical norm while a grammar for music is, by definition, neutral vis-à-vis individual compositions. Considered from the music-grammatical point of view, systemic operations as well as compositional strategies geared toward producing individual composition constitute a problem of second order in the sense that a solution to problems posed by such operators and/or strategies presuppose explicit notions of musical competence as rule-governed creativity, in contrast to the actualization of such competence in music-strategical processes. The problem of a *class of individual compositions* is an issue not principally concerning investigations into musical competence but rather studies in artistic creativity. Artistic creativity, too, can be reconstructed as a rule-governed competence; topics in the field of artistic creativity concern the individuality and finitude, not the musicality, of compositions. Although methodologically necessary, the distinction between a grammar for music and a musical poietics must not be construed as an a priori distinction. Rather, this distinction is made in order to break down into manageable portions the complex task of investigating the determinants of musical structures as they appear in individual compositions. The distinction between musical grammar and musical poietics makes it possible to explore the crucial notion of *degree of musical well-formedness* and to treat of artificially created structures as definable deviations from an explicit *grammatical norm*. (To do so presupposes that theories of individual compositions are conceived as countergrammars, i.e., as grammatical theories of contextuality.) Such a precedure is analogous to the investigation of the structure of an individual poem carried out on the basis of a generative model of linguistic competence.

In contrast to structures produced by a generative grammar for music, structures forming an individual composition constitute a finite set. However, a musical poietics is essentially not restricted to the investigation of individual compositions a certain composer is essentially able to create, given the grammatical and strategical knowledge exhibited by the products of his activity. See also note 24 below and *IGTM*, p. 84 (n. 21).

22. A program written for the analysis of a given corpus of musical structures evidently forms part of the analytic approach. This approach is geared to a definition of music rather than of musicality (understood as being the constitutive principle of things musical).

23. While analytic grammar establishing the structure of a given corpus can always be found, a generative grammar might not exist in all cases; moreover, the generative mechanism one is able to assess always underlies the limitations of a given program.

24. The conventional assumption that the study of music in general, and of musical grammar in particular, is most aptly based on the analysis of products of composition activity is prejudicial in favor of the identification of grammar and syntax, and of what is *grammatical* with what is *precompositional* (Babbitt). This assumption is methodologically all the more warranted since the strategical differences between various musical activities like composing, listening, etc. have never been explicated and can be said to be known only introspectively. Furthermore, this assumption is prejudicial in favor of individual composition as products of artistic creativity whose link with musical competence is music-theoretically incidental and music-grammatically an issue the discussion of which presupposes insights into the structure of musical competence. Finally, implying acceptance of a finite Set of historically available compositions (or, rather, scores) as the corpus of inquiry, this assumption has the tendency to conjure away the methodological necessity of explicating musical competence. (The linguistic analogue of basing a grammar on the analysis of individual compositions would be the attempt to derive French grammar from an analysis of poems by Stéphane Mallarmé.)

For suggestions concerning programmed studies in musical listening and in perception as part of sonology, see O. E. Laske, "Some Postulations Concerning a Sonological Theory of Perception," chapter II, *IGTM*, pp. 21–34.

25. The extrinsic ordering of rules does not add to the generative power of the grammar, nor does it subtract from it; however, instead of rendering only context-free languages, certain context-sensitive features can be represented by programmed grammars.

26. V_{NT} is an abbreviation for *nonterminal vocabulary*, V_T stands for *terminal vocabulary*; the symbol S represents a metamusical variable (or syntactic category of first order) functioning as the initial element of derivations; P, finally, is the set of rules underlying the derivational process.

27. If a topological orientation is introduced into a programmed grammar, it can further be specified whether the next fallowing rule appears to the left (L) or to the right (R) of the structure resulting from the previous rule; this necessitates the introduction of a set of moves which is a two-element set (L, R) of the directions which each of the rule applications can take (Rozenberg 1972).

28. See B. Brainerd, *Introduction to the Mathematics of Language Study*, New York, American Elsevier Press, 1971, pp. 247–256, especially p. 248.

29. Music-strategical systems as biological systems are best explored in the framework of systems theory which can be conceived as an *artificial biology*, see R. E. Kalman, "New Development in Systems Theory Relevant to Biology," in M. D. Mesarovic, ed., *Systems Theory and Biology*, Berlin and New York, Springer, 1968, p. 222.

30. For details concerning the nature of a cybernetic study of systems, see W. Ross Ashby, *An Introduction to Cybernetics*, London, Methuen, 1964 (1971), p. 3.

31. Goal algorithms are nondeterministic by definition; algorithms capable of only one move at a time are evidently incapable of simulating heuristic procedures.

32. This definition excludes programs written for the production of single, isolated sounds; such programs are mere software translations of single electronic generators and are of a merely technical, not inherently musical, interest.

33. Metatheoretically, the range of problems is to be defined in reference to competence constraints; musical problems in the sense of a generative theory are definable only on music-grammatical grounds. They are thus to be distinguished from problems of reasoning

about actions (Amarel) and from problems of reasoning in terms of goals and solutions such problems are of a strictly strategical nature.

34. By *sound synthesis program* is meant a fully automated composing system with synthesizing capability.

35. The first program chosen for such an investigation is G. M. Koenig's PROJECT 2 (1969), see no. 5 of the Bibliography. [A sonological observer program is presently being developed at the Institute of Sonology, Utrecht, The Netherlands; the program is based on sound synthesis facilities provided by Barry Truax's POD 5 program, a description of which appeared as *Sonological Reports*, no. 2, of the Institute of Sonology, Utrecht, The Netherlands (Summer 1973).]

36. Perceptual studies based on sound synthesis programs primarily concern topics of sonic and sonological representations as, for example, the relationship of sets of physical parameters to such sonic (i.e. mental) events as the variation in the *masse, profilet dynamique* of sounds (P. Schaeffer), their envelope characteristics. Strategically speaking, the problems involved are essentially pattern formation and pattern recognition problems. Concerning the distinction of sonic from sonological logical categories, see P. Schaeffer, *Traité des objets musicaux*, Paris, Editions Du Seuil, 1966, pp. 548–587, and O. E. Laske, PPMM, pp. 65–90. Concerning pattern recognition problems in the domain of elementary performance systems, see St. C. Fralick, "Learning to Recognize Patterns without a Teacher," *IEEE Trans. on Inf. Theory*, vol. IT-13, no. 1, New York, Institute of Electrical and Electronics Engineers (January 1967), pp. 57–64, and W. J. Steingrandt and St. S. Yau, "A Stochastic Approximation Method for Waveform Cluster Center Generation," *IEEE Trans. on Inf. Theory*, vol IT-18, no. 2 (March 1972), pp. 262–274.

37. Presumably, the same procedure can be adopted for the intended investigation of sound synthesis programs. The characteristics of the second phase of investigation in the framework of this project is the fact that the studies under (4) will above all concern the sonological, not the syntactic, component of musical competence.

Selected Bibliography

Ashby. W. Ross, *An Introduction to Cybernetics*, London, Methuen, 1964 (1971).

Banerji, R., and Mesarovic, M. D. (eds.), *Theoretical Approaches to Non-Numerical Problem Solving*, Berlin and New York, Springer, 1970.

Brainerd, B., *Introduction to the Mathematics of Language Study*, New York, American Elsevier Press, 1971.

Gross, M., and Lentin, A., *Introduction to Formal Grammar*, Berlin and New York, Springer, 1970.

Koenig, G. M., "Project 2, A Programme for Musical Composition," *Electronic Music Reports*, no. 3, Utrecht, The Netherlands, Institute of Sonology, 1970 (December).

Laske, Otto E., *On Problems of a Performance Model for Music*, Utrecht, The Netherlands, Institute of Sonology, 1972 (Spring).

Laske, Otto E., "On the Methodology and Implementation of Procedural Theory of Music," in *Proceedings*, International Conference on Computers and the Humanities (Minneapolis 1973), Edinburgh University Press, Edinburgh, Scotland, 1974.

Laske, Otto E., "Musical Semantics—A Procedural Point of View," first part to appear in *Actes du 1er Congrès International de Sémiotique Musicale* (Belgrade, 1973) Centro d'Iniziativa Culturale, Pesaro, Italie, 1974.

Laske, Otto E., "Toward a Science of Musical Problem Solving," unpublished manuscript, 1973.

Laske, Otto E., "Toward a Musical Intelligence System: OBSERVER," *Numus West*, no. 4, Mercer Island, Wash. (Fall 1973), pp. 11–16.

Laske, Otto E., "Music as a Topic of Artificial Intelligence Research," unpublished manuscript, 1974.

Lyons, J., *Introduction to Theoretical Linguistics*, Cambridge, England, Cambridge University Press, 1968.

Marcus, S., *Algebraic Linguistics: Analytic Models*, New York, Academic Press, 1967.

Mesarovic, M. D., "Systems Theory and Biology," in Mesarovic ed., *Systems Theory and Biology*, Berlin and New York, Springer, 1968, pp. 59–81.

Mesarovic, M. D., Mathematical Theory of General Systems and Some Economic Problems," in Kuhn/Szegö ed., *Mathematical Systems Theory and Economics* 1, Berlin and New York, Springer, 1969, pp. 93–116.

Mesarovic, M. D., "Systems Theoretical Approaches to Formal Theory of Problem Solving," see no. 2 of this bibliography (pp. 161–178).

Mesarovic, M. D., Macko, D., and Takahara, Y., *Theory of Hierarchical, Multi-level systems*, New York, Academic Press, 1970.

Miller, G. A., et al., *Plans and the Structure of Behavior*, New York, Holt, Rinehart & Winston, 1960.

Minsky, M., *Semantic Information Processing*, Cambridge, Mass., MIT Press, 1965.

Rosenkrantz, D. J., "Programmed Grammars and Classes of Formal Languages," *Journal of the A.C.M.*, New York, Association for Computing Machinery, vol. 16, no. 1 (January 1969), pp. 107–131.

Rozenberg, G., "Direction Controlled Programmed Grammars," *Acta Informatica* 1, Berlin, Springer (Spring 1972), pp. 242–252.

Ruwet, N., "Méthodes d'analyse en musicologie," *Revue belge de musicologie*, Bruxelles, Librarie Encyclopédique, vol. 20 (1966), pp. 65–90.

Schaeffer, P., *Traité des objets musicaux*, Paris, Editions Du Seuil, 1966.

van Leeuwen, J., *Rule-labeled Programs*, Ph.D. thesis, Utrecht, The Netherlands, Utrecht State University (Summer 1972).

Gary Rader's 1974 musical round generator is a good example of production-rule style AI programming. It uses a few layers of musical heuristics: rules that allow or disallow harmonic and melodic sequences and rules that determine the applicability and probabilities of other rules. In many cases, this lets the rule author think in terms of patterns rather than sequences of instructions or interactions between rules.

Rader cleverly begins with a solution to the "meta" problem, "How do we define a music composition task that is easily viewed as traditional problem-solving?" A request for an original composition is too vague to provide a direction; but making an *n*-part musical round, where the different voices must reveal harmony without breaking traditional counterpoint rules, provides enough constraint that Rader is then able to approach it using mid-70s style condition/action production rules.

In the development of most of the programs in this volume, there is an excitement and discovery that, as in much science, is often hidden once the research is written up. However confident a composer or improviser is, no one can be sure of knowing all the rules for making these different kinds of music. While many of Rader's rules have their origin in music texts, others result from experiments and are admittedly his own invention. Ideas that seem obvious to a theorist may more likely be missing from a music text than structures that capture musical interest.

Many are the musician/programmers who have tried an algorithm for, say, "random notes within a diatonic scale"—only to be ambushed by unforeseen effects, like unpredicted, unjustified, repeated notes, or pitches wandering to the upper or lower edge of the instrument range. In Rader's program, these are typically addressed using a modification of a rule or the addition of another rule that changes the first rule's range of applicability. The production condition/action style programming environment provides a little laboratory for these kinds of experiments. We can see certain disadvantages in the production rule format: a common requirement is to have a verbose second rule whose sole purpose is to turn the first rule on or off, when it applies only to the beginning or end of the piece and will be used at most just one time. Interestingly, Rader has not fully implemented the traditional rules of counterpoint, for avoiding parallelisms, and so forth in his program but remarks that they could be added in the same framework.

11 A Method for Composing Simple Traditional Music by Computer

Gary M. Rader

Very little work has been done to date on writing computer programs that compose noncontemporary music. An initial attempt was made in 1955 by Hiller and Isaacson (6) with their "Illiac Suite," a string quartet, part of which was based on some elementary rules of music theory. Recently Moorer (8) worked on a method to produce popular melodies. Both of these efforts were based on heuristic processes. There have also been several attempts to generate tonal music by statistical simulation, but this approach does not look promising. This chapter presents a method used to mechanically generate traditional, common practice rounds using heuristics modeled on the human composer.

Almost no one would dispute the statement that it is impossible for a machine to create any aesthetically pleasing piece of art, be it music, painting, or poetry. After all, only a very small number of people in any of these fields have ever been talented enough to be acclaimed great artists. Fundamental to this belief is the fact that art requires both conscious and unconscious evaluations along with an interfacing of the two on the part of both the artist and the perceiver and, as such, is unmechanizable because we cannot even mechanize the conscious part; let alone the whole system.

However, it is possible to talk generally about the meaning of art without going deeply into this complex system of conscious and unconscious evaluations. The cultural anthropologist Gregory Bateson (1) points out that meaning in the context of art can be thought of as being roughly synonymous with pattern or redundancy. For instance, a song can be said to have meaning if it can be separated into two connected parts so that an observer, upon hearing the first part, has a better than random chance of guessing the continuation correctly. In music, meaning usually exists on several different levels. That is, most music contains different levels of patterns (i.e., patterns of patterns, patterns of patterns of patterns, and so forth). Thus, if we can somehow formally define several levels of culturally relevant patterns, it is not entirely unreasonable to expect that a computer might be able to compose fairly pleasant music.

Copyright 1974, Association for Computing Machinery, Inc., and reproduced by permission.

Long-Range Goal

The problem is not whether computers can compose music, but how far can we go in formalizing human symbolic systems—in this case, music. The goal here is not to make aesthetically perfect music but to make it indistinguishable to the human ear from human-produced music.

With simple forms of music such as rounds, much of the multileveled structure of more complex forms of music need not be dealt with. The object of the present work is to understand better some of the simpler aspects of music and how they mutually relate. By examining the parts and their interrelationships we gain greater explanatory power of the whole. Once we are largely able to formalize the musical parameters, melody, harmony, and rhythm at the microlevel and are able to interrelate them in a common system, we will be able to begin worrying about higher level structural considerations.

Music Fundamentals

A sequence of single notes is called a line (or part). Several lines may be played at the same time. One line, usually the highest, is called the melody. Two notes that are played at a given point in time constitute a harmony. A melodic (or horizontal) interval is the interval between two successive notes in a line. A harmonic (or vertical) interval is the interval between two notes played at the same time. The name of the interval between two notes is found by counting the number of lines and spaces included by the two notes. (The interval between two notes that are one step apart is a second. A third is an interval of two steps, and so on. A unison is an interval of zero steps.) Harmonies (harmonic intervals) are either consonant or dissonant. The consonant intervals are unison, third, fourth, fifth, sixth, and octave. Dissonant intervals are second and seventh. Two lines are said to harmonize when all the harmonic intervals are consonant. The combination of two or more harmonic (vertical) intervals makes a chord. The simplest type of chord is the triad, composed of two superimposed thirds (or their octaves). Its members are called the root, third, and fifth from bottom to top, respectively. A triad with its root as the lowest note is said to be in root position. A triad with its third as the lowest note is said to be in first inversion, and a triad with its fifth as the lowest note is said to be in second inversion (figure 11.1).

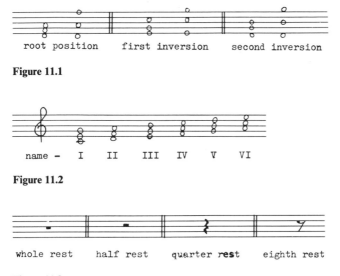

root position   first inversion   second inversion

Figure 11.1

name –   I   II   III   IV   V   VI

Figure 11.2

whole rest   half rest   quarter rest   eighth rest

Figure 11.3

For our work, we will be mainly concerned with the following chords and their inversions (figure 11.2). Chords I, II, III, IV, V, and VI are called the tonic, supertonic, mediant, subdominant, dominant, and submediant, respectively. In practice, only certain chord progressions are ever used by composers. Those mainly used are given later in the finite state graph of figure 11.5.

The term conjunct (or stepwise) motion refers to a melodic interval of a second (one step); disjunct motion refers to a melodic interval larger than a step (a leap or a jump). In general, a good melodic line contains mostly conjunct motion, with disjunct motion used cautiously for variety.

Points in a line where no tone is sounding are called rests. Rests occur in different durations just as notes do (figure 11.3).

One or more notes in a chord may be dissonant (forming a dissonant harmony with some note in the chord, usually the lowest note). The dissonant note in a chord may move to a consonant note while the other notes remain the same; this motion is called resolution and is the source of all harmonic structure. An appoggiatura is a dissonant note that resolves by movement of a step while the nondissonant notes remain stationary. It occurs on a strong beat and its resolution is on a weak beat. (In 4/4 meter,

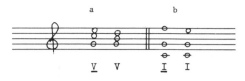

Figure 11.4

beats 1 and 3 of each measure are strong while beats 2 and 4 are weak; 1 is stronger than 3 and 2 is stronger than 4.)

The root and third of any second inversion triad are appoggiaturas that generally resolve by moving a step downward. We shall use the term V appoggiatura (and write V) to describe cases such as the first below where the appoggiatura resolves in a V chord. Similarly, we shall use the term I appoggiatura (I) where the resolution is a I chord as in the second case below. Thus the harmonic progression in figure 11.4 (a) would be V appoggiatura to V rather than I to V.

Rounds

A round is a circle canon, such as Frere Jacques, involving the sequential entrance of a number of parts with each strictly imitating only the first later in time. The amount of time between each successive entrance equals the length of the round (number of measures) divided by the number of parts.

When a part finishes, it may begin again. To end, we assume that all parts stop simultaneously just prior to an entrance point.

The reason we shall work explicitly only with rounds is this: owing to their relative shortness compared to other forms and to their built-in melodic, rhythmic, and harmonic imitation on account of repetition, rounds need not have a highly structured melody line or complex harmonic and rhythmic textures. Yet they do require an intelligent handling of these factors. However, they also require the handling of a feature not usually found in other forms. This is the obvious requirement that the melody harmonize with itself (that is, with temporal displacements of itself).

Suppose a round has n parts, where n is some positive integer. We say that this n-part round is in normal form (standard form) if it is written out in n connected staves where each succeeding staff corresponds to the entrance of the next part.

The Basic Method, Informally

The generation process is divided into two parts. Roughly speaking, starting with an empty set of staves in normal form, we first generate a harmonic framework over these staves. Then the melody is generated within this harmonic context.

The methods for generating the harmonic outline and the melody are similar. Both are based on sets of rules stating how chords or notes may be put together. The basic method is iterative and contains a set of "productions," each of which specifies a single choice for the next chord or note. It also contains a set of "applicability rules" that determine when productions may or may not be used. If at least one applicability rule specifies that a production is presently ineligible, it may not be used. The method contains a third set of "weight rules" that indicate the likelihood that an "applicable" production is applied by associating a weight with each rule. The weights are variable and may be reset prior to the initiation of any generation. These latter two sets may be viewed as sets of metarules operating on the set of productions. In general, their effects will change after each application of a production.

An example of an applicability rule would be a parallel fifth rule that would not allow the application of any productions yielding parallel fifths (two adjacent occurrences of the interval of a fifth between the same two parts). A weight rule might assign higher weights to rules resulting in stepwise rather than disjunct melodic motion. The effects of both sets of rules are dependent on what has occurred previously during a generation. If an applicability rule determines that a production may not be used, the weight of the production is multiplied by 0, otherwise by 1. A random number generator determines the sequence of applications of productions based on the weightings. A generation ends when all weights are simultaneously zero.

Harmony Generation

By harmonic framework we mean the sequence of chords that will occur on each beat of the round when written in normal form. This harmony does not include an indication of the actual positions of the chords (e.g., root, first inversion, or second inversion for triads). This will be determined later by the melody generator. This harmonic framework will be called a chord pattern.

A chord pattern shall usually consist of those triads closely related to the key of C major. The number of chords in a chord pattern equals the number of beats that any staff of a round in normal form contains.

The harmony generator consists of the following:

Productions

H1   **I** may follow any sequence of chords (even the null sequence).

H2-H5   A chord may be followed by the chord a third below, a second above, a fourth above or by itself, respectively.

H6   **I** and **IV** may be followed by **V̲** and **I̲**, respectively.

H7   **V̲** and **I̲** may be followed by V and I, respectively.

H8   **I** may precede any chord except **V̲** and **I̲**.

Applicability Rules

H9   No rule is applicable after the chord pattern has reached an initially specified length.

H10   The first chord must be **I**.

H11   The last two chords must be **I**.

H12   **I̲** and **V̲** cannot occur on the second and fourth beats.

H13   **IV, I,** and **IV** may not follow **VI, III,** and **III**, respectively.

Weight Rules

There is one weight rule for each production, which assigns a fixed weight to that rule.

We assume a meter of 4/4. H1 is used only to obtain the first chord in a chord pattern. H7 is used whenever possible (insuring resolution). The weights are usually set so that H4 or H5 is usually applied, H6 or H8 is sometimes applied, and H2 or H3 is occasionally applied. The finite state graph that follows describes all possible chord patterns the harmony generator can produce when the arrows are weighted appropriately.

H1–H8 derive in part from Piston (9) and Vauclain (14) and in part from my own musical training, H9–H11 are my own inventions, and H12–H13 are extracted from Vauclain. Other sets of rules might do just as well or even better. The relationships among the weights in the weight rules are fairly crucial.

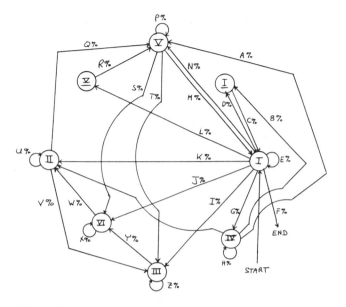

Figure 11.5

To read figure 11.5, we must follow the arrows beginning at START. Each time we come to a circle (a state), we write down the chord contained in it. If more than one arrow leads from a circle, one must be chosen and followed; the choice depends on the corresponding percentage. The chord pattern is completed when we come to END. The percentages attached to the arrows emanating from each state generally change while traversing the graph but always total 100 percent.

For example, $A + B + H + O = 100$ percent always, but B usually alternates between zero and a nonzero percentage due to rule H12. More precisely, the transition function between states is a random function with a distribution so chosen that the probability of obtaining nontraditional harmonic progressions is zero.

However, as it now stands, the harmony generator will not necessarily give a chord pattern of an initially specified length while observing the applicability rules without some sort of look ahead. To remedy this, we reverse the order of generation so that a chord pattern is produced from right-to-left beginning with the last chord. Then, since **I** can precede any chord except **V̲**, and since **V̲** cannot occur on the second beat of a measure, we can always end by choosing **I** to begin the appropriate measure.

Melody Generation

The melody generator utilizes the same basic method in producing notes
for a round. It will generate these notes within the constraints of a chord
pattern and according to practiced rules of music and a collection of
heuristic rules of melody.

Allowable notes will consist of all notes from the g below middle c
through the g two octaves above it plus the rest, which may be considered
as a null note. These notes will have a fixed duration of an eighth note. To
obtain notes with longer durations, we add a new character whose meaning will be to lengthen the duration of any note it follows by an eighth note.
In this way notes with any duration that is an integral multiple of eighth
notes can be generated.

To generate a round, the melody generator must be initially supplied
with a chord pattern, the number of parts, the maximum allowable number
of octave jumps, and the maximum allowable spread between the highest and lowest notes in the completed round. The resultant round will
have a length (ln) equal to the length of the chord pattern times the
number of parts. The round is generated in normal form, top to bottom,
left to right.

Productions

M1–M2   An eighth note on middle c or an octave above may be added
to any sequence of notes (even the null sequence).

M3   The last note may be increased in duration by a quarter note.

M4–M13   The last note may be increased in duration by an eighth note
and followed by an eighth note that is 1, 2, 3, 4, or 5 steps above or below
the last "stepwise note" (see M37).

M14–M19   The last note may be increased in duration by an eighth note
and followed by an eighth stepwise note 1, 2, or 7 steps above or below the
last stepwise note, respectively.

M20–M21   The last note may be followed by two eighth stepwise notes
moving stepwise up or down from the last stepwise note.

M22–M23   The last note may be followed by two eighth notes moving
up (down) one step and then back down (up) one step from the last stepwise
note respectively.

M24–M25   The last note may be increased in duration by an eighth note and followed by an eighth rest or an eighth note in the same position, respectively.

M26   The last note may be increased in duration by an eighth note.

Applicability Rules

M27   No rule is applicable after the length of the round equals 1n.

M25   M1 or M2 must be applied initially and never again.

M29   M26 must be the last production applied and never before.

M30   A production resulting in parallel unisons, fifths, octaves, or twelfths from the first half of a beat to the second half of the same beat or from the second half of a beat to the first half of the next beat may not be applied.

M31   A production yielding a note which is not a member of the chord corresponding to the present beat may not be applied unless it is a rest.

M32   A production yielding the harmonic interval of a fourth may not be applied unless it resolves or occurs in a first inversion triad or off the beat.

M33   If the previous chord was an appoggiatura, the present note must be a rest, the same as the last note, or move one step down.

M34   The maximum spread between the highest and lowest notes of the round may not exceed an initially specified amount.

M35   Half and dotted quarter notes may only occur on the first and third beats.

M36   The number of octave jumps may not exceed an initially specified number.

M37   (Melodic Rule) Beginning with the first note, the melody must progress stepwise or, if it jumps, it must either return and continue the stepwise movement from the point at which it jumped or move back toward this point until it does continue the stepwise motion. In the case of appoggiaturas the melody may first resolve before satisfying the above. An octave jump displaces the stepwise motion by a similar amount. An octave jump may occur only when the last note was a stepwise note (part of the stepwise motion). If continuing by two stepwise eighth notes (M20 or M21) would result in unallowed parallel motion, the melody may progress by the interval of a stepwise third (M16 or M17, respectively).

M38   An octave jump must be followed by movement in the opposite direction.

M39   Only the root of an appoggiatura chord may be doubled.

M40   M24 may be applied only if no other rule is applicable.

M41   The root of an appoggiatura chord and its resolution must be either a half note or two quarter notes.

M42   No note outside of the range from the g below middle c through the g two octaves above may be used.

Weight Rules

There are two weight rules for each production. One is used if applying the production will double a note (up to an octave); the other is used if no doubling will occur. The weights are normally set so that doubling is fairly unlikely and so that stepwise motion is much more likely than disjunct motion. We have the following additional rules.

M43   If the last note was a leading tone (♭ in the key of C), the likelihood that the next note is the root one step up is increased by an initially specified amount.

M44   The likelihood of a note being doubled is increased by an initially specified amount if that note is a c f, or g.

M45   The likelihood that the last note is c is increased by an initially specified amount.

M1–M26 are based on a combination of Vauclain (14), my own musical training, and a study I undertook of rounds and carons. M27–M43 and M45 derive from a combination of my own musical training, my imagination, and what appeared to be necessary to avoid the gross musical errors of earlier versions of this set. M44 comes from Vauclain. Again, there are indubitably other formulations of these sets of rules that would do just as well or better than the present ones. And again, the relationships among the weight settings of the weight rules are fairly crucial.

Formal Description

We now give a formal description of the basic method used in the composing process under the guise of a stochastic grammar.

A stochastic grammar is similar in its basic structure to a Chomsky grammar. It contains a terminal and a nonterminal alphabet, a set of productions, and a starting symbol. The difference lies in the fact that it also contains a set of probability functions and a set of input information. The probability functions are used to compute how probable the application of each production is at every stage in the generation process. One function is associated with each production. Generally these functions are dependent on the input information and on the past sequence of applications of productions in the current generation. (From this fact comes the name "stochastic.") The input information is a set of data supplied to the grammar before the start of a generation.

For convenience we include two more sets, a generic alphabet and a set of alphabet functions. They are not necessary but are used in production schemata to make the grammar's structure more compact and transparent. (They are also used in the computer programs to make them more efficient.) Each character in the generic alphabet represents all the members of a specified subset of the complete alphabet. When one appears in a production, it will stand as an abbreviation for the entire class of productions obtained by replacing the generic character by each member of the subset. However, if the same generic character appears more than once in a production, all occurrences must be replaced by the same member. Alphabet functions are functions from the complete alphabet into itself. As such, they may include suitable generic characters in their domains. Finally the grammar contains a bijection that associates a probability function with each production.

A stochastic grammar ς is a system of nine types of elements, $\varsigma = (\Sigma, G, V, R, S, I, F, P, M)$ where:

Σ is the terminal alphabet.

G is the generic alphabet.

V is the Complete alphabet.

R is the set of productions.

S is the starting Symbol.

I is the set of input information.

F is the set of alphabet functions.

P is the set of probability functions.

M is a bijection $M : R \to P$.

Each $p \in P$ is assumed to yield only one value at a given moment. This value is initially computed before any productions are applied and then recomputed after each application of production. The set I usually includes a probability constant for each $p \in P$. Unless otherwise stated, each generic character $g \in G$ will be considered generic over the alphabet $V-G$.

We do not restrict the usage of terminal or generic characters on the left hand side of productions. (For example, we allow $x \to aa$ and $a \to aa$ for $x \in G$, $a \in \Sigma$.) A derivation is complete when all probability functions are zero at the same instant.

The stochastic grammar is the same as the general method explained previously. The sets of applicability and weight rules are now subsumed by P.

Formal Specification of the Harmony Generator

The following stochastic grammar ς_H will determine the harmony or basic vertical structure of the rounds by outputting chord patterns. Let

$\varsigma_H = (\Sigma_H, G, V, R, S, I_H, P, M)$ where:

$\Sigma_H = (\mathbf{I}, \mathbf{II}, \mathbf{III}, \mathbf{IV}, \mathbf{V}, \mathbf{VI}, \underline{\mathbf{I}}, \underline{\mathbf{V}})$.

$G = \{x\}$

$V = \Sigma_H \cup \{S\}$.

$R = \{(1)S \to \mathbf{I}\,\mathbf{I}, (i)x\alpha \to f_i(x)x\alpha \text{ for } 2 \le i \le 8, \alpha \in V^+\}$.

S is the starting symbol.

$I_H = \{\langle \text{length} \rangle, (p_1, p_2, \ldots, p_8)\}$.

$F = \{f_i: \Sigma \to \Sigma \text{ for } 2 \le i \le 8 \text{ where}$

    $f_2: \sigma \to D^{-1}(\max\{1, (\max\{D(\sigma)\} - 6)\})$,

    $f_3: \sigma \to D^{-1}(\max\{1, (\max\{D(\sigma)\} - 4)\})$,

    $f_4: \sigma \to D^{-1}(\min\{10, (\max\{D(\sigma)\} + 2)\})$,

    $f_5: \sigma \to \sigma$,

    $f_6: \sigma \to D^{-1}(\max\{1, (\max\{D(\sigma)\} - 3)\})$,

    $f_7: \sigma \to D^{-1}(\min\{10, (\max\{D(\sigma)\} + 1)\})$,

    $f_8: \sigma \to \mathbf{I}$ for $\sigma \in \Sigma$ where D is the relation $(\mathbf{III}, 1), (\mathbf{VI}, 2), (\mathbf{VI}, 3)$,

    $(\mathbf{II}, 4), (\mathbf{II}, 5), (\underline{\mathbf{V}}, 6), (\mathbf{V}, 7), (\underline{\mathbf{I}}, 8), (\mathbf{I}, 9), (\mathbf{IV}, 10)\}$.

$P = \{(1)\, p_1 \times (\ln = 0)$,

    $(2)\, p_2 \times g \times n \times (0 < \max\{D(h)\} - 6 < 11)$,

    $(3)\, p_3 \times g \times n \times (0 < \max\{D(h)\} - 4 < 11)$,

    $(4)\, p_4 \times g \times n \times (0 < \max\{D(h)\} + 2 < 11)$,

(5) $p_5 \times g \times n$,

(6) $p_6 \times g \times n \times (0 < \max\{D(h)\} - 3 < 11)$,

(7) $p_7 \times g \times (\neg n) \times (\ln \equiv 1 (\mathrm{mod}\ 2)) \times (0 < \max\{D(h)\} + 1 < 11)$,

(8) $p_8 \times (0 \neq (g \times a + (\ln = \langle \mathrm{length} \rangle - 1)))$ where ln is defined to be the length of the partial derivation (the amount of derivation thus far completed), g is defined to be 1 if $0 < \ln < \langle \mathrm{length} \rangle - 1$; 0 otherwise, h is defined to be the left-most element of the partial derivation with **I** catenated on the right, n is defined to be 1 if $h \in \{\underline{\mathbf{I}}, \underline{\mathbf{V}}\}$; 0 otherwise, and a Boolean value of true is defined to be 1, of false, 0}.

After each calculation of the values of the above set, we must divide each by their sum (if not zero) so that they total 1.

M is defined by M: Production $(i) \rightarrow$ Probability function (i) for $1 \leq i \leq 8$.

Formal Specification of the Melody Generator

The stochastic grammar ς_M where output is the actual sequence of notes encoded is a little more complex than ς_H. The notes are labeled g, a, ..., f, g', a', ..., f', g'' beginning with the g below middle c up through the g two octaves above (see figure 11.6).

Each note will have the duration of an eighth note. In addition, an eighth note rest will be labeled r, and the letter n will stand for an extension of one eighth note to the duration of the previous note or rest. For example, c n n n r n represents a half note middle c followed by a quarter note rest.

For simplicity, we assume the notes (g through g'') are ordered as shown in figure 11.6 from left to right. The functions

R_j and $L_j : \Sigma_M - \{r, n\} \rightarrow V$ are defined by

$R_j : \sigma \rightarrow$ to the jth note to the right of σ if it exists, otherwise to g

$L_j : \sigma \rightarrow$ to the jth note to the left of σ if it exists, otherwise to g.

These functions facilitate the defining of the alphabet functions for ς_M. In the case where the jth note to the right or left, respectively, does not exist,

Figure 11.6

we do not care about the actual assignment as the probability function attached to this function will have a value of zero.

ς_M is defined to be

$\varsigma_H = (\Sigma_M, G, V, R, S, I_M, F, P, M)$ where:

$\Sigma_M = \{g, a, b, \ldots, f, g', a', \ldots, f', g'', r, n\}$.

$G = \{x\}$ where x is generic over $V - \Sigma_M \cup \{S\}$).

$V = \Sigma_M \cup \{S, [g], [a], [b], \ldots, [f], [g'], [a'], \ldots, [f'], [g'']\}$.

$R = \{(1)\ S \to [c], (2)\ S \to [c'], (3)\ \alpha x \to \alpha x nn, (i)\ \alpha x \beta \to \alpha x \beta f_i(U(x)), (26)$ $\alpha \to \alpha n (4 \le i \le 25;\ \alpha \in V^*,\ \beta \in \Sigma^*_M)\}$ where $U: V - (\Sigma_M \cup \{S\}) \to V$ by $U: [v] \to v$ (see F).

Productions 1–26 here correspond to M1–M26 given previously.
S is the starting symbol.

$I_M = \{\langle \text{length} \rangle,\ \langle \text{number of parts} \rangle,\ \langle \text{chord pattern} \rangle,\ \langle \text{spread} \rangle,$ $(p_1, p_2, \ldots, p_{26}),\ \langle \text{extra probabilities for weight rules} \rangle\}$.

$F = \{f_i : \Sigma_M - \{n, r\} \to V$ for $4 \le i \le 25$ by $f_4: \sigma \to n\smallfrown R_1(\sigma),\ f_5: \sigma \to$ $n\smallfrown L_1(\sigma),\ f_6: \sigma \to n\smallfrown R_2(\sigma),\ f_7: \sigma \to n\smallfrown L_2(\sigma),\ f_8: \sigma \to n\smallfrown R_3(\sigma),\ f_9: \sigma \to$ $n\smallfrown L_3(\sigma),\ f_{10}: \sigma \to n\smallfrown R_4(\sigma),\ f_{11}: \sigma \to n\smallfrown L_4(\sigma),\ f_{12}: \sigma \to n\smallfrown R_5(\sigma),\ f_{13}: \sigma \to$ $n\smallfrown L_5(\sigma),\ f_{14}: \sigma \to n\smallfrown R_1(\sigma),\ f_{15}: \sigma \to n\smallfrown [L_1(\sigma)],\ f_{16}: \sigma \to n\smallfrown [R_2(\sigma)],$ $f_{17}: \sigma \to n\smallfrown [L_2(\sigma)],\ f_{18}: \sigma \to n\smallfrown [R_7(\sigma)],\ f_{19}: \sigma \to n\smallfrown [L_7(\sigma)],\ f_{20}: \sigma \to$ $n\smallfrown [R_1(\sigma)]\smallfrown [R_2(\sigma)],\ f_{21}: \sigma \to [L_1(\sigma)]\smallfrown [L_2(\sigma)],\ f_{22}: \sigma \to R_1(\sigma)\smallfrown \sigma,\ f_{23}: \sigma \to$ $L_1(\sigma)\smallfrown \sigma,\ f_{24}: \sigma \to n\smallfrown r,\ f_{25}: \sigma \to n\smallfrown \sigma\}$,

where "$\smallfrown$" represents catenation. The square-bracketed characters indicate stepwise melodic progression.

Since P is rather extensive, it is not given explicitly here. In effect, P is just a mathematization of rules M27–M45 given earlier.

M is defined by M: Production $(i) \to$ Probability function $(i)\,(1 \le i \le 26)$.

To Obtain a Round

Now to obtain a round, we supply ς_H with the desired length divided by the number of parts, reset the initial weights if we wish, and initiate ς_H. This gives us a chord pattern. Then we supply ς_M with this chord pattern and the number of parts after resetting any weights that we want. ς_M will generate a sequence of encoded notes, to which we apply $U\ (U(m_1, \ldots, m_p) \equiv U(m_1) \ldots U(m_p))$ and then rectangularize. (U was defined in R of ς_M. By rectangularize, we mean reshape the vector of notes into its normal form. For a 3-part, 12 measure round, rectangularization would map measures 1–4 to the first staff, measures 5-8 to the second staff, and measures 9–12 to the third.)

Some Examples

The APL embodiment of the above process (running on an IBM 370/165) has so far generated over fifty short two- and five-part rounds. The concentration has been on three-part rounds as they are the most difficult for humans to compose. (However, 4/4 is the easiest meter for humans to compose in.) In figure 11.7 appear three of the more interesting of these. The pause ($\sim$) designates the note to be held when ending. For all, the maximum allowed spread was 11, the maximum number of octave jumps was 1, the cfg doubling weight (see M44) was 10, and the last-note-equals-c weight was 1000. The first round has weights of 1, 1, 1, 12, 4, 6, 8, and 6 for productions H1–H8, respectively. Its chord pattern is **I I V V I II V I V I I I**. The nondoubling weights for M1–M26 were 1, 1, 20000, 5000, 5000, 80, 80, 40, 40, 40, 40, 10, 10, 64000, 64000, 5000, 5000, 700, 700, 5000, 5000, 0, 0, 1, 5000, and 1, while the doubling weights were 1, 1, 200, 0, 0, 10, 10, 10, 10, 10, 10, 10, 10, 320, 320, 500, 500, 10, 10, 500, 500, 0, 0, 1, 100, and 1, respectively.

For the-second round, the weight for H5 was changed to 3, the nondoubled weights for M4, M5, M18, Ml9, M22, and M23 became 20000, 20000, 400, 400, 2500, and 2500, respectively, and the doubled weights for M6–M13, M16, M17, M20, and M21 became 40, 40, 20, 20, 3, 3, 1, 1, 50, 50, 50, and 50, respectively. Its chord pattern is **I I III VI II V I IV I I I**.

The third round is more experimental, utilizing a "key pattern," which is similar to a chord pattern but controls key modulations instead of harmony by defining a key for each vertical beat. The key pattern is CGGGGGGGGCCCC and the chord pattern **I II V V VI II V I II V I I**. Because the interfacing between the generators of these patterns has not been programmed, both patterns were human generated to insure some correspondence between them. All other relevent weights remained unchanged except that M22 and M23 were eliminated. Each round required something under 6 seconds of cpu time for generation. Output was pseudo-musical score to facilitate evaluation.

Figure 11.7

Evaluation

The best way to evaluate this music is to listen to it. Performances should be by instruments or voices of different tone qualities to allow a following of the melody line but all in the same range to prevent unwritten harmonic inversions.

Under the present rules, minor deviations from acceptable harmonic practice (such as simultaneous leaps in similar motion to the same note) are still possible, but it appears that these can be eliminated through the addition of appropriate applicability rules. The melody is a much more critical element, being generally musically acceptable but usually not very interesting. Standard melodic figures such as arpeggiation and rhythmic and melodic imitation are either impossible or very unlikely under the present rules for generating melodies.

On a higher plane, the use of probabilities in the form of weights to help decide the melodic and harmonic structures might be viewed with alarm. It might be better to use the term "guided probabilities," reflecting the use of applicability rules. Historically, both Hiller and Moorer used probabilities in their selection procedures. The musicologist Leonard B. Meyer (7, pp. 54–56) states that styles of music are in effect "complex systems of probability relationships" and gives convincing evidence in support of this. He also points out that these systems of probability relationships are explicitly acknowledged at a very general level in the names given to tones in the Western, Chinese, and Indian systems of music. (For example, in Western music the name "leading tone" reflects the fact that it usually leads up to the tonic.)

The tunings (weight settings) used are not necessarily the best. Perhaps better tunings would result in better music. It does appear that certain general styles of music may be obtained through widely different tunings. Also, the set of productions could be expanded.

Conclusion

In conclusion, the program "composes" at a mediocre level, though at a generally quite acceptable level for the man on the street. The harmony is often quite good while the melody is usually acceptable but dull. It appears that full-blown music theory is not needed for rounds—all the hardware required for structural levels is not necessary for these pieces.

Acknowledgment

The author wishes to thank Saul Gorn and Constance Vauclain for their continuing advice on the work described here.
This work was supported by the National Science Foundation under Grant GH-27 and by the US Army Research Office (Durham) under Dept. of the Army Project No. DA-31-124-ARO-D-98.

References

1. Bateson, Gregory. Style, grace, and information in primitive art. In *Steps to an Ecology of Mind*. Ballantine Books, New York 1972.

2. Brahms, J. *Kanons fur Frauenstimmen*. C. F. Peters, Leipzig, 1891.

3. Gorn, Saul. On the mechanical simulation of habit-forming and learning. *Information and Control 2* (Sept. 1959), 226–259.

4. Gorn, Saul. The computer and information sciences: a new basic discipline. *SIAM Rev. 5* (Apr. 1963), 150–155.

5. Gorn, Saul The identification of the computer and information sciences: their fundamental semiotic concepts and relationships. *Foundations of Language 4* (Nov. 1968), 339–372.

6. Hiller, L. A., and Isaacson, L. M. *Experimental Music-Composition with an Electronic Computer*. McGraw-Hill, New York, 1959.

7. Meyer, L. B. *Emotion and Meaning in Music*. Univ. of Chicago Press, Chicago, 1956.

8. Moorer J. A. Music and Computer Composition. *Comm. ACM 15*, 2 (Feb. 1972), 104–113.

9. Piston, W. *Harmony*. W. W. Norton, New York, 1941.

10. Rader, G. M. An algorithm for the automatic composition of simple forrns of music based on a variation of formal grammars. Moore School Rep. No. 73-09, Philadelphia, 1973.

11. Salomaa, A. Probabilistic and weighted grammars. *Information and Conrrol 15* (Dec. 1969), 529–544.

12. Taylor, M. C. (Ed.). *Rounds and Rounds*. Hargail Music Press, New York, 1959.

13. Taylor, M. C., Windham, M., and Simpson, C. (Eds.). *Catch That Catch Can*. E. C. Schirmer Music Co., Boston.

14. Vauclain, A. C. Music 25. Dept. of Music working paper, Univ. of Pennsylvania, Philadelphia, Pa., 1971.

Sundberg and Lindblom propose a formalization of melody. Melody in this theory exhibits "hierarchical constituent structure," projected by tranformational rules to prominence levels "identical for sentences and melodies."

The discussion draws parallels between "the level of prominence" of harmony and meter in Swedish nursery tunes. Using the theory of generative phonology (Noam Chomsky and Morris Halle, 1968) as an example, Sundberg and Lindblom suggest categorizing chords and meter by their relative stress values.

When harmonic and metric events share an equal "level of prominence," the model assigns them to each other. Chord notes from the harmony in its metric context directly produce melody.

The melodic component of the model, like the metric and harmonic components, applies rules to determine satisfactory output. Thus, the model's control flow to a satisfactory melody consists of three sequential components: metric, rhythmic, and melodic.

According to Sundberg and Lindblom, their rules produce nursery tunes typical of the style of the nineteenth-century composer Alice Tegnér. A further experiment to generate melodies with a completely randomized set of choices in the rule system also obtains satisfactory results.

12 Generative Theories in Language and Music Descriptions

Johan Sundberg and Bjorn Lindblom

Traditionally, music theory works with impressionistic, nonformalizing methods. In describing musical styles, musicologists generally content themselves with mentioning the more remarkable and apparent stylistic features, while other features taken as self-evident are considered as not worth mentioning and are disregarded. A similar attitude was adopted in linguistics some decades ago but has now been abandoned. Instead, generative methods are used, largely as a consequence of the work of N. Chomsky. The generative method may be illustrated as in figure 12.1. Observations are made and data are collected serving as the basis for the scientist's formulation of hypotheses. These hypotheses are integrated into a tentative rule system, or theory capable of generating data, or predictions. If the predictions agree with the observations, the rule system used for the predictions is a good description of reality, and knowledge is obtained. If not, the rule system contains errors that should be corrected. In this way, a generative rule system offers a unique possibility of testing hypothetical descriptions scientifically.

Generative methods in descriptions of musical styles have recently been advocated, particularly by linguists (cf. e.g., Winograd 1968, Ruwet 1972, Nattiez 1974). This chapter attempts to describe facts in musical theory by means of generative rule systems. Two rule systems will be presented, one for some Swedish nursery tunes, another for a set of different versions of an old Swedish folk song that are all felt to be melodically similar. The rule systems show striking similarities with the generative phonology of English as proposed by Chomsky and Halle (1968). The significance of these similarities will be discussed.

Formalization of Sentences

Let us start by recapitulating the major properties of generative grammar by considering the linguists' description of certain aspects of spoken sentences. Take the utterance

John beats his sister.

Copyright 1976, *Cognition*, and reproduced by permission.

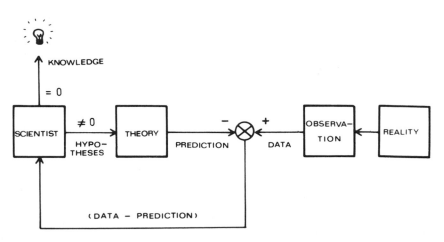

Figure 12.1
Block diagram illustrating procedure of scientific inquiry

In a traditional grammatical description of this sentence the following features might be mentioned. First, the whole string of words makes up a sentence (5). The words *beats his sister* form a verb phrase (VP) that consists of the verb (V) *beats* and the noun phrase (NP) *his sister*. The latter unit is made up by the pronoun (Proun) *his* and the noun (N) *sister*. *John* is an NP that consists of a noun. This information on the constituent structure of the sentence can be represented in the form of a tree diagram as shown in Figure 12.2.

The constituent structure of an utterance is reflected in the prosodic aspect of pronunciation, that is, intonation and stress pattern. A procedure for relating prosody and constituent structure has been proposed by Chomsky and Halle (1968). It can be diagramed as figure 12.3. Applied to the sentence *John beat his sister*, this procedure works as follows.

We can represent the distribution of stresses that might be observed in speech under normal, idealized conditions, as

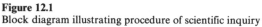

where the heaviest, main or primary stress = 1, secondary = 2, and tertiary = 3. Within the framework of Chomsky and Halle's theory of generative phonology, it has been suggested that a sequence of stresses such as

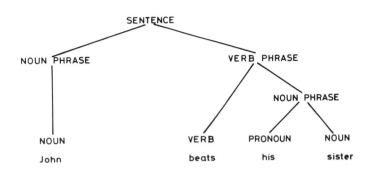

Formalization of sentences

Figure 12.2
Tree diagram of the constituent structure of the sentence "John beats his sister."

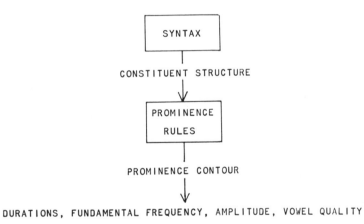

Figure 12.3
Block diagram of the Chomsky and Halle model of speech parody

```
JOHN        BEATS      HIS        SISTER
                                                     RULE:
((  1  )N ((  1   )V ((  1  )PRON(   1    )N)NP)VP)S   LEXICAL STRESS
                                                        PLACEMENT

((  1  )N ((  1   )V  (            1     )NP)VP)S

((  1  )N (   2                    1         )VP)S    RIGHT PRIORITY

(   2         3                    1            )S    RIGHT PRIORITY

OUTPUT:    2          3                 1
```

Figure 12.4
Schematical demonstration of the distribution of metric, harmonic, and tonal features
within a corpus of Swedish nursery tunes. Shaded areas indicate the position in which the
feature listed to the left has been observed to occur. Position is shown with reference to the
bars of the period (vertical dotted lines).

that proposed for *John beats his sister* be generated in the manner illustrated in figure 12.4. Here the constituent structure is represented in terms
of labeled brackets that is exactly equivalent to a tree diagram. In short,
the computation of the stress contour begins inside the innermost pair of
brackets. We start out by applying rules that assign stresses to the individual words. The deepest constituents are his and sister. The latter receives
stress on the first syllable. The former is a pronoun and does not receive
stress. Next we erase the innermost pair of parentheses and again look
for the deepest constituents. This time we find $(John)_N(beats)_V$ and (his
sister)$_{NP}$. At this level also *John* and *beats* are dealt with according to the
rule for word stress. Erase innermost parentheses once more and we get
the second line of the figure. The verb phrase, the VP, contains two main
stresses. Since it is a phrase, a right-priority rule (Nuclear Stress Rule) is
applied, that is, the rightmost stress remains and the other one is lowered
by one degree. After this operation brackets are erased and we now have
the sequence $(1\ 2\ 1)_S$. The right priority rule gives 2 3 1 and that is exactly
what we intended to get.

Two things should be observed here. One is that the prominence contour is derived automatically from the constituent structure by means of a
rule system. The second is that the prominence values determine a number
of important properties in the acoustic code. Next it will be demonstrated
that this seems to hold also in our melodies.

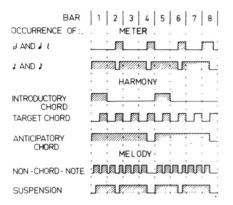

Figure 12.5
Schematical demonstration of the distribution of metric, harmonic, and tonal features within a corpus of Swedish nursery tunes. Shaded areas indicate the position in which the feature listed to the left has been observed to occur. Position is shown with reference to the bars of the period (vertical dotted lines).

Formalization of Melodies

Figure 12.5 shows an overview of the occurrence of various phenomena in meter, harmony, and tone assignment in a series of Swedish eight-bar nursery tunes, written by the composer Alice Tegnér. These melodies were composed in the late nineteenth century and they are familiar to and sung by most Swedish children even today. With respect to meter we observe that in even-numbered bars long durations occur and short notes are avoided. The chords are divided into three groups according to their harmonic functions: *Introductory chords*, which present the tonic; *target chords*, chords preceded by their dominants, and *anticipatory chords*, dominant chords followed by their own tonic. Introductory chords are found in bars I and V, and target chords may occur at the end of every bar. Anticipatory chords are not found at the end of bars IV and VIII. With melody we distinguish between chord notes and nonchord notes. The suspension is regarded as a special case of nonchord note. Suspensions seem to be avoided in approximately the same places where short durations are avoided. By and large nonchord notes occur in the same positions. These positions show a symmetrical and regular pattern. With each of these three kinds of data we see traces of a segmentation of the tune. Thus, bar VIII, particularly, but also bar IV, and bars II and VI, are treated in quite a special way. Periodicity occurs in all the diagrams. It is note-worthy that these regularities are associated with conceptions employed by musicologists for a long time: beats, subphrase, phrase, and period.

Model

Figure 12.6 shows an attempt to integrate the observations made into a generative model. At the deepest level we find the syntactic structure. Through a prominence contour this structure determines the choice of durations, chords, and pitches. We now describe in more detail the most important properties of the generative model.

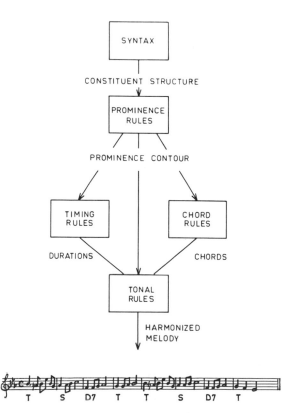

Figure 12.6
Block diagram of the generative model

A syntactic structure of the type shown in figure 12.7 can be ascribed to a typical eight-bar melody. The entire melody is a period consisting of two phrases. Each of them consists of two subphrases made up of bars, feet, and beats. The problem is to relate this constituent structure to durations, and to harmonic and tonal data. In order to do this we transform the syntactic information to a string of prominence values. This procedure is exactly the same as in the case of the linguistic example mentioned before. The procedure is illustrated step by step in figure 12.8. The top line shows the set of beats, each embedded in pairs cf parentheses. In erasing the parentheses, a left priority is applied up to the bar level and right priority at the higher levels. The final result is given in the lowest line of the figure. It gives the prominence of the beats along a scale of integers where numbers refer to rank of prominence. This prominence contour provides a method of relating the syntactic structure to the metric, harmonic, and tonal properties of the melody. It gives the raw material for the derivation of meter and harmony and for the assignment of pitches in a melody.

We should now explain in more detail the nature of the various components of the rule system. Let us do this by starting with the following question: Have we found that system of rules that automatically and completely enumerates Tegnér's nursery tunes? If we have, the rule system should be able to generate all of Tegnér's eight-bar melodies. How do we choose among the various alternatives, made available by the rules at every step of the generation, in such a way as to produce a melody that approximates as closely as possible a given Tegnér melody?

The first step is to generate the meter. An overview of the metric rules is given in the right column of figure 12.9. These rules are applied in the order shown in the figure. In the left part of the figure the derivation can be followed step by step. The top line shows the input to the rules constituted by the string of prominence values that has just been developed in figure 12.8. First, the sequence-pattern is determined. This shows which bars are to be metrically similar and which dissimilar. Two types of metrical pattern may occur, A and B, and the metrical pattern of the first four bars is obligatorily repeated in the last four bars. The next step offers three alternative choices: Delete prominence rank 5, (a) when it follows prominence rank 1, (b) when it follows prominence ranks 1 and 2, or (c) when it follows prominence ranks 1, 2, and 3. We call this deletion procedure *catalexis*, borrowing the term from the theory of verse. In the next step we may insert additional prominences of rank 6 after prominence ranks 4 and 5 in the

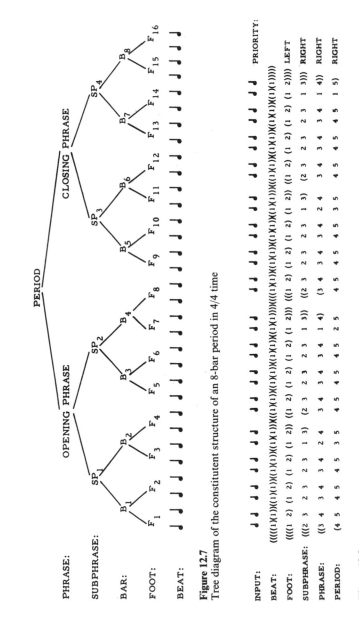

Figure 12.7
Tree diagram of the constituent structure of an 8-bar period in 4/4 time

Figure 12.8
Cyclic derivation of prominence values for the beats in the period shown in figure 12.7

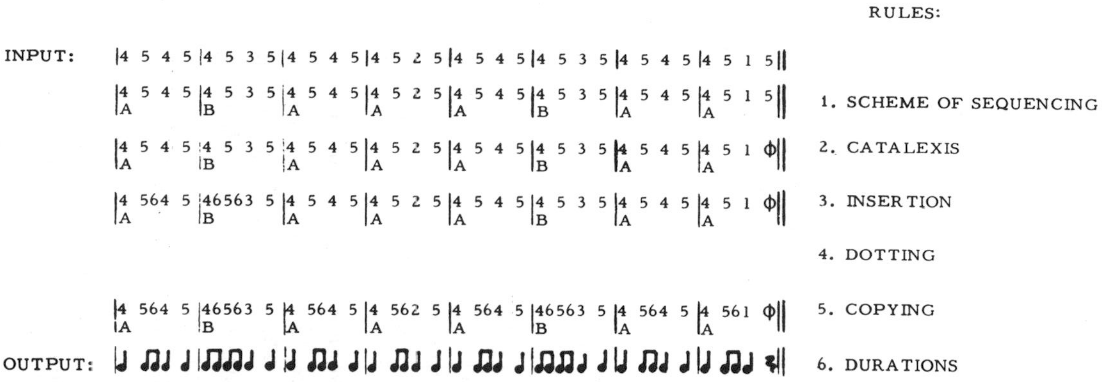
RULES:
INPUT:
|4 5 4 5 |4 5 3 5 |4 5 4 5 |4 5 2 5 |4 5 4 5 |4 5 3 5 |4 5 4 5 |4 5 1 5 ||
1. SCHEME OF SEQUENCING
2. CATALEXIS
3. INSERTION
4. DOTTING
5. COPYING
OUTPUT:
6. DURATIONS

Figure 12.9
Derivation of meter for an 8-hour period

HARMONIC TEMPO	1: DELETION OF 4'S	
	2: DELETION OF 5'S	

CADENCE STRUCTURE	3: INTRODUCTORY CHORDS	(OBLIGATORY RULE)
	4: TARGET CHORDS	(OBLIGATORY RULE)
	5: INTRODUCTORY CHORDS	(OPTIONAL RULE)
	6: EXTENDED INTRODUCTION	(OPTIONAL RULE)

ABSTRACT HARMONIC REPRESENTATION	7: HARMONIC FUNCTION	
	8: HARMONIC DISTANCE FROM THE TONIC	

REALIZATION	9: CHORD SYMBOLS

Figure 12.10
Overview of the harmonic rules

first bars marked A and B. Though not done in this case, it is possible to dot notes immediately followed by minima in the prominence contour. After this, the insertions and dottings are transferred to the other bars in accordance with the sequence-pattern. The final step is to transform the modified prominence contour into durations. Every prominence except that of rank 6, and those which have been dotted, is assigned a duration of one beat.

Figure 12.10 presents an overview of the rule system used for the chordal interpretations of prominence ranks. Here, too, the rules are applied in the order shown in the figure. Their function is to determine how often and in which way the chords change. The derivation is illustrated in figure 12.11. Once again the top line shows the input material, that is, the string of prominence values derived in figure 12.8. An obligatory rule deletes all items of prominence rank 5. After this, some items of prominence rank 4 may be deleted. Next, introductory chords, I:s, and target chords, M:s, are distributed. It would be possible to return to the introductory chord at the beginning of the closing phrase, but this has not been done in the melody considered. As a fundamental principle of the harmonic function of chords, we propose that anticipatory chords, DOM:s, must alternate with rest chords, V:s. Given the function of a chord, its harmonic distance from the tonic is determined by its relationship to the following target chord. These distances lie along a scale of integer numbers and in the figure they are given as indices.

	M1	M2	M3	M4	M5	M6	M7	
INPUT:	|4 5 4 5	|4 5 3 5	|4 4 4 5	|4 5 2 5	|4 5 4 5	|4 5 3 5	|4 5 4 5 1 5 ||	
	4 4	4 3	4 4 4	4 2	4 4	4 3	4 4 1	DELETION OF 5'S
	4	4 3	4	4 2	4	4 3	4 1	DELETION OF 4'S
	I	3	M	2	3		M	INTRODUCTORY AND TARGET CHORDS
								EXTENDED INTRODUCTION
	I	v	DOM	M	V	DOM	M	HARMONIC FUNCTION
	I	V_2	DOM_1	M_o	V_2	DOM_1	M_o	HARMONIC DISTANCE FROM THE TONIC
	T	V_2	DOM_1	T	V_2	DOM_1	T	CHORD SYMBOLS
	T	V_2	DOM_3	T	V_2	D7	T	CHORD SYMBOLS
	T	Sp	DOM_3	T	Sp	D7	T	CHORD SYMBOLS
	T |S	Sp	DOM_3 |S	T	Sp	D7	T	
OUTPUT:	T |S	Sp	T7 |S	T	Sp	D7	T	CHORD

Figure 12.11
Derivation of harmony for an 8-bar period

ORDER   CONTENTS OF RULES

1. PATTERN OF SEQUENCING

2. PROMINENCES $>$ 4   HARMONIC IMPLICATION

3. PROMINENCES $=$ 4   HARMONIC IMPLICATION
                                          TONAL ADJACENCY
                                               (SHORT-CUT PRINCIPLE)

4. PROMINENCES $<$ 4   SEQUENCING

Figure 12.12
Overview of the tonal rules

The abstract representation of the harmony obtained is then transformed, step by step, to chord symbols in a completely automatic way: When the harmony functions and distances from the tonic have been determined for a set of chords, the chords themselves can be chosen automatically.

The output of the metric and harmonic rules provides the material required for the generation of pitches. The rules applied to determine melody are those given in figure 12.12. First a sequence pattern is assigned, determining which bars are to be melodically similar. After this, pitches are assigned in an order corresponding to the order of the prominence ranks. The various lines in figure 12.13 show, step by step, the stages of the derivation. After the sequence-pattern has been determined, the pitches for prominence ranks 1, 2, and 3 are assigned in turn. The main rule allows nothing but chord notes in these cases. After this, pitches are assigned for prominence ranks of four. Here there are three guiding principles: (1) Harmonic implication (the pitch signals the underlying chord); (2) tonal adjacency or the "short-cut-principle" (when two pitches have been assigned, intermediate notes will receive intermediate pitches); and (3) the sequence-pattern. At this point it is possible to insert suspensions that represent a special case of the principles of harmonic implication and tonal adjacency. In the present example this possibility has not been used.

The next step is to choose chord notes for the introductory tones in every phrase, observing the principle of tonal adjacency. Using the same principles while taking the sequence-pattern into account, pitches are determined for the remaining notes of prominence rank 4, as illustrated in the next line of the figure. For example, the sequence-pattern dictates that the tonal relations between the tones in bar III be the same as those in bar I.

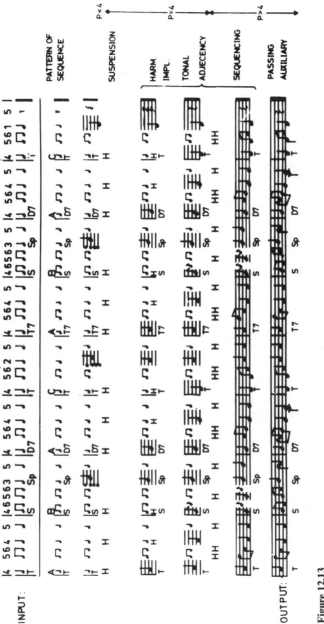

Figure 12.13
Derivation of the final melody. The derivation involves eight stages: Stage 1: determination of sequence pattern. Stage 2: assignment of chord notes to notes with higher rank of prominence than 4. Stage 4: harmonic implication (HI), tonal adjacency (TA), sequencing (S) to all sub-phase initial notes with prominence rank of 4. Stage 5: HI TA, and S applied to all remaining notes equal to 5 (only H:s chosen). Stage 7: HI TA, and S applied to the notes interpreted as H at stage 6. Stage 8: passing rule and auxiliary rule applied to the remaining notes which now all have prominence ranks lower than 5. In the cases where two notes are shown, the ones with upward lines were derived by rule, the other chosen by Tegnér.

The last step produces the realization of lesser prominence ranks—numbers greater than 4. For tones that have been assigned the role of chord notes, the rules already mentioned are applied. For nonchord notes the principle of tonal adjacency is applied. These notes are related by a scale-step to the following note. The derivation is now complete and the result is given in the bottom line in the figure.

The melody obtained differs in only a few details from "Dansa, min docka". These differences can all be accounted for by our rigorous use of the sequence-pattern. Evidently Tegnér's realization of the sequence-pattern is less rigid. We conclude that our rules can indeed generate a close approximation to one of Tegnér's melodies.

As a further test of the rule system we can generate melodies by making a completely randomized choice among the alternatives available at the various steps in our rule system. A set of melodies derived in this manner is shown in figure 12.14. The general reactions of Swedes listening to these melodies informally are that they are similar in style to those by Tegnér.

Versions of a Folk Song

Moberg (1950) has collected a large number of folk songs that he claims have a common origin. His assumption is based largely on melodical similarity and his material may in consequence be useful in an investigation of what actually makes two melodies sound melodically similar. The purpose of the study of Moberg's collection differs from that in the case of nursery tunes. What concerns us here is the fact that the melodies are felt to be similar. Here, then, we will not try to formulate a rule system describing the musical style represented by the folk song. Instead our rule system should generate only those melodies that are felt to be melodically similar to the versions given. Thus, it is not sufficient that they all belong to the same musical style.

Data

Figure 12.15 shows the versions of the folk song that will concern us here. They were selected from Moberg's material on the criterion of apparent melodical similarity. Versions with extra bars inserted, with major changes in the meter and so on were excluded. All the versions in figure 12.15 have the function of a lullaby.

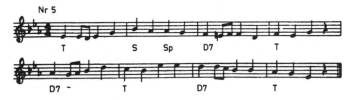

Figure 12.14
Examples of generated melodies

Figure 12.15
Eight versions of the Swedish folk song "Ro, Ro till Fiskeskär" selected from Moberg's
(1950) article on that song

An apparent common denominator of the songs is the preference for
half notes at the end of the even-numbered bars. Also, we know that all
melodies end on the fundamental of the tonic, and that all even-numbered
bars end on this note of the fifth of the dominant. A closer analysis of the
songs reveals some additional common features. Figure 12.16 gives an
overview Of them. Specific pitches, pitches belonging to a specific chord,
intervals between odd-numbered beats, and the direction of such intervals
are invariable in certain positions within the period. Also, we see that the
positions for these phenomena form a regular pattern in the period. Again,
then, the position within the period seems to be a factor of significance. In
view of our experience from the nursery tunes, it seems reasonable to
interpret this segmentation as an indication of a constituent structure.

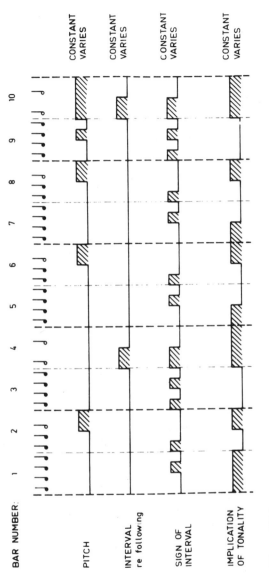

Figure 12.16
Occurrence of various phenomena in the versions of the folk song shown in figure 12.15

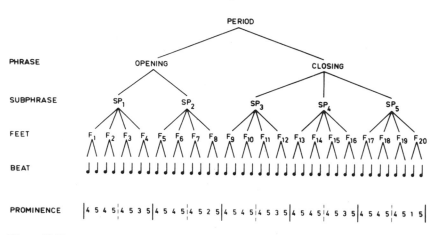

Figure 12.17
Tree diagram of the folk song. The bottom line shows the prominence values of the beats.

Rule System

In order to account for these and other observations, we again need a generative rule system. As there seem to be good reasons for assuming that a constituent structure exists that determines permissible modifications, a mapping of this structure and the generation of its prominence contour are required.

We propose that the melodies be regarded as an eight-bar structure in which bars 5 and 6 are repeated once. This agrees with the observation that, in fact, bars 7 and 8 generally repeat bars 5 and 6 metrically and melodically. The transformation needed is used so frequently in music that it has a sign of its own, $\|::\|$. The asymmetrical tree we obtain is shown in figure 12.17. The next step is to transform the tree diagram into a string of prominence values. For this, we use exactly the same procedure as in the case of the nursery tunes: labeled bracketing, erasing innermost pairs of brackets, and left and right priority up to and above the level of the bar, respectively. The output is shown in the same figure.

The rule system consists of two groups of rules, as seen in figure 12.18—one group for the tonality and the tone assignment and one for the meter.

Contrary to the nursery tunes, the harmony is rudimentary in this material. This is rather natural, since the song is normally performed without any accompaniment. However, certain rules are followed. The

TONALITY AND MELODY

$p = 1 \rightarrow$ 1 of T

$p = 2 \rightarrow \left\{ \begin{array}{l} \text{V of D} \\ \text{1 of T} \end{array} \right\}$

$p = 3 \rightarrow$ V of D

$p = 4$ A: /_ 5 q,

               $q = 1$ identical

               $q = 2$ I identical

               $q = 3 \left\{ \begin{array}{l} \text{ID identical} \\ \text{ID = 0} \end{array} \right\}$

      B: /_ 5 4 5 q,

               $q = 1$ identical

               $q = 2$ ID identical

               $q = 3 \left\{ \begin{array}{l} \text{ID identical} \\ \text{ID = 0} \end{array} \right\}$

      C: / q 5 _

               $q = \left\{ \begin{array}{l} 1 \\ 2 \end{array} \right\}$ chord note of T

               $q = 3 \left\{ \begin{array}{l} \text{identical} \\ \text{ID identical} \\ \text{identical but delayed by 1♩} \end{array} \right\}$

$p = 5$ Interval re. following is

                                   S, adjacency principle?

                                   S?

                                   0?

                                 3, adjacency principle?

                                 3?

                                 4, adjacency principle?

                                 4?

                                 5, adjacency principle?

                                 5.

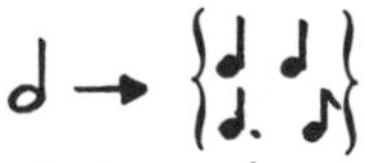

METER

$p = \left\{ \begin{array}{l} 3 \\ 4 \end{array} \right\}: \quad ♩ \rightarrow \left\{ \begin{array}{l} ♩\ ♩ \\ ♩.\ ♪ \end{array} \right\}$ second note = $\left\{ \begin{array}{l} \text{S re. following, adj. princ.} \\ \text{the first one} \end{array} \right\}$

$p = 4\ 5:$ ♫ $\rightarrow$ ♩

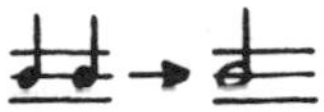

$p = \left\{ \begin{array}{l} 4 \\ 5 \end{array} \right\}: \left\{ \begin{array}{l} / 4\ \_\ q \\ /\ \_\ 5\ q \end{array} \right\}$ $q \geqslant 3$: $p \rightarrow p6$ if this gives a sequence of S ± one R

Figure 12.18
The rule system used for generating the versions of the folk song in figure 12.19. The notes constituting a chord are given by their step number (e.g., V denoting the fifth). T and D stand for the tones and dominant chords, respectively. I refers to the interval re. the nearest following note of equal or higher prominence, and ID refers to the direction of such intervals. S = step along the scale, R = repetition.

introduction of the opening and closing phrases and the beginning of the last subphrase give chord notes in the tonic. The end of each subphrase contains the fundamental rule of the tonic or the fifth of the dominant. The main function of these few rules seems to be to establish the tonality of the song.

The prominence values play an important role in the assignment of other pitches as well. The notes are treated in an order determined by the prominence rank. With the prominence rank of four, the distance to the following note of higher prominence is decisive to the order of tone assignment. The prominence rank of five is determined in relation to the following note of higher prominence. It may be observed that the rules for this prominence rank are ordered so that smaller intervals will occur more often than larger intervals.

When the tone assignment is completed, the meter may be modified. No modifications are tolerated in the bar containing prominence 1, and no insertion of prominence 6 is allowed in the bar containing prominence 2. Prominences 3 and 4 may be divided into two notes if it is a half note. If so, the extra note approaches the following by a scale tone step in accordance with the adjacency principle, or it simply repeats the preceding note. Inversely, a sequence of two identical pitches, the first of which has the prominence of 4, may melt together to a half note. Remaining notes of prominences 4 and 5 may be divided into two eighth notes, provided that this gives a sequence of scale tone steps with or without one repetition.

Another allowed alternative is that the extra note fills in a fifth interval. These restrictions as regards insertion of eighth notes are the main reason why the meter is modified after the melody in the case of the folk song. This seems logical in view of the fact that the melody is used for different texts.

As was pointed out before, our rule system does not represent more than a mere hypothetical description of the melodical similarity between the folk songs concerned. The test of the hypothesis is attained by generating versions and judging whether or not they are felt to be similar to the melodies studied. As in the case of the nursery tunes, the generation only involves random choice between the alternatives allowed by each rule. The generated melodies are shown in figure 12.19.

Regardless of whether or not we agree on the extent to which these melodies are melodically similar, we may conclude that the rule system defines the melodical similarity observed. It is interesting that this similarity is so heavily dependent upon the notion of prominence. As in the case

Figure 12.19
Examples of rule-generated versions of the folk song

of the nursery tunes the principle seems to be: The higher the prominence, the fewer alternatives are made available by the rules.

Conclusions

It has been demonstrated that the formalization of melodies and the formalization of sentences are in part strikingly similar. These similarities can be summarized as follows:

1. Melodies as well as sentences exhibit hierarchical constituent structure.

2. This constituent structure is projected onto a level of prominence by a set of tranformational rules that are identical for sentences and melodies.

It seems reasonable to hypothesize that in the case of both music and speech the function of these rules is to facilitate the generation and reception of the physical signal. In this chapter we shall not pursue our search for analogies between music and language any further. This is not to imply that such analogies are present only with respect to structure and logical organization. No doubt, parallels could be found all the way down to the physical signal.

The diagram in figure 12.20 sums up our presentation so far. As you may observe, it recapitulates features of figure 12.1. The research paradigm is

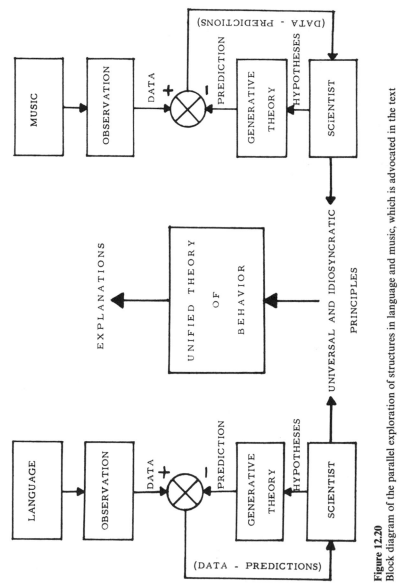

Figure 12.20
Block diagram of the parallel exploration of structures in language and music, which is advocated in the text

here applied to language on the left and music on the right. The data on music and the data on language are described in terms of two separate generative frameworks. In the construction of these theories certain principles are postulated. This parallel exploration of language and music can be expected to yield principles of varying generality. Some may be highly language specific, and others may be valid only for certain styles of music. On the other hand, some features are shared by all languages. Similarly there may be universal features that are characteristic of all styles of music. In the entire class of universals there may be some which are common to both language and music.

Examples of principles emerging from the present study are:

- Catalexis
- Harmonic implication
- Tonal adjacency
- Sequencing and other processes involving information reduction
- Marking of constituent structure.

These principles are tentative in nature. Further research is clearly needed to substantiate them or replace them by better alternatives. Nevertheless, we would claim that the hypothetic-deductive method advocated here should be substituted for traditional, impressionistic, and nonformalizing approaches.

In any case, it seems justifiable to suggest that the presence of hierarchical constituent structure is a phenomenon of considerable generality. It might be asserted that hierarchical constituent structure is a product of social and cultural conventions and largely independent of the human organism. There is, however, a large body of opinion and evidence that this interpretation is incorrect. For instance, hierarchical constituent structure appears to be a linguistic universal. The literature on music theory supports the contention that it is also widespread in various style of music. Recent psychological research by Restle (1970) on serial pattern learning shows convincingly that some structures or events are learned more easily than others by humans. A case in point is also Lashley's (1951) classical discussion of the integrative functions of the cerebral cortex where he puts forth the speculation that hierarchical syntactic arrangements are not limited to language. He mentions "the coordination of leg movements in insects, the song of birds, the control of trotting and pacing in a gaited horse, the rat running the maze, the architect designing a house, and the carpenter sawing a board." Furthermore, according to Restle, "it seems overwhelmingly obvious that long and complex serial patterns are divided into natural subparts, and that mastery is facilitated if the incoming sequence of events is somehow marked off into natural subparts." The present work may evidently serve as further support for this view.

References

Chomsky, N. and Halle, M. (1968) *Sound Pattern of English*, New York, Harper & Row.

Lashley, K. S. (1951) The Problem of Serial Order in Behavior. In L. A. Jeffres (Ed.) *Cerebral Mechanisms in Behavior*, New York, Wiley and Sons.

Moberg, C. A. (1950) Tva kapitel om svensk folkmusik, Svensk Tidskrift for Musikforskning (*Swed. J. Musicol.*), 32, pp. 5–49.

Nattiez, J. J. (1974) Semiologie Musicale, L'etat de la Question, *Acta Musicol.* 46, 2, pp. 153–171.

Restle, F. (1970) Theory of Serial Pattern Learning: Structural Trees, *Psychol. Rev.*, 77, 6, pp. 481–495.

Ruwet, N. (1972) *Language, Musique, Poesie*, Paris.

Winograd, T. (1968) Linguistics and Computer Analysis of Tonal Harmony, *J. Music Th.*, 12, 1, pp. 3–49.

Tegnér, Alice, *Sjung med oss Mamma*, vol. I–VII, Stockholm, A. B. Seelig & Co.

Fred Lerdahl and Ray Jackendoff review their generative theory of tonal music (GTTM). GTTM assigns with explicit rules hierarchical structure for grouping, meter, time-span reduction, and prolongational reduction.

The authors observe that their theory departs from previous music theories in two related ways. First, it has the psychological goal of determining why we hear particular structures beyond a "musical surface"; second, it attempts to generate a formal predictive description of the actually heard structures.

GTTM assumes four kinds of structural hierarchy in tonal composition: (1) a listener's segmentation of units, (2) a hierarchy of beats attributable to the music, (3) a hierarchy of importance for pitches in a rhythmic unit, (4) and a hierarchy of pitch stability.

Three types of rules characterize the four kinds of structural hierarchy: well-formedness rules (WFRs), transformational rules (TRs), and preference rules (PRs). WFRs determine conditions for all of the structural hierarchies; TRs "constrain" modifications for exceptional surface phenomena, for example, elision, to be classed as well-formed; PRs describe the actually heard structures for a given composition.

The authors acknowledge their indebtedness to the goals of generative linguistics. Although they realize that they focus on hierarchical rather than associational or implicative structure, they present the well-formedness condition of GTTM as a "foundation ... to approach the other, more open-ended dimension in a rule-governed way."

13 An Overview of Hierarchical Structure in Music

Fred Lerdahl and Ray Jackendoff

In our book, *A Generative Theory of Tonal Music* (GTTM), we propose a detailed theory of musical hierarchies.[1] In this chapter we (1) sketch our theoretical approach, (2) present some essentials of the theory through an analysis of a Bach chorale, and (3) discuss some general questions about musical hierarchies arising from the analysis.

Theoretical Perspective

GTTM develops a grammar of tonal music based in part on the goals, though not the content, of generative linguistics. The grammar is intended to model musical intuition. It takes the form of explicit rules that assign, or "generate," heard structures from musical surfacers. By "musical surface" we mean, broadly, the physical signal of a piece when it is played. By "heard structure" we mean all the structure a listener unconsciously infers when he listens to and understands a piece, above and beyond the data of the physical signal.

There are two related ways in which the theory differs from previous musical theories. First, it is psychological, in that it attempts to explicate a cognitive capacity. Listeners hear certain structures rather than others. How can these structures be characterized, and by what principles does the listener arrive at them? One would ultimately hope to specify these cognitive principles, or "universals," that underlie all musical listening, regardless of musical style or acculturation. Second, the theory attempts to produce formal descriptions in a scientific sense. That is, the goal is not just the description of formal relations, as happens in mathematics and in certain recent varieties of music theory. Rather, the descriptons pertain to something in the real world—even though, in this case, the reality is mental.

Thus the theory is predictive. In addition to criteria of internal coherence and parsimony, its principles can be verified or falsified by comparing the analyses it generates with one's intuitions about particular pieces of music. In addition, many of its principles can be investigated through laboratory experiment.

Copyright 1983, *Music Perception*, and reproduced by permission.

Implicit in this program of research are two simplifying idealizations familiar to cognitive science. First, we assume an "experienced listener." Obviously, no two listeners are exactly alike, nor are any two listenings by the same listener. But once the listener is familiar with a musical idiom, he is highly constrained in the ways he hears a piece in the idiom. A theory of musical understanding needs to characterize these common constraints as a foundation for the study of individual differences in hearing. Second, the theory provides structural descriptions only for the final state of a listener's understanding of a piece. In our judgment, a substantive theory of real-time listening processes cannot be constructed without first considering what information these processes must deliver.[2]

The theory is at present restricted in scope in two important ways. First, it focuses on classical tonal music. One cannot hope to address in any deep way the question of musical universals without first developing a precise theory of at least one complex musical idiom. (However, evidence toward the analysis of other tonal idioms appears at a number of points in GTTM.) Second, the present form of the grammar deals explicitly with only those aspects of heard structure that are hierarchical.

By hierarchy we mean an organization composed of discrete elements (or regions) related in such a way that one element may subsume or contain other elements. The elements cannot overlap; at any given hierarchical level the elements must be adjacent; and the relation of subsuming or containing can continue recursively from level to level.

Our theory proposes that four types of hierarchical structures are associated with a tonal piece. Grouping structure describes the listener's segmentation of the music into units of various sizes. Metrical structure describes the hierarchy of beats that he attributes to the music. Time-span reduction establishes the relative structural importance of pitch-events within the heard rhythmic units of a piece. Prolongational reduction develops a hierarchy of pitch stability in terms of perceived patterns of tension and relaxation. (This last component is the closest equivalent in our theory to Schenkerian reduction.)

Each of these structures is described formally by a separate component of the musical grammar, and within each component there are three rule types. Well-formedness rules (WFRs) provide the conditions for hierarchical structure for each component. Transformational rules (TRs) permit a constrained class of modifications on musical surfaces so that certain apparently ill-formed phenomena (such as grouping overlap and elision) can be treated as well formed. Preference rules (PRs) establish which formally possible structures correspond to the listener's actual hearing of a given piece. Thus WFRs and TRs describe formal conditions, and PPRs relate formal conditions to particular musical surfaces.

It is impossible within the space of this chapter to explain the actual rules. But a few words should be included here about the nature of the PRs, since they are an innovation as a rule-type within generative grammars. These rules, which do the major work of analysis within the theory, pick out features in musical passages that influence the listener's intuitions. In the grouping component, for example, one grouping PR marks a potential grouping boundary at a pause in the music; another detects thematic parallelism between two groups that are potentially far apart at the musical surface; a third encodes the effect of large-scale pitch structure on grouping decisions. As these instances suggest, some PRs are local in application, others are global, and some relate effects across the four components. Out of this process emerges the most "preferred," or most coherent, analysis or analyses for the piece in question. Generally, a musical passage in which the various rules are mutually reinforcing strikes the listener as clear or stereotypical. Where the rules conflict, on the other hand, the musical structure seems vague or ambiguous, and more than one overall structural description may be assigned.

Thus the grammar marks not the categorical correctness or incorrectness of an analysis but rather its relative viability. Although this characteristic may seem unusual by comparison with standard linguistic grammars, it is quite normal in theories of vision (see Koffka, 1935 and Marr, 1981, for example) and appears to be ubiquitous in cognitive systems (see GTTM, and Jackendoff, 1983).

An Analysis

We now turn to a rule-generated analysis of the Bach chorale, "Ich bin's, ich solte buessen" (from the *St. Matthew's Passion*). We have chosen this piece because it is short yet musically rich, and is easy to play at the piano; moreover, some readers may wish to make a comparison with Schenker's (1932) analysis. Our explanations will be brief; the reader is urged to follow the intuitive sense of the examples. For those interested in pursuing more closely the workings of the grammar, we will notate in parentheses those of GTTM that apply most critically.

Grouping Structure

When hearing a musical surface, listeners chunk it into motives, phrases, and sections. We represent groups by slurs placed beneath the music in an embedded fashion. Figure 13.1 gives the music of "Ich bin's ..." together with its grouping analysis.

As with most Bach chorales, the grouping of "Ich bin's ..." is simple and unambiguous. There are no salient levels beneath the phrase level. The phrase endings are marked by fermatas (GPR 2a and perhaps GPR 2b, depending on whether the fermatas are interpreted just as indicators for breathing or also as actual "holds") and by cadences (GPR 7 in conjunction with TSRPR 7). At larger levels the phrases are organized by a high degree of symmetry and parallelism (GPRs 5 and 6). In particular, the second half of the piece is melodically almost identical to the first half: phrases a and b are repeated in phrases d and e, and phrase f completes phrase c. These considerations group together a and b into g, and d and e into h; similarly, g and c group into i, and h and f into j. Finally, the whole piece is perceived as a group (group k) (GWFR 2).

Metrical Structure

Insofar as the signal permits, the listener infers from a musical surface a hierarchy of strong and weak beats. In the classical tonal idiom, beats are equidistant, and strong beats occur every two or three beats apart at any given metrical level. If a beat at a particular level is felt to be strong, it is also a beat at the next larger level; this is how metrical structure is hierarchical. The notated meter, which of course is not heard as such but is a visual cue for the performer, usually indicates an intermediate metrical level.

Because beats do not have duration but are points in time, we notate metrical structure by rows of dots, as in figure 13.2. Here beats 2, 3, 5, and 6 are weak and are beats only at the eighth-note level; beat 4 is stronger, and, along with beat 1, is also a beat at the dotted quarter-note level; beat 1 is the strongest, and is also a beat at the dotted half-note level.[3]

The metrical structure of "Ich bin's ...", shown in figure 13.3 for the first phrase only, derives in a straightforward fashion. The phrases are of equal length and exhibit considerable parallelism, so the derivation for the first phrase suffices for the whole piece (MPR 1). Here the attack patterns and the regular harmonic rhythm clearly establish the quarter-note level

Figure 13.1

Figure 13.2

Figure 13.3

(MPRs 3 and 5f). At the half-note level there is a momentary ambiguity due to the occurrence of the identical tonic sonority three and then four beats apart (MPR 9): it is initially unclear that the opening tonic is to be heard as an upbeat. But the prolongation of both the bass and the harmony in the second half of measure 1 (MPRs 5e and 6, MPR 5f), plus the long note in the melody and the suspension at the beginning of measure 2 (MPRs 5a and 8), all conspire to establish the half-note level as notated. The long melodic note and the suspension also support the given metrical structure at the whole-note level. This choice is reinforced by the general preference for strong beats relatively early in a phrase (MPR 2); the other possible choice for the whole-note level would lead to an anacrusis three quarters long, a less stable situation.

   To the analysis in figure 13.3, figure 13.4 adds the time-span segmentation, which describes the apprehended rhythmic units produced by the interaction of grouping and meter. Weak beats are bracketed with the previous strong beats as afterbeats, unless grouping boundaries intervene,

Figure 13.4

in which case they are bracketed as upbeats to the following strong beats. Besides capturing the distinction between upbeats and afterbeats, the time-span segmentation serves as input to the time-span reduction, as will be seen shortly.

Reductions

A reduction in music theory is a way to represent hierarchical relationships among pitches in a piece. Pitches perceived as relatively embellishing can be "reduced out" recursively, leaving at each stage a simplified residue of structurally more important material. At the end of this process only one event remains—the most stable structure, or tonic. The term *tonal* can be broadly defined as referring to music that is heard in such a hierarchical fashion.

In our theory we have tightened the notion of reduction by adding the following conditions: (1) pitch-events are heard in a strict (nonoverlapping) hierarchy; (2) structurally less important events are heard as elaborations of specific more important events, rather than simply as insertions or interpolations between more important events. Time-span reduction and prolongational reduction, while expressing different musical intuitions, both fulfill these conditions.

We notate reductions by means of trees. A right branch such as e2 in figure 13.5 signifies an event that is subordinate to a preceding event; a left

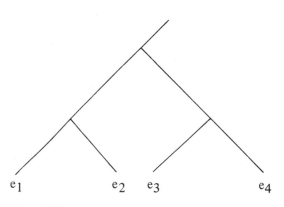

Figure 13.5

branch such as e3 signifies an event that is subordinate to a succeeding event. More specifically, e2 in figure 13.5 is subordinate to (or embellishes) e1, e3 is subordinate to e4, and e4 is subordinate to e1. Thus there is an underlying level in which e2 and e3 have been reduced out and in which e4 is adjacent to e1.

Unlike syntactic trees in linguistic theory, reductional trees do not express grammatical categories. Linguistic trees represent is-a relations: an adjective plus a noun is a noun phrase, a verb plus a noun-phrase is a verb-phrase, and so forth. A grammatical category combines with another to form a third grammatical category. Musical trees, by contrast, represent elaborational relations: e3 (figure 13.5) elaborates e4, e4 elaborates e1, and so forth. An elaborated event does not disappear or change from level to level, but proceeds intact up the tree until it too is an elaboration. The absence of grammatical categories in music marks a profound difference between music and language.[4]

Time-Span Reduction

Time-span reduction expresses the way in which pitch-events are heard in the context of hierarchically organized rhythmic units. As suggested by figure 13.4, these units, or time-spans, are determined by metrical structure at the most local levels, by a combination of meter and grouping at intermediate levels, and by grouping structure at large levels. Within each unit, events are compared in terms of mutual "stability," depending on such factors as the metrical position of the events, their intervallic configurations, voice-leading properties, and so forth. Starting at the most local levels, the most stable event in a unit is selected as the head; other events in the unit are elaborations of the head and are reduced out. Each head then goes on to the next larger time-span for comparison against another head from another time-span, and so on, until a single event is heard for the whole piece.

Figure 13.6 illustrates the first phrase of the chorale. Since the tree notation is unfamiliar, we include in the example a more traditional reductional notation beneath the music. The correspondence between the two notations is indicated by the labeling of the time-spans by level, of the nodes in the tree, and of the levels in the musical notation. For instance, level b in the musical notation consists of the heads of the time-spans labeled b. In the tree, this level consists of the branches that pass through or terminate at the node labeled b, leaving out all the branches that terminate lower. The choices for head in this passage are determined chiefly by relative local consonance (TSRPR 2), supplemented by metrical position (TSRPR 1).

To proceed further with the reduction, we must introduce the notions of structural beginning and structural ending (or cadence), which articulate grouping structure at the phrase level and all larger levels. The essential motion of a phrase takes place between these two structural points. A structural beginning is a relatively stable event appearing early in the phrase. A cadence is harmonic/melodic formula of one or two members at the end of the phrase. The structural importance of a particular structural beginning or cadence to the piece as a whole depends on its position in the larger grouping structure: if it abuts a boundary of a large-scale group, it serves as a structural beginning or cadence for that group (TSRPRs 7 and 8). Figure 13.7a shows schematically the hierarchical function of each structural beginning (marked b in the diagram) and cadence (marked c in the diagram) in the grouping structure of "Ich bin's...." Figure 13.7b translates figure 13.7a into the tree notation. Figure 13.7c adds the reduction of the two-membered final cadence as a whole.

Figure 13.8 completes figure 13.6 and figure 13.7 by giving the time-span reduction for the entire chorale. Levels a–e in figure 13.8 correspond to figure 13.7c; that is, these levels show the global hierarchical relationships among structural beginnings and cadences. Starting with level f, the branches represent local elaborations within the individual phrases. A good way to penetrate the analysis is to play at the piano the actual piece and then its successive reductional levels as represented in the musical

Figure 13.6

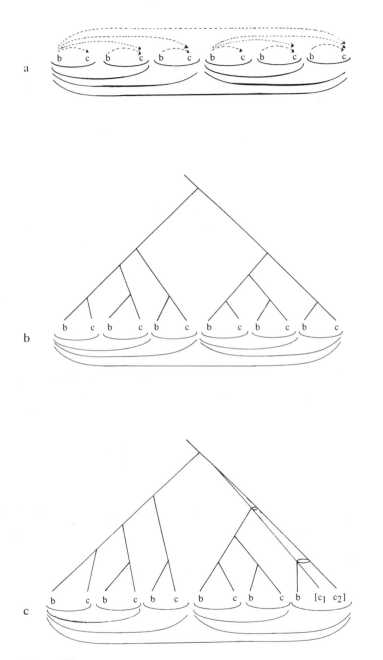

Figure 13.7

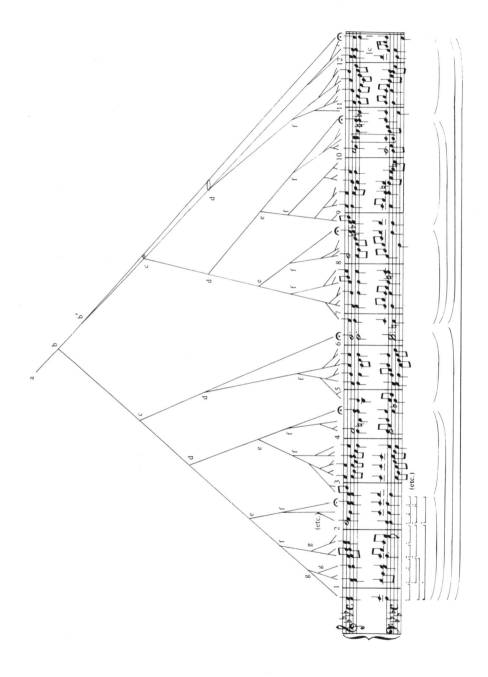

Figure 138

Figure 13.8 (continued)

notation. Each level should sound like a natural simplification of the previous level.

The naturalness of the reduction in figure 13.8 is strained in the fourth and fifth phrases (measures 7–10), due to a structural ambiguity that requires comment. The melody in these measures repeats that of the first two phrases, and implies the tonic region. But the harmonization establishes the relative minor region, while at the same time ingeniously passing through the tonic in the course of each phrase (measure 7 and measure 9). Are these phrases, then, in the relative minor, or are they in the tonic with deviant cadences? As with Wittgenstein's (1953) rabbit-duck figure, a single response is insufficient. The musical grammar mirrors this situation through conflicting rule applications: it is a question of local harmonic stability (TSRPR 2b) versus larger parallelism (TSRPR 4) In the tree we have opted for the relative-minor interpretation but have indicated the alternative in brackets in the relevant levels of the musical notation.

Prolongational Reduction

One of the most important kinds of intuition a listener has is how the motion among the pitch events of a piece tenses or relaxes. The prolongational component is intended to express such intuition explicitly and in detail. Briefly, if two events are heard as connecting prolongationally (at the musical surface or at an underlying level), and if the second event is heard as less stable than the first, the overall progression is felt as tensing. If the second event is more stable than the first, the progression is felt as relaxing. Further, the degree of tension or relaxation between two events is determined by the degree of continuity between them. In a succession of two identical events, there is little sense of tension or relaxation. If an event is followed by itself in another form (say, by a chordal inversion), there is some sense of tension or relaxation (one or the other, depending on the relative stability of the two events). If an event is followed by a completely different event, there is a stronger sense of tension or relaxation.

In the prolongational tree, we represent a tensing pattern by right branching and a relaxing pattern by left branching. Figure 13.9a–c gives right-branching patterns, 13.9d–f left-branching patterns. The various nodes in the trees indicate contrasting degrees of continuity, hence of tension and relaxation. An open circle, as in figure 13.9a and 13.9d, describes an attachment where an event is replicated (say, I–I); this is called strong prolongation. A filled-in circle, as in figure 13.9b and 13.9e, describes

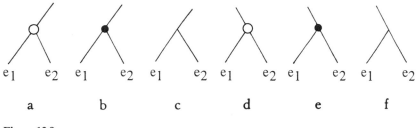

Figure 13.9

an attachment where an event progresses to another form of itself (say, I–I6 or I–I); this is called weak prolongation. A node without any circle, as in figure 13.9c and 13.9f, describes an attachment where an event progresses to a completely different event (say, I–V or ii6–V); this is called progression.

Figure 13.10 illustrates these branchings through a prolongational analysis of the first phrase of "Ich bin's. . . ." As an aid, we again supply a secondary notation beneath the music; the slurs stand for branching connections, with the dashed slurs reserved for strong prolongations. The tree twice shows a tensing-relaxing pattern—from the opening sonority to its prolongation on the third beat of the first measure, and similarly from there to the end of the phrase.

We have found that a particular pattern of tensing and relaxing is needed if the listener is to experience closure there must be at least one right-branching progression (9c) in the course of a group, followed by two left-branching progressions (9f) at the end of a group (two because the first left branch must be "prepared"). We call such a pattern normative prolongational structure (PRPR 6).

In figure 13.11, for instance, the third phrase of the chorale (11a) is incomplete not just because it lacks a final tonic but because the final event is not preceded by a sequence of two events that relax into it. By contrast, the last phrases of the chorale (11b) fulfills the branching requirement for closure.[5]

Normative prolongational structure is a shaping force at the phrase level and at all larger levels of tonal architecture. The cumulative result of such multileveled structures in a piece is to produce a complex tree that is at the same time filled with internal structural repetitions. The existence of such an organization appears to bear on why tonal music is rich yet learnable.

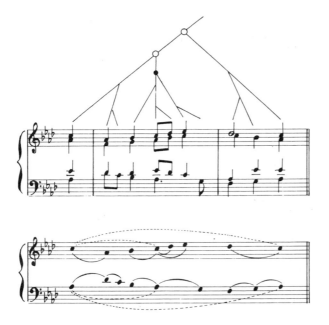

Figure 13.10

Unlike time-span trees, prolongational trees are constructed from global to local levels (i.e., from the top downward). This is necessary because the prolongational importance of an event—its role in patterns of tension and relaxation—is determined by its larger context. Further, an event's importance cannot be evaluated solely from its pitch content; rhythmic information is also needed. In our theory, the requisite contextual and rhythmic information is not a matter of the analyst's artistic intuition, as in Schenkerian analysis, but is derived formally from the time-span tree for the piece, which in turn encodes all the rhythmic information concerning grouping and meter (PRPR 1). Thus, directly or indirectly, all four components are implicated in the description of patterns of tension and relaxation.

Besides the derivation from the time-span tree, the other critical factor in building a prolongational tree is the stability of connection between two events (PRPR 3). In a tensing pattern, the least increase in tension is the most stable connection; hence a right strong prolongation (9a) is highly favored. In a relaxing pattern, the greatest increase in relaxation is the most stable connection; hence a left progression (9f) is highly favored.

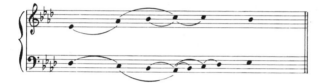

Figure 13.11

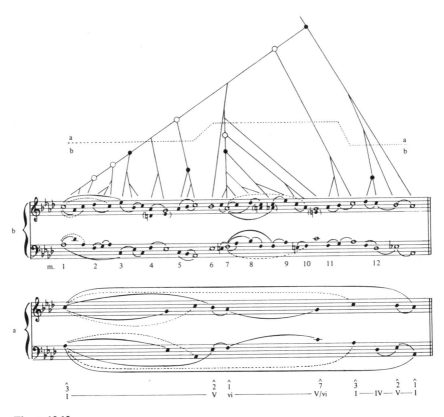

Figure 13.12

Skipping the step-by-step derivation, we offer a full prolongational reduction of the chorale in figure 13.12.[6] For simplicity, the analysis proceeds
only to a certain degree of detail. The musical notation of the reduction
appears in two stages: graph a presents those connections made above the
dashed line in the tree, graph b those made below the dashed line. As
suggested by the roman numeral and scale-step designations at the bottom of the example, graph a displays the overall linear/harmonic motion
of the piece. Note how the relative minor section (measures 7–10) tenses
off the dominant arrival in measure 6, and how all of this is enclosed within
the prolongation from measure 1 to measure 11, after which closure takes
place. Graph b reveals more local patterns of tension and relaxation.

The reader should bear in mind that the reduction in figure 13.12 is not
the only "preferred" prolongational analysis. Various details are open to

interpretation; and if the ambiguity in the time-span reduction discussed in connection with figure 13.8 were resolved otherwise, a different (though perhaps less interesting) overall prolongational tree would result.

Discussion

We alluded to the resemblance between our prolongational reduction and aspects of Schenkerian analysis. Though this resemblance is genuine, we should begin this section by pointing out various broad differences between Schenker's theory and ours. These remarks will lead gradually into brief discussions of the nonoverlapping condition on hierarchies and of the nonhierarchical dimensions of musical structure.

Some differences between the two theories are less a matter of conviction than of focus. For example, we have not developed a very interesting notion of voice-leading, a central concept in Schenker. The reason for this is that voice-leading as such is not hierarchical. On the other hand, our theory deals more centrally with rhythm and its relation to pitch than does Schenker's. Again, this is because grouping, meter, and time-span segmentation are hierarchical.

A more important contrast is that Schenker's theory, though sophisticated as an analytic system, lacks any counterpart to our musical grammar (i.e., the rule system that generates structural descriptions). It is our grammar that assigns structure, regardless of what we as analysts would personally like to say about a piece. In other words, our role is not to develop analyses but to create a system that develops analyses. This approach entails (temporarily, we hope) analyses that are limited in scope and sometimes in subtlety. But it also entails the intellectually deeper gain of putting analytic principles on a formal and generalized basis.

A still more essential difference lies in the fact that Schenker's theory is aesthetic and ours is psychological. His purpose is to illuminate musical masterpieces; ours is to find principles of musical cognition. All of our rules are motivated from simple, prosaic musical examples, of the sort a psychlogist of music perception might use in an experiment. If our theory has anything to say about masterpieces, it is because listeners make sense of Beethoven by the same cognitive principles they use in understanding trivial examples. If some of these principles relate to Schenker, it is presumably because Schenker himself was at least implicitly concerned with musical cognition.

Schenker (1935) posits the basis of his theory, the Ursatz, as an a priori aesthetic law. Whatever the value of Narmour's (1977) criticisms of this aspect of Schenker, they do not apply to our theory, which is neither a priori nor axiomatic, but empirical. For example, the Ursatz-like structures at the highest branching levels of figure 13.8 and figure 13.12 do not result from any presumed status of these structures. Rather, they arise directly out of applications of these rules, which together predict maximally stable structure. If the piece analyzed were tonally less stable, Ursatz-like structures would not appear. From our vantage, Schenker's Ursatz simply embodies many of the stability-making features of the tonal idiom.

In a similar vein, Schenker often makes transformations on a musical surface to make it conform to his aesthetic laws. (Here we mean transformation in the technical sense of some operation on a sequence that changes its order or content. A hierarchical description is not a transformation.) Though we too use transformations to explicate certain musical phenomena, their role in our theory is much more restricted. An excessive use of them leads away from the data, the musical surface, and into a priori abstractions.[7]

A technical difference between the two theories concerns our strict definition of pitch hierarchy: branches must be left or right, and they cannot overlap or intersect. Though Schenker often makes one event subordinate to another, there are numerous cases where he does not. And overlapping hierarchical interpretations for different voice-leading lines are common in Schenker's looser version of reduction. Let us consider these points in turn.

It is clear that a suspension is subordinate to its resolution (as a left branch); but what about a passing or neighboring tone? One can easily imagine a hierarchical description in which some events branch and others are simply subordinate "insertions." We have avoided this alternative because we have been able to assign structural interpretations to right and left branching that have a psychological dimension. In time-span reduction, the branchings show a position of pitch importance within grouping and meter. In prolongational reduction, they reveal patterns of tension and relaxation (even a neighboring tone tenses or relaxes as a result of rhythmic factors). Thus the case for the branching condition seems to us strong.

The nonoverlapping condition raises a number of issues. Inherent in our tree notation is the conception of a musical surface as a sequence of discrete events. This view is only partly accurate: music is also perceived as simultaneous polyphonic lines. To describe polyphony, the grammar would have to generate multiple (but related) groupings and trees, with one structural description for each line. Each such description would nevertheless continue to observe the nonoverlapping condition. We reserve for future research an extension of the theory in this dimension.

Meanwhile there are three areas in which our current theory accomodates apparent overlapping or intersecting structures. The first involves certain transformational rules. For example, one transformational rule analyzes grouping overlaps and elisions, permitting double branching for overlapped events; another treats functioning events that are literally missing from the musical surface (an instance appears in measure 10 of figure 13.8); yet another allows the fusion of arpeggiated figures and accounts for "auditory stream segregation" in music (Bregman and Campbell, 1971). In these cases the nonoverlapping condition is weakened only in a restricted manner and only for certain well-defined phenomena.

The second area where overlapping or intersecting apparently occurs is in moments of structural ambiguity for which one might seek multiple branching interpretations. As suggested for figure 13.8, however, the correct solution is not to assign crossing branches—that would tell us nothing —but to generate competing preferred structures, each of which is well formed. The competing rule applications and descriptions thereby explicate the sense of the ambiguity.

The third area has to do with the existence of four hierarchical components in a structural description. Theorists with only one hierarchical dimension at their disposal might feel compelled to cross branches (or the equivalent) in an attempt to capture their analytic intuitions. The problem lies with their impoverished theoretical model. Once grouping and meter are conceptually disentangled and the two kinds of reductions are both seen as necessary, it becomes possible to represent a variety of musical intuitions clearly and without overlapping hierarchies. Each component remains well formed but enters into a structural counterpoint with the others. Some flavor of this can be obtained by comparing the time-span and prolongational reductions of "Ich bin's ..." (figure 13.8 and figure 13.12). If superimposed, their respective branchings would cross profusely, showing how the music both articulates (time-span reduction) and progresses (prolongational reduction).[8]

Despite these remarks, let us imagine for a moment a structure characterized by the complete absence of the nonoverlapping condition, whose only constraint is noncontradiction in domination and subordination, and in which the only criterion for relationship among its elements is some kind of quasi-elaborational connection. For illustration, consider the first, third, and last phrases of the chorale. One might observe certain similarities here, such as the close melodic connections among the three phrases, the presence of a I on the third beat of the first measure in each phrase, and the parallel harmonic progressions at the ends of the first and last phrases (especially the IVs on the downbeats of their respective second measures). Similarly, the second and fifth phrases would connect, creating a structure with crossing branches. Is such a structure possible?

The chorale can also illustrate implicative structure. The melodic Bb at the end of the third phrase implies a "realization" on Ab, which arrives at the end of the sixth phrase. The inverted IV7–V–I progression at the end of the first phrase perhaps implies its realization in root position at the end of the piece; the effect of this relationship, in any case, is powerful.

Other details aside, it is apparent that associations and implications are strongly influenced by hierarchical function. For example, the final Bb in the third phrase resolves to the final Ab in the last phrase, not to any of the intervening Abs, because of their respective importance and function in the time-span reduction. This suggests that an implicative theory must take as its input not just the musical surface but the associated time-span reduction. Copnversely, our rules for parallelism in all four components demand greater specificity from an adequate associational theory.

In developing our theory of musical cognition, we have found it methodologically fruitful to concentrate on hierarchical structures at the expense of associational and implicative structures. The well-formedness conditions impose the kind of constraints in theory-building that enable progress to be made. With this relatively firm foundation, it may be possible to approach the other, more open-ended dimension in a rule-governed way.

Notes

1. Lerdahl and Jackendoff (1983). Also see Lerdahl and Jackendoff (1977, 1981), Jackendoff and Lerdahl (1981, 1982).

2. This idealization corresponds to one sense of Chomsky's (1965) notion of "competence." It is also parallel to Marr's (1981) pursuit of a "computational" level of description in the theory of vision. Marr shows how nearly every previous theory of visual processing has failed because of inadequate attention to this aspect of the problem. Along with Chomsky and Marr, we do not disparage theories of real-time processing; they are an essential part of a complete psychological theory. But, methodologically, it appears crucial to characterize

mental structures before asking how they are computed over time (see Jackendoff, 1983, for more extended remarks).

3. This notation is preferable to the traditional prosodic notation (− v), which obscures the relationship between strength of beat and hierarchical level. In Cooper and Meyer (1960), matters are further complicated by the intermingling of prosodic notation with Ihe properties of grouping structure (see GTTM for further discussion).

4. The elaborational nature of pitch hierarchies and the absence of grammatical categories in music are confirmed by more than 400 years of music theory. For support of this view from a psychological standpoint, see Deutsch and Feroe (1981). On the other hand, see Keiler (1977) for a music-theoretical approach based on quasi-linguistic trees.

5. In the figure, the dotted lines at the top indicate these branches at more global levels of the tree than is shown in the analysis (compare figure 13.12). An exclusively phrasal prolongational analysis would show all branches within a phrase as attaching locally, with no branches connecting above the phrase level. We will not pursue this possibility here.

6. The derivation for the most part follows applications of PRPRs 1 and 3, supplemented by principles not mentioned here. Readers familiar wilh GTTM will appreciate that the strong prolongational connection of the opening tonic to the I in measure 11 comes about through the Interaction Principles, since in the associated time-spall tree this I is one level below the current level of derivation. This is an excellent illustration of the Interaction Principle, supplementing those in GTTM.

7. There are many examples of transformations in Schenker's (1932) analysis of "Ich bin's...." One of them deserves special comment: he turns the IV7 on the downbeat of measure 12 into a IV–I64 progression at a background level. Assuming a transformation is required here, we would opt for a ii65, both on stylistic grounds (Bach hardly ever employs a cadential 64 in his chorales, whereas ii65–V–I is entirely typical-not that such matters would bother Schenker), and for systematic reasons (less transformation is needed, especially rhythmically, to arrive at the ii65 from the surface).

8. Incidentally, multiple tree descriptions are also necessary in linguistic theory. Recent research has shown that sentences are assigned both a syntactic tree and a phonological tree (see Liberman and Prince, 1977; and GTTM).

References

Bregman, A. A., and Campbell, J. Primary auditory stream segregation and perception of order in rapid sequences of tone. *Journal of Experimental Psychology*, 1971, 89, 244–249.

Chomsky, N. *Aspects of Theory of Syntax*. Cambridge, Mass.: The MIT Press, 1965.

Cooper, G., and Meyer, L. B. *The Rhythmic Structure of Music*. University of Chicago Press, 1960.

Deutsch, D., Feroe, J. The internal represenation of pitch sequences in tonal music. *Psychological Review*, 1981, 88, 503–522.

Jackendoff, R. *Semantics and Cognition*. Cambridge, Mass.: MIT Press, 1983.

Jackendoff, R., and Lerdahl, F. Generative music theory and its relation to psychology. *Journal of Music Theory*, 1981, 25, 45–90.

Jackendoff, R., and Lerdahl, F. A grammatical parallel between music and language. In M. Clynes (ed.), *Music, Mind, and Brain*. New York: Plenum Press, 1982.

Keiler, A. The syntax of prolongation I. *In Theory Only*, 1977, 3.5, 3–27.

Koffka, K. *Principles of Gestalt Psychology*. New York: Harcourt, Brace & World, 1935.

Lerdahl, F., and Jackendoff, R. Toward a formal theory of tonal music. *Journal of Music Theory*, 1977, 21, 111–171.

Lerdahl, F., and Jackendoff, R. On the theory of grouping and meter. *The Musical Quarterly*, 1981, 67, 479–506.

Lerdahl, F., and Jackendoff, R. *A Generative Theory of Tonal Music*. Cambridge, Mass.: MIT Press, 1983.

Liberman, M., and Prince, A. On stress and linguistic rhythm. *Linguistic Inquiry*, 1977, 8, 249–336.

Marr, D. *Vision*. San Francisco: W. H. Freeman & Co., 1981.

Meyer, L. B. *Explaining Music*. Berkeley: University of California Press, 1973.

Narmour, E. *Beyond Schenkerism*, University of Chicago Press, 1973.

Schenker, H. Fuenf Urlinie-Tafeln. New York: Dover Publications, Inc., 1969. (Originally published, Vienna: Universal Edition, 1932.)

Schenker, H. [*Der freie Satz*] (E. Oster, ed. and trans.) New York: Longman, Inc., 1979. (Originally published, Vienna: Universal Edition, 1935.)

Wittgenstein, L. *Philosophical investigations*. Oxford: Blackwell, 1953.

V AI AND MUSIC: ALTERNATIVE THEORIES

Meehan discusses the relevance for music of models for natural language processing. In particular, he addresses some of the similarities between Eugene Narmour's implication-realization theory and conceptual dependency. He describes the respective origins of both theories in Schenkerian analysis and transformational grammar.

Transformational grammar, Meehan argues, has an analogue and precedent in the theories of Heinrich Schenker. Surface details reduce via transformations in Schenkerian analysis to a smaller set of incrementally and structurally more important notes. This process continues until it reaches a "deep structure" equivalent, Schenker's Ursatz (original statement).

Whereas such transformational possibilities can demonstrate an underlying structure for musical grammaticality, Meehan observes that grammaticality is not necessary for natural language understanding. We regularly understand ungrammatical sentences in natural language.

Of the post-Schenkerian theories, two—those of Fred Lerdahl and of Eugene Narmour—share importance for Meehan. In particular, Narmour's theories, including that of "expectation," develop concepts also used by conceptual dependency to address the limits of transformational grammar.

Rather than Narmour's recursive application of rules to successively higher levels of structure, however, Meehan suggests that an "interlingua," like the semantic primitives of conceptual dependency, be developed in detail to describe a theory of meaning both for the parsing and the generation of music.

14 An Artificial Intelligence Approach to Tonal Music Theory

James Meehan

Although computers are commonly used in the composition and performance of contemporary music, there is very little computer research on models of music theory, for either analysis or composition of music. This seems surprising since tonal theory is in the standard music curriculum and shares many aspects of natural language, a favorite target from the earliest days of computer science, and since computer programs in artificial intelligence (AI) are now commonly used as process models, particularly in areas rich in symbol manipulation. There are programs that use little or no standard theory to compose nursery tunes (Pinkerton 1956), rounds (Rader 1974), and even cowboy songs (Quastler 1955). The early literature shows a strong influence of information theory and theories of composition based on Markov chains, weighted probabilities of state transitions, generate-and-test models, and so on. Few authors of such systems made claims of generality or extensibility, and indeed, no such system has caught on. There are very few analysis programs, good, bad, or otherwise, the principal exception being a 1968 paper by Terry Winograd.

If there are such strong parallels between music and natural language, what's missing?

In a review of books on computers and music, Barry Vercoe of MIT said: "We seem to be without a sufficiently well-defined 'theory' of music that could provide that logically consistent set of relationships between the elements which is necessary in order to program, and thus to specify, a meaningful substitute for our own cognitive processes" (1971). On that same point, Andy Moorer wrote in 1972: "... any attempts to simulate the compositional abilities of humans will probably not succeed until in fact the musical models and plans that humans use are described and modeled."

Schenker

The currently dominant theory of music is that of Heinrich Schenker (1868–1935), who defined a transformational system for music analysis long before Noam Chomsky did the same for linguistics (Chomsky 1957). Very briefly, the transformations reduce groups of notes on one level to

Copyright 1980, *Computer Music Journal*, and reproduced by permission.

single notes on the next higher level, in a fashion not unlike common parsing techniques for context-free grammars. The higher level notes are said to be "prolonged" by the lower level notes; a C at one level, for instance, might be prolonged by stepwise motion (C–D–E–F–G). These reduction rules theoretically apply at all levels. Finally, we are left with a two-voice structure known as the Ursatz, for which there are three possibilities: the melodic part (Urlinie) may descend a third (scale degrees 3–1), a fifth (5–1), or an octave (8–1). The Ursatz itself is a prolongation of the triad. Melodic (horizontal) motion is thus viewed as a temporal expansion of harmonic (vertical) structure. Of the many structural levels, three are distinguished: the foreground, which is the surface representation; the middleground; and the background, which is the Ursatz.

The Schenker theory has greatly enhanced our understanding of musical structure by relating the harmonic and melodic aspects of music. But as widely as the theory is accepted and taught, it remains incomplete, imprecise, and a constant subject of debate by music theorists. Two major works have appeared recently that discuss the Schenker theory from a "modern" point of view. The first is a paper by Fred Lerdahl and Ray Jackendoff (1977) [see chapter 13, this volume], who have attempted to formalize music theory, improving on Schenker, from within the paradigm of generative transformational grammar. The second is a book by Eugene Narmour, *Beyond Schenkerism* (1977), in which the author discusses numerous weak points in the Schenker theory in particular and transformational grammar in general. He also proposes a new way to look at music. Neither of the two new approaches is yet complete; both sets of authors promise upcoming books in which all the details will be worked out. Yet the two "revisions" of Schenker are utterly antithetical, a tribute, if nothing else, to Schenker's influence.

The Linguistic Approach

In transformational grammar, we seek a correspondence between deep structure and surface structure of sentences, and the issue of grammaticality is paramount. Similarly, in Schenker analysis, we seek a correspondence between the background and the foreground, already knowing what transformations are possible. If we're interested in the phenomenon of understanding, then from the fact that people often make perfect sense of sentences that are ungrammatical, we can conclude that grammar isn't very important. Likewise, not even musicians are troubled by having failed to detect the Ursatz when they hear a Beethoven symphony.

Parallels drawn between music and language often center around the issue of syntax, and linguistics seems to be a natural choice for a discipline in which both music and language might be studied. Computer science has formalized the notion of syntax, and the problem of syntax-driven translation of programming languages is now a technological skill taught to undergraduates. The problems of natural (human) language, however, are not solvable by such syntactic methods, and the split between the "computational linguists" and the traditional linguists has widened. In computer science, the area called natural language processing (NLP) shares very little with the philosophy and methodology of linguistics.

Natural Language Processing (NLP)

Narmour's theory, called the *implication-realization model*, is of special interest to AI researchers because it bears a strong resemblance to recent models of natural language processing, particularly the work of Riesbeck and Schank (1976) and Schank and Abelson (1977). In their view, the key to processing language is to look beyond syntax and to represent meaning via semantic primitives, relying on the notion that, at the literal level at least, we can get most people to agree on the meaning of simple sentences such as "John gave Mary a book" and "John gave Mary a kiss"; while the syntax of those sentences is identical, the meanings are not even close. Roger Schank developed a set of "primitive acts" to describe everyday, physical actions. The theory, conceptual dependency, has been used in various computer programs that understand newspaper stories, make inferences, translate, paraphrase, summarize, answer questions, and write stories. Neither the text-analysis programs nor the text-generation programs rely on grammars of English syntax.

Higher-Level Semantic Structures

Years of work with computer systems modeling these semantic primitives led Schank and Abelson to organize structures above the level of individual actions, particularly those that deal with aspects of human problem solving. Routine sequences of actions, such as what one normally does in a restaurant, are described as scripts. Above scripts (in the problem-solving hierarchy) are plans, which involve more choices and decisions. In theory, some scripts "evolve" from plans by learning from repeated experience. While most people understand the principle of shelving books in a library, for example, and could figure out what to do if confronted with such a task, their initial behavior would likely differ from that of skilled library workers. Plans are driven by goals, which can be permanent (e.g., staying healthy), temporary (mowing the lawn), cyclic (eating food), and so on.

Finally, themes account for behavior associated with roles (firefighter), interpersonal relationships (spouse), and lifestyle (jet set). Understanding language, in this view, requires an understanding of people; it has much to do with cognitive psychology and very little to do with grammar.

Expectation-Based Parsing

The programs that parse English into these knowledge structures are based on expectations of meaning. For example, suppose we've seen "Mary took John" as the beginning of the sentence. The conceptual dependency representation of that, so far, would be (PTRANS (ACTOR MARY) (OBJECT JOHN)) where PTRANS is the primitive act for physical motion and ACTOR and OBJECT are conceptual case names. We can now make several kinds of predictions, each expressed in the form "if X then Y." Since we've just been parsing a noun phrase ("John"), there's a pending expectation for the word and: if the next word is and, then predict another noun phrase and extend the OBJECT-filler. Another prediction is that if we see a noun phrase that has the property of being a physical object ("Mary took John the book"), then make the current OBJECTG-filler the TO-filler and make the referent of the noun phrase the OBJECT-filler: (PTRANS (ACTOR MARY) (TO JOHN) (OBJECT BOOK)).

The predictions for prepositions and adverbs are very diverse, and many of them depend on the higher-level semantic structures (contexts) described by the scripts, plans, and goals. For example, if the context is wrestling, then we can make a special prediction for the word down (a specific wrestling maneuver), entirely different from the more neutral (default) prediction about accompaniment ("Mary took John down to the harbor"). Likewise, one can establish predictions to handle the following phrases: "to task, "to Los Angeles," "to the cleaners," "to mean that...," "into her house," "into the firm," "up on his offer," "up the hill," "on," and so on.

While these contexts are useful in parsing different sentences, they also make predictions about the different interpretations of identical sentences. Compare the effects of the reply "John has a cold" to the two questions "Where's John?" and "Which of you tenors has suddenly turned tone-deaf?" Music theory texts often make the same point about pitches, chords, and sequences of chords: interpretation depends on context.

Although these expectations deal primarily with the parameter of meaning, as opposed to focus or, for that matter, rhythm (e.g., dactyls in "Mary took John to the home of the president"), there is no reason in principle why the technique could not be applied to other parameters as well. AI has yet to tackle such other parameters in language in as well-organized a fashion, defining higher-level structures and coordinating the expectations from different parameters.

Narmour's Theory of Music

Is it possible, then, to define an expectation-based procedure for analyzing music? Narmour seems to think so. (There is a difference in terminology between Narmour and the AI researchers. To Narmour, the term *expectation* means prediction with absolute certainty, which is not the AI sense. As I understand it, his implications are possible consequences, and realizations are actual consequences.)

In an example discussed at length in his book, Narmour describes the following implications after the first three chords of Schumann's *Soldier's March* (figure 14.1). The next soprano note may be an E (B–C–D–E). If so, the next bass note may be a C (parallel 10ths). The soprano may eventually reach a rhythmically accented high G (B–D–G triad). The next chord may be more stable than the current I6 (I → IV), and so on. The

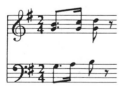

Figure 14.1

musical "semantic primitives" are what Narmour calls style forms, "those parametric entities in the piece which achieve enough closure [local explanation] to enable us to understand their intrinsic functional coherence without reference to the functionally specific, intraopus context from which they come" (Narmour 1977, p. 164). They are patterns that "make sense" by themselves, and they are associated with the parameters of music: melody, harmony, rhythm, meter. When we say that a certain piece is more interesting harmonically than rhythmically, for example, what we mean is that the rhythmic patterns are simple, whereas the harmonic patterns are not. Bach four-part chorales, for example, exhibit less variety in rhythm than in harmony.

Recursive Rules and High-Level Representation

A major point of disagreement that I have with both the Narmour system and the Lerdahl-Jackendoff system is something on which they surprisingly agree. They each describe analysis as a process that uses rules recursively, implying that music analysis starts from notes and applies rules to transform these into other notes, which are further transformed by the same rules, and on and on. The idea has a certain mathematical appeal to it, but it is unlike the situation in NLP, where sentences are not "reduced" to other sentences but are represented in terms of an interlingua, corresponding to no particular human language. Inferences, for example, are not keyed by specific English sentences but rather by the representation of meaning. Otherwise, all synonymous sentences would have to be listed explicitly, which is not simply inefficient but also psychologically dubious.

Only if the language for high-level musical structures is the same as for the "foreground" will it be possible to use the same rules ("recursively" in Narmour's usage) for further analysis, although there is no particular evidence, much less a guarantee, that this should be so. It is precisely this characteristic that Schenker uses to reach the Ursatz. It predisposes us to reduce the number of structures we transform into, although, as Narmour has corrected me, it does not require that the analysis terminate in any specific top-level set such as Schenker's three Ursaetze.

To me, the lower levels of Schenker analysis are the most convincing, the explanations of the local connections between melody and harmony. By the same token, some of the Lerdahl-Jackendoff theory seems usable, particularly their preference rules. It is much more useful to know the principles of metrical grouping, for example, than to see a transformation that enforces conformity with the data structure of trees, which seems an exercise in notational convenience, at best.

Differences

Since even the simplest music has aspects of melody and harmony, it is more complex than the natural language that can be currently processed by machine. There are good AI models of what we might describe as environments rich in problem-solving behavior. That is, NLP efforts have concentrated first (and necessarily so) on meaning, and they work well on ordinary prose such as newspaper stories. What will they do with literature, either prose or poetry? They cannot yet recognize literature because there's no representation of those domains that define literature as something beyond simple prose. That's not a criticism of the Schank-Abelson work; they never set out to process art. For that matter, nor has anyone else in AI. Of course, just as there are programs that compose nursery tunes, there are programs that produce poetry, too, but they're on equally weak foundations. It's hard enough to model the literal-meaning domains and, logically, that must precede the modeling of other parameters or knowledge domains. The richness of the real world, even in simple texts, makes that problem very hard indeed.

Simple tonal music, in contrast, would seem to have more domains but less complexity within each domain. Musical scripts abound (e.g., cadences). The few, common meters provide "solutions" that make rhythmic expectations very simple. (Of course, just as in language, one aspect of what it means to be interesting is to avoid the easy solutions, which explains why so much of the popular music of the 1950s, with endless repetitions of I–vi–IV–V7, is mind-numbing.) Integration of domains is a more obvious problem in music than in language, but I believe that the similarities exist. Narmour, among others, points out the differences between music and the linguists' view of language, and I certainly agree with him. It is not at such a low level as syntax that the two are similar, and I find Smoliar's comparison of the language of computer programs and the language of music inappropriate (Smoliar 1971).

Another difference in theories of music and language is the synchronic/diachronic contrast. In any system it is tempting to seek a set of factors that, with one set of values, describes one historical point or style, and with another set of values, a different point, and so on. You can then invent a theory about the nature of the changes from one set to the next, and you claim you have a diachronic model, an epistemological philosopher's stone. Narmour hopes to do the same with compositional styles: what distinguishes Beethoven's *Fifth* from the *Sixth*? In natural language processing, this is viewed as part of the language of learning. It's hard enough, right now, to model how people use knowledge structures, for instance; modeling how they acquire them is a higher-level problem, requiring a synthesis of all the experience gained from building many individual models. In other words, it's too soon to expect any significant answers about The Big Problem, the "universals" of music. One seriously doubts Lerdahl and Jackendoff's claim: "Preliminary investigation has indicated that the theory can be modified to produce structural descriptions of pieces as diverse as Macedonian folk music, North Indian music, and 14th-century French music, by changing various specifics of rhythmic and pitch structure" (Lerdahl and Jackendoff 1977, p. 166).

Composition

A language parser is not also a language generator, even though the two may share a theory of meaning. Current generators start with a representation of the meaning of what it is to be said, as provided by a paraphrase program, an inference mechanism, an event simulator, or a question-answerer, for example. That is, they don't start from scratch. In fact, they make the need for higher-level structures (e.g., problem solvers) even more apparent.

There are musical composition tasks that provide some direction, such as the harmonization of a given melody. As any music student knows, musical knowledge is as easily tested by composition as by analysis, and the same holds true; certainly, in NLP.

Conclusion

Where does an AI person start, then? With a music theory textbook, perhaps, but reading it with the task in mind of representing the information there in a computer program. To what end? A theory of music should certainly explain aspects of the undeniably tonal popular music with which we are bombarded daily. But my own preference is to concentrate on harmony and melody—it is difficult to model even the simplest tonal music without them—and, to a lesser extent, rhythm, with an initial goal of writing chorales. This is the type of experiment in choosing semantic primitives, forms of representation, and control structure for which there is ample precedent in AI. What music theory lacks is not the concept of expectations or semantic primitives, but rather the organized and detailed specification of such concepts, which would lead to higher-level information structures and reasonable process models for analysis and composition. If our analogy with research in natural language processing is valid, such a knowledge-based system will provide better results than previous attempts.

Acknowledgments

This paper is a revision of Information and Computer Science Technical Report 124. I would like to thank Eugene Narmour, Otto Laske, Stephen Smoliar, the ACM reviewers, and the many correspondents who made valuable suggestions for improving it.

References

Chomsky, Noam. 1957. *Syntactic Structures*. The Hague: Mouton.

Laske, Otto E. 1977. "Understanding the behavior of Users of Interactive Computer Music Systems." Revised version. Mimeographed. Urbana, Illinois: School of Music, University of Illinois.

Lerdahl, Fred, and Jackendoff, Ray. 1977. "Toward a Formal Theory of Music." *Journal of Music Theory* 21(1): 111–172.

Moorer, James Anderson. 1972. "Music and Computer Composition." *Communications of the ACM* 15(2): 104.

Narmour, Eugene. 1977. *Beyond Schenkerism*. Chicago: University of Chicago Press.

Pinkerton, R. C. 1956. "Information Theory and Melody." *Scientific American* 194(2): 77.

Quastler, H. 1955. Discussion following "Mathematics Theory of Word Formation" by W. Fucks. In *Information Theory—Third London Symposium*, ed. E. C. Cherry. New York: Academic Press, p. 168. Cited in Cohen, Joel E. 1962. "Information Theory and Music." *Behavioral Science* 7:63.

Rader, Gary M. 1974. "A Method for Composing Simple Traditional Music by Computer." *Communications of the ACM* 17(11): 631–642.

Riesbeck, Christopher K., and Schank, Roger C. 1976. "Comprehension by Computer: Expectation-Based Analysis of Sentences in Context." Research Report 78, Yale Computer Science Department.

Schank, Roger C., and Abelson, Robert P. 1977. *Scripts, Plans, Goals and Understanding*. Hillsdale, New Jersey: Erlbaum.

Smoliar, Stephen W. 1971. "A Parallel Processing Model of Musical Structures." Ph.D. dissertation, M.I.T.

Truax, Barry. 1976. "A Communicational Approach to Computer Sound Programs." *Journal of Music Theory* 20(2):227–300.

Vercoe, Barry. 1971. "Harry B. Lincoln, *The Computer and Music*, and Barry S. Brook, *Musicology and the Computer*." *Perspectives of New Music* 9(1)–10(2):323–330.

Winograd, Terry. 1968. "Linguistics and the Computer Analysis of Tonal Harmony." *Journal of Music Theory* 12(1):2–49.

"Music, Mind, and Meaning" asks the question, "Why do we like music?" Minsky posits that music's large role in everyday life makes it an important subject for the study of mind. Although we are accustomed to thinking that emotion in music and art can not be understood, Minsky observes that what we now know of humor and children from Freud and Piaget once "seemed too humorous ... and too childish" to be taken seriously by science. He emphasizes the need to understand the "process" of music, the general mental and "psychological details of its creation and absorption," more than the "surface" music, to do more than study music in isolation "the way scientists analyze the spectrum of a distant star."

Minsky gives the example of a sonata exposition to describe how music impresses our minds. With the teaching devices of repetition and the dramatic emphasis of themes, a sonata teaches the mind its "basic stuff." Minsky comments that the variations of basic thematic material give us an understanding of the musical material commensurate with the understanding we get of something when we have more than one perspective of it and can "turn it around in our minds," can "think" about it. He argues that the creation, required for musical understanding and evidenced by thematic variation, of at least two meanings for musical "stuff" generates a network, "a web ... whose meanings and significances depend on one another."

To explain the hierarchies of mental network interrelationships, Minsky applies his concept of an "agent." Each agent has a specific role in a "society of agents" in this theory; each agent has interactions with a subset of the other agents of the society. Of central importance to the society are the "managing agents" that assign parts of a problem to other agents. Interagent messages need not be in "surface music languages" but can communicate in codes that influence particular agents to respond to surface languages.

Minsky asks, "How do both music and vision build things in our minds?" How does music create a sense of a greater entity than the few notes we can hear at any given time? An agent may do nothing more than notice that there is a particular rhythm. Minsky calls such agents *measure-takers*. Other agents perceive small musical patterns (*structure-builders*) or detect differences (*difference-finders*), for example, that a pattern remains the same except for being a fifth higher. "Music, Mind, and Meaning" suggests that higher order agents serve to recognize larger sections of music and that visual parallels exist for such higher order agents when, for instance, we recognize a table from only one angle at a given point in time.

Minsky does not insist upon but rather hints at the validity of his approach. "Societies of agents" have a physical counterpart in the nerve networks of the brain, and music does seem to be "composed" of multiple hierarchies of interrelated phenomena.

15 Music, Mind, and Meaning

Marvin Minsky

Why Do We Like Music?

Why do we like music? Our culture immerses us in it for hours each day, and everyone knows how it touches our emotions, but few think of how music touches other kinds of thought. It is astonishing how little curiosity we have about so pervasive an "environmental" influence. What might we discover if we were to study musical thinking?

Have we the tools for such work? Years ago, when science still feared meaning, the new field of research called *artificial intelligence* (AI) started to supply new ideas about "representation of knowledge" that I'll use here. Are such ideas too alien for anything so subjective and irrational, aesthetic, and emotional as music? Not at all. I think the problems are the same and those distinctions wrongly drawn: only the surface of reason is rational. I don't mean that understanding emotion is easy, only that understanding reason is probably harder. Our culture has a universal myth in which we see emotion as more complex and obscure than intellect. Indeed, emotion might be "deeper" in some sense of prior evolution, but this need not make it harder to understand; in fact, I think today we actually know much more about emotion than reason.

Certainly we know a bit about the obvious processes of reason—the ways we organize and represent ideas we get. But whence come those ideas that so conveniently fill these envelopes of order? A poverty of language shows how little this concerns us: we "get" ideas; they "come" to us; we are "reminded of" them. I think this shows that ideas come from processes obscured from us and with which our surface thoughts are almost uninvolved. Instead, we are entranced with our emotions, which are so easily observed in others and ourselves. Perhaps the myth persists because emotions (by their nature) draw attention, while the processes of reason (much more intricate and delicate) must be private and work best alone.

The old distinctions among emotion, reason, and aesthetics are like the earth, air, and fire of an ancient alchemy. We will need much better concepts than these for a working psychic chemistry.

Much of what we now know of the mind emerged in this century from other subjects once considered just as personal and inaccessible but which

Copyright 1981, Marvin Minsky, and reproduced by permission.

were explored, for example, by Freud in his work on adults' dreams and jokes, and by Piaget in his work on children's thought and play. Why did such work have to wait for modern times? Before that, children seemed too childish and humor much too humorous for science to take them seriously.

Why do we like music? We all are reluctant, with regard to music and art, to examine our sources of pleasure or strength. In part we fear success itself—we fear that understanding might spoil enjoyment. Rightly so: art often loses power when its psychological roots are exposed. No matter; when this happens we will go on, as always, to seek more robust illusions!

I feel that music theory has gotten stuck by trying too long to find universals. Of course, we would like to study Mozart's music the way scientists analyze the spectrum of a distant star. Indeed, we find some almost universal practices in every musical era. But we must view these with suspicion, for they might show no more than what composers then felt should be universal. If so, the search for truth in art becomes a travesty in which each era's practice only parodies its predecessor's prejudice. (Imagine formulating "laws" for television screenplays, taking them for a natural phenomenon uninfluenced by custom or constraint of commerce.)

The trouble with the search for universal laws of thought is that both memory and thinking interact and grow together. We do not just learn about things, we learn *ways to think* about things; then we learn to think about thinking itself. Before long, our ways of thinking become so complicated that we cannot expect to understand their details in terms of their surface operation, but we might understand the principles that guide their growth. In much of this article I will speculate about how listening to music engages the previously acquired personal knowledge of the listener.

It has become taboo for music theorists to ask why we like what we like: our seekers have forgotten what they are searching for. To be sure, we can't account for tastes, in general, because people have various preferences. But that means only that we have to find the causes of this diversity of tastes, and this in turn means we must see that music theory is not only about music, but about how people process it. To understand any art, we must look below its surface into the psychological details of its creation and absorption.

If explaining minds seems harder than explaining songs, we should remember that sometimes enlarging problems makes them simpler! The theory of the roots of equations seemed hard for centuries within its little world of real numbers, but it suddenly seemed simple once Gauss exposed the larger world of (so-called) complex numbers. Similarly, music should make more sense once seen through listeners' minds.

Sonata as Teaching Machine

Music makes things in our minds, but afterward most of them fade away. What remains? In one old story about Mozart, the wonder child hears a lengthy contrapuntal mass and then writes down the entire score. (I do not believe such tales, for history documents so few of them that they seem to be mere legend, though by that argument Mozart also would seem to be legend.) Most people do not even remember the themes of an evening's concert. Yet, when the tunes are played again, they are recognized. Something must remain in the mind to cause this, and perhaps what we learn is not the music itself but a way of hearing it.

Compare a sonata to a teacher. The teacher gets the pupils' attention, either dramatically or by the quiet trick of speaking softly. Next, the teacher presents the elements carefully, not introducing too many new ideas or developing them too far, for until the basics are learned, the pupils cannot build on them. So, at first, the teacher repeats a lot. Sonatas, too, explain first one idea, then another, and then recapitulate it all. (Music has many forms, and there are many ways to teach. I do not say that composers consciously intend to teach at all, yet they are masters at inventing forms for exposition, including those that swarm with more ideas and work our minds much harder.)

Thus *expositions* show the basic stuff—the atoms of impending chemistries and how some simple compounds can be made from those atoms. Then, in *developments*, those now-familiar compounds, made from bits and threads of beat and tone, can clash or merge, contrast or join together. We find things that do not fit into familiar frameworks hard to understand—such things seem meaningless. I prefer to turn that around: a thing has meaning only after we have learned some ways to represent and process what it means, or to understand its parts and how they are put together.

What is the difference between merely knowing (or remembering, or memorizing) and understanding? We all agree that to understand something we must know what it means, and that is about as far as we ever get. I think I know why that happens. A thing or idea seems meaningful only when we have several different ways to represent it—different perspectives and different associations. Then we can turn it around in our minds, so to speak: however it seems at the moment, we can see it another way and we never come to a full stop. In other words, we can *think* about it. If there were only one way to represent this thing or idea, we would not call this representation thinking.

So something has a "meaning" only when it has a few; if we understood something just one way, we would not understand it at all. That is why the seekers of the "real" meanings never find them. This holds true especially for words like *understand*. That is why sonatas start simply, as do the best of talks and texts. The basics are repeated several times before anything larger or more complex is presented. No one remembers word for word all that is said in a lecture or all notes that are played in a piece.

Yet if we have understood the lecture or piece once, we now "own" new networks of knowledge about each theme and how it changes and relates to others. No one could remember all of Beethoven's *Fifth Symphony* from a single hearing, but neither could one ever again hear those first four notes as just four notes! Once a tiny scrap of sound, these four notes have become a known thing—a locus in the web of all the other things we know and whose meanings and significances depend on one another (figure 15.1).

Learning to recognize is not the same as memorizing. A mind might build an agent that can sense a certain stimulus, yet build no agent that can reproduce it. How could such a mind learn that the first half-subject of Beethoven's *Fifth*—call it *A*—prefigures the second half—call it *B*? It is simple: an agent *A* that recognizes *A* sends a message to another agent *B*, built to recognize *B*. That message serves to "lower *B*'s threshold" so that after *A* hears *A*, *B* will react to smaller hints of *B* than it would otherwise. As a result, that mind "expects" to hear *B* after *A*; that is, it will discern *B*, given fewer or more subtle cues, and might "complain" if it cannot. Yet that mind cannot reproduce either theme in any generative sense. The point is that interagent messages need not be in surface music languages, but can be in codes that influence certain other agents to behave in different ways.

(Andor Kovach pointed out to me that composers do not dare use this simple, four-note motive any more. So memorable was Beethoven's treatment that now an accidental hint of it can wreck another piece by unintentionally distracting the listener.)

If sonatas are lessons, what are the subjects of those lessons? The answer is in the question! One thing the *Fifth Symphony* taught us is how to hear

Figure 15.1
Introductory measures of Ludwig van Beethoven's *Symphony No. 5 in C Minor*

those first four notes. The surface form is just descending major third, first tone repeated thrice. At first, that pattern can be heard two different ways: (1) fifth and third in minor mode or (2) third and first, in major. But once we have heard the symphony, the latter is unthinkable—a strange constraint to plant in all our heads! Let us see how it is taught.

The *Fifth* declares at once its subject, then its near-identical twin. First comes the theme. Presented in a stark orchestral unison, its minor mode location in tonality is not yet made explicit, nor is its metric frame yet clear: the subject stands alone in time. Next comes its twin. The score itself leaves room to view this transposed counterpart as a complement or as a new beginning. Until now, fermatas have hidden the basic metric frame, a pair

Figure 15.1 (continued)

of twinned four-measure halves. So far we have only learned to hear those halves as separate wholes.

The next four-measure metric half-frame shows three versions of the subject, one on each ascending pitch of the tonic triad. (Now we are sure the key is minor.) This shows us how the subject can be made to overlap itself, the three short notes packed perfectly inside the long tone's time-space. The second half-frame does the same, with copies of the complement ascending the dominant seventh chord. This fits the halves together in that single, most familiar, frame of harmony. In rhythm, too, the halves are so precisely congruent that there is no room to wonder how to match them — and attach them into one eight-measure unit.

The next eight-measure frame explains some more melodic points: how to smooth the figure's firmness with passing tones and how to counterpoise the subject's own inversion inside the long note (I think that this evokes a sort of sinusoidal motion-frame idea that is later used to represent the second subject). It also illustrates compression of harmonic time, seen earlier; this would obscure the larger rhythmic unit, but now we know enough to place each metric frame precisely on the afterimage of the one before.

Cadence. Silence. Almost. Total.

Now it is the second subject-twin's turn to stand alone in time. The conductor must select a symmetry: he or she can choose to answer prior cadence, to start anew, or to close the brackets opened at the very start. (Can the conductor do all at once and maintain the metric frame?) We hear a long, long unison F (subdominant?) for, underneath that silent surface sound, we hear our minds rehearsing what was heard.

The next frame reveals the theme again, descending now by thirds. (We see that it was the dominant ninth, not subdominant at all. The music fooled us that time, but never will again.) Then *tour de force*: the subject climbs, sounding on every scale degree. This new perspective shows us how to see the four-note note theme as an appogiatura. Then, as it descends on each tonic chord-note, we are made to see it as a fragment of arpeggio. That last descent completes a set of all four possibilities, harmonic and directional. (Is this deliberate didactic thoroughness, or merely the accidental outcome of the other symmetries?) Finally, the theme's melodic range is squeezed to nothing, yet it survives and even gains strength as single tone. It has always seemed to me a mystery of art, the impact of those moments in quartets when texture turns to a single line and forte-piano shames sforzando in perceived intensity. But such acts, which on the surface only cause the structure or intensity to disappear, must make the largest difference underneath. Shortly, I will propose a scheme in which a sudden, searching change awakes a lot of mental *difference-finders*. This very change wakes yet more difference-finders, and this awakening wakes still more. That is how sudden silence makes the whole mind come alive.

We are "told" all this in just one minute of the lesson, and I have touched but one dimension of its rhetoric. Besides explaining, teachers beg and threaten, calm and scare, use gesture, timbre, quaver, and sometimes even silence. This is vital in music, too. Indeed, in the *Fifth*, it is the start of the subject! Such "lessons" must teach us as much about triads and triplets as mathematicians have learned about angles and sides! Think how much we can learn about minor second intervals from Beethoven's *Grosse Fuge in E-Flat, Opus 133.*

What Use Is Music?

Why on earth should anyone want to learn such things? Geometry is practical—for building pyramids, for instance—but of what use is musical knowledge? Here is one idea. Each child spends endless days in curious ways; we call this play. A child stacks and packs all kinds of blocks and boxes, lines them up, and knocks them down. What is that all about? Clearly, the child is learning about space! But how on earth does one learn about time? Can one time fit inside another? Can two of them go side by side? In music, we find out! It is often said that mathematicians are unusually involved in music, but that musicians are not involved in mathematics. Perhaps both mathematicians and musicians like to make simple things more complicated, but mathematics may be too constrained to satisfy that want entirely, while music may be rigorous or free. The way the mathematics game is played, most variations lie outside the rules, while music can insist on perfect canon or tolerate a casual accomplishment. So mathematicians might need music, but musicians might not need mathematics. A simpler theory is that since music engages us at earlier ages, some mathematicians are those missing mathematical musicians.

Most adults have some childlike fascination for making and arranging larger structures out of smaller ones. One kind of musical understanding involves building large mental structures out of smaller, musical parts. Perhaps the drive to build those mental music structures is the same one that makes us try to understand the world. (Or perhaps that drive is just an accidental mutant variant of it; evolution often copies needless extra stuff, and minds so new as ours must contain a lot of that.)

Sometimes, though, we use music as a trick to misdirect our understanding of the world. When thoughts are painful, we have no way to make them stop. We can attempt to turn our minds to other matters, but doing this (some claim) just submerges the bad thoughts. Perhaps the music that some call background music can tranquilize by turning underthoughts from bad to neutral, leaving the surface thoughts free of affect by diverting the unconscious. The structures we assemble in that detached kind of listening might be wholly sophistic webs of meaninglike cross-references that nowhere touch "reality." In such a self-constructed world, we would need no truth or falsehood, good or evil, pain or joy. Music, in this unpleasant view, would serve as a fine escape from tiresome thoughts.

Syntactic Theories of Music

Contrast two answers to the question, Why do we like certain tunes?

Because they have certain structural features.
Because they resemble other tunes we like.

The first answer has to do with the laws and rules that make tunes pleasant. In language, we know the forms sentences must have to be syntactically acceptable, if not the things they must have to make them sensible or even pleasant to the ear. As to melody, it seems, we only know some features that can help—we know of no absolutely essential features. I do not expect much more to come out of a search for a compact set of rules for musical phrases. (The point is not so much what we mean by a rule, as how large a body of knowledge is involved.)

The second answer has to do with significance outside the tune itself, in the same way that asking, Which sentences are meaningful? takes us outside shared linguistic practice and forces us to look upon each person's private tangled webs of thought. Those private webs feed upon themselves, as in all spheres involving preference: we tend to like things that remind us of the other things we like. For example, some of us like music that resembles the songs, carols, rhymes, and hymns we liked in childhood. All this begs this question: If we like new tunes that are similar to those we already like, where does our liking for music start? I will come back to this later.

The term resemble begs a question also: What are the rules of musical resemblance? I am sure that this depends a lot on how melodies are "represented" in each individual mind. In each single mind, some different "mind parts" do this different ways—the same tune seems at different times to change in rhythm, mode, or harmony. Beyond that, individuals differ even more. Some listeners squirm to symmetries and shapes that others scarcely hear at all, and some fine fugue subjects seem banal to those who sense only a single line. My guess is that our contapuntal sensors harmonize each fading memory with others that might yet be played; perhaps Bach's mind could do this several ways at once. Even one such process might suffice to help an improviser plan what to try to play next. (To try is sufficient since improvisers, like stage magicians, know enough "vamps" or "ways out" to keep the music going when bold experiments fail.)

How is it possible to improvise or comprehend a complex contrapuntal piece? Simple statistical explanations cannot begin to describe such processes. Much better are the generative and transformational, e.g., neo-Schenkerian) methods of syntactic analysis, but only for the simplest analytic uses. At best, the very aim of syntax-oriented music theories is misdirected because they aspire to describe the sentences that minds produce without attempting to describe how the sentences are produced. Meaning is much more than sentence structure. We cannot expect to be able to describe the anatomy of the mind unless we understand its embryology. And so (as with most any other very complicated matter), science must start with the surface systems of description. But this surface taxonomy, however elegant and comprehensive in itself, must yield in the end to a deeper causal explanation. To understand how memory and process merge in "listening," we will have to learn to use much more "procedural" descriptions, such as programs that describe how processes proceed.

In science, we always first explain things in terms of what can be observed (earth, water, fire, air). Yet things that come from complicated processes do not necessarily show their natures on the surface. (The steady pressure of gas conceals those countless, abrupt microimpacts.) To speak of what such things might mean or represent, we have to speak of how they are made.

We cannot describe how the mind is made without having good ways to describe complicated processes. Before computers, no languages were good for that. Piaget tried algebra and Freud tried diagrams; other psychologists used Markov chains and matrices, but none came to much. Behaviorists, quite properly, had ceased to speak at all. Linguists flocked to formal syntax and made progress for a time but reached a limit: transformational grammar shows the contents of the registers (so to speak) but has no way to describe what controls them. This makes it hard to say how surface speech relates to underlying designation and intent—a baby-and-bathwater situation. The reason I like ideas from AI research is that there we tend to seek procedural description first, which seems more appropriate for mental matters.

I do not see why so many theorists find this approach disturbing. It is true that the new power derived from this approach has a price: we can say more, with computational description, but prove less. Yet less is lost than many think, for mathematics never could prove that much about such complicated things. Theorems often tell us complex truths about the simple things, but only rarely tell us simple truths about the complex ones. To believe otherwise is wishful thinking or "mathematics envy." Many musical problems that resist formal solutions may turn out to be tractable anyway, in future simulations that grow artificial musical semantic networks, perhaps by "raising" simulated infants in traditional musical cultures. It will be exciting when one of these infants first shows a hint of real "talent."

Space and Tune

When we enter a room, we seem to see it all at once; we are not permitted this illusion when listening to a symphony. "Of course," one might declare, for hearing has to thread a serial path through time, while sight embraces a space all at once. Actually, it takes time to see new scenes, though we are not usually aware of this. That totally compelling sense that we are conscious of seeing everything in the room instantly and immediately is certainly the strangest of our "optical" illusions.

Music, too, immerses us in seemingly stable worlds! How can this be, when there is so little of it present at each moment? I will try to explain this by arguing that hearing music is like viewing scenery and by asserting that when we hear good music our minds react in very much the same way they do when we see things.[1] And make no mistake; I meant to say "good" music! This little theory is not meant to work for a senseless bag of musical tricks, but only for those certain kinds of music that, in their cultural times and places, command attention and approval.

To see the problem in a slightly different way, consider cinema. Contrast a novice's clumsy patched and pasted reels of film with those that transport us to other worlds so artfully composed that our own worlds seem shoddy and malformed. What "hides the seams" to make great films so much less than the sum of their parts so that we do not see them as mere sequences of scenes? What makes us feel that we are there and part of it when we are in fact immobile in our chairs, helpless to deflect an atom of the projected pattern's predetermined destiny? I will follow this idea a little further, then try to explain why good music is both more and less than sequences of notes.

Our eyes are always flashing sudden flicks of different pictures to our brains, yet none of that saccadic action leads to any sense of change or motion in the world; each thing reposes calmly in its "place"! What makes those objects stay so still while images jump and jerk so? What makes us such innate Copernicans? I will first propose how this illusion works in vision, then in music.

We will find the answer deep within the way the mind regards itself. When speaking of illusion, we assume that someone is being fooled. "I know those lines are straight," I say, "but they look bent to me." Who are the different I's and me's? We are all convinced that somewhere in each person struts a single, central self, atomic, indivisible. (And secretly we hope that it also indestructible.)

I believe, instead, that inside each mind work many different agents. (The idea of societies of agents [Minsky 1977, 1980a, 1980b] originated in my work with Seymour Papert.) All we really need to know about agents is this: each agent knows what happens to some others, but little of what happens to the rest. It means little to say, "Eloise was unaware of X" unless we say more about which of her mind-agents were uninvolved with X. Thinking consists of making mind-agents work together; the very core of fruitful thought is breaking problems into different kinds of parts and then assigning the parts to the agents that handle them best. (Among our most important agents are those that manage these assignments, for they are the agents that embody what each person knows about what he or she knows. Without these agents we would be helpless, for we would not know what our knowing is for.)

In that division of labor we call seeing, I will suppose that a certain mind-agent called feature-finder sends messages (about features it finds on the retina) to another agent, scene-analyzer. Scene-analyzer draws conclusions from the messages it gets and sends its own, in turn, to other mind-parts. For instance, feature-finder finds and tells about some scraps of edge and texture; then scene-analyzer finds and tells that these might fit some bit of shape.

Perhaps those features come from glimpses of a certain real table leg. But knowing such a thing is not for agents at this level; scene-analyzer does not know of any such specific things. All it can do is broadcast something about shape to hosts of other agents who specialize in recognizing special things. (Since special things—like tables, words, or dogs—must be involved with memory and learning, there is at least one such agent for every kind of thing this mind has learned to recognize.) Thus, we can hope, this message reaches table-maker, an agent specialized to recognize evidence that a table is in the field of view. After many such stages, descendents of such messages finally reach space-builder, an agent that tries to tell of real things in real space.

Now we can see one reason why perception seems so effortless: while messages from scene-analyzer to table-maker are based on evidence that feature-finder supplied, the messages themselves need not say what feature-finder itself did, or how it did it. Partly this is because it would take scene-analyzer too long to explain all that. In any case, the recipients could make no use of all that information since they are not engineers or psychologists, but just little specialized nerve nets.

Only in the past few centuries have painters learned enough technique and trickery to simulate reality. (Once so informed, they often now choose different goals.) Thus space-builder, like an ordinary person, knows nothing of how vision works, perspective, foveae, or blind spots. We only learn such things in school: millenia of introspection never led to their suspicion, nor did meditation, transcendental or mundane. The mind holds tightly to its secrets not from stinginess or shame, but simply because it does not know them.

Messages, in this scheme, go various ways. Each motion of the eye or head or body makes feature-finder start anew, and such motions are responses (by muscle-moving agents) to messages that scene-analyzer sends when it needs more details to resolve ambiguities. Scene-analyzer itself responds to messages from "higher up." For instance, space-builder may have asked, "Is that a table?" of table-maker, which replies (to itself), "Perhaps, but it should have another leg—there," so it asks scene-analyzer to verify this, and scene-analyzer gets the job done by making eye-mover look down and to the left. Nor is scene-understander autonomous: its questions to scene-analyzer are responses to requests from others. There need be no first cause in such a network.

When we look up, we are never afraid that the ground has disappeared, though it has certainly has "disappeared." This is because space-builder remembers all the answers to its questions and never changes any of those answers without reason; moving our eyes or raising our heads provide no cause to exorcise that floor inside our current spatial model of the room. My paper on frame-systems (Minsky 1974) says more about these concepts. Here we only need these few details.

Now, back to our illusions. While feature-finder is not instantaneous, it is a very, very fast highly parallel pattern matcher. Whatever scene-analyzer asks, feature-finder answers in an eye flick, a mere tenth of a second (or less if we have image buffers). More speed comes from the way in which space-builder can often tell itself, via its own high-speed model memory, about what has been seen before. I argue that all this speed is another root of our illusion: If answers seem to come as soon as questions are asked, they will seem to have been there all along.

The illusion is enhanced in yet another way by "expectation" or "default." These agents know good ways to lie and bluff! Aroused by only partial evidence that a table is in view, table-maker supplies space-builder with fictitious details about some "typical table" while its servants find out more about the real one! Once so informed, space-builder can quickly move and plan ahead, taking some risks but ready to make corrections later. This only works, of course, when prototypes are good and are rightly activated—that is what intelligence is all about.

As for "awareness" of how all such things are done, there simply is not room for that. Space-builder is too remote and different to understand how feature-finder does its work of eye fixation. Each part of the mind is unaware of almost all that happens in the others. (That is why we need psychologists; we think we know what happens in our minds because these agents are so facile with "defaults," but we are almost always wrong.) True, each agent needs to know which of its servants can do what, but as to how, that information has no place or use in those tiny minds inside our minds.

How do both music and vision build things in our minds? Eye motions show us real objects; phrases show us musical objects. We "learn" a room with bodily motions; large musical sections show us musical "places." Walks and climbs move us from room to room; so do transitions between musical sections. Looking back in vision is like recapitulation in music; both give us time, at certain points, to reconfirm or change our conceptions of the whole.

Hearing a theme is like seeing a thing in a room, a section or movement is like a room, and a whole sonata is like an entire building. I do not mean to say that music builds the sorts of things that space-builder does. (That is too naive a comparison of sound and place.) I do mean to say that composers simulate coherency by engaging the same sorts of interagent coordinations that vision uses to produce its illusion of a stable world using, of course, different agents. I think the same is true of talk or writing, the way these very paragraphs make sense—or sense of sense—if any.

Composing and Conducting

In seeing, we can move our eyes; lookers can choose where they shall look, and when. In music we must listen here; that is, to the part being played now. It is simply no use asking music-finder to look there because it is not then, now.

If composer and conductor choose what part we hear, does not this ruin our analogy? When music-analyzer asks its questions, how can music-finder answer them unless, miraculously, the music happens to be playing what music-finder wants at just that very instant? If so, then how can music paint its scenes unless composers know exactly what the listeners will ask at every moment? How to ensure—when music-analyzer wants it now— that precisely that "something" will be playing now?

That is the secret of music; of writing it, playing, and conducting! Music need not, of course, confirm each listener's every expectation; each plot demands some novelty. Whatever the intent, control is required or novelty will turn to nonsense. If allowed to think too much themselves, the listeners will find unanswered questions in any score; about accidents of form and figure, voice and line, temperament and difference-tone.

Composers can have different goals: to calm and soothe, tell tales, stage scenes, teach new things, or tear down prior arts. For some such purposes, composers must use the known forms and frames or else expect misunderstanding. Of course, when expectations are confirmed too often, the style may seem dull; this is our concern in the next section. Yet, just as in language, one often best explains a new idea by using older ones, avoiding jargon or too much lexical innovation. If readers cannot understand the words themselves, the sentences may "be Greek to them."

This is not a matter of a simple hierarchy, in which each meaning stands on lower-level ones, for example, word, phrase, sentence, paragraph, and chapter. Things never really work that way, and jabberwocky shows how sense comes through though many words are new. In every era some contemporary music changes basic elements yet exploits established larger forms, but innovations that violate too drastically the expectations of the culture cannot meet certain kinds of goals. Of course this will not apply to works whose goals include confusion and revolt, or when composers try to create things that hide or expurgate their own intentionality, but in these instances it may be hard to hold the audience.

Each musical artist must forecast and predirect the listener's fixations to draw attention here and distract it from there—to force the hearer (again, like a magician) to ask only the questions that the composition is about to answer. Only by establishing such preestablished harmony can music make it seem that something is there.

Rhythm and Redundancy

A popular song has 100 measures, 1000 beats. What must the martians imagine we mean by those measures and beats, measures and beats! The words themselves reveal an awesome repetitiousness. Why isn't music boring?

Is hearing so like seeing that we need a hundred glances to build each musical image? Some repetitive musical textures might serve to remind us of things that persist through time like wind and stream. But many sounds occur only once: we must hear a pin drop now or seek and search for it; that is why we have no "ear-lids." Poetry drops pins, or says each thing once or not at all. So does some music.

Then why do we tolerate music's relentless rhythmic pulses or other repetitive architectural features? There is no one answer, for we hear in different ways, on different scales. Some of those ways portray the scans of time directly, but others speak of musical things, in worlds where time folds over on itself. And there, I think, is where we use those beats and measures. Music's metric frames are transient templates used for momentary matching. Its rhythms are "synchronization pulses" used to match new phrases against old, the better to contrast them with difference and change. As differences and changes are sensed, the rhythmic frames fade from our awareness. Their work is done and the messages of higher-level agents never speak of them; that is why metric music is not boring!

Good music germinates from tiny seeds. How cautiously we handle novelty, sandwiching the new between repeated sections of repeated stuff! The clearest kind of change is near identity, in thought just as in vision. Slight shifts in view may best reveal an object's form or even show us whether it is there at all.

When we discussed sonatas, we saw how matching different metric frames helps us to sense the musical ingredients. Once frames are matched, we can see how altering a single note at one point will change a major third melodic skip at another point to smooth passing tones, or will make what was there a seventh chord into a dominant ninth. Matching lets our minds see different things, from different times, together. The fusion of those matching lines of tone from different measures (like television's separate lines and frames) lets us make those magic musical pictures in our minds.

How do our musical agents do this kind of work for us? We must have organized them into structures that are good at finding differences between frames. Here is a simplified four-level scheme that might work. Many such ideas are current in research on vision (Winston 1975).

• Feature finders listen for simple time-events, like notes, or peaks, or pulses.

• Measure-takers notice certain patterns of time-events like 3/4, 4/4, 6/8.

• Difference-finders observe that the figure here is same as that one there, except a perfect fifth above.

• Structure-builders perceive that three phrases form an almost regular "sequence."

The idea of interconnecting feature-finders, difference-finders, and structure-builders is well exemplified in Winston's work (1975). Measure-takers would be kinds of frames, as described in "A Framework for

Representing Knowledge" (Minsky 1974). First, the feature-finders search the sound stream for the simplest sorts of musical significance: entrances and envelopes, the tones themselves, the other little, local things. Then measure-takers look for metric patterns in those small events and put them into groups, thus finding beats and postulating rhythmic regularities. Then the difference-finders can begin to sense events of musical importance, imitations and inversions, syncopations and suspensions. Once these are found, the structure-builders can start work on a larger scale.

The entire four-level agency is just one layer of a larger system in which analogous structures are repeated on larger scales. At each scale, another level of order (with its own sorts of things and differences) makes larger-scale descriptions, and thus consumes another order of structural form. As a result, notes become figures, figures turn into phrases, and phrases turn into sequences; and notes become chords, and chords make up progressions, and so on and on. Relations at each level turn to things at the next level above and are thus more easily remembered and compared. This "time-warps" things together, changing tone into tonality, note into composition.

The more regular the rhythm, the easier the matching goes, and the fewer difference agents are excited further on. Thus once it is used for "lining up," the metric structure fades from our attention because it is represented as fixed and constant (like the floor of the room you are in) until some metric alteration makes the measure-takers change their minds. Sic semper all Alberti basses, um-pah-pahs, and ostinati; they all become imperceptible except when changing. Rhythm has many other functions, to be sure, and agents for those other functions see things different ways. Agents used for dancing do attend to rhythm, while other forms of music demand less steady pulses.

We all experience a phenomenon we might call persistence of rhythm, in which our minds maintain the beat through episodes of ambiguity. I presume that this emerges from a basic feature of how agents are usually assembled; at every level many agents of each kind compete (Minsky 1980b). Thus agents for 3/4, 4/4, and 6/8 compete to find best fits. Once in power, however, each agent "cross-inhibits" its competitors. Once 3/4 takes charge of things, 6/8 will find it hard to "get a hearing" even if the evidence on its side becomes slightly better.

When none of the agents has any solid evidence long enough, agents change at random or take turns. Thus anything gets interesting, in a way, if it is monotonous enough! We all know how, when a word or phrase is repeated often enough it, or we, begin to change as restless searchers start to amplify minutiae and interpret noise as structure. This happens at all levels because when things are regular at one level, the difference agents at the next will fail, to be replaced by other, fresh ones that then re-present the sameness different ways. (Thus meditation, undirected from the higher mental realms, fares well with the most banal of repetitious inputs from below.)

Regularities are hidden while expressive nuances are sensed and emphasized and passed along. Rubato or crescendo, ornament or passing tone, the alterations at each level become the objects for the next. The mystery is solved; the brain is so good at sensing differences that it forgets the things themselves; that is, whenever they are the same. As for liking music, that depends on what remains.

Sentic Significance

Why do we like any tunes in the first place? Do we simply associate tunes with pleasant experiences? Should we look back to the tones and patterns of our mother's voice or heartbeat? Or could it be that some themes are innately likable? All these theories could hold truth, and others too, for nothing need have a single cause inside the mind.

Theories about children need not apply to adults because (I suspect) human minds do so much self-revising that things can get detached from their origins. We might end up liking both *Art of Fugue* and *Musical Offering*, mainly because each work's subject illuminates the other, which gives each work a richer network of "significance." Dependent circularity need be no paradox here, for in thinking (unlike logic) two things can support each other in midair. To be sure, such autonomy is precarious; once detached from origins, might one not drift strangely awry? Indeed so, and many people seem quite mad to one another.

In his book *Sentics* (1978), Manfred Clynes, a physiologist and pianist, describes certain specific temporal sensory patterns and claims that each is associated with a certain common emotional state. For example, in his experiments, two particular patterns (that gently rise and fall) are said to suggest states of love and reverence; two others (more abrupt) signify anger and hate. He claims that these and other patterns—he calls them sentic—

arouse the same effects through different senses—that is, embodied as acoustical intensity, or pitch, or tactile pressure, or even visual motion—and that this is cross-cultural. The time lengths of these sentic shapes, on the order of 1 sec, could correspond to parts of musical phrases.

Clynes studied the "muscular" details of instrumental performances with this in view and concluded that music can engage emotions through these sentic signals. Of course, more experiments are needed to verify that such signals really have the reported effects. Nevertheless, I would expect to find something of the sort for quite a different reason: namely, to serve in the early social development of children. Sentic signals (if they exist) would be quite useful in helping infants to learn about themselves and others.

All learning theories require brains to somehow impose "values" implicit or explicit in the choice of what to learn to do. Most such theories say that certain special signals, called reinforcers, are involved in this. For certain goals it should suffice to use some simple, "primary" physiological stimuli like eating, drinking, relief of physical discomfort.

Human infants must learn social signals, too. The early learning theorists in this century assumed that certain social sounds (for instance, of approval) could become reinforcers by association with innate reinforcers, but evidence for this was never found. If parents could exploit some innate sentic cues, that mystery might be explained.

This might also touch another, deeper problem: that of how an infant forms an image of its own mind. Self-images are important for at least two reasons. First, external reinforcement can only be a part of human learning, the growing infant must eventually learn to learn from within to free itself from its parents. With Freud, I think that children must replace and augment the outside teacher with a self-constructed, inner, parent image. Second, we need a self-model simply to make realistic plans for solving ordinary problems. For example, we must know enough about our own dispositions to be able to assess which plans are feasible. Pure self-commitment does not work; we simply cannot carry out a plan that we will find too boring to complete or too vulnerable to other competing interests. We need models of our own behavior. How could a baby be smart enough to build such a model?

Innate sentic detectors could help by teaching children about their own affective states. For if distinct signals arouse specific states, the child can associate those signals with those states. Just knowing that such states exist, that is, having symbols for them, is half the battle. If those signals are uniform enough, then from social discourse one can learn some rules about the behavior caused by those states. Thus a child might learn that conciliatory signals can change anger to affection. Given that sort of information, a simple learning machine should be able to construct a "finite-state-person-model." This model would be crude at first, but to get started would be half the job. Once the baby had a crude model of some other, it could be copied and adapted in work on the baby's self-model. (This is more normative and constructional than it is descriptive, as Freud hinted, for the self-model dictates more than portrays what it purports to portray.)

With regard to music, it seems possible that we conceal, in the innocent songs and settings of our children's musical cultures, some lessons about successions of our own affective states. Sentically encrypted, those ballads would encode instructions about conciliation and affection, aggression and retreat—precisely the knowledge of signals and states that we need to get along with others. In later life, more complex music might illustrate more intricate kinds of compromise and conflict, ways to fit goals together to achieve more than one thing at a time. Finally, for grown-ups, our Burgesses and Kubricks fit Beethoven's *Ninths* to *Clockwork Oranges*.

If you find all this far-fetched, so do I. But before rejecting it entirely, recall the question, Why do we have music and let it occupy our lives with no apparent reason? When no idea seems right, the right one must seem wrong.

Theme and Thing

What is the subject of Beethoven's *Fifth Symphony*? Is it just those first four notes? Does it include the twin, transposed companion too? What of the other variations, augmentations, and inversions? Do they all stem from a single prototype? In this case, yes.

Or do they? For later in the symphony the theme appears in triplet form to serve as countersubject of the scherzo: three notes and one, three notes and one, three notes and one, still they make four (figure 15.2). Melody turns into monotone rhythm; meter is converted to two equal beats. Downbeat now falls on an actual note, instead of a silence. With all of those changes, the themes are quite different and yet the same. Neither the form in the allegro nor the scherzo alone is the prototype; separate and equal, they span musical time.

Is there some more abstract idea that they both embody? This is like the problem raised by Wittgenstein (1953) of what words like game mean. In my paper on frames (Minsky 1974), I argue that for vision, chair can be described for no single prototype; it is better to use several prototypes connected in relational networks of similarities and differences. I doubt that even these would represent musical ideas well; there are better tools in contemporary AI research, such as constraint systems, conceptual dependency, frame-systems, and semantic networks. Those are the tools we use today to deal with such problems. (See *Computer Music Journal* 4[2] and 4[3], 1980.)

What is a good theme? Without that bad word good, I do not think the question is well formed because anything is a theme if everything is music!

So let us split that question into (1) What mental conditions or processes do pleasant tunes evoke? and (2) What do we mean by pleasant? Both questions are hard, but the first is only hard; to answer it will take much thought and experimentation, which is good. The second question is very different. Philosophers and scientists have struggled mightily to understand what pain and pleasure are.

I especially like Dennett's (1978) explanation of why that has been so difficult. He argues that pain "works" in different ways at different times, and all these ways have too little in common for the usual definition. I agree, but if pain is no single thing, why do we talk and think as though it were and represent it with such spurious clarity? This is no accident: illusions of this sort have special uses. They play a role connected with a problem facing any society (inside or outside the mind) that learns from its experience. The problem is how to assign the credit and blame, for each accomplishment or failure of the society as a whole, among the myriad agents involved in everything that happens. To the extent that the agents' actions are decided locally, so also must these decisions to credit or blame be made locally.

How, for example, can a mother tell that her child has a need (or that one has been satisfied) before she has learned specific signs for each such need? That could be arranged if, by evolution, signals were combined from many different internal processes concerned with needs and were provided with a single, common output—an infant's signal of discomfort (or contentment). Such a genetically preestablished harmony would evoke a corresponding state in the parent. We would feel this as something like the distress we feel when babies cry.

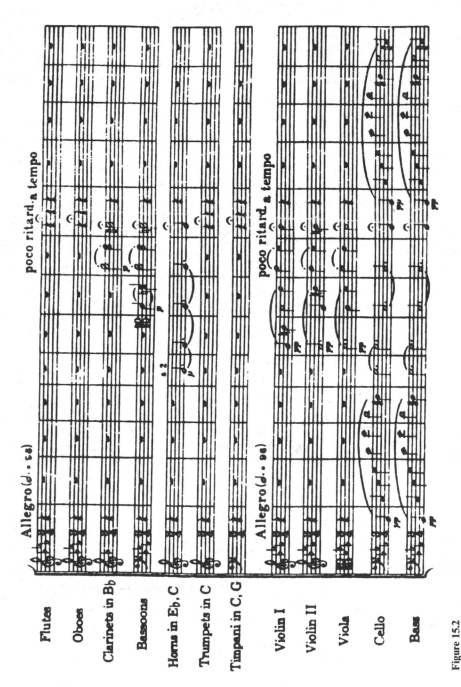

Figure 15.2
Introductory measures of the third movement of Ludwig van Beethoven's *Symphony No. 5 in C Minor*

Figure 15.2 (continued)

A signal for satisfaction is also needed. Suppose, among the many things a child does, there is one that mother likes, which she demonstrates by making approving sounds. The child has just been walking there, and holding this just so, and thinking that, and speaking in some certain way. How can the mind of the child find out which behavior is good? The trouble is, each aspect of the child's behavior must result from little plans the child made before. We cannot reward an act. We can only reward the agency that selected that strategy, the agent who wisely activated the first agent, and so on. Alas for the generation of behaviorists who wastes its mental life by missing this plain and simple principle.

To reward all those agents and processes, we must propagate some message that they all can use to credit what they did, the plans they made, their strategies and computations. These various recipients have so little in common that such a message of approval, to work at all, must be extremely simple. Words like good are almost content-free messages that enable tutors, inside or outside a society, to tell the members that one or more of them has satisfied some need, and that tutor need not understand which members did what, or how, or even why.

Words like satisfy and need have many shifting meanings. Why, then, do we seem to understand them? Because they evoke that same illusion of substantiality that fools us into thinking it tautologous to ask, Why do we like pleasure? This serves a need: the levels of social discourse at which we use such clumsy words as like, or good, or that was fun must coarsely crush together many different meanings or we will never understand others (or ourselves) at all. Hence that precious, essential poverty of word and sign that makes them so hard to define. Thus the word good is no symbol that simply means or designates, as table does. Instead, it only names this protean injunction. Activate all those (unknown) processes that correlate and sift and sort, in learning, to see what changes (in myself) should now be made. The word like is just like good, except it is a name we use when we send such structure-building signals to ourselves.

Most of the "uses" of music mentioned in this chapter—learning about time, fitting things together, getting along with others, and suppressing one's troubles—are very "functional" but overlook much larger scales of "use." Curt Roads remarked, "Every world above bare survival is self-constructed; whole cultures are built around common things people come to appreciate." These appreciations, represented by aesthetic agents, play roles in more and more of our decisions: what we think is beautiful gets linked to what we think is important. Perhaps, Roads suggests, when groups of mind-agents cannot agree, they tend to cede decisions to those others more concerned with what, for better or for worse, we call aesthetic form and fitness. By having small effects at many little points, those cumulative preferences for taste and form can shape a world.

That is another reason why we say we like the music we like. Liking is the way certain mind-parts make the others learn the things they need to understand that music. Hence liking (and its relatives) is at the very heart of understanding what we hear. Affect and aesthetic do not lie in other academic worlds that music theories safely can ignore. Those other worlds are academic self-deceptions that we use to make each theorist's problem seem like someone else's.[2]

Acknowledgments

I am indebted to conversations and/or improvisations with Maryann Amacher, John Amuedo, Betty Dexter, Harlan Ellison, Edward Fredkin, Bernard Greenberg, Danny Hillis, Douglas Hofstadter, William Kornfeld, Andor Kovach, David Levitt, Tod Machover, Charlotte Minsky, Curt Roads, Glorla Rudisch, Frederic Rzewski, and Stephen Smoliar. This article is in memory of Irving Fine.

Notes

1. Edward Fredkin suggested to me the theory that listening to music might exercise some innate map-making mechanism in the brain. When I mentioned the puzzle of music's repetitiousness, he compared it to the way rodents explore new places: first they go one way a little, then back to home. They do it again a few times, then go a little farther. They try small digressions, but frequently return to base. Both people and mice explore new territories that way, making mental maps lest they get lost. Music might portray this building process, or even exercise those very parts of the mind.

2. Many readers of a draft of this chapter complained about its narrow view of music. What about jazz, "modern" forms, songs with real words, monophonic chant and raga, gong and block, and all those other kinds of sounds? Several readers claimed to be less intellectual, to simply hear and feel and not build buildings in their minds. There simply is not space here to discuss all those things, but:

• What makes those thinkers who think that music does not make them do so much construction so sure that they know their minds so surely? It is ingenuous to think you "just react" to anything a culture works a thousand years to develop. A mind that thinks it works so simply must have more in its unconscious than it has in its philosophy.

• Our work here is with hearing music, not with hearing "music"! Anything that we can all agree is music will be fine—that is why I chose Beethoven's *Fifth Symphony*. For what is music? All things played on all instruments? Fiddlesticks. All structures made of sound? That has a hollow ring. The things I said of words like theme hold true for words like music too: it does not follow that because a word is public, the ways it works on minds is also public. Before one embarks on a quest after the grail that holds the essence of all "music," one must see that there is as signficant a problem in the meaning of that single sound itself.

References

Clynes, M. 1978. *Sentics*. New York: Doubleday.

Dennett, D. 1978. "Why a Machine Can't Feel Pain." In *Brainstorms*: *Philosophical Essays on Mind and Psychology*. Montgomery, Vermont: Bradford Book.

Minsky, M. 1974. "A Framework for Representing Knowledge." AI Memo 306. Cambridge, Massachusetts: MIT Artificial Intelligence Laboratory. Condensed version in P. Winston, ed. 1975. *The Psychology of Computer Vision*. New York: McGraw-Hill, pp. 211–277.

Minsky, M. 1977. "Plain Talk About Neurodevelopment Epistemology." In *Proceedings of the Fifth International Joint Conference on Artificial Intelligence*. Cambridge, Massachusetts: MIT Artificial Intelligence Laboratory. Condensed in P. Winston and R. Brown, eds 1979. *Artificial Intelligence*. Cambridge, Massachusetts. MIT Press, pp. 421–450.

Minsky, M. 1980a. "Jokes and the Logic of the Cognitive Unconscious." AI Memo 603. Cambridge, Massachusetts: MIT Artificial Intelligence Laboratory.

Minsky, M. 1980b. "K-lines: A Theory of Memory." *Cognitive Sciences* 4(2):117–133.

Roads, C. ed. 1980. *Computer Music Journal* 4(2) and 4(3).

Winston, P. H. 1975. "Learning Structural Descriptions by Examples." in P. Winston, ed 1975. *Psychology of Computer Vision*. New York: McGraw-Hill, pp. 157–209.

Wittgenstein, L. 1953. *Philosophical Investigations*. Oxford: Oxford University Press.

VI AI AND MUSIC: COMPOSITION TOOLS

Ames describes the machine model used to generate *Protocol*, a composition for solo piano. To implement desired compositional features, Ames abandons the conventional approaches of purely "random selection and rigid determinism."

Ames defines the protocol of a set of algorithmic tests as a preference ranking. By evaluating a "repertory of alternatives" according to a protocol of tests of harmonic quality, voice-leading, and so forth, a search will find "the best of the imperfect choices."

Production of *Protocol* divides into five phases: (1) generate the material, (2) organize the material, (3) compose the global form, (4) compose the median form, (5) compose the local form. Ames provides an overview for the flow of control used by his modular system.

The generation of *Protocol* includes manual composition, for example, for the sequence of modules in the global form. Ames emphasizes that such a "manually" executed stage has primary relevance as the composer's input rather than "heuristic" assumptions.

The article describes automated compositional techniques, useful per se and as tools for composing with a computer in an "artistically meaningful way." Finally, Ames presents *Protocol*, the composition itself.

16 *Protocol*: Motivation, Design, and Production of a Composition for Solo Piano

Charles Ames

Motivation

Protocol is a work for solo piano composed using a digital computer. Its underlying compositional image deals with a universal concern: our subjective impression of time. I based the work rhythmically upon regular pulsations, exploiting frequent and abrupt modulations between rates as the principle compositional focus. Depending upon its predecessor, each entering rate of pulsation functions either to compress or to expand subjective time. Assertive contrasts in extra-rhythmic domains establish each rate as an independent frame of reference, equivalent to all other rates within the structural context.

The piano is not only especially well suited to this idea; it is also a fairly "idiomatic" instrument for this sort of automated composition. Its rich timbre fatigues a listener far less over an extended form than synthetic timbres do. Its percussive envelope brings the attack of each note into relief and so helps project the pulse. It can also support modulations between rates with perceptual cues from several independent and easily formalized domains. Its scales of register, dynamics, and articulation are both uniform and extensive, while its polyphonic capabilities open up myriads of sonorous resources.

Complementing my arrival at *Protocol*'s time-compression image was my discovery that algorithmic methods of composition could be much more powerful than had previously been demonstrated. I had long been uncomfortable with methods depending heavily either on random selection or on rote determinism, since both of these approaches are highly limiting to a composer with clear stylistic objectives. When the random-number generator selects the details of a musical passage as in Xenakis's 1962 ST series (described 1971), the composer exerts little control beyond the gross characteristics—the means and variances—of the result. More elaborate applications of random selection such as the rule-filtered randomness of Hiller and Isaacson's 1957 *Illiac Suite* (described 1959) and the top-down hierarchical strategies of my own *Crystals* (1980, described 1982) do impose loose stylistic constraints, but they remain capricious within

Previously published in the *Proceedings* of the 1981 International Computer Music Conference and in *INTERFACE: Journal of New Music Research*. Revised 1990.

these constraints. Rote determinism in the manner of Boulez's *Structures*, Book I (described in Ligeti, 1958) almost invariably leads to conflicts. For example, if one wishes to subject the voices in a passage independently to rote inversions, retrogrades, and/or transpositions, then one must generally relinquish control over the resulting sonorities and their progression.

Artistic values suggest that even in automated composition, some choices will be better—in the sense of being more appropriate to the composer's stylistic intent—than others. They also suggest that whether any given choice is optimal or even suitable will depend upon its context. As an alternative to the preceding methods, suppose it is possible to enumerate a *protocol* of algorithmic tests, that is, a collection of tests ranked in significance according to the composer's priorities. Included might be tests of harmonic quality, tests of dependent or independent voice-leading, tests for horizontal octaves, even tests of statistical balance. Then one can direct the computer to search among a substantial repertory of candidates for the solution best fitting all these criteria.[1] If there is a choice passing all tests, then an exhaustive search must find it; otherwise, the search can provide the best of the imperfect choices. Such an approach allows the computer wide flexibility in adapting its solutions to individual contexts. It guarantees a high level of integrity in the composed product. It also simulates actual creative decision-making much more closely than either random selection or rote determinism. In those situations where the optimal solution is unique (always assuming that the protocol of tests accurately reflects the composer's values), the computer will meet or surpass human capabilities in finding that solution.

Design

Protocol's modular design is somewhat idiosyncratic, so before sketching out this design it will be helpful to establish the scheme of definitions summarized in table 16.1. Notice that this scheme distinguishes between *forms*, which depend upon temporal sequence, and *material*, which in *Protocol* exists independently of time. Among the three levels of formal design, the local pulse—while requiring the most intensive computation sheerly as the level of greatest detail—holds the least significance in projecting the major compositional focus of the work. It was not the pulses or rates of pulsation per se that concerned me the most, but rather the

Table 16.1
Scheme of definitions

Level of design	Forms	Material
Global	A *packet* is a sequence of 3 to 5 *units*, all drawing material from the same *module*.	A *module* combines 4 *components* with 2 adjacent dynamics and 1 mode of articulation
Median	A *unit* is a sequence of 3 or more *pulses*, unified by a consistent *rate of pulsation* and a common *chord*; these attributes are both drawn from a single *component*.	A *component* combines 1 *rate of pulsation* with 1 *chord* of 7 pitches.
Local	A *pulse* combines a *duration* with a *sonority* of 1 to 4 pitches. The *rate of pulsation* at the median level determines the *duration* at the local level. Similarly, the *chord* at the median level supplies all pitches for the *sonority* at the local level.	

modulations between rates, and it is at the median level where these modulations come under scrutiny. The global level performs its usual role of shaping the work as a whole. However, it remains ancillary to the median level in an important sense, for many compositional decisions at the global level simply provided a congenial environment for median-level decisions.

There are 32 rates of pulsation in *Protocol*. When arranged in order of increasing speed, these rates proceed geometrically. The slowest rate is 1 pulse every two seconds. the fastest is 8 pulses each second, and the proportion between consecutive rates is 31/16. This mathematically irrational proportion approximates the ratio 12:11, so gradations between consecutive rates are rather subtle despite the wide overall compass. Excepting the two extreme rates, there is no common factor to link one rate to another. Polyrhythms do not occur in this work; they would have been mathematically impossible to coordinate.

In order to clarify and enhance the rhythm, I made each of the 32 rates correspond to a distinct chord and maintained this correspondence throughout all of the work but the coda. Since *Protocol* is of fairly substantial duration (17 minutes), it was also necessary that consecutive pulses exploit constantly varying material. For this reason, a chord only becomes manifest as an arpeggiation over the course of a unit; the sonorities articulating successive pulses each present different subsets of the complete 7-pitch collection. Such arpeggiations are especially suitable because although the chordal material is fairly specific in its definition, it remains malleable to demands imposed by context. I honor pairings of rate and chord by designating them as *components*, both of the material in general and of the specific *modules*. The modules provide comprehensible references to unify the work as a whole. They are established as familiar global entities by three factors: consistent proximity between the 4 components of a module, a restricted set of dynamics, and a consistent mode of articulation.[2]

Figure 16.1 illustrates the global form of *Protocol*. There is a total of 64 packets in the work, 8 packets drawing material from each of the 8 modules. The work exhibits informal characteristics of exposition and development in its modular layout. With a few exceptions, repetitions confirm each module to the ear after the module first enters. The layout also sets up interactions between pairs of modules, thus establishing broad associations. The frequent proximity of modules 1 and 2 or 3 and 4, for example, associates them as familiar combinations throughout the course of the work. On an even broader scale of perception, similar associations through proximity establish modules 1–4 and modules 5–8 as familiar groups. Such associations, in fact, suggest the hierarchy of groups diagrammed in figure 16.2, where the single, double, (and triple) primes indicate groups at successively broader scales of perception. This hierarchy strongly influences the strategies for distributing material among the 8 modules.

The coda to *Protocol* abandons the modular design exploited throughout the main body of the work as well as the formerly consistent pairings of rate and chord. Here, the work simply presents all 32 rates, in order from slowest to fastest, and all 32 chords, in order from lowest register to highest. This closing gesture is frankly evocative of similar endings by J. J. Froberger and by a contemporary influence, Morton Feldman.

Production

Figure 16.3 summarizes the stages of production involved in creating *Protocol*. Arrows connecting program names indicate which programs depended upon information generated by preceding programs and stored as intermediate data files. The stages defining material come first, after

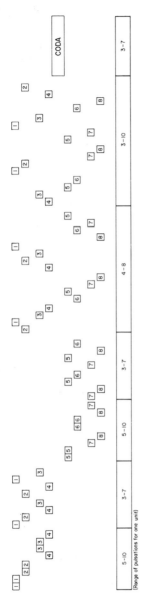

Figure 16.1
Global form of *Protocol*

Number of Components	Organization							
(32)	(I'''')							
16	I''				2''			
8	I'		2'		3'		4'	
4	1	2	3	4	5	6	7	8

Figure 16.2
Hierarchical organization of modules

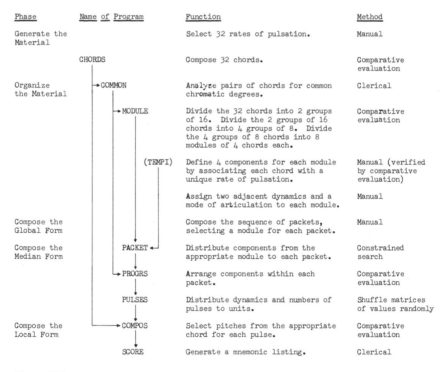

Phase	Name of Program	Function	Method
Generate the Material		Select 32 rates of pulsation.	Manual
	CHORDS	Compose 32 chords.	Comparative evaluation
Organize the Material	COMMON	Analyze pairs of chords for common chromatic degrees.	Clerical
	MODULE	Divide the 32 chords into 2 groups of 16. Divide the 2 groups of 16 chords into 4 groups of 8. Divide the 4 groups of 8 chords into 8 modules of 4 chords each.	Comparative evaluation
	(TEMPI)	Define 4 components for each module by associating each chord with a unique rate of pulsation.	Manual (verified by comparative evaluation)
		Assign two adjacent dynamics and a mode of articulation to each module.	Manual
Compose the Global Form		Compose the sequence of packets, selecting a module for each packet.	Manual
Compose the Median Form	PACKET	Distribute components from the appropriate module to each packet.	Constrained search
	PROGRS	Arrange components within each packet.	Comparative evaluation
	PULSES	Distribute dynamics and numbers of pulses to units.	Shuffle matrices of values randomly
Compose the Local Form	COMPOS	Select pitches from the appropriate chord for each pulse.	Comparative evaluation
	SCORE	Generate a mnemonic listing.	Clerical

Figure 16.3
Stages of production

which the process moves on to describe features of the global, median, and finally local levels of the form. The methods range from manual decisions through the clerical procedures of COMMON and SCORE, through the random shuffling of PULSES and the constrained search of PACKET, to *comparative evaluation*, by which I refer to the method of exhaustive search described in the opening of this chapter. The last is clearly the most pervasive technique used by the various programs; indeed, one may even regard the constrained search in PACKET as a degenerate—though still extremely powerful—application of the same strategy.

Figure 16.4 charts the flow of an exhaustive search applied to the general problem of optimizing a collection of elements in response to a protocol of tests. In practice, the number of elements and the number of values each element may assume must be small. One application of this algorithm is CHORDS, where the "values" are pitches and the "collection of elements" is the collection of 7 voices that comprise a chord. Another application is MODULE, which divides a group of chords into two smaller groups. Here the "values" are the chords themselves while the "elements" are member-ships in one or the other of the smaller groups. In the third application, PROGRS, the "values" again are chords but the "elements" are positions in a progression.

According to figure 16.4, the search advances through the elements in the collection, assigns values to each element, and evaluates the results. Evaluations take the general form of a cumulative *measure* (in the non-musical sense of measure) that reflects the number of times the values currently under scrutiny violate tests in the protocol. The objective of the search is to minimize this measure. Whenever it manages to assign values to every element in the collection, the search stores these values and their associated measure as a potentially optimal solution. Usually, however, the current measure will grow to exceed the one in storage before all elements have received values; in this circumstance it becomes pointless to proceed to other elements. When the search either discovers a new solution or bumps up against too large a measure, it then retreats back to preceding elements, substitutes new values, and attempts to find another solution. It continues in this manner until all possible configurations of values and elements have been exhausted. Upon completion, the solution in storage becomes truly optimal.

If the cumulative measure is not very discriminating, the result will be substantially affected both by the order in which the search considers

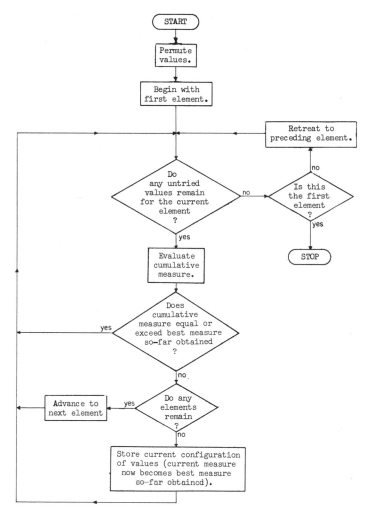

Figure 16.4
Flow of exhaustive search

elements and by the orders in which values are considered for each element. In some applications it may therefore be desirable to permute elements, values (as in figure 16.4), or both, randomly.

Generating the Material

I have already described the rhythmic material of *Protocol*, the 32 rates of pulsation. Following from the rhythmic conception of the work, the 32 chords are all dissonant, so as to bring each pulse into relief. Each chord also provides sufficient tonal resources for internal contrast while retaining its own identity against the other chords.[3]

The web of logarithmic curves illustrated in figure 16.5 determined voicings for each chord. This web spreads chord in lower registers more widely than chords in each registers—four octaves in the lowest extreme versus two octaves in the highest—to maintain uniform clarity of relationships between pitches. When sequences of pitches are widely spaced in register, we generally perceive them as having a chordal, rather than melodic, character; here, the wide span of each voicing impresses a vertical orientation upon the ear as the chord arpeggiates.[4] A tolerance of three semitones to either side of the curve provided flexibility in adapting this registral information to other criteria. Since there are 7 curves (that is, 7 voices per chord) and since this tolerance results in 7 possible pitches around a curve, there was a repertory of $7^7 = 823,543$ possible candidates for each chord.

The protocol of tests used to evaluate these candidates greatly emphasized considerations of dissonance, but they also included tests to contrast adjacent chords in the sequence. Highest in significance was a proscription against assigning the same degree of the chromatic scale to more than one voice. Next came a rule against three contiguous voices forming either a major or minor triad. Contiguous diminished triads or triads with two perfect intervals (e.g., C–F–Bb) followed. Subsequent tests discouraged the sharing of chromatic degrees by many chords in succession, certain instances of parallel voice-leading, and so on.

My technique for measuring a chord with respect to multiple, prioritized tests worked as follows: Assume a protocol of N tests. Let F_n be the number of times a chord fails the nth test in the protocol. Let A be the maximum possible value of F_n for any n and for any chord. Add one to this value to include the case where a chord meets the test perfectly. Expression 1 then weights each F_n so that the weighted number will swamp all possible

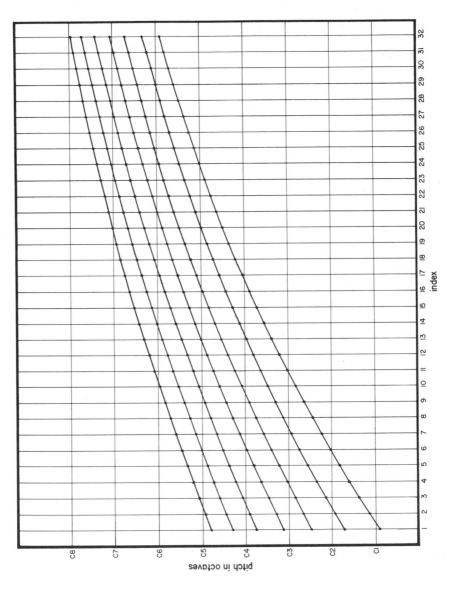

Figure 16.5
Voicings

contributions from less significant tests in the protocol—even when a chord fails all of these less significant tests in every possible way.

$$\sum_{1 \leq n \leq N} F_n \cdot (A + 1)^{N-n} \tag{1}$$

Expression 1 enabled CHORDS to compare any two candidates for a given chord in such a manner that whenever both candidates equally met all tests preceding the nth one in the protocol, CHORDS favored the candidate meeting the nth test more consistently. For example, suppose a pair of candidates both had 7 distinct chromatic degrees (test 1) and both contained an identical number of contiguous major or minor triads (test 2). Suppose further that the first candidate contained two contiguous diminished triads—or triads with two perfect intervals—while the second contained only one (test 3). Then expression 1 would have favored the latter.

Often it was possible to eliminate many candidates in a single stroke, thanks to the cumulative nature of the measure. Suppose for example that at some point CHORDS found a candidate with 7 distinct chromatic degrees (test 1) and no contiguous triads of the types listed above (tests 2 and 3). Then from that point onward the search could apply alpha-beta pruning to reject any partial chord as soon is one unacceptable triad was detected. If it discovered that its tentative selections for the first three pitches were a G, an Eb, and a C, then it could reject the entire class of candidates containing these first three pitches. From all 823,543 candidates, my personal computer could usually produce an optimal chord in a matter of minutes—not impressive by computer standards, but quite competitive with manual efforts. Figure 16.6 presents the results of all 32 searches.

Organizing the Material

The fact that the four components of a module appear consistently together in figure 16.1 provided a welcome opportunity to control typical progressions in advance of specific decisions. Having MODULE organize chords into complementary groups insured that the later stage of composing the median form (implemented by PROGRS) would be able to draw upon resources worthy of its discrimination. It was also necessary at this point to select characteristic dynamics and articulations for each module. Since the global form first presents modules 1 through 8 sequen-

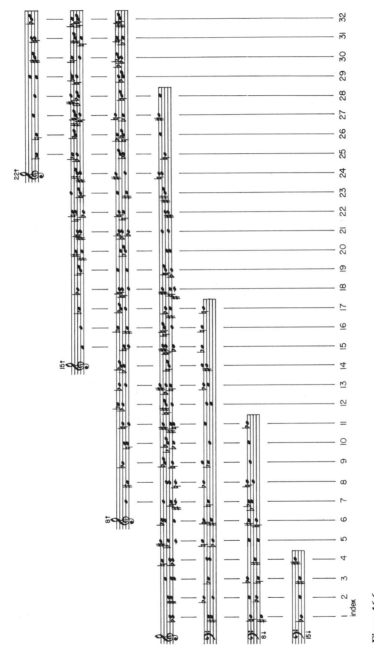

Figure 16.6
Chordal material

Table 16.2
Rates in the eight modules

module 1	55	(8)	114	(16)	125	(17)	256	(25)
module 2	51	(7)	104	(15)	137	(18)	280	(26)
module 3	46	(6)	95	(14)	149	(19)	306	(27)
module 4	42	(5)	87	(13)	163	(20)	335	(28)
module 5	39	(4)	80	(12)	179	(21)	366	(29)
module 6	35	(3)	73	(11)	196	(22)	401	(30)
module 7	32	(2)	66	(10)	214	(23)	438	(31)
module 8	29	(1)	61	(9)	234	(24)	480	(32)

tially, in an expository manner, I cultivated a module-to-module progression of increasing disparities, holding off the more dramatic contrasts until later in the sequence.

Distributing Rates among Modules Table 16.2 shows which modules contain which rates. It details each rate both in pulses per minute and, in parentheses, as an ordinal position in the sequence from the slowest rate to the fastest. I first selected this arrangement manually. Then, feeling I should be truer to the comparative approach, I developed a measure of rhythmic disparity in a module and implemented an exhaustive search (program TEMPI) to select an arrangement for me. The result was the same.

Distributing Chords among Modules In order for each chord to exert its own identity as fully as possible within a module—or within one of the groups of modules shown in figure 16.2—I had MODULE suppress the most blatant common-degrees linkages between chords in the same group. This procedure involved first developing a way of measuring such linkages over a collection of chords. MODULE then used this measure to evaluate alternative ways of arranging 32 chords into two mutually exclusive collections of 16 chords each. For collections of this size it was simply not feasible to evaluate *all* possible arrangements; my recourse was to generate many arrangements randomly and take the best of these random candidates. Next, MODULE exhaustively evaluated ways of arranging each group of 16 chords into two collections of 8 chords each, for a total of four 8-chord groups. Finally, it divided each 8-chord group into two 4-chord groups, with the net result of one 4-chord group for each module.

I derived my measure of common-degree relationships as follows: Assume each collection under scrutiny has M chords. It was not necessary to examine pairs of chords with any regard to order, since to say that one chord should lead but not follow another would have been contrary to my stated intention of making all components structurally equivalent. Thus given two equally sized collections of chords, I only needed to insure this requirement: if the number of pairs sharing k degrees was the same in both collections for each k greater than some number n, and if the first collection had fewer pairs sharing n degrees than the second collection, then the first collection would receive the lower measure. Expression 2 gives an appropriate weighting factor W for the above requirement, as the number of unordered pairs in a collection of M elements, plus 1:

$$W = \frac{M!}{2!(M-2)!} + 1 = \frac{M(M-1)}{2} + 1 \tag{2}$$

Now, let C_n be the number of pairs in the collection sharing exactly n degrees of the chromatic scale, then expression 3 weights C_n so that even if every pair of chords in the collection shared $n - 1$ degrees, the contribution C_{n-1} would make to expression 3 would still be less than the contribution C_n would make, if positive:

$$\sum_{1 \leq n \leq 7} C_n \cdot W^{n+1} \tag{3}$$

MODULE evaluated potential arrangements by measuring each half of the total group and by using the maximum of the two measures to characterize the whole arrangement. It then compared this value to the best measure so far obtained. Whenever the old measure exceeded the new one, the new arrangement became the standard.

Figure 16.7 illustrates the common-degree linkages between the chords of modules 3 and 4, respectively. Under each chord is an index showing the chord's position in the sequence of figure 16.6. It will be instructive to compare these two modules using expression 3; however, readers should remember that the actual search judged each of these illustrated collections to be optimal and that intermodular comparisons were not at issue. Since both collections have 4 chords each, we obtain $W = (4(4 - 1)/2) + 1 = 7$. Module 3 therefore has a measure of

$$0.7^0 + 1.7^1 + 3.7^2 + 1.7^3 + 1.7^4 + 0.7^5 + 0.7^6 = 2898,$$

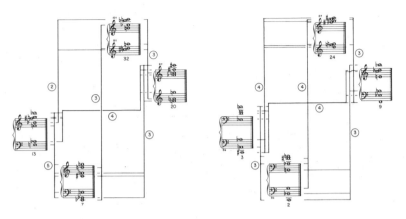

Figure 16.7
Common degrees in module 3 and module 4

while module 4 has a measure of

$$0.7^0 + 0.7^1 + 3.7^2 + 3.7^3 + 0.7^4 + 0.7^5 + 0.7^6 = 1176.$$

Notice that the rightmost nonzero term swamps all other terms in the two polynomials above. Had both collections been vying for the same module, MODULE would have judged the chords of module 4 superior to those of module 3, because module 4 has no pairs sharing five degrees while module 3 has one such pair. It does not matter that module 3 has a pair sharing only two degrees while module 4 has none; this measure does not sacrifice tonal contrast within a single pair to improve results for the remainder. Only when two measures have equal high-order terms do lower order terms take on significance.

Having divided the 32 chords recursively into groups of 16, 8, and 4 chords, MODULE exhaustively shuffled these groups around, always maintaining the hierarchical organization of figure 16.2, until it found the best progression of registral disparities. In the final sequence, the chords of module 1 have the most similar registers. As the sequence proceeds, the contrast between registers becomes more apparent. MODULE also assigned one chord to each of the rates in table 16.2, avoiding any correspondence between particular extremes of rate and particular extremes of register. Figure 16.8 presents the result, indicating rates in pulses per minute and chords according to their registral indices in figure 16.6.

Module	Articulation	Dynamics	Rates	Chords
1		$mf-f$	55	18
			114	22
			125	28
			256	30
2		$mp-mf$	104	10
			51	11
			280	14
			137	26
3		$p-mp$	149	7
			306	13
			46	20
			95	32
4		$mp-mf$	335	2
			163	3
			87	9
			42	24
5		$ppp-pp$ (una corda)	80	16
			366	21
			39	23
			179	29
6		$f-ff$	35	4
			196	5
			73	12
			401	25
7		$pp-p$ (una corda)	438	8
			66	15
			214	17
			32	31
8		$ff-fff$	234	1
			29	6
			480	19
			61	27

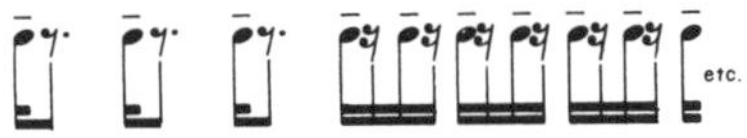

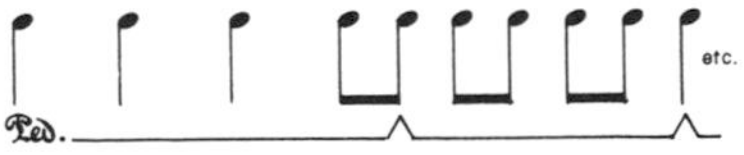

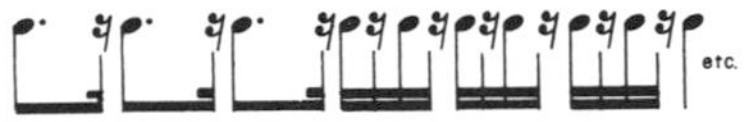

Figure 16.8
The eight modules

Selecting Ancillary Attributes for Modules   The major perceptual factor establishing the eight modules as familiar entities is their consistent proximity in the music. However, the components of a module also share a characteristic dynamic range and mode of articulation. Figure 16.8 details these characteristic attributes in addition to listing rates and chords. The attributes assigned to modules 5–8 are more disparate than those assigned to modules 1–4, in spirit with the other progressions of the sequence.

Composing the Global Form

The global form of *Protocol* has already been presented in figure 16.1 and in its accompanying discussion. I composed this sequence of modules manually with the expository principle in mind and with the intent of suggesting the hierarchical relationships shown in figure 16.2.

Composing the Median Form

Composing the forms of *Protocol* at the median level of design involved assigning to each unit of a packet one component drawn from the appropriate module. This process was undertaken in three stages. The first median stage, implemented by PACKET, was to determine *how often* each component would appear in a packet. The demands of sustaining interest over a long piece required that the material vary in its distribution around the form. In particular, while each packet would only exploit components from the appropriate module, different packets drawing material from the same module would not duplicate one another exactly. The second median stage, implemented by PROGRS, determined the *order* in which these components would appear. Here, my concern that each new rate of pulsation enter assertively led to a search for progressions of greatest tonal contrast. The third median stage, implemented by PULSES, selected a dynamic for each unit and determined how long a unit would last, in pulses.

Selecting Material for Packets   Table 16.3 gives the number of units occurring in each of the packets shown in figure 16.1. Notice the 4 × 4 arrays resulting when one tacks either modules 1–4 or modules 5–8, as a group, against either packets 1–4 or packets 5–8, also as a group. Each row and column in these 4 × 4 arrays contains one 3, two 4s, and one 5. This arrangement helped balance the placement of values with respect

Table 16.3
Lengths of packets

Module	Packet							
	1	2	3	4	5	6	7	8
1	5	4	4	3	4	5	3	4
2	4	5	3	4	4	3	5	4
3	4	3	5	4	3	4	4	5
4	3	4	4	5	5	4	4	3
5	5	3	4	4	3	4	4	5
6	4	4	3	5	4	3	5	4
7	3	5	4	4	4	5	3	4
8	4	4	5	3	5	4	4	3

both to sequences of packets representing the same module and to sequences of packets representing distinct, but associated, modules.

The process of selecting components for packets dealt with each module independently and isolated packets 1–4 for a module from packets 5–8. Within this limited scope, PACKET created a list with sixteen entries representing the module's four components four times in random order. Drawing its candidates from this randomized list, PACKET then searched for a sequence of components fitting the following three constraints:

1. When there were only 3 units in a packet, no component could repeat within that packet.

2. When there were 4 units, up to one component could repeat, but it could not occur more than twice.

3. When there were 5 units, up to two components could repeat, but neither could occur more than twice.

These constraints had the objective of insuring diverse material within individual packets while also allowing variety from packet to packet.

A constrained (depth-first) search of this nature is both quicker and simpler than a fully exhaustive search; however, the algorithm for a constrained search closely resembles the one charted in figure 16.4. One needs only to dispense with the cumulative measure, forsaking advancement to the next element whenever a constraint is violated, and to terminate the search as soon as it has assigned a legal value to every element.

Chordal Progression It was insufficient to let the chords progress arbitrarily within a packet. While MODULE encouraged a fair amount of tonal contrast between chords in a module, chords 7 and 13 in module 3 (see figure 16.7) demonstrate that some combinations remain much less effective than others. In order to present modulations between rates assertively, I worked out a procedure that would avoid using pairs such as these consecutively in a packet. This procedure worked as follows: PROGRS initially selected the first component for the leftmost packet in figure 16.1 at random from module 1. It then proceeded to step through packets, evaluating every possible assignment of components to unit 2 of the current packet, to unit 3, and so on, while also evaluating components for unit 1 of the *next* packet. The measure used to evaluate progressions was similar to the one used to distribute chords to modules. The objective here, however, was to suppress the most blatant cases where two *consecutive* chords shared many chromatic degrees; the tonal environment of the module accounted for relationships between nonconsecutive chords.

Dynamics and the Number of Pulses Two attributes not completely determined for a unit by its assigned component or by the corresponding module both substantially affect the contextual emphasis of material in *Protocol*: the dynamic and the number of pulses. This latter is the final determinate of rhythm. Although dynamics are an effective means of emphasis in a local context, the ear adjusts to dynamics over time. Rhythmic emphasis, especially repetition, is a much more potent means of bringing musical ideas into relief against their surroundings.

Because no component of any module exerts structural priority over any other component, it was desirable to keep the emphasis upon various components in balance. This attitude led me to devise methods of distributing dynamics and numbers of pulses to individual units, methods that would treat all gradations uniformly in two ways: (1) in each packet, and (2) over the complete set of occurrences for each component of a module. (My image of each rate as an "independent frame of reference" precluded balancing units with respect to duration.) The program responsible both for distributing dynamics and for distributing pulses—PULSES—used a strategy quite different from the searches used in other stages of *Protocol*'s genesis. This strategy involved setting up a matrix

Component		Unit							
rate	chord	1	2	3	4	5	6	7	8
333	2	*mf*	*mp*	*mp*	*mf*	*mf*	*mp*	*mp*	*mf*
163	3	*mf*	*mp*	*mf*	*mp*	*mf*	*mf*	*mp*	*mp*
87	9	*mp*	*mf*	*mf*	*mp*	*mp*	*mp*	*mf*	*mf*
42	24	*mp*	*mf*	*mp*	*mf*	*mp*	*mf*	*mf*	*mp*

Figure 16.9
Dynamics for module 4

representing all gradations in each row and column, then permuting the rows and columns at random.

The matrix for dynamics held sixteen entries arranged in the following 4×4 pattern:

```
0  0  1  1
0  1  0  1
1  1  0  0
1  0  1  0
```

These entries represented the lower (0) and the higher (0) of the two dynamics characterizing the module, as listed in figure 16.8. Each module required a random permutation of rows and columns for packets 1–4 and a second permutation for packets 5–8. Figure 16.9 details what this process yielded for module 4: chord 2's first occurrence is played *mf*; its second occurrence is *mf*; chord 9's first occurrence is *mp*; its second occurrence is *mf*; and so on.

Figure 16.10 illustrates the functions used to transform uniformly distributed values between zero and unity into discrete numbers of pulses. The various minima and maxima indicated beneath the sequence of packets in figure 16.1 determined which function from figure 16.10 would be applied to any specific unit. My concern in selecting values to drive these functions was not only that consecutive units within a packet receive their fair share of low and high values, but also that any nonconsecutive group of eight units drawing material from the same packet would also receive its fair share. I could not trust the random number generator to produce

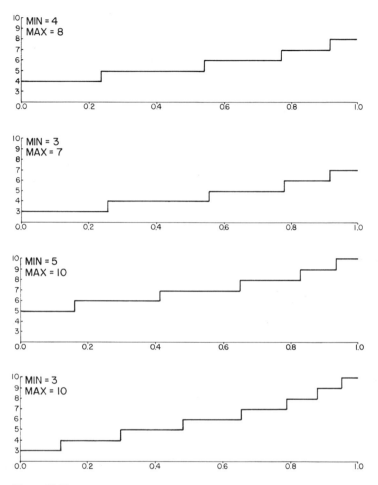

Figure 16.10
Statistical transforms controlling the number of pulses in a unit

UNIVERSITY OF HOUSTON
MUSIC LIBRARY
106 FINE ARTS BLDG.
HOUSTON, TX 77204-4893

suitable values directly, so instead I divided the interval from zero to unity into segments of length 1/8. Next I represented each of these eight segments exactly once in each row and each column of an 8 × 8 matrix. One edge of this matrix corresponded to two sets of four components in a pair of associated modules (module 1 was paired with module 2, module 3 with 4, etc.), while the other edge corresponded to the eight units. Permuting rows and columns at random eliminated all implications of sequential causality divorced from the work's stated concerns.

Composing the Local Form

The first step in composing a sonority for a pulse was to choose the number of pitches in the sonority. In most cases, COMPOS selected a number K uniformly from 2, 3, and 4. Since there were only seven pitches per chord, however, it was necessary to make a special exception following a four-pitch sonority. In this situation, PULSES set K to either 1 or 2.

The next steps were to shuffle the seven pitches into random order and then to exhaustively consider ways of selecting K distinct pitches from this shuffled list. The protocol of tests used to evaluate these selections most greatly emphasized the practical problem of keeping sonorities within the reach of a pianist's hands. Tests of descending significance encouraged tonal contrast with preceding sonorities, dissonance, and assertive voice-leading. For example, one high-priority test discouraged sonorities in which every chromatic degree had been anticipated in the preceding two sonorities. Other tests discouraged consonant triads, horizontal octaves, and blatant parallelism. In a substantial majority of instances no candidate met all tests perfectly, so COMPOS had to provide the best compromise. However, when this compromise had three or more pitches, yet failed to satisfy even the most significant tests—roughly the tests of practicality and dissonance, combined with the test described above against too many anticipated degrees—COMPOS reduced K by one and tried again.

Figures 16.11a and b illustrate the final product of all stages of production, as manifest in measures 399–422 of *Protocol*. This music initiates the sixth of the seven sections marked off in figure 16.1. It exploits material from modules 4, 3, and 5, in that order. The notation approximates all rhythms in divisions of a strict quarter note. The analytic strip underneath each system of music indicates rates, chords, and modules according to the conventions established in figure 16.8.

Closing Remarks

This chapter has had three objectives: first, to present the more significant features of a work that I feel attains artistic standards of contemporary literature for the piano, regardless of its genesis; second, to describe some potent new techniques for composing music by computer; and third, to illustrate—through example—a methodology of automated composition that enables a composer to use technology in an artistically meaningful way. This methodology encompasses three phases of creation:

1. Motivation: Conception of the work's compositional image or focus.

2. Design: Determination of stylistic principles and of a form suitable for projecting this image.

3. Production: Development of automated procedures to realize the above style and form by computer.

I like to believe that the first two of these phases happen independently of the machine. However elaborate or sophisticated a generative process may be, it is the result that matters, and we must ultimately judge any composition according to aesthetic, rather than technical, criteria. It is quite possible for the last step to influence the first ones positively, as when practical limitations force one to refine a concept, to eliminate extraneous concerns, or to discover creative solutions one would not otherwise have considered. What is equally likely, however, is that one's imagined limitations turn out in truth to signal deficiencies in programming technique. To assume such limitations at the outset is to preclude all imperatives to overcome them.

The responsibility for all three phases remains firmly with the composer. In the case of the programming (phase 3), solutions of compositional and technical problems are often inextricably linked. Works composed using generic "utilities" for generating musical scores are therefore of dubious propriety. How can one truly claim authorship to a work whose entire genesis is pervasively conditioned by some independent programmer's a priori assumptions about what constitutes a musical idea, about how such an idea grows into a tangible composition, and about what vocabulary of techniques and operations should facilitate that growth? If one accepts composition as a creative act, one can make no such claim.

Protocol received its first performance on November 8 at the 1981 International Computer Music Conference in Denton, Texas. The pianist

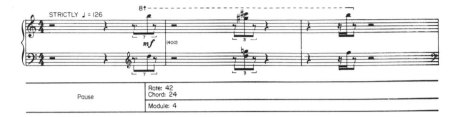

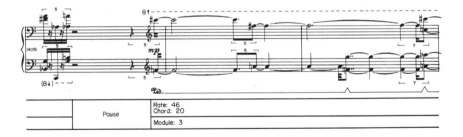

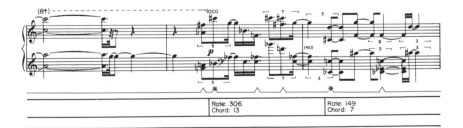

Figure 16.11a
Charles Ames, *Protocol*, measures 399–410. Copyright Charles Ames 1981.

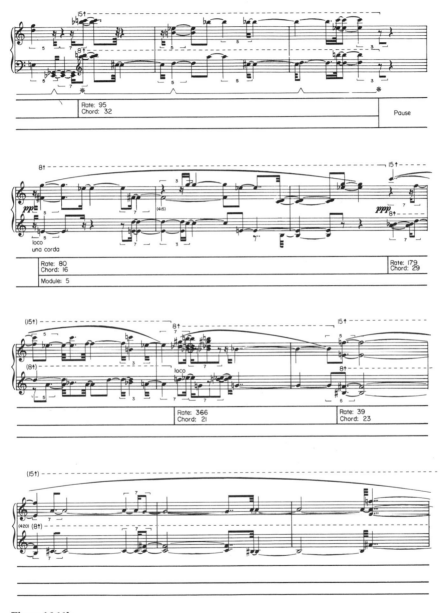

Figure 16.11b
Charles Ames, *Protocol*, measures 411–422. Copyright Charles Ames 1981.

was Jack Behrens, Dean of the Faculty of Music at the University of Western Ontario, Canada. As an expression of my warm appreciation for the great amount of time and effort Jack Behrens expended to prepare this lengthy and difficult score, I have dedicated *Protocol* to him.

Acknowledgments

I would like to thank Lejaren Hiller and John Myhill for their encouragement and their many helpful suggestions toward preparing this article.

Notes

1. This approach parallels the chess-playing strategies which gave birth to artificial intelligence (Shannon, 1950). A more immediate influence was Kemal Ebcioglu's 1980 program for two-part species counterpoint over a cantus firmus, which used a constrained search and did not optimize its solutions.

2. In considering the factors binding musical elements into larger perceptual aggregates, I was strongly guided by Tenney's 1961 applications of Gestalt psychology to musical experience.

3. I use the word "tonal" here in its most general sense, to denote concepts relating to "tone" or to degree, rather than key.

4. Robert Erickson's 1975 discussion of perceptual "channelling" (an insight from Gestalt psychology) was influential here and elsewhere.

References

Ames, Charles, 1982. "*Crystals*: Recursive structures in automated composition," *Computer Music Journal* vol. 6, no. 3, pp. 46–64.

Ebcioglu, Kemal, 1980. "Computer Counterpoint," *Proceedings of the 1980 International Computer Music Conference* (San Francisco: Computer Music Association).

Erickson, Robert, 1975. *Sound Structure in Music* (Berkeley: University of California Press), pp. 117–119.

Hiller, Lejaren, and Leonard Isaacson, 1959. *Experimental Music* (New York: McGraw-Hill).

Knuth, Donald, and Ronald Moore, 1975. "An analysis of alpha-beta pruning," *Artificial Intelligence* vol. 6, no. 4.

Ligeti, György, 1958. "Pierre Boulez: Entscheidung und Automatik in der Structure Ia," *Die Reihe*, no. 4 (Universal Edition).

Shannon, Claude, 1950. "Automatic Chess Player," *Scientific American*, vol. 182, no. 48.

Tenney, James, 1961. META + HODOS: *A Phenomenology of 20th Century Musical Materials and an Approach to the Study of Form* (Berkeley: Frog Peak Music).

Xenakis, Iannis, 1971. "Free stochastic music by computer," chapter V of *Formalized Music* (Bloomington: Indiana University Press).

Ebcioglu's expert system CHORAL, implemented in his own Backtracking Specification Language (BSL), harmonizes chorales in the style of J. S. Bach. CHORAL takes a chorale melody as input and gives as output the harmonization of the chorale in conventional notation and a hierarchical voice-leading analysis in "slur-and- notehead notation."

Designed by Ebcioglu to render more efficiently the significant backtracking required for generating tonal music, BSL represents a logical programming language. A feature of BSL—its representation of subprograms as assertions to be proved—allows the convenient scheduling of multiple generate-and-test processes.

"Multiple viewpoints" of the compositional process define Ebcioglu's approach to harmonizing a chorale. For each "viewpoint," CHORAL divides logical assertions into three groups: production rules, constraints, and heuristics.

To divide the chorale harmonization into manageable units, Ebcioglu represents such viewpoints as chord-skeleton view, fill-in view, time-slice view, melodic-string view, and Schenkerian analysis view. Cyclical scheduling of the viewpoint processes themselves defines CHORAL's overall process.

Ebcioglu reports that in tests of over 70 chorales, CHORAL's level of competence "approaches that of a talented student of music." While not claiming the cognitive accuracy of the CHORAL model, results included in the chapter demonstrate characteristic musical output as well as the ability to bypass rules, for example, the rule against parallel fifths in chorale no. 75, in appropriate situations.

17 An Expert System for Harmonizing Four-Part Chorales

Kemal Ebcioglu

In this chapter, we will report on a rule-based expert system called CHORAL for harmonization and Schenkerian analysis of chorales in the style of J. S. Bach. We will first briefly compare our approach with some current trends in algorithmic composition and music analysis, and we then will describe the CHORAL system itself.

Overview of Current Approaches to Algorithmic Music

Quite a few trends in algorithmic composition today are based on a streamlined formalism, for example, in the form of random generation of note attributes using elegant statistical distributions (Xenakis 1971), terse and powerful formal grammars (Jones 1981), elegant mathematical models (Kendall 1981, Vaggione 1984), or generalizations of serial composition procedures (Laske 1981). The economy and elegance of the formal representation underlying these musical styles (which are not in the least less respectable than traditional styles of music), may often have an aesthetic appeal in and of themselves. On the other hand, traditional music, and most of modern music, which are usually composed without a computer, do not seem to permit such economical representations. In the traditional style, the typical basic training the composer has to go through in harmony, strict counterpoint, fugue, and orchestration, already imposes a certain minimal complexity on the amount of knowledge required to describe such a style.

Also, many will agree that a similar complexity can be observed in the works of modern "noncomputer" composers like Karlheinz Stockhausen, Pierre Boulez, Gyorgi Ligeti, Jan Rychlik, and Steve Reich (his later compositions). It seems that musical composition is a hard mental task that requires a substantial amount of knowledge, and any serious attempt to simulate "noncomputer" music composition on the computer would have to face the task of constructing a formal model of considerable complexity. In fact, we have found that even the algorithmic representation of the knowledge underlying the seemingly simple Bach chorale style is a task that already borders the intractable.

As for the music analysis field, the prevailing trends seem to emphasize selective and unobvious properties of music; for example, a golden section in some motets of Dufay (Sandreski 1981), or a surprising log-normal distribution in the dissonances within some chorales of Bach (Knopoff and Hutchinson 1981). Even the analysis approaches that capture a profound structure in tonal music, such as reduction techniques (Schenker 1979, Lerdahl and Jackendoff 1983), are still based on finding a selective property (the property that the piece has a plausible parsing). These properties, although interesting in their own right, do not constitute a satisfactory explanation of the music in question, in the sense that there exist many pieces that have these properties, but that have no relationship with the style.

An alternative approach that would perhaps provide a more satisfactory understanding of the music is to attempt to algorithmically generate pieces in the same approximate style. There have already been some attempts at this analysis by synthesis approach to music in some simpler traditional styles, such as folk melodies (Zaripov 1960), or the first two phrases of Bach chorale melodies (Baroni and Jacoboni 1976). But there are two problems associated with extending this approach to more substantial traditional styles. First, it may be difficult to prevent the designer of such a resynthesis algorithm from introducing traits that would distort the style in an unscholarly fashion (this unscholarliness may be trivially removed by resynthesizing only the original pieces of the composer in some interesting way—but we feel that the approach of synthesizing new pieces is also worthwhile). The second and more fundamental problem is that, although there has been good progress in the automated synthesis of sound (Mathews et al. 1969, Roads and Strawn 1985), the automated composition of nontrivial tonal music is to date not sufficiently understood (and is still regarded with some suspicion in the traditional circles). The present research is an attempt to further our understanding of the mechanical generation of music, by extending the analysis by synthesis approach to a more complex style, the style of the Bach chorale harmonizations. To cope with the complexity of the problem, we have developed a rule-based approach inspired from recent research in artificial intelligence, as well as from a heuristic search method that we had used in an earlier, smaller-scale strict counterpoint program (Ebcioglu 1979, 1980).

BSL: An Efficient Logic Programming Language

Perhaps because of its inherent difficulty, the generation of nontrivial tonal music appears to require large computational resources. In typical computing environments, artificial intelligence (AI) languages such as Prolog or Lisp tend to be too slow for implementing our particular approach to the algorithmic generation of music. More efficient languages such as C or Fortran are not viable alternatives, since they in turn tend to be too low-level for the task of coding a large music expert system. At the outset of our research, we decided to represent musical knowledge using first-order predicate calculus; and in order to cope with the large computational requirements of tonal music generation, we have designed BSL (Backtracking Specification Language) (Ebcioglu 1986, 1987a, 1987b, 1988), a new and efficient logic programming language that is fundamentally different from Prolog. From the execution viewpoint, BSL is a nondeterministic Algol-class language where variables cannot be assigned more than once except in controlled contexts. However, BSL has a desirable relationship with first-order predicate calculus that makes it a new kind of logic programming language: namely, each BSL program corresponds to an assertion in first order logic, and executing the BSL program amounts to proving the corresponding assertion. More precisely, the semantics of a BSL program F is defined via a ternary relation Ψ, such that $\Psi(F, \sigma, \tau)$ means program F leads to final state τ when started in initial state σ, where a state is a mapping from variable names to elements of a "computer" universe, consisting of integers, arrays, records. There is a simple mapping $\lambda u[u']$ that translates a BSL program to a formula of a first-order language, such that if a BSL program F terminates in some state σ, then the corresponding first-order formula F' is true in σ (where the truth of a formula in a given state σ is evaluated in a fixed "computer" interpretation involving integers, arrays, records, and operations on these, after replacing any free variables x in the formula by $\sigma(x)$). Thus, successfully executing a BSL program without free variables amounts to constructively proving that the corresponding first-order sentence is true in the fixed computer interpretation, or in all models of a suitably axiomatized theory of integers, arrays, and records.

A formal and rigorous description of BSL, in a style inspired from de Bakker (1979), can be found in Ebcioglu (1987a). To implement BSL on real computers, we wrote a compiler, in Lisp, that translates BSL programs into very efficient backtracking programs in C. Except for a few C routines for reading in the melody and for graphics, the CHORAL expert system has been coded entirely in BSL.

A Knowledge Representation Technique for Music

An ambitious music expert system somehow has to deal with the problem of representing a large amount of complex musical knowledge. Even when one has avoided the approach of coding the rules directly in a conventional language, and one has chosen to represent musical knowledge declaratively, in logic, the complexity of the knowledge base may still be far from being conquered. To represent substantial amounts of musical knowledge in first-order logic, it appears necessary to divide up the logical assertions into groups that observe the music from multiple viewpoints. Using a small and nonredundant set of primitive functions and predicates to represent music, although mathematically appealing, does not seem to be suitable for expressing all the required viewpoints of the music in a natural way. For example, a set of primitive functions $\{p, a, d\}$, that observe each voice as a linear sequence of notes, such that $p(0, v), p(1, v), \ldots, a(0, v), a(1, v), \ldots,$ $d(0, v), d(1, v), \ldots$ are the pitches, accidentals, and durations of the notes of voice v, would certainly be sufficient to describe a simple vocal piece and would also be suitable for expressing horizontal, melodic relationships in each voice; but the same primitives would be somewhat clumsy for expressing vertical, harmonic relationships between voices, since the i'th note of one voice obviously does not in general line up with the i'th note of another voice. Similarly, a large-scale work may require several hierarchical viewpoints that may constitute successively refined plans of the piece. So we opted for a knowledge representation that used *multiple sets of logical primitives* to represent the different viewpoints of the music. Each set of primitives was deliberately made richer than required by incorporating all the musical attributes that we felt we could need while writing rules.

The viewpoints used by our CHORAL system include one that observes the chord skeleton of the chorale, another that observes the individual melodic lines of the different voices, and another that observes the Schenkerian voice leading within the descant and bass. The need for using multiple viewpoints of the solution object has arisen in expert systems in other domains as well—for example, the Hearsay-II chain. Among the processes, there is a specially designated *clock* process, which executes exactly one step when it is scheduled; all other processes depend on inputs produced by this process and thus become blocked whenever they need an input that has not yet been produced by the clock process. Thus, each step of the clock process determines the total amount of work done in one complete trip around the round-robin scheduling chain. The process scheduling paradigm described here is *backtrackable*, as will be explained.

Knowledge Base of the Viewpoints

The knowledge base of each viewpoint is expressed in three groups of logic assertions (BSL subformulas), which determine the way in which the n'th generate-and-test step is executed.

1. Production rules: These are the formal analogs of the production rules that would be found in a production system for a generate-and-test application, such as Stefik's GA1 system that solves a search problem in molecular genetics (Stefik 1978). The informal meaning of a production rule is IF certain conditions are true about the partial solution (elements 0, ..., $n - 1$, and the already assigned attributes of element n) and external data structures, THEN a certain value can be added to the partial solution (assigned to a group of attributes of element n). Their procedural effect is to generate the possible assignments to element n of the solution array.

2. Constraints: These side-effect-free subformulas assert absolute rules about elements 0, ..., n of the solution array and external data structures. They have the procedural effect of rejecting certain assignments to element n of the solution array (this effect is also called *early pruning* in AI literature speech understanding system (Erman et al. 1980) observed the input utterance as mutually consistent streams of syllables, words, and word sequences, and the *constraints* system of (Sussman and Steele 1980) used equivalent circuits for observing a given fragment of an electrical circuit from more than one viewpoint.

We will now describe one possible way of implementing multiple viewpoints of the music in BSL. In this method, which was used in the CHORAL system, each viewpoint is represented by a different data structure, typically an array of records (called the solution array of that viewpoint), which serves as a rich set of primitive pseudofunctions and predicates for that view. This multiple view paradigm has the following procedural aspect: it is convenient to visualize a separate process for each viewpoint, which incrementally constructs (assigns to) its solution array, in close interaction with other processes constructing the irrespective solution arrays. Each process executes a series of generate-and-test steps. At the n'th generate-and-test step of a process, $n = 0, 1, \ldots$, a value is selected and assigned to the n'th element of the solution array of the viewpoint, depending on the elements $0, \ldots, n - 1$ of the same solution array, the currently assigned elements of the solution arrays of other viewpoints, and the program input. The processes behave somewhat like the multiple processes that are scheduled on a single CPU in a time-sharing operating system, and they are arranged in a round-robin scheduling chain. Each process (implemented as a BSL predicate), whenever it becomes active (is given the CPU), first attempts to execute zero or more generate-and-test steps until all of its inputs are exhausted, and then gets blocked, relinquishing the CPU to the next process in the (Hayes-Roth, Waterman and Lenat 1983) since it removes certain paths from the search tree that are guaranteed not to lead to any solution).

3. Heuristics: These side-effect-free subformulas assert desirable properties of the solution elements $0, \ldots, n$ and external data structures. They have the procedural effect of having certain assignments to element n of the solution array tried before others are. The purpose of the heuristics is to guide the search so that the solution first found is hopefully a good solution. Here is how the n'th generate-and-test step of a process is executed: first, all possible assignments to the n'th element of the solution array are generated via the production rules. If a candidate assignment does not comply with the constraints, it is thrown away, otherwise its *worth* is computed by summing the weights of the heuristics that it makes true (the heuristics are weighted by different powers of two, with the most important heuristic having the greatest weight, etc.). Assuming that at least one choice was found for the n'th element, the generate-and-test step is then completed by assigning the best choice to the n'th element of the solution array (with ties being resolved randomly). At the same time, the current state of all the processes and the list of remaining choices for this generate-and-test step are pushed down, so that the current state of all the processes can later be recovered and the execution of the current process can be restarted by choosing the next best alternative for this generate-and-test step. Later on, if an impasse is encountered, that is, some process fails to find any acceptable values for an element of its solution array, control returns to the most recent step among the history of the steps of all the processes, which is estimated to be responsible for the failure. This is not necessarily the immediately preceding step, which could be irrelevant to the failure; BSL uses an intelligent backtracking algorithm. Execution then continues with

the next best choice at the step where the return has been made to (assuming that there is a remaining choice at this step. If there is none, further backtracking occurs.)

The generate-and-test method described here is based on the idea of producing the solution incrementally and backing up where necessary. An alternative search technique in the field of algorithmic music is to repetitively generate (with a nonbacktracking algorithm) a new random solution and test it, until an acceptable solution is found (e.g., Baroni and Jacoboni 1976); but this latter technique is difficult to use when the acceptable solutions are extremely few in comparison to the generable solutions, which we feel is a common situation in complex styles of music. Generate-and-test is a basic search technique used in expert system design (Hayes-Roth, Waterman, Lenat 1983). Studies on other relevant search techniques of artificial intelligence can be found in, for example, (Nilsson 1971, Pearl 1983). This style of incorporating heuristics in a generate-and-test method for producing music, was used in our earlier strict counterpoint program (Ebcioglu 1979, 1980) and was also independently used by B. Schottstaedt in another larger scale, strict counterpoint program (Schottstaedt 1984). (Ames 1983) used a similar technique for generating music in a more contemporary contrapuntal style.

In certain cases a viewpoint may be completely dependent on another, that is, it may not introduce new choices on its own. In the case of such redundant views, it is possible to maintain several views (solution arrays) in a single process, provided that one master view is chosen to execute the process step and comply with the paradigm. This can be done as follows: As soon as a possible assignment to the n'th element of the solution array of the master viewpoint is generated via the production rules of the master viewpoint, the subordinate views are tentatively updated according to this new element of the master viewpoint. The subordinate views may advance by zero, one, or more than one steps, even though the master view advances by one step. Then the constraints and heuristics of the subordinate views are used in conjunction with the constraints and heuristics of the master view in order to determine the acceptability of the current tentative assignment to the n'th element of the master view, and to compute how desirable this assignment is. Note that the subordinate views do not have production rules, since the new addition to the master view completely determines all attributes of the new element(s) of the subordinate views.

In the generate-and-test technique described here, the heuristics constitute the most crucial ingredient for obtaining musical results. It is a known fact that absolute rules, such as those found in a treatise, are not sufficient for producing beautiful music. Composers use much additional knowledge (roughly termed as "talent") for choosing among the "correct" extensions of a partial composition at each stage of the compositional process. While our limited powers of introspection prevent us from replicating the thought process of such choices in an algorithm, we conjecture that a good algorithmic approximation can be obtained by using a large number of prioritized heuristics, or recommendations, based on style-specific musical knowledge. The heuristics used in our music generation algorithm help to prevent the search process from taking correct but unmusical paths (these paths could easily be followed if absolute rules and random search were used alone), and they guide the music in the preferred direction.

The Viewpoints of the CHORAL System

We are now in a position to discuss the knowledge models, or viewpoints, of the CHORAL system. The CHORAL system knowledge base, which was developed over a period of several years, is based on our study of the Bach chorales (Terry 1964), our personal intuitions, and traditional treatises such as (Louis and Thuille 1906, Koechlin 1928). We will give here only a brief overview of the knowledge base of CHORAL, which is in reality very long and complex. The CHORAL system uses the backtrackable process scheduling technique described above to implement the following viewpoints of the chorale: The *chord skeleton* view observes the chorale as a sequence of rhythmless chords and fermatas, with some unconventional symbols underneath them, indicating key and degree within key. This is the clock process, and it produces one chord per step. The primitives of this view allow referencing attributes such as the pitch and accidental of a voice v of any chord n in the sequence of skeletal chords. Although some harmony treatises tend to omit rules about degree transitions (e.g., Dubois 1921), keeping track of the key and degree within key, and imposing careful rules for the transitions between the different degrees, were found to be necessary for maintaining a solid sense of tonality early during our research; since without key and degree information, progressions tend to sound "Gregorian." Similarly, implementing modulations turned out to be no simple matter, and a literal implementation of the definition of modulation as in a treatise was found to be too permissive and to give unacceptable results. Instead, we have implemented a complex set of production rules for generating a set of style-specific modulating progressions, constraints for filtering out the unacceptable modulating progressions, and heuristics for choosing the desirable modulating progressions. The chord skeleton view is the view where we have placed, for example, the production rules that enumerate the possible ways of modulating to a new key, constraints about the preparation and resolution of a seventh in a seventh chord, and heuristics that prefer Bachian cadences.

The *fill-in* view observes the chorale as four interacting automata that change states in lockstep, generating the actual notes of the chorale in the form of suspensions, passing tones, and similar ornamentations, depending on the underlying chord skeleton. For each voice v at fill-in step n, the primitives allow referencing attributes of voice v at a weak eighth beat and an immediately following strong eighth beat, and the new state that voice v enters at fill-in step n (states are suspension, descending passing tone, and normal). At each of its steps, the fill-in view generates the cross product of all possible inessential notes (passing tones, neighbor notes. suspensions other chorale-specific ornamentations) in all the voices, discards the un-acceptable combinations of inessential notes, and selects the desirable combinations, via a complex set of production rules, constraints, and heuristics.

We felt that bold clashes of simultaneous inessential notes were indispensable for achieving the effect of a Bachian harmonic-melodic flow. The harmonization task would have been greatly simplified if we had avoided simultaneous inessential notes, but we felt that we then probably would not obtain music. Note that precise rules about simultaneous inessential notes were not at all readily available: the typical treatise on school harmony gives precise rules on severely restricted forms of simultaneous inessential notes (e.g., Bitsch 1957). In other traditional studies on passing notes in Bach, (e.g., Koechlin 1922, McHose 1947) authors tend to merely give examples of clashes of simultaneous inessential notes from Bach, which the talented music student will nevertheless digest in an unconscious way, but which are not of suitable precision for programming.

The fill-in view reads the chord skeleton output. This is the view where we have placed, for example, the production rules for enumerating the long list of possible inessential note patterns that enable the desirable bold clashes of passing tones, a constraint about not sounding the resolution of a suspension above the suspension, and a heuristic on following a suspension by another in the same voice (a Bachian cliché).

The *time-slice* view observes the chorale as a sequence of vertical time-slices, each of which has a duration of an eighth note, and imposes harmonic constraints. This view is redundant with and subordinate to fill-in. The primitives of this view allow referencing attributes such as the pitch and accidental of a voice v at any time-slice i, and whether a new note of voice v is struck at that time-slice. We have placed, for example, a constraint about consecutive octaves and fifths in this view. The *melodic string* view observes the sequence of individual notes of the different voices from a purely melodic point of view. The primitives of this view allow referencing attributes such as the pitch and accidental of any note i of a voice v. The *merged melodic string* view is similar to the melodic string view, except that the repeated adjacent pitches are merged into a single note. The merged melodic string view was necessary for recognizing and advising against bad melodic patterns that are not alleviated even when there are repeating notes in the pattern. These views are also redundant with, and subordinate to fill-in. These are the views where we have placed, for example, a constraint about sevenths or ninths spanned in three notes, some other highly difficult constraints for enforcing "melodic interest" in the inner voices. (The melodic interest constraint of the merged melodic string view indicates that in any voice, when a note has occurred as a *high corner* [sandwiched between two notes of lower pitch], then it cannot occur as a high corner for at least two measures. Notes that occur in high-corner positions are perceived to be more salient than notes that are, for example, in the middle of a linear progression. This rule prevents the monotony arising from the repetition of the same pitch in the salient high-corner positions.)

The *Schenkerian analysis* view is based on our formal theory of hierarchical voice leading, inspired from Schenker (1979) and also from Lerdahl and Jackendoff (1983). The core of this theory consists of a set of rewriting rules that, when repeatedly applied to a starting pattern, can generate the bass and descant lines of a chorale. The Schenkerian analysis view uses our rewriting rules to find separate parse trees for the the bass and descant lines of the chorale, employing a bottom up parsing method, and using many heuristics for choosing (among the alternative possible actions at each parser step) the action that would hopefully lead to the musically most plausible parsing. Unlike Lerdahl and Jackendoff's theory, which is based on a hierarchy of individual musical events (e.g., chords, noteheads), our theory is based on a hierarchy of slurs and is more in line with Schenker's theory. The discussion of our voice-leading theory is beyond the scope of this paper, and the details can be found in Ebcioglu (1987a).

The Schenkerian analysis view observes the chorale as the sequence of steps of two nondeterministic bottom-up parsers for the descant and bass. This view reads the fill-in output. The primitives of this view allow referencing the output symbols of a parser step n, the new state that is entered after executing step n, and the action on the stack at parser step n. The rules and heuristics of this view belong to a new paradigm of automated hierarchical music analysis and do not correspond to any rules that would be found in a traditional treatise. In this view we have placed, for example, the production rules that enumerate the possible parser actions that can be done in a given state, a constraint about the agreement between the fundamental line accidentals and the key of the chorale, and a heuristic for proper recognition of shallow occurrences of the Schenkerian D–C–B–C ending pattern.

The fill-in, time-slice, and melodic string views are embedded in the same process, with fill-in as the master view among them.

The order or scheduling of processes is cyclical: chord skeleton, fill-in, Schenker-bass, Schenker-descant. Each time chord skeleton is scheduled, it adds a new chord to the chorale; each time fill-in is scheduled, it fills-in the available chords and produces quarterbeats of the actual music until no more chords are available. Each time a Schenker process is scheduled, it executes parser steps until the parser input pointer is less than a lookahead window away from the end of the currently available notes for the descant or bass. (The lookahead window gradually grew bigger as our ideas evolved, and in the recent versions, for the sake of reducing module sizes, we have found it expedient to place the Schenker processes in a separate postprocessing program that reads its input from a file produced by the other views.) When a process does not have any available inputs to enable it to execute any steps when it is scheduled, it simply schedules the next process in the chain without doing anything. The chorale melody is given as input to the program.

Chorale no. 286

Figure 17.1

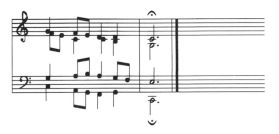

Chorale no. 75

Figure 17.2

Results and Conclusions

BSL and the CHORAL system are presently running on the IBM 3081-3090 computers at the IBM Thomas J. Watson Research Center, under CMS and Lisp/VM and the AT&T C compiler. The program takes as input an alphanumeric encoding of the chorale melody and outputs the harmonization in conventional music notation and the hierarchical voice-leading analysis in slur-and-notehead notation. The output can be viewed on a graphics screen or can be printed. The inputs typically take three to thirty minutes of IBM 3081 CPU time to get harmonized, but some chorales have taken several hours. At the end of the chapter we give two output examples, harmonizations of chorales no. 286, and no. 75 (Terry 1964). In these harmonizations, the voices are not in the proper ranges, but the program writes the harmonizations in such a way that there exists a transposition interval that will bring them to the proper ranges. Note that the parallel fifths between the soprano and tenor accompanying the antici-pation pattern in the soprano at the end of the second phrase of no. 75, are allowable in the Bach chorale style (see, e.g., no. 383 (Terry 1964)). Many more output examples and the complete list of rules of the program can be found in Ebcioglu (1987a). The program has presently been tested on over seventy chorale melodies and has reached an acceptable level of compe-tence in its harmonization capability; we can say that its competence approaches that of a talented student of music who has studied the Bach chorales. While the heuristically guided generate-and-test method described in this paper is not necessarily an accurate cognitive model of the human compositional process, it seems to work, and it seems to be capable of producing musical results. We hope that our techniques will be of use to researchers in algorithmic composition who may be seeking alternative approaches.

Acknowledgments

I am grateful to Professor Lejaren Hiller for encouraging me to study computer music. I am also grateful to the late Professor John Myhill for getting me interested in the mechanization of Schenkerian analysis.

Note

This research was supported by NSF grant DCR-8316665, and a major portion of it was done at the Department of Computer Science, S.U.N.Y. at Buffalo, under the direction of my advisor, the late Prof. John Myhill. A preliminary version of this paper appeared in the proceedings of the 1986 International Computer Music Conference.

References

Ames, C. 1983. "Stylistic Automata in *Gradient*." *Computer Music Journal.*, 7(4):45–56.

Baroni, M. and Jacoboni, C. 1976. *Verso una Grammatica della Melodia*. Università Studi di Bologna.

Bitsch, M. 1957. *Précis d'Harmonie Tonale*. Paris: Alphonse Leduc.

de Bakker, J. 1979. *Mathematical Theory of Program Correctness*. Amsterdam: North Holland.

Dubois, T. 1921. *Traité d'Harmonie Théorique et Pratique*. Paris: Heugel.

Ebcioglu, K. 1979. "Strict Counterpoint: A Case Study in Musical Composition by Computers." M.S. thesis (in English), Department of Computer Engineering. Ankara: Middle East Technical University.

Ebcioglu, K. 1980. "Computer Counterpoint" in H. Howe, ed. *Proceedings of the 1980 International Computer Music Conference*. San Francisco: Computer Music Association.

Ebcioglu, K. 1986. "An Expert System for Chorale Harmonization." *Proceedings of the AAAI-86*. Los Altos: Morgan Kaufmann.

Ebcioglu, K. 1987a. "Report on the CHORAL project: An Expert System for Chorale Harmonization." Research report no. RC 12628, IBM, Thomas J. Watson Research Center, Yorktown Heights, March 1987. (This is a revised version of the author's Ph.D. thesis [1986], "An Expert System for Harmonization of Chorales in the Style of J. S. Bach." Technical Report no. 86–09, Department of Computer Science. S.U.N.Y. at Buffalo.)

Ebcioglu, K. 1987b. "An Efficient Logic Programming Language and its Application to Music." *Proceedings of the 4th International Conference on Logic Programming*. Cambridge, Mass: MIT Press.

Ebcioglu, K. 1990. "An Expert System for Chorale Harmonization in the Style of J. S. Bach." *Logic Programming* 1990:8; pp. 145–185.

Erman, L. D., et. al. 1980. "The Hearsay-II Speech Understanding System: Integrating Knowledge to Resolve Uncertainty." *Computing Surveys* 12(2):213–253.

Hayes-Roth, F., Waterman, D, and Lenat, D. B. (eds.) 1983. *Building Expert Systems*. Reading, Mass.: Addison-Wesley.

Jones, K. 1981. "Compositional Applications of Stochastic Processes" 5(2):45–61.

Kendall, G. S. 1981. "Composing from a Geometric Model: *Five-leaf Rose*." *Computer Music Journal* 5(4):66–73.

Knopoff, L. and L. Hutchinson. 1981. "Information Theory for Musical Continua." *Journal of Music Theory* 25(1).

Koechlin, C. 1922. *Étude sur les Notes de Passage*. Paris: Éditions Max Eschig.

Koechlin, C. 1928. *Traité de l'Harmonie*. Volumes I, II, III. Paris: Éditions Max Eschig.

Laske, O. 1981. "Composition Theory in Koenig's Project One and Project Two." *Computer Music Journal*. 5(4):54–65.

Lerdahl, F. and R. Jackendoff 1983. *A Generative Theory of Tonal Music*. Cambridge, MA: MIT Press.

Louis, R. and L. Thuille, 1906. *Harmonielehre*. Stuttgart: C. Grüninger.

Mathews, M. V., et. al. 1969. *The Technology of Computer Music.* Cambridge, MA: MIT Press.

McHose, A. I. 1947. *The Contrapuntal Harmonic Technique of the 18th Century.* Englewood Cliffs: Prentice-Hall.

Nilsson, N. J. 1971. *Problem Solving Methods in Artificial Intelligence.* New York: McGraw-Hill.

Pearl, J. (ed.) 1983. *Artificial Intelligence* 21. Special Issue on Search and Heuristics.

Roads, C. and J. Strawn (eds.) 1985. *Foundations of Computer Music.* Cambridge, MA: MIT Press.

Sandresky, M. V. 1981. "The Golden Section in Three Byzantine Motets of Dufay." *Journal of Music Theory.* 25(2).

Schenker, H. 1979. *Free Composition (Der freie Satz)* Trans. and ed. by Ernst Oster. New York: Longman Press.

Schottstaedt, B. 1984. "*Automatic Species Counterpoint.*" CCRMA, Report no. STAN-M-19, Stanford: Department of Music, Stanford University.

Stefik, M. 1978. "Inferring DNA Structures from Segmentation Data" *Artificial Intelligence.* 11:85–114.

Sussman, G. J. and G. L. Steele, 1980. "Constraints—A Language For Expressing Almost-Hierarchical Descriptions." *Artificial Intelligence* 14:1–39.

Terry, C. S. (ed.) 1964. *The Four-voice Chorals of J. S. Bach.* Oxford: Oxford University Press.

Vaggione, H. 1984. "Fractal C" *Program notes.* International Computer Music Conference, Paris, October 1984.

Xenakis, I. 1971. *Musique-Architecture.* Casterman.

Xenakis, I. 1974. *Formalized Music.* Bloomington: Indiana University Press.

Zaripov, R. K. 1960. "On Algorithmic Expression of Musical Compositions." Doklady, Akademii Nauk, 132(6).

Cope describes his Experiments in Music Intelligence (EMI) project. To understand algorithmic composing in various styles, EMI projects focus on the stylistic replication of individual composers.

The discussion pertains to the EMI modeling projects in three contexts: possibilities, examples, and usefulness. EMI's generated styles include Albinoni, Mozart, Brahms, and Debussy.

Defining compositional style largely as the adjustments to "inherited material," Cope focuses on reused ideas within a given composer's works. EMI's paradigm for a given composer requires the input of at least two compositions in a similar style.

Analysis of two or more stylistically similar compositions determines "musical signatures" and compositional rules. To determine the musical signatures of a composition, EMI maps it by pitch and duration to a similar composition; frequency weights of patterns shared in common by the compositions then create a stylistic "image" of the composition. To analyze compositional rules, EMI compiles statistics of voice-leading characteristics, for example, the use of repeated notes, independent of the musical signatures.

EMI composes by fixing signatures in a given stylistic framework and composing music in an Augmented Transition Network (ATN) between the musical signatures according to the constraints determined in the rule-analysis phase. Characteristic output in a given style thus represents a typical departure for the composer.

18 A Computer Model of Music Composition

David Cope

Experiments in Music Intelligence (EMI) began in 1981 as an algorithmic composing tool. Work has centered on approaches to the understanding of musical style. Replication of various composers' styles is the essence of the work at EMI. Ultimately, tools thus created should be useful for composers, theorists, and musicians.

Computers at EMI have thus far successfully replicated music in the styles of a number of composers (Cope 1987, 1988, 1989, 1990). It may now be useful to look closely at the models used for these purposes to discover if they in fact parallel those of human composers and if so, what these models tell us about how we listen to music, how we should analyze music, and even how we think about and understand music. To these ends, this chapter describes: (1) possibilities of computer composition, (2) examples of computer composition, and (3) the usefulness of computers composing music.

Possibilities of Computer Composition

A Composing Paradigm

Composers invest in each of their works a combination of new and inherited materials. New materials are created by inspiration. Codifying inspiration in terms of computational means seems improbable, even impossible. Inherited materials, however, consist of ideas proven successful over a period of time and include traditional gestures of other composers (as in "common practice") as well as once-original ideas. Defining processes of inheritance in machine terms seems a logical and practical goal. It can be accomplished by searching many works for repeated and almost repeated ideas. In terms of machine composition, they can then be reused in order to replicate a composer's style.

A Machine Model

One of the many algorithms of the EMI program is shown in figure 18.1. It consists of two major branches. The left-hand branch consists of a pattern matching process. The patterns or motives thus discovered are considered to be signatures. The right-hand branch consists of a rules analyzer that discovers the constraints used in the music provided as a

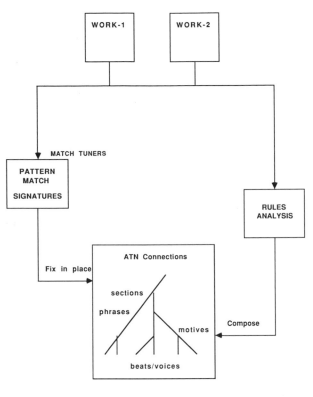

Figure 18.1

database. Composing using this algorithm is achieved by (1) "fixing" signatures in an otherwise empty work, and (2) connecting them with newly created music based on the rules analysis. Proper interpolation of this new music relies on an "augmented transition network" (ATN) (see Cope 1990). The ATN operates hierarchically by building the new work top-down. This is shown in figure 18.1 as a tree of successively smaller musical increments: sections down to voices.

The Process in More Detail

1. Use real music in a given style. While it may seem obvious, it must be noted that the music that is entered into this program must have both rules and signatures (i.e., style). The program can detect rules and signa-

Figure 18.2

tures only to the extent that they are present in the original works. A minimum of two works of a single style must be present before EMI can emulate it. The more closely the works resemble one another in terms of meter, tactus, mode, etc., the more stylistically faithful will be the program's output. Also, the more examples of a particular style present, the more convincingly the program imitates it. Music is coded into memory as numbers representing pitches and durations. The style of the music under analysis must therefore reside in these two categories (i.e., pitch and duration). Musical styles that are distinguished principally by their timbral or dynamic qualities are not susceptible to analysis in this program.

2. Make the examples compatible.   The works of music entered into the database will have a number of similarities and dissimilarities. In order to make the similarities clear, the works must be forced to conform with each other in certain respects, with one of them (arbitrarily the first) being used as the standard.

On the simplest level, this means eliminating pitches shorter than a certain duration. Typically notes less a sixteenth in duration are shed to make pattern matching easier. On a more complex level, the rhythm must be synchronized. Figures 18.2a and 18.2b should clarify this. The first example (from Mozart's Sonata K. 279, first movement) is predominantly in sixtieth notes, while the second (from Mozart's familiar Sonata K. 545, first movement) is in eighth notes. Because of differences in duration of the notes in each piece, almost nothing matches. However, if the second example is rhythmically transposed, as shown in figure 18.2c, relationships become evident. For example, the opening five notes in the left hand, with the appropriate allowances for pitch variation, have similarity.

The mode must also be made to match. If the first composition entered is in a major key and the second in a minor key, the second must be made major. Patterns are also easier to detect if both works are in the same key, the key of C major being most logical.

3. Pattern match for signatures. Pattern matching is a powerful technique for attempting to discover the reasons why composer's styles are distinctive. Pattern-matching is achieved through a process of "almost" matching, since in music perceived patterns are rarely exactly the same. This is accomplished by setting a series of "tuners," each of which signifies the amount of variation that can exist for a match to be captured. Patterns that occur in different works of a composer constitute signatures.

These patterns are recognized by shape and size, allowing for intervening pitches and other variations. They are analyzed in three different ways: pitch alone, rhythm alone, and pitch and rhythm together. These enable EMI to discover patterns in materials where widely varying pitch or rhythms have been employed for variation. Patterns are weighted by how often they appear. Hence, what is called an "image" of a work is formed. An image is the result of a full-scale pattern matching of an entire composition. It consists of frequency lists of captured patterns.

When two or more images have been completed, EMI superimposes them to reveal an important distinction. First it discovers which patterns are local to a given work (i.e., patterns and variations related only to the *thematic* peculiarities of one of the stored works). These will not increase significantly in number during superimposition. Then EMI tags any of the patterns whose number of occurrences has increased significantly in the superimposition. These are, by definition, *signatures* of the composer's style.

4. Musical rules analysis. Next, a rules analysis takes place. This is a series of mathematical subprograms that compute percentages of certain aspects of music such as voice leading directions, use of repeated notes, triad outlining, leaps followed by steps, etc. Unlike pattern matching, the constraint analysis is not concerned with signatures. It merely counts musical events and represents them as a statistical model of the works being analyzed.

The results of the rules analysis are used to compose music that conforms to the melodic, harmonic, and voice-leading rules present in the music in the database. It contributes "correct" but styleless music between the signatures (see 6—"Recompose using constraint analysis"). Most important, it relieves the machine-composed music from becoming too intensely saturated with signatures.

5. Fix signatures in an empty form.   Since signatures are often location dependent, the program "fixes" them to their same locations in an otherwise empty form based on the form of the first of the input works. Since the matched signatures derive from this and not the succeeding works, the location of the fixed signatures will retain the musical value of their original positions. Thus the new work begins as a skeletal frame with music in some locations and not others. This corresponds to the "section" level shown in the lowest box in figure 18.1.

6. Recompose using rules analysis.   At this point, the program composes rules-based music in the intervening spaces between signatures. This process follows the rules discovered by the statistical model resulting from rules analysis. It completes phrases by inserting logical motives into vacant beats in the fledgling composition.

Proper interpolation of this new music relies on an ATN. By following protocols similar to those found in linguistics (Woods 1970), the program orders and connects appropriately composed materials and fleshes out a new work. The problems that must be overcome include: linking both the initial and concluding parts of the signatures to the surrounding materials, creating new material that follows the style of the original material closely enough to avoid stylistical anomalies, and maintaining range, function, and voice motions.

A texture is also generated at this point. This involves the shaping of the music into one or more voices according to the texture of the first of the input works. It maps by slimming thick textures or doubling thin textures. Textures of signatures are not changed during this process. This works on a phrase-by-phrase basis.

7. Ensure proper performance.   Performance aspects of music never seem more critical than when dealing with computer replications of musical styles. If one employs synthetic sounds and inflexible rhythms while replicating music, stylistically valid works may not be recognized. Proper timbral choices, use of live performers, and attention to performance practice are highly recommended.

A Musical Example

Figure 18.3 roughly demonstrates the just described process in terms of music. In 18.3a and 18.3b, the music is by Mozart. Both 18.3c and 18.3d are EMI-culled motives of 18.3a and 18.3b respectively. The music of 18.3c can be found beginning on the second half of beat one in bar one of 18.3a. The repeated two beats of 18.3d are the first two beats of 18.3b. The motives sound very similar (though they look different) because both melodies land on the beat with the chromatic lower neighboring tone C♯. These would qualify as signatures in a pattern-matching routine. The music in 18.3e, then, shows Mozart's signature resting in its proper place in a measure otherwise devoid of musical material except rests. In 18.3f, the signature lies between musically correct material derived from the rules analysis of the music in the database and the previously described texture mapping. This last example is a theme from the third movement of an EMI-composed sonata in the style of Mozart.

Examples of Code

The code provided here is written in Common LISP and should function in any Common LISP implementation. Note that this represents only a small fraction of what is necessary for a functioning compositional tool for music output. It does, however, illustrate one of the basic concepts alluded to previously in this chapter: finding signatures, one of the most important aspects of the EMI algorithm. Higher level function descriptions are preceded by sample runs to show the nature and type of data used. The process uses intervals instead of pitches (as in 0 = no motion, 1 = half-step up, − 1 half-step down, etc).

Figure 18.4a gives the definition of the function *find-signatures*. This top-level function superimposes (see line 2) the analysis of two works. "Type," here, allows melodic, harmonic, or rhythmic signature gathering. These are very different concepts in the EMI program and must be treated uniquely, even at a very high level. The "window" tuner adds inclusive intervals so that new pitches are considered in relation to the first, not the

a)

b)

c)

d)

e)

f)

Figure 18.3

a)

```
;(find-signatures 'melody '(1 2 1 2 3 2) '(1 3 2 3 2 1) 3 1 0)
;= (((1 3) 2) ((2 3) 2) ((2 1) 2) ((1 5) 2) ((2 5) 2) ((2 3) 2) ((3 2) 2))
;(analyze 'melody 3 '(1 2 1 2 3 2) 0)
;= (((1 3) 1) ((1 2) 1) ((2 3) 1) ((2 1) 1) ((1 5) 1) ((1 2) 1) ((2 5) 1)........
;(analyze 'melody 3 '(1 3 2 3 2 1) 0) = (((1 5) 1) ((1 3) 1) ((3 5) 1) ((3 2) 1).....
;(find-signatures 'melody '(1 2 1 2 3 2) '(1 3 2 3 2 1) 3 3 0) = NIL
;(find-signatures 'melody '(1 2 1 2 3 2) '(1 3 2 3 2 1) 3 2 0)
;= (((1 3) 2) ((2 3) 2) ((2 1) 2) ((1 5) 2) ((2 5) 2) ((2 3) 2) ((3 2) 2)) and
;(find-signatures 'melody '(1 2 1 2 3 2) '(1 3 2 3 2 1) 3 4 0) = NIL
;(find-signatures 'harmony a b 3 2 0) with a and b obviously setq's
;((((((1 2 3) (2 3 4)) ((1 2 3) (2 3 4))) (((1 2 3) (2 3 4)) ((1 2 3)
;(2 3 4)))) 2))

1.(defun find-signatures (type first-work second-work window threshold
allowance)
2.      (superimpose (analyze type window first-work allowance)
3.                   (analyze type window second-work allowance)
4.                   threshold))
```

b)

```
1.(defun superimpose (image-one image-two threshold)
2.    (if (null image-one) ()
3.          (let ((test (assoc (very-first image-one) image-two :test 'equal)))
4.              (if (null test)(superimpose (rest image-one) image-two threshold)
5.                  (let ((test-1 (+ (very-second image-one)(second test))))
6.                   (if (> threshold test-1)
7.                       (superimpose (rest image-one) image-two threshold)
8.                      (cons (list (first test) test-1)
9.                          (superimpose (rest image-one) image-two
threshold))))))))))
```

Figure 18.4

intervening pitches. The "threshold" tuner discounts found patterns for minimal use. The "allowance" tuner signifies the amount of variation possible for recognizing patterns—the higher the number, the more acceptable possibilities.

In *find-signatures*, the function *superimpose*, shown in figure 18.4b, superimposes the motivic lists produced by *analyze* so that one can observe the increase in global signatures in comparison with the static nature of local thematic motives. The use of the LISP primitive *assoc* in line 3 here is critical to the operation of the function since it discovers similar motives. When "associations" are found (see the conditional in line

4), then the frequency of occurrence of both of the motives are added together (line 5). If this number exceeds that of the "threshold" tuner (line 6), then the motive is captured through the *cons* (lines 8 and 9) as a signature.

The function *analyze*, see figure 18.5a, distinguishes the way it returns harmonic versus melodic motives through its "type" argument. The function *collect-motive-lists* in line 3 collects lists of motives using the window tuner and returns them to the local variable "motive-lists." The function *count-all-occurrences* in figure 18.5b then counts all of the similar occurrences of the motive based further on various tuner settings accessed by lower level functions. The results of this process are then given to the composing routine for recomposition into a new work. The function *add-numbers* in figure 18.5c adds the rest of the motives so that groups of numbers become one.

The function *collect-motive-lists* shown in figure 18.6a lists groups of motives using *collect-motives* shown in figure 18.6b. The latter function collects successively smaller (minimum two) groups of its argument. This function applies the window tuner to data determined by the length of the list provided it from *collect-motive-lists*.

The function *match* shown in figure 18.7 is the central matching function of the find-signatures program. It applies the test case (line 2), which is the very first element of the analyzed first argument, to a number of conditions (lines 3 through 11), each designed to check it against one or more possibilities. It tests true if (in line 3) it proceeds through each step and becomes empty (meaning all tests have succeeded).

The functions shown in figure 18.8a through 18.8f represent utilities required by the find-signatures program in order to operate. For the most part the names of these functions indicate what they do, which usually equates to a simple process required by a number of higher level functions. The last two examples, 18.8e and 18.8f, are simple synonyms for less readable code.

Examples of Computer Composition

Albinoni

EMI was given only the *Adagio for Strings* by Tomaso Albinoni. It was deliberately broken into two parts synthetically forming two quasia)

```
;(analyze 'melody 3 '(1 3 2 2 12 1 3 2 1) 0)
;= (((1 5) 1) ((1 3) 1) ((3 4) 1) ((3 2) 1) ((2 14) 1) ((2 2) 1) ((2 13) 1) ((2 12)
; 1) ((12 4) 1) ((12 1) 1) ((1 5) 1) ((1 3) 1) ((3 3) 1) ((3 2) 1) ((2 1) 1))

1.(defun analyze (type window list-of-numbers allowance)
2.   (let ((motive-lists (collect-motive-lists window list-of-numbers)))
3.      (count-all-occurances (if (equal type 'harmony) motive-lists
4.                                (funcall 'add-numbers motive-lists)) allowance
type)))
```

b)

```
;(count-all-occurances '(2 3 3 3 4 4 3 5) 0 'melody) returns ((2 1) (3 4) (4 2) (5
1))

1.(defun count-all-occurances (list-of-numbers allowance type)
2.      (if (null list-of-numbers) ()
3.          (cons (list (first list-of-numbers)
4.                 (if (equal type 'harmony)
5.                     (count-them (first list-of-numbers) list-of-numbers
allowance)
6.                     (count (first list-of-numbers) list-of-numbers)))
7.                (count-all-occurances (remove (first list-of-numbers)
8.                                      list-of-numbers)
9.                                      allowance type))))
```

c)

```
;(add-numbers (collect-motive-lists 3 '(1 2 3 4 5))) returns
;((1 5) (1 2) (2 7) (2 3) (3 9) (3 4) (4 5)) and by itself
;(add-numbers '((1 2 3 4)(2 3 4)(2 3))) returns
;((1 9) (2 7) (2 3))

1.(defun add-numbers (motive-list)
2.      (if (null motive-list) ()
3.          (cons (list (very-first motive-list)
4.                 (apply '+ (rest (first motive-list))))
5.                (add-numbers (rest motive-list)))))
```

Figure 18.5

a)

```
;(collect-motive-lists 3 '(1 2 3 4 5)) returns
;((1 2 3) (1 2) (2 3 4) (2 3) (3 4 5) (3 4) (4 5))

1.(defun  collect-motive-lists  (window  list)
2.     (cond ((null list) ())
3.               ((< (length list) window)
4.                  (collect-motive-lists (1- window) list))
5.               (t (append (collect-motives (firstn window list))
6.                             (collect-motive-lists window (rest list))))))
```

b)

```
;(collect-motives '(1 2 3 4)) returns
;((1 2 3 4) (1 2 3) (1 2))

1.(defun  collect-motives  (number-list)
2.     (if (null (rest number-list)) ()
3.               (cons number-list (collect-motives (butlast number-list)))))
```

Figure 18.6

independent "works." As a result, the replicant shown in figure 18.9 sounds very much like the original, even though the actual notes differ. Both works have falling stepwise lincs followed by leaping rising ones and sequence almost excessively. The middle section of the EMI-Albinoni (not shown here) includes a violin duet while the Albinoni has a violin solo. The last section repeats the first in the EMI-Albinoni followed by a simple solo coda that resembles the real Albinoni. The differences include contrasting rhythms, textures, incipient notes, etc. The similarities, however, are unmistakable. Differences could be reduced by increasing the number of works by Albinoni in the database.

Mozart

Figure 18.10 shows the beginning of a third movement of an EMI-composed sonata in the style of Wolfgang Amadeus Mozart. Completed in early summer of 1988, the sonata follows standard Allegro-Andante-Presto forms. Three Mozart sonatas (*K. 283, 309, and 457*) were used for signature gathering. Cadences, textures, sequenced gestures, and various ostinati show evidence of the rules derived from the works in the database, while themes and harmonic progressions demonstrate the influence of

```
;(match '((1 2 3)(4 5)) '((1 2 3)(4 5)) 0) = t
;(match '((1 2 3)(4)) '((1 2 3)(4 5)) 0) = t
;(match '((1 2 3)(4 5)) '((1 2 3)(4)) 0) = ()
;changing the accuracy level, however, allows for subtle variations
;(match '((1 2 3)(4 5)) '((1 2 3)(4)) 1) = t
;again, more in the second argument allows for match
;(match '((1 2)(4 5)) '((1 2 3)(4 5)) 0) = t
;again, a great deal more in the second allows for match
;(match '((1 2 3)(4 5)) '((1 2 3 4 5)(4 5)) 0) = t
;minimum not met here
;(match '((1 2 3)(4 5)) '(()(4 5)) 0) = NIL
;with accuracy lowered, however, it allows for match
;(match '((1 2 3)(4 5)) '(()(4 5)) 3) = t
;the following lowered accuracy will not quite bring it to threshold, ;however!
;(match '((1 2 3)(4 5)) '(()(4 5)) 2) = NIL

1.(defun match (list-1 list-2 allowance)
2.     (let ((test (very-first list-1)))
3.       (cond ((all-nullp list-1) t)
4.                ((null (first list-1))(match (rest list-1)(rest list-2) allowance))
5.                ((all-nullp (nthcdr allowance (first list-1)))
6.                 (match (rest list-1)(rest list-2) allowance))
7.                ((and (null (rest list-1))(null (nthcdr allowance (first list-1)))) t)
8.           ((all-nullp list-2) ())
9.                ((anyp (list test) (first list-2))
10.                (match (list (remove-one test (first list-1))(second list-1))
11.                          (list (remove-one test (first list-2))(second list-2))
allowance))
12.            (t ()))))
```

Figure 18.7

signatures. Note the variation of the signature demonstrated in figure 18.3 in bars 2, 4, and 6.

The overall form of this movement is a standard rondo, with the first theme stated at the outset and the second beginning in bar 17. The form follows closely that of the first Mozart sonata used during composition. Beyond this the inner structure of cadences and the actual notes originated with the machine. Weaknesses of style inheritance include the lack of variations in texture and the range of the chordal accompaniment near the end of the example. The energy of the theme and the logic of the accompaniment appear to be strengths.

Brahms

The example shown in figure 18.11, an EMI intermezzo in the style of Brahms, is the result of pattern-matching parts of several different piano works. Thus the resultant form (not shown in its entirety here) is an

a)

```
;(count-them   '((1  2  3)(4  5  6))  '(((1  2  3)(4  5  6))((1  3  3)(4  5  6))((1  2  3)(3  3  3))) 2) =
;2

1.(defun  count-them    (object  list  allowance)
2. ·     (cond ((or (atom  list)(not (listp (first list)))) 0)
3.              ((match object list allowance) 1)
4.               (t (+ (count-them  object (first list) allowance)
5.                  (count-them  object (rest list) allowance)))))
```

b)

```
1.(defun  all-nullp  (lists)
2.   (cond ((null  lists) t)
3.               ((null (first lists))(all-nullp (rest lists)))
4.          (t nil)))
```

c)

```
1.(defun  anyp  (find  stuff)
2.   (cond ((null  find)())
3.              ((member (first find) stuff) t)
4.              (t (anyp (rest find) stuff))))
```

d)

```
1.(defun  firstn  (number  list)
2.    (butlast  list (- (length  list) number)))
```

e)

```
1.(defun  very-first  (list)
2.   (caar  list))
```

f)

```
1.(defun  very-second  (list)
2.   (cadar  list))
```

Figure 18.8

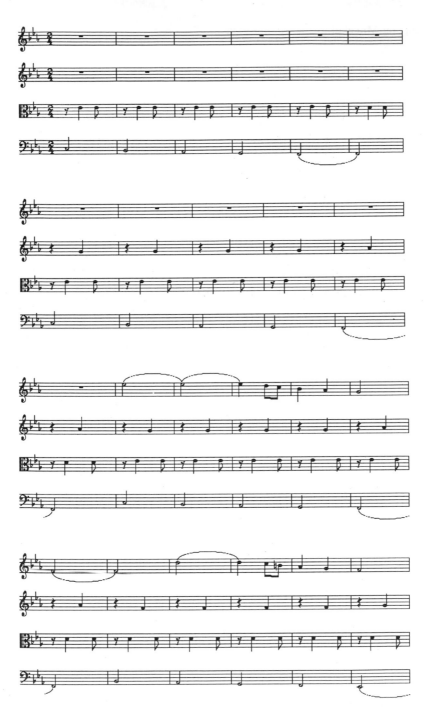

Figure 18.9

Figure 18.10

Figure 18.11

average of those present in his intermezzi, waltzes, ballades, and rhapsodies rather than that of any single work. As well, many of the input works (see particularly his *Ballade* in B major, Opus 10, Number 4, Waltz Number 9, Opus 39 and *Rhapsody* in G minor, Opus 79, Number 2) have uncharacteristically thin textures compared to his more typical fecund harmonies. Hence, in comparison to the actual appearance of a work by Brahms, the resultant machine composition looks relatively barren. Hearing it, however, gives a different impression, as the steady driving rhythm and repeating accompaniment provide almost immediate recognition of Brahms's style.

Debussy

The EMI-composed Debussy shown here in figure 18.12 is based on twelve of his preludes as well as his *Suite bergamasque*. It shows the definite influence of the *Claire de lune* of *Suite bergamasque* in the rising thirds, even though in this case they reside a tritone apart. The triplet in measure three here alludes to the 9/8 meter of the original and even follow its motivic stepwise motion.

The four stave notation is due to the complicated voicing. The use of dorian mode (C–C with two flats) is typical of the modal resources Debussy often employed in his works. The extended range, "rolled" accompaniment, and complicated ninth chord harmonic vocabularies all tend to confirm the Debussy style. The poor idiomatic writing and voicing are uncharacteristic of Debussy and owe entirely to machine ignorance of human limitations.

Cope

Figure 18.13 is page 1 of the score of the third movement of *Vacuum Genesis*. Composition involved the composer using a "computer-assisted" version of the EMI algorithm. This version of the program stops at the end of various levels and does not continue until instructed to do so. In the meantime, the co-composer has access to all of the data thus far composed and may alter it in any manner.

The more one knows about how the program operates, the more effectively changes can be made. Certainly the more changes made, the more dynamic the compositional process becomes and the more intense the computer/human relationship becomes. The computer processes immense

Figure 18.12

Figure 18.13

amounts of data quickly and accurately; the human partner uses personal aesthetics to judge and revise the results.

The Usefulness of Computers Composing Music

Composers

Beyond simply providing enjoyable musical output, studies of algorithmic composition have created a renewed interest in approaches to music composition. Models have been based on, among others, language (Cope 1988 and Lerdahl 1983) and mathematical processes such as stochastics (Xenakis 1971) and fractals (Dodge 1986). None, however, address the human dimension as directly as those programs that deal with musical style itself. It is with style that one learns directly about music perception and aesthetics.

However, learning about one's own style can resemble psychoanalysis. The knowledge of what constitutes one's style can be liberating and suffocating at the same time. The author can testify to the self-criticism aroused when confronted by conscious knowledge of subconscious musical tics that revealed themselves as signatures during computer-assisted composition. On the other hand, knowledge certainly should not be considered dangerous. Interplay between man and machine, however confusing it may be, should produce nontrivial results, especially when liberally doused with the inspiration noted at the outset of this chapter.

Most of the controversies surrounding computer composition seem to intensify in the context of commercial music. For example, while programs such as EMI may further the career of one composer experiencing a block, might not they also put dozens of others out of work? Would it be in the best interests of, for example, a motion picture studio to purchase a computer program and avoid paying living composers salaries for new scores for its films? Yet, have recordings put living performers out of business? Has electronic music lowered the production of acoustic instruments?

This returns us to the issue of computer-assisted music. Here, the hand of the composer is less absent from the finished product. With experience it is possible that musicians and music lovers alike will forgive the machine extension and consider it to be a composer's tool in the same manner that a camera serves the artist's eye. We may even come to appreciate that, as expressed in the previous paragraph, even machine-composed music is really only computer-assisted.

Even plagiarism can be positive when seen from a perspective of humans stealing from machines. It is not at all clear what legal and moral implications exist concerning new music created based on works of other composers. Mixtures of styles (Cope 1991) pose yet further complications.

Theorists

To date, music theory, as taught by most in the profession, has been concerned with analysis based on traditional part-writing rules. By nature, it is a general study of approaches toward pitch, function, and rhythm (primarily) as well as dynamics, texture, orchestration, and form (secondarily) and what composers have in common in these areas. Studies of what differentiates one style from another should, however, not be ignored. The very definition of what constitutes musical style has a somewhat confused history, combining the rhetorics of aesthetics and "ology."

Computers have allowed enormous strides in the understanding of idiosyncrasies and lead to deeper understanding of musical style. Signatures can differentiate styles and can, for example, identify diagnostic characteristics of Baroque versus Classical styles, of German Baroque versus Italian Baroque, of individual German Baroque composers, of Bach versus Handel, of early Bach from late Bach, and finally one Bach invention from another.

Such discrimination need not replace broader definitions of style but augment them. It is unproductive to rely solely on generalizations of musical grammars rather than develop strategies for describing specific examples of the patterns of originality within such constraints. It is, in fact, the differences between such patterns of originality that makes music interesting in the first place. Common-practice music, when taken as a body of general voice-leading rules, produces little more than musically correct realizations of those rules: neither good music nor musically good realizations. It is often the unique interpretations or even exceptions to rules that provide insight into the style of individual composers.

Performers

As previously mentioned, performance by living musicians can be an important test of algorithmic composition emulating musical style. To separate composition from performance divorces the two most eminently important factors in the realization of the art form. To make this separation also means that certain musical concepts fundamental to style throughout music history will be lost. For instance, it is imperative that *physical* constraints be factored into the compositional process.

The tactile nature of performance, the physical limitations of human performers, the layout of the instruments, etc., combine to create a cumulation of limitations often difficult to describe in machine terms. A fingering, for example, is possible in one circumstance and not another. One approach in dealing with this problem rests with the concept of *musical sense*. This parallels the model of the AI "blocks world" where one does not describe the infinite number of sizes and weights of blocks which, when stacked off center, may or may not fall down. Rather, the concepts of gravity, balance, and leverage are given, with all of the *situational* conditions removed from the problem. For the musical examples already given, this means that the computer should be taught to think like a cellist with no situation rules given at any time.

The aspects of this approach most useful for compositional problems suggest that computers could be instructed to reason in musical terms rather than just plodding through a list of endless rules and regulations about when and where they might allow a certain action to take place.

Since the computer can allow anything, the concept here is to teach it that in, the human world, some things are more musical (and possible) than others and that musicality can originate in physical as well as intellectual terms.

For example, implementing a model of the human voice in a computer could force composition toward more musical output. Even a description of the human ear would be useful in order for this real-world parallel to become fully possible. Hence one could coax the computer to incorporate the concept of range so important (and taken for granted) in our human world. There are, for example, gradations of vibrato, intonation, etc., that the human ear simply cannot detect. Knowing these would reduce the number of variations with which the computer must deal.

Obviously, the intricate balance between intellectual potential and physical limitation is difficult to describe. Also, knowing these potentials and limitations is no guarantee that the results of composition will be good music (history abounds with good orchestrators who were poor composers). However, with this added intelligence the computer could create more musically viable examples by applying a flexible computational world to real-world limits of human perception and performance.

One can imagine a system wherein users simply perform naturally on their instruments with the computer program keeping track of both the current state of the work being improvised and the broader sweep of style of the improviser. Any time computer-composed music is desired, it could be requested and performed. This would be immediate and *conversational*. Such requests could be due to "composer's block" or just to satisfy curiosity. Computer-generated music could be supplied in any amount from a single pitch to the rest of the work.

Such imaginings are not far from reality. As programming environments become more and more user friendly, computer-assisted composition in different musical styles could allow the real-time control of musical nuance on profound levels. Such programs could become the perfect composing partner, working hand in hand with composers to achieve the best and most musical results. Such programs would truly emulate musical *intelligence*.

Bibliography

Cope, David. "Experiments in Music Intelligence." *Proceedings of the International Computer Music Conference*. Computer Music Association, 1987.

Cope, David. "An Expert System for Computer-Assisted Music Composition." *Computer Music Journal.* 11/4, Winter, 1987:30–46

Cope, David. "Music and LISP." *AI Expert.* vol. 3, no. 3, March, 1988.

Cope, David. "Music: The Universal Language." *Proceedings of the American Association of Artificial Intelligence Workshop on Music and AI.* Menlo Park, CA: AAAI, August, 1988.

Cope, David. "Experiments in Musical Intelligence (EMI): Non-linear Linguistic-based Composition." *Interface.* vol. 18, no. 1–2, 1989.

Cope, David. *Proceedings of the Glasgow International Computer Music Conference* "Pattern Matching as an Engine for the Computer Simulation of Musical Style" Computer Music Association, 1990.

Cope, David. *Computers and Music Style.* Madison, WI: A-R Editions, 1991.

Dodge, Charles and Curtis Bahn. "Musical Fractals." *BYTE Magazine,* June 1986.

Lerdahl, Fred, and Ray Jackendoff. *A Generative Theory of Formal Music.* Cambridge, MA: The MIT Press, 1983.

Woods, William. "Transition Network Grammars for Natural Language Analysis." *Communications of the ACM.* vol. 13, no. 10, pp 591–606.

Xenakis, Iannis. *Formalized Music.* Bloomington: Indiana University Press, 1971.

Fry's original, information-intensive work has noticeably advanced the state of the art in computer generated music improvisations, especially in jazz. His 1980 paper, *Computer Improvisation*, is one of the first serious jazz improvisation efforts in the literature. Reprinted here, Fry's 1984 paper, *Flavors Band: A Language for Specifying Musical Style*, provides a look at his most complex work in the field, one of the most advanced composing/improvising systems.

Fry's explicitly stated goal for the research is *precision of specificity*—the ability to design an arrangement by describing particular elements and leaving others to defaults and chance.

The Flavors Band software is organized around structures called *phrase-processing networks*. Such a network is a complex function or procedure, similar in purpose to the functions and constraints in Levitt's style generator. Fry emphasizes the ability to add random functions as well as use defaults. However, Fry's approach is distinctly procedural rather than functional. For example, Fry describes certain phrase processors as "note modifiers" and assumes modifications will be performed in sequence rather than composed functionally. One can think of functional versus procedural approaches as describing the intentions versus the sequential behavior of musicians developing a phrase.

As with most composition programs originating in a jazz framework, the Flavors Band usually starts with an input tune and produces a number of choruses of output in the given style. Like Charles Ames, Fry benefits greatly from careful transcriptions of a few arrangements, reusing structural elements and solo licks to construct new arrangements in each rather specific style.

Fry also sought to create a composing environment that required very little Lisp programming, after the first few hundred phrase processors had been defined. As the figures show, Flavors Band made extensive use of the hierarchical and pop-up menu capabilities of the Symbolics/Lisp Machine software system, one of the first commercial software environments to make wide use of bitmap graphics. However, we note that Flavors Band did not attract an audience beyond its inventor, and today the Lisp Machine interface itself is viewed as user-hostile to nonprogrammers. Fry's interface work may seem dated to a modern audience spoiled by the Apple Macintosh interface.

Fry's success is in the selection and quality of the arrangements. By choosing famous hits like The Doors's "Light My Fire," Coltrane's "Giant Steps," and the Beatles' "Norwegian Wood," Fry fearlessly courts comparison with the originals, while simultaneously creating a common frame for listeners to fit with what they're hearing and to unconsciously fill in gaps. The synthetic solos are orchestrated like the originals, and a typical listener recognizes the 'goal' tune and, the original style immediately. Since the detailed effects in the originals remain subconscious for most audiences, a typical listener might not like Fry's version as much as the original, without being able to say why.

The size of the starting databases, and thoughtful use of phrase processors, combined with the selection and orchestration, makes Fry's recordings among the more convincing in the literature.

19 Flavors Band: A Language for Specifying Musical Style

Christopher Fry

The Problem

One of the tasks of music composition is the precise expression of a tremendous number of sonic events. Traditional notation does not permit composers to communicate precise sonic details to the performers of their works. The composer uses the performers to interpret the unwritten details of the score. Composers who use computers must somehow teach the computer-performer exactly what to play. For a large score this is a burden.

Many operations on scores are conceptually simple yet difficult to realize using conventional music media. Transposing of whole sections, global articulation modifications, insertion of several bars in all parts, and filling in harmonies are all examples of processes that are easy to specify, yet hard to implement using pen and paper or even scores typed into a word-processor-like musical interface. More difficult to specify but still imaginable are operations that generate original melodies and harmonies and produce variations on themes.

The Goal

Precision of specificity is a term I use to describe the degree of detail in the plan for a final product (which could be a musical score, a building, or anything). The composer should be able to choose the precision of specificity for each piece. Some pieces may require every nuance of every sonic event to be described exactly from the beginning. Alternatively, the composer might want to start with a very sketchy description by specifying a composition whose only important qualities are a duration of five minutes and a common time signature. Values for tempo and amplitude as well as note durations and pitches could come from default values. Defaults are preset values that are used in the absence of a composer's explicit specification. Incremental modifications could be made to the entire score, refining it from the top down, rather than making hundreds of separate, local changes to achieve the same end.

Copyright 1984, Christopher Fry, and reproduced by permission.

Typically the composer would want to specify certain sections very carefully, while other sections need not have the same accuracy. The precision of specificity would vary throughout the piece as well as from part to part.

Features of Languages

Completely general composition programs are impossible to design because the problem space of composition is unbounded. The programmer can't know in advance what algorithms a composer would like to use, even if the programmer is the composer (as in my case). However, for certain styles of music, the programmer can guess the functionality of some likely to be desired compositional algorithms. These algorithms should be configurable in a wide variety of juxtapositions. The program should also allow hooks to a general-purpose programming language to aid the construction of new algorithms.

Flavors Band: A Solution

Flavors Band is a language for specifying jazz and popular musical styles procedurally. The procedural representation allows the generation of a large number of scores in a specified style by making only minor changes to a score specification. A style can be specified very narrowly such that all tunes generated by a style sound similar (Levitt 1981, 1984). A broader specification allows more diverse compositions to come from the same specification. Since the precision of specificity is easily controlled in Flavors Band, styles often have some tightly controlled aspects and some loosely described aspects that can provide musical scores with a predetermined amount of self-similarity. (For a discussion of musical styles and their relationship to natural language, see Moorer 1972.)

Flavors Band is embedded in Lisp. The languages are entwined such that each may call the other in a structured but flexible way. A Flavors Band construct can explicitly evaluate a composer-specified Lisp expression that itself uses a second Flavors Band construct, and so on.

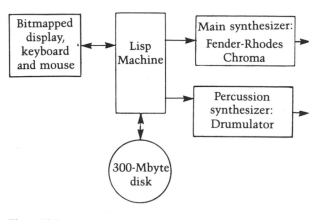

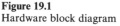

Figure 19.1
Hardware block diagram

System Overview

The essential hardware of Flavors Band consists of a Lisp Machine with a bitmapped display, alphanumeric keyboard and mouse, and a sound synthesizer for realizing scores. I also use a drum synthesizer in addition to the main synthesizer (figure 19.1).

Inside the Lisp Machine, Flavors Band organizes musical structure into a tree topology (figure 19.2). Modifiers of musical structure can be applied to each level of a Flavors Band score, from the entire score, to its sections, parts, and phrase processors.

A musical style is represented as a *phrase processing network*. Each phrase processor exhibits a particular low-level musical behavior. By interconnecting phrase processors in various ways, different higher-level musical behaviors are specified. Currently about 60 kinds of phrase processors are implemented in Flavors Band. Since all phrase processors conform to the same input/output (I/O) conventions, a new phrase processor can be added to Flavors Band and used in conjunction with the existing phrase processors without modification.

Pitch-Time Events

Phrase processors manipulate *event streams*. In Flavors Band, a note is specified by two events, an "on" event and an "off" event. Each event has

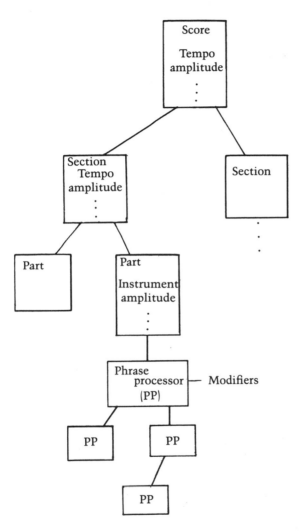

Figure 19.2
Flavors Band Score topology. (PP = Phrase Processor.)

a time (in beats), a flag indicating whether the event is an on event or an off event, a pitch-class (0–11), an octave (0–10), another flag indicating whether it is a rest or not, and a note identification number (ID). The two events of a note travel independently through a phrase processing network. The only way a phrase processor can tell whether two events are for the same note is to check if they have the same ID. IDs are manufactured in such a way as to guarantee that each note's ID is unique.

An optional characteristic of an event is a property list that can hold any number of additional properties. (Read any text on Lisp for an explanation of property lists.) Properties may be added, deleted, and read by phrase processors as an event progresses through a network.

Flavors Band deals primarily with the pitch-time structure of a score. The property list could be used to hold timbre modifications, but the synthesizers in the current system support few such modifications. Frequently the property list is used to hold amplitude, and sometimes scales, or voicings of chords. Two languages that go beyond Flavors Band from the standpoint of timbre modifications are FORMES (Rodet and Cointe 1984), and Pla (Schottstaedt 1983).

The Anatomy of a Phrase Processor

Each phrase processor produces an event stream that becomes the input to another phrase processor. Most phrase processors have one input event stream and act like a black box whose behavior depends on the kind of phrase processor used and the parameter values used to refine the behavior of the phrase processor. Some phrase processors have more than one input event stream, where the output events are some combination of the input events. Other phrase processors have no event streams as inputs. This kind of phrase processor acts more like a generator than a filter (figure 19.3).

Phrase Processing Networks

A connected set of phrase processors forms a network. Scores are specified in terms of such networks. When a score specified by a network is computed, an array of events suitable for performance by a synthesizer is created (figure 19.4). These events are stored in the *events* slot of the part that made them. Thus the output of Flavors Band is stored in the same

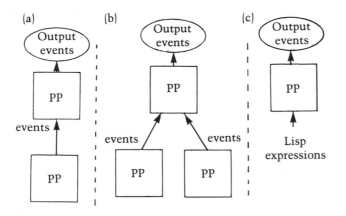

Figure 19.3
Phrase processor input types. (a) Single event stream input. The normal case. (b) Multiple event stream input. (c) No event stream input. An event generator.

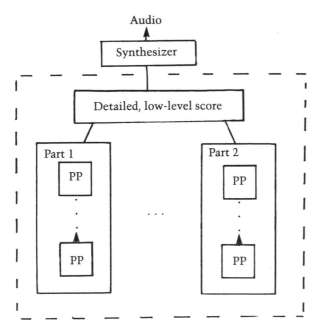

Figure 19.4
Phrase processing networks

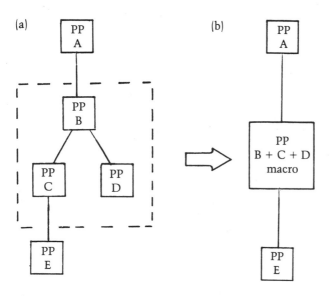

Figure 19.5
Macro phrase processor (a) complex network (b) simplified network.

data framework used for input and computation. This insures the association between a score specification and the computed score, as well as facilitating inheritance (described later). The input and output behavior of a phrase processing network is no different in syntax from that of a single phrase processor. A sophisticated user can build a small network containing several phrase processors that can then become a construct in the language. This new construct performs semantically just as the subnetwork it was constructed from and syntactically just like other single phrase processors (figure 19.5).

Kinds of Phrase Processors

Phrase processors fall logically into three categories: *note modifiers*, *control flow modifiers*, and *accessors* to precomputed event arrays. Phrase processors typically have several arguments, one of which is a phrase processor from which to get the input event stream, and the rest of which are Lisp expressions that customize the phrase processor for each particular use. Any number of a particular kind of phrase processor can be used in a network, as can any mix of phrase processor types. In the rest of this section, I describe some of the more interesting phrase processors.

Note-Modifier Phrase Processors

notes is a phrase processor that allows the specification of the begin-end pairs of events that make up a note. Each of the characteristics of a note (duration, pitch, octave, and rest) has a Lisp expression associated with it that is evaluated to yield the value for the characteristic. For example, the value for pitch must be a number, typically between 0 and 11. The specification for pitch could be any of the following:

3	The pitch E-flat
e-	A Flavors Band global variable representing the pitch E-Flat
my-favorite-pitch	A user-declared global variable
(+1 my-favorite-pitch)	One greater than the above

The important point here is that all of the expressive power of Lisp can be used with little effort on the part of Flavors Band. **notes** allows the specification of the start time as either an absolute time (in beats) or as the ending time of the previous note. The ending time of a note may be specified either as a duration from the starting time or as an absolute time. **notes** is an event generator rather than a filter since it has no event stream as input. It creates events as they are requested from the phrase processor controlling **notes**.

Several phrase processors use pitch modes and scales (Coker 1964, Russell 1959). Modes are formal objects in Flavors Band. Each mode contains a set of intervals in semitones specified by integers between 0 and 11 inclusive. Certain mode objects include just the chord tones of seventh chords while others include more than seven intervals that represent altered jazz modes (figure 19.6). Additional modes are easily specified by the user.

A scale in Flavors Band is a mode with an associated pitch class that is designated as the root of the scale. Scales with any defined mode containing any root are easy to specify.

transpose has the arguments of *interval*, *scale*, and an *input phrase processor*. It requests events from its *input phrase processor* and adds *interval* to the pitch of the incoming events before returning them. The

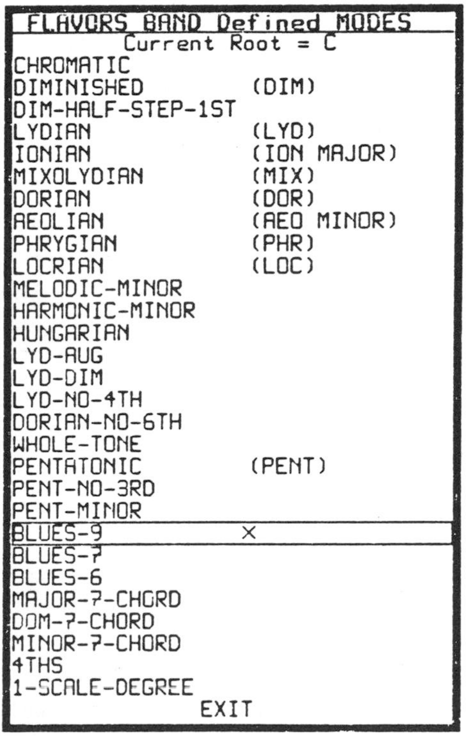

```
┌─────────────────────────────────────────────┐
│ FLAVORS BAND Defined MODES                   │
│            Current Root = C                  │
│ CHROMATIC                                    │
│ DIMINISHED            (DIM)                   │
│ DIM-HALF-STEP-1ST                            │
│ LYDIAN                (LYD)                   │
│ IONIAN                (ION MAJOR)             │
│ MIXOLYDIAN            (MIX)                   │
│ DORIAN                (DOR)                   │
│ AEOLIAN               (AEO MINOR)             │
│ PHRYGIAN              (PHR)                   │
│ LOCRIAN               (LOC)                   │
│ MELODIC-MINOR                                 │
│ HARMONIC-MINOR                                │
│ HUNGARIAN                                     │
│ LYD-AUG                                       │
│ LYD-DIM                                       │
│ LYD-NO-4TH                                    │
│ DORIAN-NO-6TH                                 │
│ WHOLE-TONE                                    │
│ PENTATONIC            (PENT)                  │
│ PENT-NO-3RD                                   │
│ PENT-MINOR                                    │
│ BLUES-9               ×                       │
│ BLUES-7                                       │
│ BLUES-6                                       │
│ MAJOR-7-CHORD                                 │
│ DOM-7-CHORD                                   │
│ MINOR-7-CHORD                                 │
│ 4THS                                         │
│ 1-SCALE-DEGREE                               │
│                 EXIT                          │
└─────────────────────────────────────────────┘
```

Figure 19.6

interpretation of *interval* depends on *scale*. If the interval is 1, the scale is C Chromatic, and the input pitch is D, the output pitch will be D-sharp. However, if the scale is C Ionian, the output pitch will be E. Since *interval* is evaluated for each event, the transposition need not be by a constant value throughout the life of an instance of the **transpose** phrase processor.

harmonize is similar to **transpose** except that it takes a list of intervals rather than just one interval as an argument. For each input event, **harmonize** puts out an event for each of the intervals in the list transposed by that interval from the original input event. Thus with the intervals of (0 2 4 6) and the scale D Lydian, **harmonize** will output a major seventh chord for each input event. The root of the chord will be the same pitch as the incoming event (transposed by the 0 interval), and the rest of the pitches will be above that root using every other scale degree in D Lydian.

coerce-into-scale takes as arguments a *scale* and an *input phrase processor*. If the pitches of the input events are not in the *scale*, they are modified by the smallest amount to make them be in the *scale*. This phrase processor can correct the output of a previous phrase processor that plays "out of key."

shift-time adds one number to the time of an ending event and the time of the next starting event. The number may be negative and expressed as a floating point number or as a rational (-0.5 and $1/3$ are legal values). Shifting the onset times of a melody by varying amounts can cause it to lag behind the original, then get ahead of the original, a technique used frequently in jazz performance.

swing represents a more specialized functionality. It adds the value of its *time-increment* argument to the times of events that occur halfway between beats. For example, with a time-increment of $1/6$, an event at beat 2 1/2 will be shifted to 2 2/3. Events on the beat such as events at time 2 or 31 will be unmodified.

phrase-gap makes it easy to insert rests periodically in a long phrase. One motivation for this phrase processor is to give the effect of a horn player taking a breath.

context-mapper is a very general phrase processor. It takes as its arguments a *Lisp expression* and an *input phrase processor*. The *Lisp expression* is evaluated during the processing of each input event. Before evaluation of the *Lisp expression*, certain variables are bound to the characteristics of the current event as well as the two previous and two next events (the event's context). The *Lisp expression* can read and/or modify these variables. In computing the characteristics for the current event, **context-mapper's** ability to read the values of the surrounding events' characteristics gives it a limited context within which it can operate. For example, **context-mapper** could be used to limit melodic leaps in the input event stream by coercing the pitch of the current event to be no more than a certain interval from the previous event. A smarter use of **context-mapper** might choose to smooth out leaps by placing the current pitch between the previous pitch and the next pitch. The *Lisp expression* can access both the previous events from its input stream and the previous events in its output stream. The **context-mapper** can generate precisely one output event for each input event.

embellish initializes and runs an entire subnetwork of phrase processors for each input event. The phrase processors in the subnetwork can read the values of characteristics in the input event as well as a limited context surrounding it. When the subnetwork is done, a new input event is acquired and the subnetwork is computed all over again. One of my uses for **embellish** is to add off-beat eighth notes to a walking bass line that originally contained only quarter notes.

Control Flow Phrase Processors

concat is used to put together serially two or more event streams. This permits phrase processors to generate events with a time base of zero and yet still have their output appended onto that of another phrase processor rather than played concurrently with it.

repeat allows its argument *phrase processor* to be reinitialized and run a specified number of times. (Without **repeat**, most phrase processors finish when their input stream is used up.) If **repeat** is given an argument of *forever* instead of a number, it will continue reinitializing and running its input phrase processor until either the machine's memory is full, the user kills the process, or a controlling phrase processor somewhere up the network kills the **repeat**.

coerce-time passes events from its *input phrase processor* until an event more than a *specified time* is produced. **coerce-time** then kills its input phrase processor and returns an event equal to the *specified time*. **coerce-time** can also be used to pad short phrases with rests, should the input processor die a natural death before it reaches the specified time. **repeat** *forever* phrase processors are often limited by a **coerce-time** processor. For example, the user could have an ostinato bass figure that he or she wanted to repeat many times. If the user didn't know the number of times to repeat, but did know how long the entire bass line must be, a **repeat** *forever* controlled with a **coerce-time** phrase processor is called for. This does more than simply save the user from doing some arithmetic. If the duration of the ostinato figure is not a whole number multiple of the entire bass line duration, or the user simply can't figure out the duration of the ostinato figure before the score is computed, the functionality of **coerce-time** is needed.

gate behaves like a transistor. It takes two arguments, both of which are phrase processors. The event stream from one phrase processor the (*control stream*) allows the events from the other phrase processor (the *main stream*) to pass through the gate only when there is an ongoing note in the control stream that is not a rest. The control stream can be modified just like any other event stream. The **invert** phrase processor was initially designed to invert the control stream to a **gate** phrase processor, allowing events from the main stream to pass when there are no ongoing notes in the control stream. These phrase processors used in conjunction with **filter** (which conditionally removes events based on a Lisp expression) and **merge** (which combines two event streams into one) allow a user to construct phrase processing networks analogous to the networks that synthesizers use for generating sound.

Event Array Accessors

Event array accessors are designed to store intermediate event streams to be used and modified in numerous other places.

   set-events passes its input unmodified, but has the side-effect of storing copies of the events that go through it into an array. These events may be accessed with the **use-events** phrase processor from anywhere in the network after the **set-events**, or by the phrase processing network of another part.

   As an example of the use of event array accessors, a bass part might generate roots of chords in its early processing. These roots could be saved, and the bass part could go on to transpose its events such that it played only the thirds and fifths of the roots. Meanwhile a melody part could extract the roots from the saved array and embellish them to form a melody. Both parts used a musical skeleton that was never explicitly output by any part. For accessing the final score of a part, **use-events** can be applied since the data format for storing a part's completed score is an array of events.

Lisp Functions

Most of the arguments to most of the phrase processors can be passed by arbitrary Lisp expressions. Some of the more commonly used expressions have been coded into Lisp functions and made available for use in constructing a network. Currently there are about 30 of these functions. Like phrase processors, these functions can be added to Flavors Band with no modification to the rest of the language. Calls to these functions can occur everywhere that Flavors Band calls the Lisp evaluator, which is just about anywhere within a network. Here are descriptions of two particularly interesting user functions.

make-line-envelope makes line-segment envelopes from specified points. It is used by sending it a value (the *address* or *x* value). It returns a value (the *y* or *data* value). The address can come from anywhere, but usually comes from the time of an event. A melody with a particular pitch contour can be generated by making an envelope of the desired contour, generating an event stream, using the events' times as addresses into the envelope, and assigning the events' pitches to the output of the envelope. Only the rhythm of the input event stream is important, which can come from anywhere, for instance from another part. Inputs and outputs of the envelope generator can be scaled and offset with common Lisp functions.

sequencer is used because sometimes an application calls for a series of numbers that are not easily specified as an envelope, or may require a series of objects that are not numbers. **sequencer** can contain a list of any number of objects to sequence through. Each object has a *count* and a *value specification*. Each time the sequencer is asked for a value, the *count* of the current object is decremented, and its *value specification* is evaluated and returned. When the current object's *count* reaches 0, the next object is made the current object. The evaluation of an object's *value specification* can modify the *count* of the object. Thus the sequencer can modify itself as it is run. **sequencer** is an experiment in sequencer autonomy.

Use of Indeterminacy

The user can allow Flavors Band to choose from among a constrained set of values to generate arguments to phrase processors or other Lisp functions. This makes it possible to construct a network that has bounded indeterminacy, permitting the specification of a potentially wide range of musical styles with a comparatively short and simple syntax.

fb-random, the Flavors Band random number generator, takes as its arguments a *minimum output value*, a *maximum output value*, a *granularity*, and a *seed*. If this were used for note duration, a composer could say, "I want the duration of each note to be between 1/4 and 1 with a granularity of 1/8." The possible values would all be multiples of 1/8. Changing the seed would change the sequence of numbers, but not their other specified characteristics. Another Flavors Band generator allows the user to specify the probability that a particular value will be returned. In the previous example on duration, the user might wish to specify that half of the durations be 1/4, and assign correspondingly smaller probabilities to the remaining possible durations. The value returned from this probability generator could be any Lisp object, not simply a number. The value could even be a phrase-processing subnetwork, effectively allowing Flavors Band to choose a composition strategy based on user-supplied probabilities. An extension to this probability generator allows the user to specify the number of times a particular value is returned once it is selected. This lends consistency to the output values.

random-segment allows the network to determine which one of a number of subnetworks is to be used, based on user-supplied probabilities. A repeat wrapped around a random-segment phrase processor allows the generation of event streams that are composed using the variety of techniques specified by the phrase processors selected by **random segment**.

Phrase Network Architectures

An instance of a phrase processor with its arguments could be thought of as a sentence in the Flavors Band language. Most sentences can be placed adjacent to most other sentences, permitting an unlimited variety of paragraphs. However, as in natural languages, only a small subset of such paragraphs are likely to be coherent and/or interesting. This section examines how meaningful paragraphs are constructed in the Flavors Band language.

Example 1: Deriving Pitch from Envelope

An interesting pitch generation technique is to get a value from an envelope and add a slight amount of deviation to it. If the deviation comes from a random number generator, then each pass through the envelope will produce a phrase with a similar pitch contour as the previous pass, but not exactly the same (figure 19.7). Figure 19.7a is a block diagram of such a network; 19.7b gives the actual code; 19.7c is an unmodified random melody; 19.7d is a random melody modified by a pitch envelope.

In figure 19.7b a random number between 0 and 3 (with a granularity of 1) is generated with **fb-random** and assigned to pitch in the **notes** phrase processor. Seventy-two of such notes are made by the **repeat** phrase processor. In **context-mapper**, the starting time of each note is used as an index into the envelope generator specified in the **init-expression** of this part. The

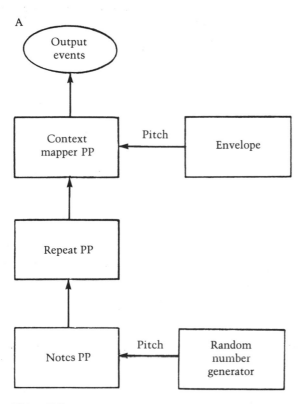

Figure 19.7

output of the envelope generator is added to the pitch that was assigned in **notes**. Since the envelope is just 24 beats long, and the last note will end on beat 72, three groups of notes will have the general pitch contour specified by the envelope. Each of the three groups will be slightly different due to the deviation from the **fb-random** function.

Example 2: Phrase Libraries

Long phrases can be constructed out of short phrases whose notes are specified directly. The particular combination of the short phrases to form longer phrases can be determined by a Flavors Band network. I call a group of fully specified phrases a *phrase library* from which a network may borrow. There can be any number of phrase libraries in Flavors Band, each of which can contain any number of phrases. In my use of this technique,

```
(shift-time 1/8 ;minimum-duration
          (random-alist '((.8 0) (.9 -1/4) (1 1/4)))
          (REPEAT 32 ;number of repetitions
                  (random-segment
                  13 ;seed
                  ;phrase library with probabilities
                  '((.3 (NOTES (N (S 0.))
                               (N (S 0.5))
                               (N (S 1.) (E 2.))))
                    (.6 (NOTES (N (S 0.))
                               (N (S 0.5))
                               (N (S 1.))
                               (N (S 1.5) (E 2.))))
                    (1. (NOTES (N (S 0.))
                               (N (S 1.) (E 2.)))))))))
```

Figure 19.8

each library rarely contains over 20 phrases. Phrase libraries allow a user to precisely specify the details while imprecisely specifying the higher-level structure of the phrase being constructed (figure 19.8).

The phrase library contains three phrase processing subnetworks, each made from **notes** phrase processors. (Syntactically, any one of these could be replaced by an arbitrary network.) Each of the three **notes** phrase processors has about an equal probability of occurring. (Actually the probability for the third is $1.0 - 0.6 = 0.4$.) Thirty-two times during this score, **random-segment** selects one of the three subnetworks and returns the events generated by it. The times of these events are subject to possible modification by **shift-time**. Eight percent of the events' times go unmodified, while 10 percent are retarded by 1/4 and 10 percent are advanced by 1/4. Since this net doesn't vary pitch at all, it would most likely be used as a drum part or the rhythm generator in a larger net.

Nonstandard Communication

Typically, the topology of a phrase-processing network is a tree where the highest processor on the tree is the processor between the rest of the network and the output event stream of the network (figure 19.9). The flow of control is from the later, higher phrase processors to the earlier processors near or at the leaves of the tree.

Events move opposite to the direction of control, from the earlier processors (at the bottom of the tree) through the later processors. A surprising variety of composition algorithms can be supported with this

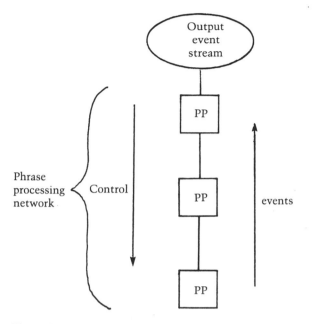

Figure 19.9

architecture, but not all. For example, many levels of nested repeats work well in the Flavors Band treelike topology. However, some kinds of networks whose control-flow branches dynamically are difficult to implement as a treelike topology. Such an architecture might occur if you wanted to design a network containing subnetworks that are not yet fully specified at the time of initialization of the whole network. Branching based on events to be computed is also a difficult architecture. You might want to do this if the technique to be used next depends on the last note of the previous technique.

For miscellaneous communication between processors, Lisp global variables can be used. A processor can set a flag during the course of computation of an event. That flag can be read by any other processors that choose to at any time after the flag is set. Sometimes I pass starting times or indicate the current pitch mode (e.g., Ionian or Dorian) via a global variable. A variable can contain a subnetwork.

As previously mentioned, event array accessors can conveniently store and retrieve event arrays. The reading phrase processor can be placed anywhere in the network (before as well as after the writer) or in the network of a different part. Thus event streams, as well as control information, may move nonhierarchically within a score's phrase processing networks.

Event arrays can be used to store themes to be read by another phrase processor in order to generate a variation. A subnetwork whose output is fed back into its input constitutes a *phrase-locked loop*. A predecessor to Flavors Band, the program called Computer Improvisation (Fry 1980) could create original phrases but didn't have the ability to make variations on them.

Within a section, parts are computed in parallel such that no part computes far ahead or behind the other parts. This permits parts to share recently computed events among themselves.

Defaults and Inheritance

Scores, sections, and parts have ten to fifteen characteristics each. For a score of several sections with several parts each, a large number of parameters must be specified. To automate this task, all parameters have default values. A human composer can start with a procedural outline of a score and then fill in particular characteristics as desired, some of which are available via menus.

There is still a complexity problem with default values that must be explicitly overridden. Frequently a new score will have characteristics in common with previously computed scores. Flavors Band takes advantage of this by permitting inheritance of characteristics between scores.

The entire score, individual sections, or whole parts can be inherited from a previously computed score. The user can specify that only particular characteristics are inherited. Most importantly, the set of defaults can come from other scores, sections, or parts. This permits easy construction of a new score that behaves just like a previous score except for certain characteristics. Being able to use pieces of existing scores facilitates the specification of a new musical style that has similarities to a previously-coded style.

The entire description of a phrase-processing network can be inherited from one part to another. But if the new part is really supposed to behave exactly as its parent did, it can inherit the output events of that part as well. This saves redundant computation and facilitates building very large scores by combining smaller, previously debugged, and computed scores.

User Interface

Flavors Band uses a careful interaction between custom menus (Symbolics 1984a) and a text editor (Symbolics 1984b) as its user interface. A user remains continually in the text editor while constructing and performing Flavors Band scores. Over twenty menus are used in Flavors Band (figure 19.10). All of them are accessible through the Flavors Band Command Menu, which pops up on the screen via a keystroke. The Flavors Band Command Menu allows access to the following:

Documentation (including this chapter on-line)

Examples of score descriptions

Menus of phrase processors and user functions

Evaluation of the current score description

Performance of computed scores

Modifications of computed scores

Debugging aids

For each phrase processor type and user function, the user can get via menu: documentation, the argument list, the source code, or insert the name of the processor or function into the current text buffer. Examples of the use of every phrase processor can be found in the examples file that is accessible via menu. For beginning users, two simple examples can be inserted directly into the current buffer via menu.

Once a score has been computed, it can be played as many times as desired via menu. Certain parts of the score can be modified without complete recomputation. Instruments can be assigned to parts via menu; approximately a hundred instruments are available. The amplitude of each part can be modified via a simple "mixing console" menu. Each part can also have its octave offset modified via menu without recomputation of the whole part.

A history list of the previously computed scores during the current terminal session is maintained. Any previously computed score can be selected via menu as the current score and have all of the aforementioned operations performed on it.

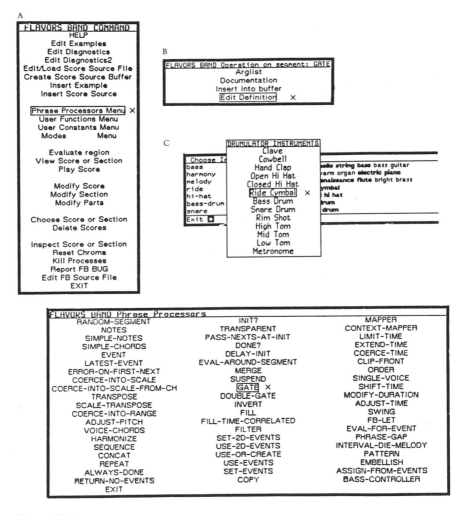

A

FLAVORS BAND COMMAND
HELP
Edit Examples
Edit Diagnostics
Edit Diagnostics2
Edit/Load Score Source File
Create Score Source Buffer
Insert Example
Insert Score Source

Phrase Processors Menu ×
User Functions Menu
User Constants Menu
Modes   Menu

Evaluate region
View Score or Section
Play Score

Modify Score
Modify Section
Modify Parts

Choose Score or Section
Delete Scores

Inspect Score or Section
Reset Chroma
Kill Processes
Report FB BUG
Edit FB Source File
EXIT

B

FLAVORS BAND Operation on segment: GATE
Arglist
Documentation
Insert into buffer
Edit Definition   ×

C

DRUMULATOR INSTRUMENTS
Clave
Cowbell
Hand Clap
Open Hi Hat
Closed Hi Hat
Ride Cymbal   ×
Bass Drum
Snare Drum
Rim Shot
High Tom
Mid Tom
Low Tom
Metronome

Choose I
bass
harmony
melody
ride
hi-hat
bass-drum
snare
Exit ■

ello string bass bass guitar
arm organ electric piano
naissance flute bright brass
ymbal
hi hat
rum
drum

FLAVORS BAND Phrase Processors

RANDOM-SEGMENT	INIT?	MAPPER
NOTES	TRANSPARENT	CONTEXT-MAPPER
SIMPLE-NOTES	PASS-NEXTS-AT-INIT	LIMIT-TIME
SIMPLE-CHORDS	DONE?	EXTEND-TIME
EVENT	DELAY-INIT	COERCE-TIME
LATEST-EVENT	EVAL-AROUND-SEGMENT	CLIP-FRONT
ERROR-ON-FIRST-NEXT	MERGE	ORDER
COERCE-INTO-SCALE	SUSPEND	SINGLE-VOICE
COERCE-INTO-SCALE-FROM-CH	GATE ×	SHIFT-TIME
TRANSPOSE	DOUBLE-GATE	MODIFY-DURATION
SCALE-TRANSPOSE	INVERT	ADJUST-TIME
COERCE-INTO-RANGE	FILL	SWING
ADJUST-PITCH	FILL-TIME-CORRELATED	FB-LET
VOICE-CHORDS	FILTER	EVAL-FOR-EVENT
HARMONIZE	SET-2D-EVENTS	PHRASE-GAP
SEQUENCE	USE-2D-EVENTS	INTERVAL-DIE-MELODY
CONCAT	USE-OR-CREATE	PATTERN
REPEAT	USE-EVENTS	EMBELLISH
ALWAYS-DONE	SET-EVENTS	ASSIGN-FROM-EVENTS
RETURN-NO-EVENTS	COPY	BASS-CONTROLLER
EXIT		

Figure 19.10

Implementation

I started coding Flavors Band in the fall of 1982. The core of the program is fairly stable, although extensions occur regularly. Currently about 35 source code and peripheral files contain over 10,000 lines of code. I have been the sole programmer up to now. Flavors Band is written entirely in Lisp Machine Lisp (Symbolics 1984c, Symbolics 1984d). It runs on both the Symbolics LM-2 and 3600 systems.

A Fender-Rhodes Chroma synthesizer is connected to the Lisp Machine for sound output. The Chroma is a digitally-controlled analog synthesizer. It can produce eight voices (with eight different instruments) in real time, with each voice consisting of several oscillators, filters, and envelopes (Fender Rhodes 1982). An E-mu Drumulator synthesizer (E-mu 1983) provides realistic percussion sounds.

The Flavors Band software takes advantage of numerous Lisp Machine system features making the code both powerful and unportable. Flavors, the Lisp Machine mechanism for object-oriented programming, is used extensively (Cannon 1982). (The "Band" part of "Flavors Band" is a pun on the term *band* used to refer to a disk partition on the Lisp Machine.) Each phrase processor is implemented as a flavor. Most communication between phrase processors occurs via message-passing.

Each musical part is implemented as a process with its own stack. The scheduling of these processes is determined by a combination of the Lisp Machine scheduler and a special scheduler inside the Flavors Band interpreter.

Musical Applications

I am still at an early stage of musical application. So far, most of the scores made with Flavors Band have been developed for experimentation with compositional algorithms and for diagnostic purposes. A few short works have been produced and are described in this section.

My Favorite Things

In the Flavors Band arrangement of *My Favorite Things* (written by Richard Rodgers and adapted from John Coltrane's arrangement), the melody and chords were coded directly. One verse of the melody was constructed by merging the rhythms from a phrase library with the pitches from the original melody. Another verse used **shift-time** on the original rhythms with sporadic applications of **transpose** to pitches. The piano part used **harmonize** on the supplied chords with nonmetrical starting times for the chords. The bass player arpeggiated the chords with a certain amount of deviation rhythmically and harmonically. For drums I used only a brushlike sound. The drummer played a traditional ride cymbal figure by attacking on every beat and playing a high percentage of the swing eighth notes between beats.

Norwegian Wood

As an experiment, I decided to reuse the score description of *My Favorite Things* to arrange *Norwegian Wood* (written by John Lennon and Paul McCartney). I changed only the input melody and chords. Both pieces are in related meters (*My Favorite Things* in 3/4 time and *Norwegian Wood* in 12/8) and have a two-part structure (A and B sections). The similarities between the two pieces end there. The chord structures and melodies are very different. Recorded versions of the compositions also have very different arrangements and instrumentation.

What I had really done in arranging *My Favorite Things* in Flavors Band was to specify a style in machine-readable form. One way to observe the essential characteristics of that style was to listen to more than one piece in the style. I do not consider the Flavors Band version of *Norwegian Wood* as played in the style of the Flavors Band version of *My Favorite Things* to be a musical success. *My Favorite Things* sounds better. Perhaps this is primarily due to the fact that I developed this style with *My Favorite Things* in mind.

Regardless of this result, the technique of using a style adapted from one piece to realize another piece is still a fascinating concept. For once, the phrase "as played in the style of" is not ambiguous. Moreover, the building of libraries of networks, each of which concretely describes a style, is both technically feasible and conceptually powerful as a composition technique.

Light My Fire

The longest piece I have produced with Flavors Band is an attempt to capture the style of the guitar solo section of the long version of *Light My Fire* (written by The Doors). The bass plays an embarrassingly consistent one-measure line throughout on the record, so I simply used **repeat** on those notes. The organ part uses numerous two-measure licks selected from a phrase library. The drummer plays both a bass drum and a snare drum. The snare drum part is minimally conscious of phrasing: a short fill is played every four measures, and a longer fill is played every sixteen measures. The lead guitarist knows eight one-measure licks. They are coded in scale degree rather than chromatic notation. As a lick is selected, it is transposed based on previous transpositions and the location of the current measure in the current four-measure phrase. Quite a bit of the code is devoted to making certain that phrasing over four-measure periods is consistent with the style being imitated.

Giant Steps

The most advanced use of Flavors Band is an arrangement of *Giant Steps* (by John Coltrane). *Giant Steps* is a classic, fast (285 beats per minute) jazz composition with many II–V–I chord progressions. The most interesting parts of the Flavors Band arrangement are the bass line and the improvised solo, played on the Chroma synthesizer.

To create a walking bass line, I use a special phrase processor called the **bass-controller**. The **bass-controller** sets up a context in which a bass style computes. The **bass-controller** provides its bass style with the current chord, the next chord, the pitch of the expected first bass note to be played during the chord, and the pitch of the expected first bass note for the next chord.

It is the responsibility of each bass style to choose the notes to be played during the chord. For walking bass, Flavors Band uses a bass style that makes a trajectory of pitches aiming toward the expected first note of the next chord. The pitches are usually constrained to be within the scale indicated by the current chord. Constraining the legal scale degrees to the root, the third, the fifth, and the seventh produces a more conventional-sounding bass line.

Although the improvised solo does not occur in the bass register, it uses the **bass-controller** and a bass style that is similar to the one mentioned in the previous paragraph. The main difference is that the expected first pitch of each chord is not the root of the chord as it is in the bass part. It is rather a pitch that is a small interval from the last pitch of the previous chord. This causes the solo to wander more freely through the chord changes than the bass part.

Not surprisingly, the resulting score did not sound as good as the John Coltrane Quartet. However, except for the unnatural sound of the Chroma synthesizer, it is conceivable that the piece could have been performed by a human jazz band.

Original Compositions

Flavors Band has also been used to produce original pieces. Chord progressions, melodies, and rhythms can be made via complex use of phrase libraries, envelopes, sequencers, probability functions, and other phrase processors.

Conclusions

The core of Flavors Band is a framework upon which many kinds of phrase processors can be hung in a wide variety of configurations. The architecture has proven successful with respect to extensibility.

Flexibility is more difficult to measure. When constructing compositional algorithms, it is much easier to build them from the bottom up based on the tools immediately available. If you attempt to build them to conform to an existing style, as I chose to in the aforementioned compositions, the task is considerably more difficult. Deficiencies in the toolkit become apparent and suggest the need tor new constructs in the language.

For each of the pieces described previously, I built new phrase processors or adopted new styles of using the language. Flavors Band was able to accommodate concepts I had not considered before completing the majority of the code. Given the impossibility of predicting future uses, this is a necessary characteristic of any flexible language.

Throughout the implementation of Flavors Band, flexibility had a higher priority than ease of use. Consequently, despite my efforts at user interface, Flavors Band is not simple to use. Maintaining the ability to have a widely variable precision of specificity means that when a high-level construct is built, all of the obvious levels below that high level must be accessible. This increases generality at the expense of complexity and size of the language. No doubt simplifications could be made to Flavors Band that would both increase flexibility and reduce complexity to the user. Such elegant solutions are difficult to discover. If they are not found, Flavors Band will continue to have the trait of complexity in common with the domain it attempts to describe.

Acknowledgments

Tom Trobaugh is to be credited with random theoretical insights. Jim Davis developed key parts of the Flavors-Band-to-synthesizer software interface. Curtis Roads, Jim Davis, and Gareth Loy made comments on drafts of this chapter. John Coltrane and The Doors provided musical inspiration. David Clark and John Voigt gave me insights into jazz bass theory. Most importantly, my thanks to David Levitt and Bill Kornfeld for Lisp Machine tutorials over the last three years along with essential friendship.

References

Cannon, H. 1982. "Flavors: A Nonhierarchical Approach to Object-oriented Programming." Cambridge, Massachusetts: Symbolics.

Coker, 1. 1964. **Improvising Jazz**. Englewood Cliffs, New Jersey: Prentice-Hall.

E-mu. 1983. *Drumulator Service Manual*. Santa Cruz. California E-mu Systems Inc.

Fender-Rhodes. 1982. *Chroma Programming Manual*. Fullerton, California: Fender-Rhodes.

Fry, C. 1980. "Computer Improvisation." *Computer Music Journal* 4(3):48–58.

Jackson, C. P. 1980. *How to Play Jazz Basslines*. Boston, Massachusetts: Hornpipe Music Publishing.

Levitt, D. 1981 "A Melody Description System for Jazz Improvisation." M.S. thesis, Cambridge, Massachusetts: Massachusetts Institute of Technology.

Levitt, D. 1984. "Machine Tongues X: Constraint Languages." *Computer Music Journal* 8(1):9–21.

Moorer, J. A. 1972. "Music and Computer Composition." *Communications of the Association for Computing Machinery*." 15(2):104–113.

Rodet, X., and P. Cointe. 1984. "Formes: Composition and Scheduling of Processes." *Computer Music Journal* 8(3):32–50.

Russell, G. 1959. *The Lydian Chromatic Concept of Tonal Organization*. New York, New York: Concept Publishing.

Schottstaedt, B. 1983. "Pla: A Composer's Idea of a Language." *Computer Music Journal* 7(1):11–20.

Symbolics. 1984a. "User Interface Support." *Symbolics 3600 Documentation, Release 5.0 version*. Cambridge, Massachusetts: Symbolics.

Symbolics. 1984b. "Program Development Tools." *Symbolics 3600 Documentation. Release 5.0 version*. Cambridge, Massachusetts: Symbolics.

Symbolics. 1984c. "Lisp Language." *Symbolics 3600 Documentation, Release 5.0 version*. Cambridge, Massachusetts: Symbolics.

Symbolics. 1984d. *Symbolics 3600 Technical Summary*. Cambridge, Massachusetts: Symbolics.

VII AI AND MUSIC: NEW DIRECTIONS

Like several other contributors to this volume, David Levitt has written a number of works on music modeling. His work emphasizes constraint-based description of musical dialects or styles. *Constraints* are declarative relationships that might be satisfied through a variety of different procedures. By developing a description language broad enough to encompass different kinds of music, Levitt's software expresses the dialect as a transformation of inputs, like chord progressions and melodies, through a series of constraint relationships collectively called a *style template*.

Perhaps the strongest contrast in Levitt's work, relative to Fry's, Moorer's, Hiller's, and most other automatic composition work, is his avoidance of pseudorandom number selection anywhere in the composition process. Throughout his work Levitt has argued that use of pseudorandom number generators tends to obscure rather than reveal the musical constraints needed to represent simple musical structures.

The examples are excerpted from a late chapter in Levitt's doctoral thesis at the MIT Artificial Intelligence Laboratory. In detail impossible to reproduce here, Levitt has by this time defined rhythmic elements such as metric hierarchy, syncopation, and swing; harmonic concepts like quality (such as Major or Dominant7th), mode, chord, key, scale degree, and motion along the circle of fifths both in chromatic degrees and scale degrees; melody shape (the pattern of ups and downs) and parallel, oblique, and contrary melodic motion among voices. The examples describe a traditional jazz walking bass player simulation and a more complex two-handed ragtime piano simulation.

Descriptions appear in a spreadsheet-like formula notation, intended for computer scientists more than musicians, developed throughout the thesis. A variable like Pitches refers to a sequence of pitch values. A formula referring to Pitches[i] is a constraint on every pitch in the sequence. Variables with the suffix "Sched" like PitchSched refer to a schedule, a function of time. The shorthand "@ <" is used to index the most recent element in a schedule, the element "at or before" a given time. Variables like Chords and Modes are sequences of harmonic qualities, constructed from periodic arrays of pitch classes, typically of three and seven tones, respectively.

In contrast with Longuet-Higgins, Levitt's software makes no direct attempt to represent traditional notation with correctly spelled accidentals. Musical results appear in limited music notation (in fact, MacroMind's MusicWorks notation) and show progressive functional variations on successive patterns. The chapter begins with a brief description of this notation for non-musicians. By adding constraints to the description, a simple initial pattern becomes increasingly complex.

20 A Representation for Musical Dialects

David A. Levitt

Introduction: Musical Dialects

Suppose we ask a musician to play a melody and accompanying chords. The most literal piano amateur will simply play the chords in root inversion with the left hand and the melody with the right. But a more expert pianist will introduce new rhythmic elements in the left hand, and perhaps add a parallel melody or a countermelody in the right; the expert will improvise a complex piano arrangement of the tune. A versatile pianist may, on request, produce syncopated jazz swing arrangements; elaborate classical arrangements with many suspensions, passing tones and other devices; reharmonized romantic versions; and so on.

What sort of knowledge makes this behavior possible? What concepts and mental data structures does the musician consider and build? What are good descriptions of a musical genre or arrangement style? This paper addresses these questions. A range of structure is captured in a *music constraint language*—a few dozen descriptive terms that make musically significant distinctions explicit, using many of the terms and concepts of traditional music theory. The music terms are constructed from more primitive arithmetic and set-theory *constraints*, each with several corresponding *enforcement procedures* that satisfy them. A musical dialect is described by connecting musical constraints into a network of relationships, *a model* depicting a partial description of a musical situation. The music template determines how enforcement procedures will construct a musical variation or arrangement when given a melody and/or chord progression.

The system is designed to support a wider range of dialect description, but only a few experiments have yet been performed. The music constraint language has also been applied to partial harmonic, melodic, and rhythmic analysis of examples, and high-level control of musical constraints in designs for novice musical instrument interfaces.

Scenarios

We alternate between music notation and a spreadsheet-like formula notation. Above many of the figures we use a linear format for the melodies, a

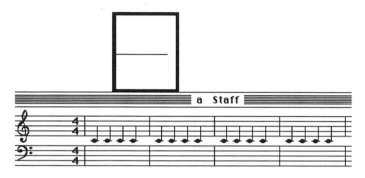

Figure 20.1

notation like the pattern on a paper piano roll, which sometimes makes elements of the shape and timing of the melodies more evident.

We construct an increasingly complex description of a melody. We start with the simplest of descriptions for one voice.

LENGTH(Pitches) = 8
LAST(MetricTimes) = 2

We are telling the system we want an eight-note melody, two measures (we assume a time signature of 4/4) long. The system infers from the standard melody model that LENGTH(MetricTimes) is also eight and employs default values to build a satisfactory melody at the user's request. As shown in figure 20.1, this is quite a dull melody. Taking a first pass at improving it, we might say that pitches shouldn't repeat consecutively:

Pitches[i] $\neq$ Pitches[i − 1]

This produces the melody in figure 20.2. How does the system construct such melodies automatically when given an underconstrained description? To select a pitch in a melody, the system ordinarily searches with respect to a reference pitch. The value for the reference pitch is one of the following: the previously entered or computed pitch; the middle range pitch of the instrument; out of context, C4; the user may select the reference pitch. To construct a sequence of pitches for the underconstrained description, the system searches through candidate pitches, beginning with the reference pitch, for a pitch that does not apparently violate any of the constraints on it or on the structures that contain it.

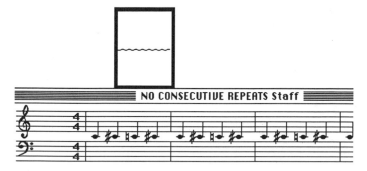

Figure 20.2

The search proceeds in alternating directions from the reference pitch, first in a user-specified default direction (toward C4), then in the opposite, then further in the default direction again; so the effect is to choose the satisfactory pitch nearest to the reference pitch in either direction, with a user-determined preference in the event of a tie. Next we begin enforcing harmonic constraints. In the example, at first there is only one chord, and one key.

LENGTH(Chords) = LENGTH(Keys) = 1
ChordRoots[1] = C
ChordQualities[1] = Major
KeyRoots[1] = C
KeyQualities[1] = Ionian

These do not affect the suggestion for a pitch sequence until we say something like

KeyConsonant?[i] = TRUE

which restricts the melody to the C Ionian scale (figure 20.3), or

ChordConsonant?[i] = TRUE

which restricts us to C Major arpeggios (figure 20.4). This still isn't very musical. Let's introduce a chord progression with more than one element. Like the simple melodies above, the chord progression can be constructed largely by default; to make a typical song progression we have to add a few constraints. First we indicate that the initial chord is the same stable chord

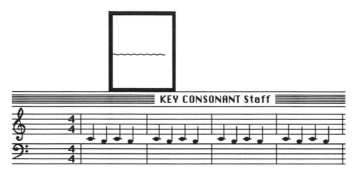

Figure 20.3

Figure 20.4

as the final one—that together they provide a harmonic center for the piece.

$$\text{FIRST(Chords)} = \text{LAST(Chords)}$$
$$\text{STABLE?(LAST(Chords))} = \text{TRUE}$$

Next we describe the default motion of the chord roots along the circle of fifths. In the most typical, classical harmony, the chord root moves *cadentially*, in a descending trajectory along the degree circle of fifths. We establish this and allow the total length of the progression to vary.[1]

Now there is slack for chord sequences of any length. We have yet to place any constraint on the chord qualities, but we have already outlined the root motion of a large class of popular songs. Gershwin's "I Got Rhythm" and the "Heart and Soul" duet some children play on the piano both follow [C A D G C A D G ...]; "Five Foot Two," "Basin Street

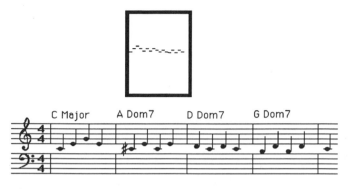

Figure 20.5

Blues," and "No Regrets" follow the six chord circle, [C E A D G C], each with its own solution for fitting the sequence of six roots into eight bars; and chord progressions for many other popular songs can easily be viewed as elaborations of this basic structure. We will use this for the system's default progression structure. Furthermore, we'll set the default ChordTimeIntervals[i] to 1 (a whole note), and by default we'll select the chord qualities from the most common unstable qualities. Again, we treat the first and last elements differently by creating a new sequence variable: here MiddleQualities excludes both the first and last elements of the main progression.

MiddleQualities = HEAD(TAIL(ChordQualities))
MEMBER?(MiddleQualities[i], {Dominant7 Minor7 HalfDiminished7}
  = TRUE
ChordTimeIntervals[i] = 1
LENGTH(Chords) = 4

The resulting melody constructed by the simple algorithms shown in figure 20.5 has considerably more structure. The progression is quite common; the unstable Dominant7 quality was chosen for every chord except the endpoints. Alternatively, it is also common to require chords to fall within the key.

Bass Player

Next we construct a harmonic anchoring voice like the New Orleans tuba or the bass in a jazz or rock band. These employ a regular pulse in the low register, playing the root of the chord whenever the chord changes. This will be our first use of subsequences and hierarchy in the system. First we construct an outline, a structure-capturing melody that is never played, which will be used to build other melodies. Then we construct a second-level embellishment of the outline melody. Here, the pitches in the outline melody are targets or trajectory points for the embellished melody. There may be many levels of outline/embellishment in different parts of a piece.

We introduce several new melody variables. The BO prefix identifies the Bass Outline voice the way integer suffixes were used to distinguish voices in earlier examples. The outline follows the timing of the chord progression itself.

BOTimes = ChordTimes

The pitches in the outline are constrained to the low register, and in accordance with the bass's usual harmonic role, the pitch class of each pitch in the outline must be the root of the corresponding chord.

BOPitches[i] ≤ C3
BOPitchClassSched[t] = ChordRootSched[ChordTimes@ < t]

The system constructs a corresponding bass outline, shown in figure 20.6. We then embellish the bass melody with trajectories toward each of the outline pitches. This is similar to the earlier construction of chord roots leading toward the final chord, but now we construct such a sequence for every element in the outline and use chromatic or degree steps rather than steps along the Pythagorean circle.

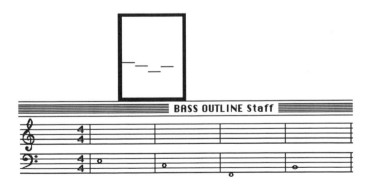

Figure 20.6

The actual melody in the bass, BassPitches, is constructed from a sequence of pitch sequences, BassPhrases, which is in turn described in terms of the Bass Outline. We use the prefix BP to indicate BassPhrases variables. The bass line itself proceeds at regular intervals, 1/4 notes.

$$\text{BassPeriod}[i] = 1/4$$
$$\text{BassTimeIntervals}[i] = \text{BassPeriod}$$
$$\text{BassTimeIntervals}[i] = \text{BassTimes}[i + 1] - \text{BassTimes}[i]$$

The number of events in each phrase is then determined by the amount of time between successive events in the outline (which here correspond to the chord changes).

$$\text{LENGTH}(\text{BPPitches}[i]) = \text{BOTimeIntervals}[i]/\text{BassPeriod}$$

The outline pitch is the last note in each phrase.

$$\text{LAST}(\text{BPPitches}) = \text{BOPitches}[i + 1]$$

The unity offset is required since in the description the first pitch in the outline is not used to construct a phrase; it is a left-hand fence post. Finally, we must indicate that the pitches in the phrases are the same elements, in the same order, as the pitches in the bass melody itself. We construct a delimiting sequence of Boolean values, PhraseEnd?, synchronized with the outline sequence to use as the delimiter in a DELIMIT expression. As usual, the X prefix indicates a version of the chord progression resynchronized to the indices of the bass melody. A change in the chord delimits the last event in the phrase.

$$\text{PhraseEnd?}[i] = (\text{XChords}[i - 1] \neq \text{XChords}[i])$$
$$\text{BPPitches} = \text{DELIMIT}(\text{TAIL}(\text{BassPitches}), \text{PhraseEnd?})$$

This describes the construction of BassPitches from BPPitches, except for the first element, which should be the first outline pitch.

$$\text{FIRST}(\text{BassPitches}) = \text{FIRST}(\text{BOPitches})$$

Now if we ask the system to construct BassPitches, it may do so from BOPitches. Since only the last pitch in any of the phrases is constrained, the system constructs the phrases in figure 20.7. The outline appears again in gray, raised up one octave for visibility. This still isn't very "musical"; the root of each new chord is appearing too early. The bass line is antici-

Figure 20.7

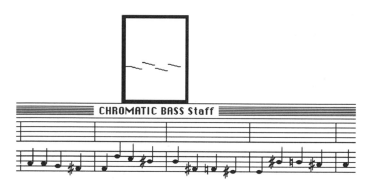

Figure 20.8

pating the chord root, when in the bass we seek the suspense of a trajectory *toward* it. The repeated notes are inappropriate. We might fix this by saying

BPPitches[i,j] ≠ BPPitches[i,j − 1]

Or by constraining the corresponding Contour variable forBass Phrases: following our conventions, BPContour is a sequence of sequences corresponding to the melodic pattern of each phrase. Thus the constraint above might also appear simply as

BPContour[i,j] ≠ 0

The resulting bass line in figure 20.8 is more reasonable. The algorithm constructs the outline pitches in the usual way, then constructs each phrase in reverse order, beginning with the already-known final pitch. Since there is no constraint except that pitches in the phrase not repeat, the search always terminates with the pitch immediately above its neighbor; the effect in the melody is a descending chromatic trajectory. In musical context, the

Figure 20.9

effect is one of slight suspense—of purposeful motion toward a rhythmically and harmonically important event from the outline. The pattern is
quite common, especially in double bass accompaniments in jazz bands.

Several simple variants of this bass model form other familiar patterns
of bass motion. The phrases above descended because, under partial constraint, the chromatic neighbor nearest to C4 was chosen. If, in recognition
of the bass instrument range, we change the default position to C2, the bass
trajectories ascend as in figure 20.9. We can add a constraint that makes
each trajectory proceed in the same direction as the outline.

$$BPContour[i,j] = BOContour[i]$$

Alternatively, the local chromatic motion can proceed in the direction
opposite from the outline.

$$BPContour[i,j] = -BOContour[i]$$

As shown in figure 20.10, the example is full of jumps since the trajectories are contrary to the natural motion of the outline melody. The
pattern is less typical. Each of the above is a parody, an extended repetition
of a particular constraint on the bass pattern. Musicians keep a vocabulary
of many such alternative methods for satisfying a particular constraint,
and they select different ones as their attention shifts, or in the course of
solving some other problem—though simple variety may be the further
goal.

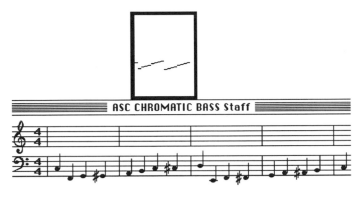

Figure 20.10

Ragtime Left Hand

The next example includes construction of ragtime piano left- and right-hand patterns, each of which may include several simultaneous pitches. We construct the left- and right-hand patterns separately, fitting them to a concurrent harmonic progression. The ragtime piano left hand is periodic, like the bass above, and also has a characteristic "Oom-Pah" alternating pattern. The left hand may play as many as three pitches at once, so we distinguish the melodies with the prefixes LH1, LH2, and LH3. The "Oom" part of the pattern functions much like the bass in the earlier examples; it is often helpful to view it as a separate outlinelike melody. Most commonly, the Oom and Pah sounds fall on strong and weak beats respectively. First we indicate the constant rate of bass over all.

LHTimeIntervals[i] = 1/8
LHTimeIntervals[i] = LHTimes[i + 1] − LHTimes[i]

We could define the alternating Ooms in terms of beat strength, but since the left hand is periodic we can do it even more easily, and without moving into the schedule representation: odd sequence elements are Ooms, even ones are Pahs.

Oom?[i] = (MOD i 2)=1)
Pah?[i] = NOT(Oom?[i])
Oom1Pitches[i] = LH1Pitches[(2*i) − 1]
Pah1Pitches[i] = LH1Pitches[2*i]
Oom2Pitches[i] = LH2Pitches[(2*i) − 1]

...

Figure 20.11

Figure 20.12

In our simplified Joplin-style ragtime, an Oom is generally a pair of low pitches separated by an octave (twelve chromatic steps), while a Pah is three pitches, somewhat higher, spanning less than an octave and all consonant with the chord. We let LH1 be the lowest pitch for both of these, with LH2 and LH3 the successively higher ones.

$$\text{Oom1Pitches}[i] < C2$$
$$\text{Oom2Pitches}[i] = \text{Oom3Pitches}[i] = \text{Oom1Pitches}[i] + 12^2$$

$$\text{Pah1Pitches}[i] < F3$$
$$\text{Pah3Pitches}[i] > \text{Pah2Pitches}[i] > \text{Pah1Pitches}[i]$$

$$\text{CONSONANT?}(\text{Pah1Pitches}[i], \text{XChords}[i]) =$$
$$\quad \text{CONSONANT?}(\text{Pah2Pitches}[i], \text{XChords}[i]) =$$
$$\quad \text{CONSONANT?}(\text{Pah3Pitches}[i], \text{XChords}[i]) = \text{TRUE}$$

Finally, like some of the earlier bass instruments, we require that the Oom melody not repeat pitches consecutively and that it play either the root or the fifth scale degree of the voice.

$$\text{Oom1Pitches}[i] \neq \text{Oom1Pitches}[i - 1]$$
$$\text{MEMBER?}(\text{Oom1ScaleDegrees}[i], \{1 \ 5\}) = \text{TRUE}$$

Combined with the chord progression, this results in the gradual construction of the ragtime left-hand pattern shown in figures 20.11 through 20.15.

Figure 20.13

Figure 20.14

Figure 20.15

Ragtime Right Hand

In the final synthesis example, we construct a typical ragtime right-hand pattern using the same description language. Having explained the use of the language in the previous examples, we return to the briefer, informal verbal description format. Also, we use a different chord progression, beginning with a root on degree four rather than degree one of the key.[3]

The default range of the right hand will be higher than for the left; we set the reference pitch to E5 and again describe an outline pattern that is consonant with the given chord. Since in ragtime we presume the chord root and quality are indicated by the left hand, we don't require the right hand to serve any specific harmonic role; we simply don't want to purposelessly violate the harmonic structure that the left hand establishes. Here we constrain the outermost outline to be consonant with the chord and to change when the chord changes. Figure 20.16 shows the outline moving from one chord consonance to nearest adjacent one.

The right-hand texture we have in mind is syncopated at the next level of elaboration. The details of the syncopation pattern may vary; here we

Figure 20.16

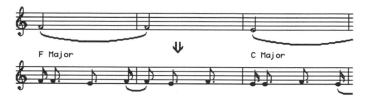

Figure 20.17

Figure 20.18

Figure 20.19

choose a simple method of filling the rhythmic intervals with a regular 3/16 pattern, which will precess with respect to the binary meter. As with the chord root motion constraints above, we relax the 3/16 constraint for the first interval, truncating to fit the two-measure intervals roundly. We also constrain the pitches at this level to fall on the scale, C Ionian. Figure 20.17 shows the previous outline and the resulting new embellishment.

In the last embellishment that will affect the rhythm, we insert ascending 1/16 note (chord consonant) arpeggios—elaborations of the most recent pitch at the previous level. Figure 20.18 again shows contrast between the two levels.

We add one more characteristic elaboration for this ragtime pattern: we accent the syncopated outline melody by doubling it with pitches one octave above. The new before/after picture is shown in figure 20.19. Finally, combining this with the ragtime left-hand version of the same chord progression, we obtain the two-handed fragment shown in figure 20.20.

This combination of patterns—derived from manual analysis of parts of Joplin's pieces *Maple Leaf Rag* and *Elite Syncopations*—creates a distinctly ragtime effect. The template is a not a definition of ragtime, but the use of syncopation, three-note arpeggio patterns, doubled octaves, and oom-pahs are typical of Joplin's and James Scott's ragtime work.

This concludes our treatment of musical examples. I have performed several experiments with genre in the lab by devising models and applying them to various chord progressions. The genre simulations included a few jazz bass player simulations like those described; an up-tempo bebop horn player that produced long phrases of rapid (1/16th notes), hierarchically structured lines; and a three-voice band simulation that included a bass player and two upper voices.

Figure 20.20

Notes

1. For reasons of space, the detailed development of the DegreeCircleMotion constraints described in Levitt's thesis has been omitted here.

2. During Ooms, when only two left-hand pitches are playing, we say the LH3 pitch is the same as LH2 to indicate its effective silence. This is somewhat different from the approach taken in standard music notation, where there are explicit silences (rests) and where a melody or voice may take on a varying number of pitches under some conditions. But this alternative description would complicate the model without providing much musical or computational insight.

3. The progression itself here is of little significance; it originates from an experiment in which a program harmonically analyzed part of Joplin's *Elite Syncopations*, and reused the progression to produce new ragtime in the manner shown.

H. Christopher Longuet-Higgins's "The Perception of Melodies" (1976) describes a program that makes a "typical" Western musician's transcription of a melody played on an electronic keyboard. Most transcription programs, such as Moorer's 1975 thesis, focus on the difficult problem of extracting one or more simultaneous pitches from a recording of an acoustic signal. Instead, Longuet-Higgins focusses on how the way a simple melody is notated reflects the data structures we've already built in our minds for describing it—what the main key area is, what the metrical structure is, and so on. The program works at several levels—harmonic, rhythmic, and melodic.

Longuet-Higgins and his well-documented programs have provided some of the most insightful, practical representations of musical "common sense" in the literature. While this is not explicitly a composing program, it captures basic, multilevel musical common sense in a way that makes the implicit knowledge of every songwriter visible.

Like Lerdahl and Jackendoff, Longuet-Higgins brings musical sophistication to the task. More important, he focusses on basic problems—such as, how does someone listening to a melody guess what key it is in, and when it modulates?—in a way that makes major presumptions about "already given" knowledge of music or linguistics. The final result, an operating transcription program, forces him to make explicit all the assumptions a theoretical linguist might be tempted to take for granted. An example as simple as the default notation for "Shave and a Haircut—two bits" is laden with meaning, and Longuet-Higgins presents it in a way that is intuitive to almost any musician. At the paper's end, automatic transcription of parts of Wagner's *Tristan und Isolde* demonstrate the application of the same principles in more complex examples.

The chapter introduces several themes that appear throughout Longuet-Higgins's extensive music work, in particular a multidimensional representation of harmony. He shows how, by viewing harmony as a multidimensional space with various projections, the problem of finding the key or following a modulation becomes one of setting limits on the step size within that space. Several music representation and music education projects (Levitt 1985, Holland 1987) have demonstrated further uses of this approach. The paper also provides a strong example of rhythm transcription: the tempo is assumed to be fixed within certain error limits, until strong enough evidence indicates either a syncopation or a tempo change.

The appendix showing Longuet-Higgins's program, written in the POP2 language, offers programmers a much clearer idea of how the programs work and how simple the algorithms are. For a complete selection of Longuet-Higgins's writing in artificial intelligence, music, linguistics, vision, and memory, *Mental Processes: Studies in Cognitive Science* (1987) is a rich resource. The chapters "The Three Dimensions of Harmony" (1965) and "Two Letters to a musical friend" (1962) provide a look at Longuet-Higgins's original thoughts on the topics applied in "The Perception of Melodies."

21 The Perception of Melodies

H. Christopher Longuet-Higgins

A searching test of practical musicianship is the "aural test" in which the subject is required to write down, in standard musical notation, a melody he has never heard before. His transcription is not to be construed as a detailed record of the actual performance, which will inevitably be more or less out of time and out of tune, but as an indication of the rhythmic and tonal relations between the individual notes. How the musical listener perceives these relationships is a matter of some interest to the cognitive psychologist. In this chapter, I outline a theory of the perception of classical Western melodies and describe a computer program, based on the theory, that displays, as best it can, the rhythmic and tonal relationships between the notes of a melody as played by a human performer on an organ console.

The basic premise of the theory is that in perceiving a melody the listener builds a conceptual structure representing the rhythmic groupings of the notes and the musical intervals between them. It is this structure that he commits to memory, and which subsequently enables him to recognize the tune, and to reproduce it in sound or in writing if he happens to be a skilled musician. A second premise is that much can be learned about the structural relationships in any ordinary piece of music from a study of its orthographic representation. Take, for example, the musical cliche notated in figure 21.1.

The way in which the notes are rhythmically grouped is evident from the disposition of the bar lines and the "beams" linking the notes of the first bar. The rhythm is, in this case, a binary tree, each terminal of which is a note or a rest, but more generally such a tree may have ternary as well as binary nodes.

The tonal relations between the notes in figure 21.1 are also indicated by the symbolism, but more subtly. It is a common mistake to suppose that the position of a note on the five-line stave (and its prefix, if any) indicates merely the approximate pitch of the note—where it would be located on the keyboard. If that were true, an equally acceptable alternative to figure 21.1 would be figure 21.2, in which the Ab has been written as a G, with the same location on the keyboard. But a music student who offered figure 21.2 as his transcription would lose marks for having misrepresented the

Copyright 1987, H. Christopher Longuet-Higgins, and reproduced by permission.

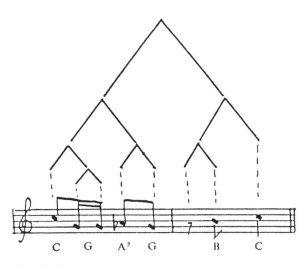

Figure 21.1

Figure 21.2

tonal relation of the fourth note to its neighbors (though he could hardly be imagined not to have perceived it properly).

The problems posed by melodic perception are not dissimilar to those that arise in perception of speech. The distinction between the Ab in figure 21.1 and the G♯ in figure 21.2 is analogous to the difference between the homophones "here" and "hear" in English; though these words sound exactly alike, they are interpreted and spelled quite differently according to the context in which they are heard. Another problem in speech perception, which has its counterpart in the perception of melody, relates to the timing of successive acoustic events. The way in which the syllables of a poem are perceptually grouped into "feet" is largely unaffected by variations in rate of delivery, and the same applies to the rhythmic grouping of the notes of a melody. Notes, which on paper are of equal length, will in a live performance be sounded at quite unequal intervals of time, particularly in an "expressive" performance. A change of meter from duplets to triplets can, nevertheless, usually be distinguished quite clearly from a mere quickening of tempo, in a reasonably competent performance. Previous programs for the automatic transcription of music have required the performer to maintain a fairly constant tempo (Styles 1973, Askenfelt 1976); but human listeners have no difficulty in discerning the rhythms of melodies played by performers who are free from this constraint.

The third premise of the theory is that the perception of rhythm and the perception of tonal relationships can be viewed as independent processes. This strong claim (which is not to be misunderstood as referring to the process of musical composition) may be weakly supported by two observations. First, a given melodic sequence such as the ascending major scale will be heard as such by a Western musician regardless of the rhythm in which it is played. Conversely, a "dotted" rhythm, for example, will be clearly recognizable for what it is, regardless of the musical intervals between the successive notes. To say this is not, of course, to deny that higher cognitive processes can and will operate on the "surface structure" generated by rhythmic and tonal perception, to reveal musically significant relations between the rhythm and the tonality. But one may reasonably suppose that such processes of musical appreciation can begin only when some structure has been created on which they can get to work.

Rhythm

One might imagine that to discern the rhythm of a melody the listener must be able to perceive differences in loudness between successive notes. This may be true on occasion, but it fails as a generalization for two reasons. First of all, performers do not as a rule thump out every note that occurs on a beat or at the beginning of a bar; to do so would be as tiresome as to accent, in reading a poem, every syllable that occurred at the beginning of a foot. But more decisively, there are instruments, such as the organ and harpsichord, on which it is physically impossible for the performer to vary the acoustic intensity of each individual note; all he can control is the time of onset of the note and its temporal duration. It is nevertheless quite possible for a listener to perceive correctly the rhythm of a melody played on such an instrument; we conclude that temporal information alone is enough for the purpose, except in special circumstances.

The basic assumption underlying the rhythmic component of the program is that the first necessity in perceiving the rhythmic structure of a

melody is to identify the time of occurrence of each "beat." Music in which
the beat is irregular falls outside the scope of the theory, which therefore
has nothing to say about the rhythmic perception of recitative or of music
in which the beats alternate in length. The grouping of the beats into higher
metrical units such as "bars" raises issues that have been discussed elsewhere (Longuet-Higgins and Steedman 1971, Steedman 1973); the principal concern of the present study is with the manner in which each beat
should be subdivided and with the problem of keeping track of the beat
through unforeseen changes in tempo.

In Western music, by far the commonest subdivisions of the beat are into
two and into three shorter metrical units; these in turn can be further
subdivided into two or three. Whether a beat or a fraction of a beat is
perceived to be divided depends, according to the theory, on whether or
not it is interrupted by the onset of a note. What counts as an "interruption" is a matter of some delicacy to which I shall return in a moment.

After such a process of division and subdivision, every note will find
itself at the beginning of an uninterrupted metrical unit. It is the relations
between these metrical units that constitute the rhythm of the tune; the
metrical units can be thought of as the nodes of a tree in which each
nonterminal node has either two or three descendants. Every terminal
node in the tree will eventually be attached either to a rest or to a note
(which may be sounded or tied) in the manner of figure 21.1. The program
does not actually draw such trees nor print out a musical stave; it represents the rhythm in a nested bracketed notation. It also indicates the
phrasing; if the offset of a note occurs earlier than halfway through its
allotted time, or else appreciably before the end of that time, the note is
marked "stc" standing for "staccato," or "ten," for "tenuto."

We now return to the question. What counts as an interruption? By
what criterion could a listener judge whether the onset of a note occurs
during the current metrical unit rather than *at* its beginning or its end?
Plainly there must be some upper limit to the temporal discrepancies he
can disregard, just as there is a lower limit to those he can detect. The
former limit—the listener's "tolerance"—must obviously exceed the latter.
It must be small enough to permit the structuring of rapid rhythmic
figures, but large enough to allow a reasonable degree of flexibility to the
tempo. In the program the tolerance can be preset to any desired value.
Experiments with the program indicate that for reasonably careful perfor-

mances a tolerance of about 10 centiseconds meets both criteria, but that for more expressive performances of relatively sedate melodies a greater tolerance is needed if an obvious rubato is not to be misconstrued as a variation in rhythm.

In order to perceive the rhythm clearly a listener must, it is assumed, take account of the precise onset time of every note within any metrical unit in predicting when the unit could end. The rule eventually adopted for making such predictions was as follows: If, in the course of a binary metrical unit, a note which terminates the first subunit begins a little less than halfway through, then the expected further duration of the unit is reduced in magnitude to the mean of its original value and the value implied by the time of onset of the note in question. Corresponding remarks apply, of course, in cases where the note is slightly late or the current metrical hypothesis assigns a ternary rather than a binary structure to the metrical unit in question. In fact the program also allows for the termination of a metrical unit, not by the actual onset of a note, but by the anticipated end of a lower metrical unit that is itself interrupted by the onset of one or more notes. Such procedures are, unfortunately, much more difficult to specify precisely in English than in a suitably designed programming language, but this fact only underlines the value of casting perceptual theories in computational form.

Finally, it is necessary to commit oneself, in writing such a program, to a view as to what counts as good perceptual evidence for a change in meter. It is here assumed that the listener initially expects a pure binary meter, but is prepared to change his mind at any level in the metrical hierarchy. The evidence for a change in meter may be of two kinds: that the current meter implies a "syncopation," in which the beginning of the next beat, or higher metrical unit, is not accompanied by the onset of a note; or that it implies a "distortion" in which an excessively large change of tempo is required to accommodate the current metrical hypothesis. Each of these outcomes represents a flouting of the listener's expectations, and either may, according to the theory, lead him to change his opinion about the meter if the other possible division of the current metrical unit (ternary instead of binary, or vice versa) does not imply a distortion or a syncopation. Lastly, it is assumed that, once having changed his mind, the listener does not change it back again until he encounters positive evidence for doing so.

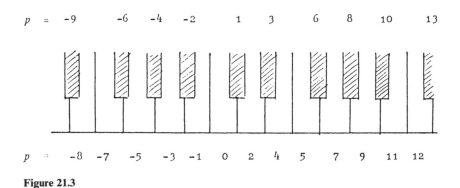

$p = $ -9   -6   -4   -2   1   3   6   8   10   13

$p = $ -8   -7   -5   -3   -1   0   2   4   5   7   9   11   12

Figure 21.3

Tonality

In committing a melody to memory, the listener must not only create a rhythmic structure of the kind depicted in figure 21.1; he must also identify the tonality of each note which is to be attached to it. This tonal information should ideally suffice, not only for the transcription of the melody into standard notation, but also for the purpose of evaluating the intonation of a performance on, say, the violin, which permits fine distinctions of pitch that cannot be made explicit on a keyboard instrument. (See figure 21.3.) To appreciate what is involved in this task, it is necessary to formalize the classical theory of tonality developed by Rameau (1721), Bosanquet (1876), Helmholtz (1885), and other writers. In the formal theory (Longuet-Higgins 1962,1972) every musical note is assigned coordinates (x, y, z) in a "tonal space" of three dimensions, corresponding to the perfect fifth, the major third, and the octave, respectively. (The ideal frequency ratios of these intervals are 3/2, 5/4, and 2/1 respectively—involving the first three prime numbers—so that they are strictly incommensurable when not distorted by equal temperament.) Thus in figure 21.4, if the origin is taken as "middle C," the tonal coordinates of the various notes are as shown in the first three rows of the table. The following points may be noted:

1. It is the relative values of the coordinates (x, y, z), not their absolute values, which characterize the melodic sequence. Thus, increasing all the z values by 1 would merely put the melody up one octave.

2. The numerical values of the coordinates (x, y, z) are all small; this is evidently the result of having chosen middle C as origin.

x	0	1	0	1	.	1	0	(0)
y	0	0	-1	0	.	1	0	(2)
z	1	0	1	0	.	0	1	(0)
p	12	7	8	7	.	11	12	(8)
q	0	1	-4	1	.	5	0	(8)
N	C	G	A♭	G	.	B	C	(G♯)

Figure 21.4

3. The "position" p of each note on the keyboard, that is, its distance above middle C in keyboard semitones, is given by $p = 7x + 4y + 12z$, so that there are arbitrarily many different notes (x, y, z) with the same value of p.

4. The conventional name of any note is determined not by its keyboard position p but by its "sharpness" q, defined as $q = x + 4y$. The name N of the note is such that there are q sharps, or $-q$ flats, in the key signature of N major. Thus an "A" is a note with $q = 3$, and an "Ab" is one with $q = -4$.

The task of naming the notes of a melody played on the keyboard, or of notating them correctly on the five-line stave, therefore involves the apparently insoluble problem of determining the three coordinates (x, y, z) of each note from its keyboard position p, so as to be able to determine its sharpness q. The problem is analogous to the visual problem of adding an extra dimension to the two-dimensional image of a three-dimensional scene, except that a keyboard performance of a melody supplies the listener with only one directly audible dimension, to which he must add two more to identify each note uniquely.

There is in fact a short cut to the solution of this problem, arising from the mathematical fact that a given choice of p severely restricts the range of possible values of q. A little simple arithmetic shows that q must differ from $7p$ by a multiple of 12. If, therefore, we can find independent grounds for limiting q to one of a fairly small set of values, we can determine it uniquely from the remainder upon division of p by 12. A survey of the published scores of classical melodies reveals (Longuet-Higgins 1962, 1972) that the value of q (which can be directly determined from the notation) never changes from one note to the next by more than eleven units of sharpness. As a consequence, if δq is the "span" of any interval between two successive notes, then the "degree" oq of that interval is restricted to the following alternative values when δq lies in the range -11 to $+12$:

By far the commonest intervals occurring in classical and traditional melodies are "diatonic" intervals, with $|\delta q| < 6$. "Chromatic" intervals, with $|\delta q| > 6$, and "diabolic" intervals, with $|\delta q| = 6$, are relatively rare. If they were nonexistent, the degree Coq of each interval would be uniquely determined by its span p, and one could infer the sharpness of each note in any melody from its position relative to its immediate predecessor. Such a "Markovian" theory of tonal perception would, as it happens, correctly predict the q values in figure 21.4. It would, however, fail dismally for melodies containing chromatic scales, because each keyboard semitone in such a scale would be assigned the same value of δq, and this would lead to absurd tonal interpretations such as that shown in figure 21.5.

An alternative, and musically much more plausible, hypothesis is that the listener identifies the sharpness of each note by placing it within a diatonic interval of the very first note (or perhaps an interval of degree 6 if the span indicates that the interval is diatonic). Such a rule would account equally well for the q values of the notes in figure 21.4. It would, further-more, account very nicely for the sharpness of the notes in the theme of Bach's Musical Offering (figure 21.6). In this melody there are in fact four chromatic intervals—a diminished seventh between the fourth and fifth notes, of degree $q = 9$, and three chromatic semitones, of degree -7. Such intervals could not, for obvious reasons, be correctly identified by the "Markovian" procedure.

It will not do, however, to assume that the first note is invariably the "keynote" to which every other note should be referred in order to deter-mine its sharpness, first because melodies very often begin on notes other

Figure 21.5

than the keynote, or "tonic," and second because the tonic may very well seem to change in the course of a melody, when we speak of a "modulation" having occurred.

A good example of an indisputable modulation is to be found in the subject of the B minor fugue in the first book of Bach's *Wohltemperierte Klavier*. (See figure 21.7.) The first three notes clearly establish the tonic as B ($q = 5$), and all the other notes in bars 1 and 2 are related to it by nonchromatic intervals ($|\delta q| < 7$). But the first note of bar 3, though in the same keyboard position as the C in bar 2, is notated differently. To have written it as a C would have produced the sequence C♯ C C♯ calling for two chromatic semitones in succession. But in unaccompanied classical melodies such an event never seems to occur, for the very good reason that if X Y Z are three successive notes of a melody which, on paper, are separated by chromatic intervals X Y and Y Z, then there is always an alternative, simpler, interpretation of the middle note Y which transforms both intervals into diatonic ones. Generally speaking, then, the tonal identity of a note cannot be finally established until the following note is heard. In figure 21.7 the offending note has become transformed into a B♯ making both the neighboring intervals into diatonic semitones, of degree 5 and -5 rather than -7 and 7 respectively. But a B♯ is too far from the old tonic B to belong to its key, so that a modulation is perceived to occur to a new key, that of F, such that the value of oq for the new note B is only 6, which is just close enough for comfort.

There seem to be other general restrictions upon the contexts in which chromatic intervals occur in classical melodies. The most important of

| p | 0 | 3 | 7 | 8 | -1 | 7 | 6 | 5 | 4 | 3 | 2 | 1 | 0 | -1 | -3 | -5 | 0 | 5 | 3 | 2 | 0 |
| q | 0 | -3 | 1 | -4 | 5 | 1 | 6 | -1 | 4 | -3 | 2 | -5 | 0 | 5 | 3 | 1 | 0 | -1 | -3 | 2 | 0 |

Figure 21.6

Figure 21.7

these relates to four-note sequences W X Y Z in which the middle interval is chromatic. In such a sequence not only must both W X and Y Z be nonchromatic, but at least one of the intervals W Y and X Z must be diatonic. If the interpretations of W, X, Y, and Z based on the current key violate this rule, then the tonality of the note Y is reinterpreted in such a way as to make X Y a diatonic interval, and to force a modulation into a key to which Y belongs. As implied by what has been said, a note is regarded as belonging to a given key if its sharpness relative to the tonic lies in the range -5 to $+6$ inclusive.

Another rule that seems to be necessary in order to account for the notation of chromatic scales, particularly in music of the period following Bach, concerns the tonal interpretation of ascending semitones. If such a semitone ends on the note of a key whose sharpness relative to the tonic is 2, 3, 4, or 5, then its first note is to be assigned a relative sharpness 7, 8, 9, or 10. Though this reassignment places the note outside the key, it does not by itself precipitate a modulation; if it did, then an ascending chromatic scale of any length would trigger a whole sequence of modulations into progressively sharper and sharper keys.

Two further rules are necessary, and sufficient, for determining the relative sharpnesses of the notes in most classical melodies. The first is a rule to the effect that for the purposes of establishing tonality one may conflate repeated notes, or notes separated by an octave (the second and third notes in figure 21.4 provide an example). The other rule, which is theoretically less satisfactory, is that the tonic may be determined from the first two notes, and that it will be either the first note itself or the note a fifth below it. This rule, and the absence of any more delicate tests of modulation than those already described, are undoubtedly the weakest links in the tonal section of the program.

Before I describe the program in detail, a few words of caution may be in order. First, the tonal rules outlined above must not be expected to apply to accompanied melodies, where the accompaniment supplies tonal information that may not be implicit in the melody itself. Nor must it be supposed that the rules necessarily hold for covertly polyphonic melodies in which, for example, alternate notes really belong to two different melodies. Further, the contextual constraints on chromatic intervals will often be violated at phrase boundaries, marked by rhythmically prominent rests, though this is not always the case. And finally, one must allow for the possibility that in a musical score a radical change of notation (such as occurs between the first and second sections of Chopin's "*Raindrop*" *Prelude*) does not signify a real change in tonality, but merely an enharmonic change designed to simplify the reader's task. Only if such qualifications are borne in mind can the program safely be used to indicate how a melody performed on the keyboard should be transcribed into conventional notation.

The Program

The program accepts as input a list of sublists, each of which comprises three numbers. The first number is the keyboard position of the corresponding note and lies in the range 0 to 48, there being four octaves on the organ console. The second number is the time in centiseconds at which the note was depressed, and the third number indicates the time at which the note was released. The order of the notes on the list is the order of their times of onset. The list itself is generated from a live performance of a melody on an electronic organ connected, through an analogue-to-digital converter, to a high-speed paper-tape punch. The information on the paper tape is equivalent to the information that would be recorded on a player piano roll, and no more. The preprocessing of the paper tape is an entirely automatic matter, which simply involves constructing the above-mentioned list from the paper-tape record and transferring it to disk storage.

The performer is required, by the present version of the program, to establish the initial tempo and the number of beats in a bar by prefacing his performance of the melody by a bar's worth of beats on some low note, which may conveniently be positioned an octave below the first note of the melody, so as not to prejudice the tonality.

The program itself is written in POP2, the high-level programming language designed and developed in Edinburgh by Burstall and Popplestone (Burstall et al. 1971). It is relatively short and is structured as follows. First, the list of sublists is converted into a list of records, each of which has a "slot" indicating the pitch, onset time, and offset time of a particular note, and further slots which are to hold and span p and the degree cq of the interval between the note and its predecessor. The keynote is then fixed by the positions of the first two notes, and the relative sharpnesses of all the notes are determined from their keyboard positions by an algorithm based on the theory of tonality outlined in the previous section. The next stage is a rhythmic analysis (which could have been carried out first, as it is indifferent to the results of the tonal routines). Each beat is examined in turn, by a combination of "top down" and "bottom up" analysis in which the time of onset of each note is used both for establishing the structure of the rhythmic hierarchy and for correcting the estimated tempo. In the course of this analysis the time of offset of each note is used for determining how the note was phrased.

The final stage in the operation of the program corresponds to the exercise of musical literacy; it consists of displaying, on paper, the essential features of the structure created by the rhythmic and tonal analyses as a sequence of nested lists of symbols. The innermost symbols name the individual notes as, for example, "D" (D natural), "DS" (D sharp), or "DB" (D flat); the word REST is self-explanatory. Each name is preceded by either the word TIED if the note is tied to its predecessor or a number indicating the span (not the degree, which is implicit in the name of the note) of the interval from the preceding note; this is needed for identifying the octave in which the note occurs. Finally, a note that is not tied may be followed by the abbreviation STC or TEN indicating that the note was played *staccato* or *tenuto*; the absence of either abbreviation implies that the note was played *legato*.

Figures 21.8, 21.9, and 21.10 provide examples of the program's performance. Each figure indicates (a) the "raw" input, in which each set of three numbers gives the keyboard position of a note and its times of onset and offset in centiseconds, (b) the output generated by the program from the input (a), and (c) the result of transcribing the output (b) by hand into ordinary stave notation.

The performance of the tune shown in figure 21.8 was prefaced by a single low C, and the time between the onset of this note and the next was arbitrarily taken as a "minim" in adopting the note values indicated in (c); it will be noted that in (b) the outermost brackets enclose a minim's worth

Figure 21.8

```
: printlist(tris);
```

```
[  12  24  114]
[  12 148  238]
[  24 274  399]
[  31 400  554]
[  34 551  587]
[  32 586  671]
[  27 669  711]
[  32 707  794]
[  26 795  831]
[  31 829  860]
[  24 863  895]
[  29 895  989]
[  31 987 1021]
[  29 1020 1145]
[  27 1140 1242]
[  26 1268 1282]
[  24 1289 1298]
[  22 1308 1320]
[  29 1332 1452]
[  26 1450 1495]
[  22 1508 1517]
[  21 1528 1536]
[  20 1546 1556]
[  27 1570 1696]
[  24 1692 1734]
[  20 1752 1762]
[  19 1774 1782]
[  18 1792 1808]
[  26 1815 1930]
[  29 1928 1934]
[  27 1932 2062]
[  26 2059 2188]
[  25 2183 2446]
[  24 2491 2628]
```

a

```
: 13->tolerance; notate(tris);
```

```
[ 12 C][ 7 G]

[[[TIED G] [ 3 BB]] [-2 AB]][[[TIED AB] [-5 EB]] [ 5 AB]]

[[[TIED AB] [-6 D]] [[ 5 G] [-7 C]]][[ 5 F] [[TIED F] [ 2 G]]]

[-2 F][-2 EB TEN]
```

b

```
[[[-1 D] [-2 C STC] [-2 BB]] [ 7 F]][[TIED F] [-3 D TEN]]

[[[-4 BB STC] [-1 A STC] [-1 AB]] [ 7 EB]][[TIED EB] [-3 C TEN]]

[[[-4 AB STC] [-1 G STC] [-1 FS]] [ 8 D]][[TIED D] [ 3 F -2 EB]]

[[TIED EB] [-1 D]][[TIED D] [-1 DB]]

[TIED DB][TIED DB]

[-1 C]
```

c

Figure 21.9

```
: printlist(stan);

[ 19  148  190]
[ 31  280  287]
[ 29  302  309]
[ 27  322  329]
[ 34  347  466]
[ 31  474  518]
[ 27  538  548]
[ 26  559  566]
[ 25  578  586]
[ 33  605  648]
[ 30  646  657]
[ 26  669  678]
[ 25  687  696]
[ 24  707  714]                          a
[ 32  729  760]
[ 29  769  777]
[ 25  791  801]
[ 24  811  820]
[ 23  830  839]
[ 31  856  987]
[ 27  986  1027]
[ 24  1049  1054]
[ 23  1068  1075]
[ 22  1087  1096]
[ 29  1111  1153]
[ 26  1152  1157]
[ 22  1174  1183]
[ 21  1194  1202]
[ 20  1211  1220]
[ 27  1232  1270]
[ 24  1272  1279]
[ 20  1295  1304]
[ 19  1316  1325]
[ 18  1336  1348]
[ 26  1360  1619]
```

```
: 13->tolerance; notate(stan);

[[[ 12 G STC] [-2 F STC] [-2 EB STC]] [ 7 BB]]

[[TIED BB] [-3 G TEN]]

[[[-4 EB STC] [-1 D STC] [-1 CS STC]] [[ 8 A] [TIED A] [-3 FS]]]      b

[[[-4 D STC] [-1 CS STC] [-1 C STC]] [[ 8 AB] [REST] [-3 F STC]]]

[[[-4 DB STC] [-1 C STC] [-1 B STC]] [ 8 G]]

[[TIED G] [-4 EB TEN]]

[[[[-3 C STC] [-1 B STC]] [-1 BB STC]] [[ 7 F] [TIED F] [-3 D STC]]]

[[[-4 BB STC] [-1 A STC] [-1 AB STC]] [[ 7 EB] [TIED EB] [-3 C STC]]]

[[[-4 AB STC] [-1 G STC] [-1 FS]] [ 8 D]]
```

c

Figure 21.10

of notes. The interpretation (b) was obtained from the input (a) with a tolerance of 10 cs; with a tolerance of 15 cs the program would assign the two semiquavers to the same node. The actual times of onset of the first four quaver units differed in the performance by 37, 27, and 35 cs, respectively, the separation between the last two notes being 39 cs. The considerable discrepancy between these numbers clearly illustrates the acute difficulty which would confront any attempt to determine the rhythm without taking account of its hierarchical structure.

Figure 21.9 shows how the program handled a performance of part of the long *cor anglais* solo from the prelude to Act III of Wagner's *Tristan und Isolde*. This example is interesting in two particular respects. First, it involves the perception of a change from a binary to a ternary meter in the fifth bar; secondly, the published score indicates a grace note at the end of the seventh bar, to which it would be inappropriate to assign a separate place in the rhythmic structure. The program's output agrees fully with the score in its rhythmic and tonal indications. There are slight discrepancies in the marks of phrasing—Wagner marked all the triplet quavers as staccato—but for this the performer is clearly to blame, not the program.

Finally, figure 21.10 illustrates the program's handling of a later section of the same melody (prefaced, this time, by only one "cue" note, which is why each line of the output contains only one, not two, minim units). Again the rhythm is correctly represented, though there are minor discrepancies in phrasing. As for the tonality, the main point to note is the perceptual problem presented by the rapid succession of modulations beginning in the second bar. There is, nevertheless, only one note to which the program assigns a tonality at variance with that indicated by Wagner: he wrote the second C♯ in the second bar as a D♭.

Conclusions

The domain of competence of the program is, of course, very restricted; it cannot be expected to reveal significant tonal or rhythmic relations between the notes of "atonal" or "arhythmic" melodies, for example. But the perceptual theory on which it is based does seem worthy of serious consideration, in that up to the present time no detailed suggestions seem to have been offered as to how a listener builds an internal representation of a melody from a live performance. The most significant rhythmic hypothesis in the theory is that the rhythm of a melody is conceptualized as a structural hierarchy, and that the onset of each note provides important predictive information about the time of onset of the following note at every level in the hierarchy. The hypotheses underlying the tonal section of the program are presumably limited in application to the kind of music that has been developed in the West; but for such music one conclusion at least seems secure, namely, that the tonality of any note cannot in general be established unambiguously until the following note has been heard. It is perhaps surprising that such a limited amount of context should usually suffice for the purpose, but it should be remembered that it is really the key of the melody that creates the tonal context in the first place. It seems altogether possible that the principles of operation of the program's rhythmic component will apply to other temporal processes, such as the perception of speech.

Acknowledgments

I thank D. C. Jeffrey, M. J. Steedman, B. C. Styles, O. P. Buneman, and G. E. Hinton for practical assistance and helpful discussions, and the Royal Society and the SRC for research support.

References

Askenfelt, A. 1976. Quarterly Progress and Status Report, Speech Transmission Laboratory, Royal Institute of Technology, Stockholm 1:1.

Bosanquet, P. H. M. 1876. *Elementary Treatise on Musical Intervals and Temperament.*

Burstall, R. M., J. S. Collins, and R J. Popplestone. 1971. *Programming in POP-2.* Edinburgh University Press.

Helmholtz, H. L. F. 1885. *On the Sensations of Tone* (tr. Ellis), second edition.

Longuet-Higgins, H. C. 1962. *Music Review* 23 (August) 244, 23 (November) 271.

Longuet-Higgins, H. C. 1972. *Proc. R. Inst.* 45:87.

Longuet-Higgins, H. C., and M. J. Steedman. 1971. *Machine Intelligence* 6, p. 221.

Rameau, M. 1721. *Traite de l'harmonie reduite a des principes naturels.*

Steedman, M. J. Thesis, Edinburgh University.

Styles, B. C. 1973. Thesis, Cambridge University.

Appendix A: The Program "music.p"

recordclass note pitch onset offset span deg index;
function sift notefile = > notefile;

```
   maplist (notefile, lambda x;
   if x.tl.tl.hd — x.tl.hd < 5 then else x. close
   end) —> notefile;
end;

function takein notefile => nlist;
   maplist (notefile, lambda x;
       consnote (applist(x, identfn), undef, undef, undef)
   end) —> nlist;
end;

function res x;
   loopif x < 0 then x + 12 —> x close;
   erase (x//12);
end;

function int x;
   res(7 * x + 5) — 5;
end;

vars flag k l m n;

function modulate;
   if m > 2 then y — 1 —> k
   elseif m < (—1) then y + 6 —> k
   else exit;
   int (x — k) —> l; int(y — k) —> m; int(z — k) —> n;
end;

function hark;
   m —> l; n —> m; int(z — k) —> n;

   if flag and abs(n — 1) > 6 then .modulate
   close; false —> flag;

   if abs(n — m) < 7 then return
   elseif abs(m — l) > 6 then .modulate
   elseif abs(n — l) > 6 and l < 7 then true —> flag
   elseif n — m = 7 and n < 6 then m + 12 —> m
   close;
end;
```

```
function simplify tune; vars y;
   tune.hd − 1 −> y;
   maplist (tune, lambda x;
   if res(x − y) > 0 then x
   close; x −> y; end)
end;

function intervals tune; vars ints x y z;
   tune.simplify −> tune;
   false −> flag; nil −> ints;
   tune.hd −> y; tune.tl −> tune;
   if tune.null then return
   else tune.hd −> z; tune.tl −> tune
   close;
   y −> k; 0 −> m; int(z − k) −> n;
   if n = 3 or n < 0 and not(n = (−3))
      then k + 5 −> k; 1 −> m; n + 1 −> n
   close;
   loopif tune.null.not
   then y −> x; z −> y;
      tune.hd −> z; tune.tl −> tune;
      .hark; (m − 1)::ints −> ints
   close;
   rev((n − m)::ints);
end;

vars place;

function tuneup nlist; vars ints x0;
   maplist(nlist, pitch).intervals −> ints;
   nlist.hd −> x0; x0.pitch.int −> place
   applist(nlist, lambda x;
      x.pitch − x0.pitch − x .span;
      if res(x.span) = 0 then 0
      else ints.hd; ints.tl −> ints
      close −> x.deg;
      x −> x0;
   end);
end;
```

```
vars start beat position number group last metre nlist sequence;
function startup;
    nil -> sequence; nlist.hd.onset -> start;
    nlist.tl,hd.onset - start -> beat;
    nlist.hd.pitch -> position;
    nil -> group; nil -> last; 0 -> number;
    loopif nlist.hd.pitch = position then
        nlist.tl -> nlist; number + 1 -> number
    close;
end;

vars tol metre; 13 -> tol; nil -> metre;

function singlet -> stop -> fig;
    vars period mark;
    if group.null.not then
        if group.hd.offset < stop - period/2 then "stc"
        elseif group.hd.offset < stop - tol then "ten"
        else "leg"
        close -> mark;

        group.rev -> last; nil -> group, mark::last;
    else
        [%"tac", applist(last,lambda x;
        if x.offset > start + tol then x
        close end)%]
    close -> fig;
    if nlist.null or nlist.hd.onset > stop + tol then 0
    else nlist.hd.onset
    close -> stop;
end;

function rhythm start period -> stop -> fig; vars stop;
    start + period -> stop;
    if nlist.null.not and nlist.hd.onset < start + tol
    then nlist.hd::nil -> group; nlist.tl -> list;
    else goto label
    close;
    loopif nlist.null.not and nlist.hd.onset < stop + tol
        and nlist.hd.onset < group.hd.onset + tol
```

```
    then nlist.hd: group −> group; nlist.tl −> nlist;
    close;
    if group.hd.onset > stop − tol
    then group.hd::nlist −> nlist; group.tl −> group
    close;
label;
    if nlist null or nlist.hd.onset > stop − tol
    then .singlet
    else .tempo
    close −> stop −> fig;
end;

function tempo −> stop −> figure;
    vars new old again pulse time count fig syncop;
    [%nlist,last,group%] −> old; 0 −> again;
loop:
    if metre.null then 2::nil −> metre
    close;
    metre.hd −> pulse; metre.tl −> metre;
    nil −> figure; period −> time;
    0 −> count; start −> stop;
    loopif count < pulse
    then
        count + 1 −> count;
        rhythm(stop,time/pulse) −> stop −> fig;
        fig::figure −> figure;
        if stop = 0 then start + count ∗ time/pulse −> stop; true
        else stop − start + (pulse − count) ∗ time/pulse −> time; false
        close −> syncop;
    close;
    again + 1 −> again;
    if not(syncop or stop > start + period + tol or stop < start + period − tol)
    then figure.rev −> figure; pulse::metre −> metre;
    exit;
    if again = 1 then
        [%nlist,last,group,figure.rev,stop,pulse::metre%] −> new;
        old.destlist −> group −> last −> nlist;
        (5 − pulse)::nil −> metre; goto loop;
```

```
    else
      new.destlist − > metre − > stop − > figure − > group − > last − > nlist;
    close;
  end;

function tapout nlist − > sequence;
  vars start beat tol group last stop figure;

  loopif nlist.null.not
  then
    rhythm(start,beat) − > stop − > figure;
    figure::sequence − > sequence;

    if stop = 0 then start + beat
    else (stop − start + beat)/2 − > beat; stop
    close − > start;
  close;
  nil − > metre;
  sequence.rev − > sequence;
end;

vars max min; 17 − > max; − 13 − > min;

vars symbols: [Fbb Cbb Gbb Dbb Abb Ebb Bbb Fb Cb Gb Db Ab Eb Bb
    F C G D A E B Fs Cs Gs Ds As Es Bs Fx Cx Gx Dx Ax Ex Bx]
    − > symbols;

vars symbol; newarray([% − 15,19%],
    lambda x; symbols.hd; symbols.tl − > symbols end) − > symbol;

function name note:
  place + note.deg − > place;
  if place > max then "enh"; − 12
  elseif place < min then "enh"; 12
  else 0
  close + place − > place;

  place − > note.index;
  note.span; place. symbol;
end;

function describe fig; vars word;
  fig.hd − > word; fig.tl − > fig;
```

```
    if fig.null then [rest]
    elseif word = "tac" then
        "tied"::maplist(fig,index < > symbol)
    elseif word = "leg" then maplist(fig,name)
    else [%applist(fig,name),word%]
    close;
end;

function reveal figure;
    if figure.hd.isword
    then figure.describe
    else maplist(figure,reveal)
    close;
end;

function typeout seq; vars count;
    0 −> count; 1.nl;
    applist(seq, lambda x;
        if count = number then 1 −> count; 2.nl
        else count + 1 −> count
        close; x.reveal .pr
    end); 2.nl;
end;

function notate notefile;
    notefile.takein −> nlist;
    .startup;
    nlist.tapout −> sequence;
    nlist.tuneup;
    sequence.typeout;
end;

function printlist 1;
    2.nl;
    applist(1,lambda x; x.pr; 1.nl end);
    2.nl;
end;

$
```

Appendix B: Comments on the Program "music.p"

The program, which was originally named "music.pop", combines a number of hypotheses about melodic perception, most of which are highly provisional but all of which are readily falsifiable in principle (which is all one can ever expect of scientific theories). The following things are assumed:

a. The processes of rhythmic and tonal perception are independent, rhythmic perception being represented by the line

nlist.tapout — > sequence;

and tonal perception by the following line,

nlist.tuneup.

b. A tonal interval may be adequately characterized by its "span" (in keyboard semitones) and its "degree," which is the difference in the indices of the notes involved, the index of a note being the number of sharps in the key signature of its major key. Thus the upward diminished third from F♯ to A♭ is of span 2 and degree $-10 (=(-4) - 6)$.

c. The tonality of the sequence $X\ Y\ Z$ is unaffected by repetition of one of its notes (say Y) at the unison or the octave. (See the note on *simplify* below.)

d. Melodic rhythms are parsed "bottom-up" (this is certainly an oversimplification), the precise time of onset of each note being taken into account in predicting the time of onset of the next metrical unit.

e. Our judgments of articulation are based not on the gaps between notes but on the gap between the end of a note and the start of the next metrical unit.

f. A rest is what separates the beginning of a metrical unit from the first note that interrupts it.

g. Rhythmic perception proceeds recursively (each of the functions *rhythm* and *tempo* calls the other) under the guidance of a structural preconception, the *meter*, which is changed only reluctantly. (The time signatures $\frac{3}{4}$ and $\frac{6}{8}$ correspond to the metres [3 2] and [2 3] respectively.) Only binary and ternary groupings are permitted by the program.

Now for some comments on the individual functions:

1. *sift* removes from a *file* all notes of duration less than 5 centiseconds. If this procedure is deemed necessary (to remove accidentally touched notes), *sift* must be called before *notate*.

2. The highest-level function is called *notate*; it takes as argument a *note-file* consisting of a list of lists. Each sublist gives the keyboard *pitch*, time of *onset*, and time of *offset* of a note played on the organ console; the times are measured in centiseconds. The output of the function is a sequence of lists, each of which represents the rhythm, tonality, and phrasing of the notes occurring in a single beat.

3. *sequence* is the data structure to be created from the file.

4. *nlist* is to be a list of notes, each being a record with six entries: a note's *pitch* (its position on the keyboard), its times of *onset* and *offset* (in centiseconds), the *span* and the *degree* of the interval from the preceding note. and the *index* (which is 0 for a C, 1 for a G and so on).

5. *takein* creates *nlist*.

6. *place* stores the index of the first note.

7. *tuneup* uses the musical intervals between the notes to assign a *span* and a *degree* to each note.

8. *intervals* takes as argument the pitches of the notes. It chooses a keynote k, studies each set of three notes in turn, and creates a list of the (nonzero) musical intervals between the notes (in the range -11 to $+11$ inclusive).

9. *simplify* removes any note separated from its predecessor by a whole number of octaves.

10. *res x* is the remainder on division of x by 12.

11. *int x* is the diatonic interval between two notes separated by x keyboard semitones.

12. *hark* studies a set of three successive notes and evaluates the intervals between them; *flag* indicates whether the third note seems remote from the first two.

13. *modulate* alters the keynote when appropriate and makes consequent changes in the positions of the three notes relative to the keynote.

14. *tolerance* is the permissible discrepancy between an observed and a predicted time (in centiseconds); it and *meter* can be preset as desired.

15. *tapout* studies each beat in turn, taking the beat length initially from the first two notes. At the end of each beat, the *beat* length is adjusted if necessary and a rhythmic *figure* is appended to *seq*.

16. *rhythm* does four things: (a) If its allotted *period* begins with the onset of a note, this note is placed in *group*. (b) If any more notes follow in rapid succession, these are added to *group*. (c) If the last such note might be the beginning of the next metrical unit, it is removed from *group*. (d) If the next note begins before the end of the unit, *tempo* is called; otherwise *singlet* is called.

17. *singlet* places a *mark* of phrasing at the beginning of the current *group* if it is non-null; otherwise it harks back to any notes that may still be sounding (*tac* stands for "tacet"). It leaves on the stack a marked group and a finishing time (or zero). *mark* is taken as *stc* (staccato) if a note lasts less than half its allotted time, *ten* (tenuto) if it lasts nearly its allotted time, otherwise *leg* (legato).

18. *tempo* divides its time into *pulse* parts and uses the intervening notes to gauge the starting time of the next unit. If the unit fails to end with the onset of a note, or ends rather early or rather late, a different *metre* is tried; if this gives no better results, the original metre is accepted. It leaves on the stack a rhythmic figure and a finishing time, discovered or estimated.

19. *typeout* types out the sequence generated by *tapout*.

20. *reveal* is defined recursively, the lowest level being attended to by *describe*.

21. *describe* translates each figure composed of a word followed by a sequence of notes into a list of words and numbers.

22. *max* and *min* delimit the extremes of sharpness and flatness permitted in the output symbols, and may be preset at will. *place* may also be reset before any call of *typeout*; the effect is to make the tune start on the corresponding note.

23. *name* indicates the occurrence of an enharmonic change with the word *enh*, and gives (for nontied notes) the keyboard interval up to the note from its predecessor, and the appropriate *symbol*. In the list of *symbols*, *Eb* stands for E flat, *Fs* for F sharp, *Cx* for C double sharp, *Bbb* for B double flat, etc.

Bharucha proposes a connectionist explanation for the acquired intuitions of harmonic expectancy and consonance. By linking keys, chords, and tones as units, his network learns regularities by reacting to musical events and adjusting connection strengths among units as it reverberates to equilibrium.

Bharucha's model focuses on "schematic" rather than "sequential" musical structures, with schematic structures defined as musical relationships, for example, chord combinations, that transcend individual compositions. The information learned by his network is thus, by definition, general.

To model the acquisition of schematic harmonic expectations, Bharucha assumes the proportionality of a musical event's consonance and expectancy. Bharucha observes that a strength of his network, a standard connnectionist network of elementary processing units connected by weighted links, is its ability to account for a listener's tacit knowledge of musical structures.

The network's architecture comprises three layers of units: tones, chords, and keys. Input to the network is an event sequence, with each event as a synchronized cluster of tones; output from the network is a "pattern of activation" of the chord and key units.

The network creates "graded" musical expectations for given harmonic contexts. One result of the network's satisfaction of tonal clustering constraints is the circle of fifths.

22 MUSACT: A Connectionist Model of Musical Harmony

Jamshed J. Bharucha

Several features of connectionist models—in which simple processing units, connected by weighted links in a network, activate each other in parallel—recommend them as models of music cognition. First, they are highly interactive, so that low-level processes can influence higher level processes and vice versa. Thus, a sequence of tones can imply a chord or a key, and the implied chord or key can in turn influence the perception of tones that follow. Second, the architecture of a connectionist system hooks up naturally with a sensory front end that codes frequency as a (spatial or temporal) pattern of activations of neurons in the inner ear. Third, pattern matching of a currently heard sequence can be achieved in parallel by content-addressing all similar memory traces, enabling recognition of sequences and variations thereof. Finally, connectionist networks can learn persistent regularities, such as occur in our musical environment, without explicit instruction.

A network's ability to learn regularities—by altering the strengths of connections between units[1]—enables the parsimonious view that music cognition is a learned consequence of general principles of cognition operating on structural regularities in the environment. The average listener has little, if any, explicit knowledge of musical structure, yet shows evidence of considerable tacit knowledge. For example, even listeners with no formal training in music show systematic differences in processing time for chords as a function of the prior harmonic context (Bharucha and Stoeckig 1986, 1987).

The model proposed here, MUSACT, is designed to capture musical intuitions and psychological data concerning expectancy and context-dependent consonance in Western harmony. Schenker (1906–1954) observed that one of the qualities of the dominant chord is "to indicate that the tonic is yet to come" (p. 219). Expectancies of this sort are driven by cognitive structures and processes that have encoded regularities in the musical environment in order to facilitate subsequent perception. Hand in hand with expectancies are intuitions about context-dependent consonance. The greater an event's expectancy, the greater its consonance (Bharucha and Stoeckig 1986, 1987). A composer may choose to satisfy or violate these expectancies to varying degrees, thereby evoking varying degrees of consonance or dissonance. The aesthetic value of subtle departures from the expected has figured in numerous theoretical writings about music and emotion (e.g., Mandler 1984, Meyer 1956). A new piece is heard as culturally anomalous to the extent that expectancies are violated. Indeed, the connection strengths between units in a network that learns sequences are assumed to be learned by minimizing, over the history of one's exposure, the discrepancy between expectancies generated by the network and transitional probabilities in the music of one's culture.[2]

The model assumes that people exposed to Western music acquire a network representation of chord functions (hereafter referred to as chords) and their organization in the form of keys, which serves to schematize subsequent perception. Constraints on the combining of tones into chords and constraints on the sequencing of these chords are among the more obstinate regularities in Western music. Every amateur musician knows that a mastery of only six chords enables you to accompany a vast majority of popular songs. Given the pervasiveness of these regularities, and given the evidence of tacit knowledge of them (Bharucha and Stoeckig 1986, 1987), it is reasonable to conclude that they have been internalized (through perceptual learning) as cognitive structures that facilitate and bias subsequent perception.

Schematic and Sequential Structures: Schematic and Veridical Expectancy

Two broad classes of cognitive structures for music are envisioned: schematic structures, which represent abstract structural regularities (sometimes formalized as grammars) of the music of one's culture, and sequential structures, which represent particular musical sequences (Bharucha 1984b). The former embody typical relationships between types or classes of events, and the latter embody relationships between particular event tokens. The expectation generated by a dominant chord for the tonic to follow arises from schematic structures that encode the typicality of relationships, whereas the expectation for a VI chord to follow a particular dominant chord in a particular familiar piece arises from sequential structures that encode the particular events in that piece. The former generate schematic expectancies and the latter veridical expectancies. The two are usually in agreement but often in conflict, giving rise to the peculiar effect known as the deceptive cadence (a dominant chord followed by a VI chord). The unavoidable effect of schematic expectancies, even when listening to a piece that violates them, provides a resolution of Wittgenstein's puzzle (see Dowling and Harwood 1985) concerning the possibility of violating expectancies when listening to a familiar piece. The present paper focuses only on the schematic structure.

The Model

Architecture

We have the sense that certain typical tone clusters, such as major and minor chords, are heard as unitary. We also have the sense of an even more abstract state called a key. Sequences or clusters of tones may unavoidably suggest a chord or several alternative chords, and combinations of chords establish a sense of key. One of the advantages of the model is that it enables chord and key instantiations to be graded and ambiguous. These ambiguities are an important feature of music, exploited during modulations or other transitions, and used to create graded degrees of expectancy violation.

The schematic network consists of three layers of units, representing tones, chords, and keys (see figure 22.1). There are symmetric links between units of adjacent layers (i.e., between tone units and chord units, and between chord units and key units) but no links between units within a layer. The links between tone and chord units reflect the relationships

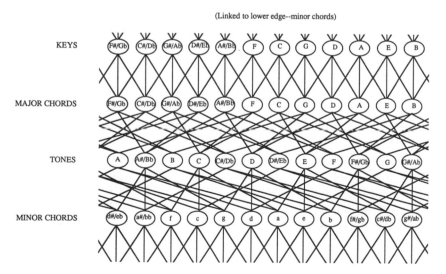

Figure 22.1

between tones and the chords of which they are components. The links between chord and key units reflect the relationships between chords and their parent keys. In the current version of the model, only major and minor chords are implemented, and only major keys.

The input to the network is a sequence of events, each event being a simultaneous cluster of tones. Input is received via the tone units, which represent the twelve octave-equivalent pitch categories. This layer constitutes a discrete pitch schema to which the pitch continuum is assimilated (see Shepard and Jordan 1984). The frequency responses of these units are equally spaced along a logarithmic scale of frequency and are fixed only relative to each other, underlying the relational nature of pitch memory. The sensory front end that provides the input to these units is beyond the present scope, but neural net models that extract octave-equivalent pitch categories (see Deutsch 1969) can be adapted quite naturally to a connectionist model of more abstract phenomena as proposed here.

The output of the model is the pattern of activation of the chord and key units. A chord unit is activated either by the explicit sounding of some or all of its component tones, or by indirect influences, via its parent keys, from related chords. When only some of the chord's component tones are sounded, the context may help disambiguate the chord by top-down activation from parent key units. A key unit is activated by some or all of its daughter chords, or by indirect influences, via its daughter chords, from related keys. Indirect activation of chord units permits smooth excursions (such as secondary dominants and modulations) from the focus of activation.

Phasic Activation

After an event is heard, activation spreads through the network, via the weighted links, reverberating back to units that were previously activated. In this model, activation is phasic, meaning that units respond only to *changes* in activation of neighboring units. Phasic activation was selected because of the salience of event onsets in music. On each cycle, units are synchronously updated on the basis of activation levels, from the previous cycle, of neighboring units. Phasic activation eventually dissipates until the network settles into a state of equilibrium. The network will settle if no unit transmits more phasic activation than it received on the previous cycle. This requirement is easily satisfied if the weights are small relative to the fan-in or fan-out.

Activation, Tonality, and Expectation

The pattern of activation of key units represents the degree to which keys are established. Tonal music will tend to build up activation in one region of the network, such that one key unit is most highly activated, with activation tapering off with increasing distance from the focal key. Atonal music will typically induce a less, focused pattern, and polytonal music would result in multiple, though not very strong, foci. The model thus allows for gradations of key, and for multiple keys, consistent with the findings of Krumhansl (Krumhansl and Kessler 1982, Krumhansl and Schmuckler 1986).

The pattern of activation of chord units represents the pattern of expectancies for chords to follow. A chord whose unit is highly activated is strongly expected, and a strongly expected chord is heard as consonant. The pattern of activation of chord units thus underlies our harmonic expectations as well as our intuitions of context-dependent sequential consonance.

Weights

All links between tone units and chord units are assumed to have equal weights. There are six classes of weights between chord units and key units, corresponding to the six chords in each key. All the links of the same class must have the same weight, resulting in a repeating pattern of weights over the network. (For example, the G major chord has the same relationship—the dominant—to the key of C as the C♯ major chord has to the key of F♯.) In music-theoretic terms, a chord's relationships to its parent keys are its functions in those keys. The six classes of weights thus correspond to the six chord functions. Since some chord functions are stronger instantiators of key than others (e.g., the key of C is more strongly instantiated by the C major chord—the tonic   than by the F major chord—the subdominant—even though both are daughter chords), it would be reasonable to assume that links for stronger functions have higher weights. However, it turns out, that the model can exhibit all the essential qualitative patterns of behavior even when the weights are not differentiated according to function. Thus, the typical hierarchy of strengths of the three major chord functions (tonic, dominant, subdominant) emerges even if their weights are equal. The pattern of connectivity alone is sufficient to bring about functional differentiation. The model thus generates the desired functional hierarchy of chords simply by knowing which chords are members of which keys and which tones are components of which chords. This is a remarkable and unanticipated property of the model and points to its power.

The weights are assumed to be higher for major chord units than for minor chord units, since major chords are stronger instantiators of key. As discussed below, with only these elementary constraints on links and their weights, based on fundamental tenets of music theory, a set of weights can be found that enable the model to account for a complex array of psychological data on the perception of harmony as well as some subtle aspects of music theory. Indeed, one of the advantages of a connectionist model is that complexities and interactions may emerge naturally from simple constraints on architecture.

The Spread of Activation

The activation, $a_{i,e}$, of the ith unit after the network has reverberated to equilibrium following the eth event is

$$a_{i,e} = a_{i,e-1}(1 - d)^t + sA + \sum_{c=1}^{\text{equil}} \Delta a_{i,e,c},$$

where d is the rate of decay ($0 < d_i < 1$) for one time unit, t is the time elapsed since the offset of the last event, A is the source activation due to the stimulus, and s is 1 if the unit is receiving environmental input and 0 otherwise. (For simplicity, the present version of the model assumes that all events are of equal duration; duration is varied simply by repeating events.) $\Delta a_{i,e,c}$ is the change in activation after reverberation cycle c, and is the output of the unit on cycle $c + 1$. $\Delta a_{i,e,c}$ is the sum of the outputs of its n neighboring units, weighted by their links, w_{ij}, ($0 < w_{ij} < 1$). Thus,

$$\Delta a_{i,e,c} = \sum_{j=1}^{n} w_{ij} \Delta a_{j,e,c-1}.$$

Simulations

The simulation results reported below were obtained with a weight assignment in which all chord units of the same mode (major or minor) have equally weighted links with their parent keys. This enables us to observe the differentiation of chord functions without forcing their differentiation via the weights. Major chord units were assigned more strongly weighted links (0.244) with their parent key units than were minor chord units (0.22, 90% of 0.244), since major chords more strongly establish their parent keys. Links between tone units and chord units were also uniform (0.0122, 5% of 0.244), with no preference given to the root of the chord. This weight assignment yields an initial strong influence of the input tones on their local regions of the network, followed by an extended percolation during which the two more abstract layers exert their influence. Thus, if the input tone cluster is $\{C, E, G\}$, i.e., a C major chord, the chord units linked to these tone units show an initial prominence, so that, for example, the A major chord unit is more highly activated than the D major chord unit. However, after the activation has had a chance to reverberate for a number of cycles, the D major chord unit overtakes the A major chord unit, by virtue of its greater proximity to the eventual activation peak, which is at C major. Within 40 cycles, all constraints inherent in the network are satisfied, and the pattern of activation does not change qualitatively. Within 50 cycles, the phasic activation has dissipated to the point at which the ratio $\Delta a_{i,e,c}/A$ does not exceed 0.005 for any unit. For the results discussed below, the equilibrium state is stipulated to be the state of the network when this 0.005 criterion is reached.

The tone cluster $\{C, E, G\}$, that is, a C major chord, played without any prior context, generates the following pattern of activation (see figure 22.2). The most highly activated key is C, of which the source chord is the tonic. Activations of other key units decrease monotonically with distance from C, the lowest being F♯. The pattern of activation of the chord units mirrors that of the key units with the same alphabetic name.

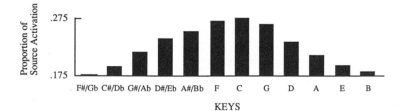

Figure 22.2

Even though the weights between the source chord, C major, and its parent keys, F, C, and G, are equal, the parent keys are not activated to the same degree. In decreasing order, the activations of these three keys are C, F, and G, which are the keys in which the source chord is the tonic, dominant, and subdominant, respectively. This is exactly the hierarchy of harmonic functions to be expected from music theory.

There seems at first to be a paradox here. On the one hand, a chord more strongly instantiates the key of which it is the dominant than the key of which it is the subdominant. On the other hand, the key of the dominant is generally thought to be closer to the current key than is the key of the subdominant and should therefore have a higher activation. This paradox is not peculiar to the present model; the model simply forces us to confront it. (Interestingly, the model conforms to the latter alternative if the link between a tone unit and a chord unit is weighted more heavily for the root of the chord than for the other tones, illustrating the unanticipated interdependence of apparently disparate factors.) The resolution of the paradox lies in the fact that dominant chords typically occur much more often than subdominant chords in a piece of music, presumably because dominant chords contribute to a more stable key. Given the high frequency of dominant chords, the dominant builds up more activation than the subdominant.

For an input consisting of a sequence of events, the rate at which activation decays between events was set at 0.3. If the input sequence is the tone cluster $\{F, A, C\}$ followed by $\{G, B, D\}$, that is, an F major chord followed by a G major chord, the model shows the most highly activated key unit to be C, even though the tonic chord of that key, the C major chord, has not occurred. This, again, is consistent with what would be expected from music theory.

Psychological Data

The model's performance in experiments eliciting rating judgments and memory confusions is qualitatively equivalent to human performance on these tasks. In a series of experiments on the perception of harmony (Bharucha and Krumhansl 1983; Krumhansl, Bharucha, and Castellano 1982), the perceived relationship between chords as a function of context was studied using these tasks.

Rating Judgments

In the rating task, subjects were presented with two chords in succession and rated, on a scale from 1 to 7, how well the second followed the first. For the simulation, the rating judgment consisted of reading off the level of activation of the last chord. On this assumption, the observed rating judgments are equivalent to judgments of expectancy or sequential consonance.

When both chords of the pair shared a parent key, subjects gave higher judgments when the last chord was major than when it was minor. This result was particularly interesting for a pair consisting of one major chord and one minor chord, because the same two chords elicited different judgments depending upon their temporal order. In the model, a major chord activates its unit slightly more than does a minor chord, even though the source activation, A, is the same, because of more reverberatory activation from its parent keys. This asymmetry doesn't require asymmetric links since it follows directly from the fact that major chords establish their parent keys more strongly than do minor chords. In music, this translates into a tendency to end with a major chord, often even if the key is minor.

When the two chords were preceded by a context that established a key, subjects gave higher judgments the more closely related the last chord was to the key of the context. In the model, this occurs because the context activates closely related chords more than distantly related chords. An interesting asymmetry was contained in this result as well: two chords of the same mode (major or minor) elicited a higher judgment if the one closer to the key of the context was played last. Thus, in the key of C, an F major chord followed by a C major chord is a more stable ending than the reverse, even though the reverse may be true in the absence of a prior context.

Recognition Memory

Memory for a sequence does not take the form of an explicit representation, but rather is encoded by weight increases of links between the units in the network and episodic units that are temporally organized. Each event in a sequence increases the weights of links between a proprietary episodic unit and the schematic units, in proportion to the activations of these latter units. The episodic units are then activated every time the tone, chord, or key units to which they have strong links are highly activated.

Once activated, the episodic units in turn activate the schematic units. This architecture can accomplish pattern completion (recalling a piece given only a few notes or a sketchy rendition), recognition of variations, and retrieval of past musical memories in a parallel, content-addressable fashion rather than through serial search.

In the present implementation, episodic units serve only to simulate short-term recognition of a sequence. Consider a to-be-remembered sequence of chords. Each chord token in the sequence has its proprietary episodic unit. Links between this unit and the schematic units have their weights increased in proportion to the phasic activations of the schematic units after that chord is heard. In this way, the pattern of activation of the network after hearing a particular chord token can be recovered simply by activating its episodic unit.

Data from experiments on recognition memory for chord sequences show trends similar to those observed for rating judgments (Bharucha and Krumhansl 1983; Krumhansl, Bharucha, and Castellano 1982). In these experiments, subjects judged whether two presentations of a sequence of chords were identical or had different chords (the target chords) in one serial position. If the sequence as a whole established a key, a change was less likely to be detected the more closely related the second target was to the key. This manifested itself in two ways. First, a change was less likely to be detected if both targets were closely related to the key than if both were distantly related to the key. Second, if one target was more closely related to the key than the other, a change was less likely to be detected when the more closely related one occurred in the second presentation rather than the first. In general, if a change is made to a sequence, it is less likely to be detected if it renders the sequence more coherent than more anomalous. Coherence is a consequence of the strong activation of a subsuming unit, such as a key unit in music, or a subsuming semantic unit in language (Bharucha, Olney, and Schnurr 1985), relative to the other subsuming units in the network.

In the model, the probability with which the second target is judged to be the same as the first is monotonically related to the activation of the unit representing the second target, relative to the activations of the other chord units, when the first target was heard. Since the more closely related the second target is to the key of the context, false alarm rates increase with closeness of the second target to the key of the context.

This short-term memory architecture also predicts that if the second presentation is transposed to a different key, false alarm rates should decrease with the distance (along the network) between the two keys. This would be consistent with recognition memory results for sequences of tones (Cuddy, Cohen, and Miller 1979).

Evidence of Spreading Activation: Priming

Evidence that chords indirectly activate representations of related chords comes from experiments on priming. Bharucha and Stoeckig (1986) presented subjects with two major chords in succession, the first called the prime and the second the target. On half the trials, the chord in the target position was a mistuned foil. Subjects were instructed to judge, as fast as possible, whether the chord in the target position was in-tune or out-of-tune. Subjects first practiced without the prime until a criterion level of accuracy was reached. In the main task, response times were significantly faster when the prime and target were close together along the network than when they were distant. This demonstrates that the prime activates units corresponding to closely related targets, as would be predicted by the model. Error rates mirrored response times, so that the target was more likely to be judged in-tune the closer it was (along the network) to the prime. The response time and error rate data measure the prime's influence on the target's expectancy and sequential consonance, respectively.

An alternative explanation of the above results is that the priming is due to overlapping harmonic spectra between closely related prime and target chords. In a subsequent study (Bharucha and Stoeckig 1987), harmonics that overlapped were removed from the stimuli and priming was still observed. This demonstrates that there must be a spread of activation at a fairly abstract cognitive level.

Conclusion

Harmonic expectations can be modeled by a constraint-satisfaction network whose only constraints are the clustering of tones to form chords and the clustering of chords to form keys. The model generates graded expectations in response to a harmonic context and predicts graded implications of musical key. For tonal music, the circle of fifths emerges from the joint satisfaction of clustering constraints. The patterns of expectation generated by the model are borne out by psychological experiments employing rating judgments, memory, and reaction time.

Notes

This paper was presented in 1987 at the Ninth Annual Conference of the Cognitive Science Society and is reprinted here, with minor changes, from the proceedings (published by Lawrence Erlbaum Associates, copyright 1987, Cognitive Science Society). The author thanks Katherine Olney for early assistance in this work.

The reader is directed to more recent papers for developments since this paper. For a broader discussion of the theoretical and empirical context of the MUSACT model, see Bharucha (1987) "Music Cognition and Perceptual Facilitation: A Connectionist Framework," *Music Perception*, 5, 1–30. A mechanism by which a structure such as MUSACT might be learned through self-organization, along with a discussion of alternative neural net representations of pitch, is reported in Bharucha (1991) "Pitch, Harmony, and Neural Nets: A Psychological Perspective," in Todd and Loy (eds.), *Connectionism and Music*, MIT Press. A network that can learn simple musical sequences using the backpropagation algorithm, and that acquires schematic properties as a result, is reported in Bharucha and Todd (1989) "Modeling the Perception of Tonal Structure with Neural Nets," *Computer Music Journal*, 13, 44–53.

1. For example, the algorithms of Fukushima (1975), Grossberg (1976), Kohonen (1984), Rumelhart, Hinton and Williams (1986), Rumelhart and Zipser (1985), von der Malsberg (1973).

2. For a subsequent development of a model that learns musical sequences in this way, see Bharucha and Todd (1989) "Modeling the Perception of Tonal Structure with Neural Nets," *Computer Music Journal, 13*, 44–53.

References

Bharucha, J. J. (1984a). Anchoring effects in music: The resolution of dissonance. *Cognitive Psychology*, 16:485–518.

Bharucha, J. J. (1984b). Event hierarchies, tonal hierarchies, and assimilation: A reply to Deutsch and Dowling. *Journal of Experimental Psychology: General*, 113:421–425.

Bharucha, J., and Krumhansl, C. L. (1983). The representation of harmonic structure in music: Hierarchies of stability as a function of context. *Cognition*, 13:63–102.

Bharucha, J. J., Olney, K. L, and Schnurr, P. P. (1985). Coherence-disrupting and coherence-conferring disruptions in text. *Memory and Cognition*, 13:573–578.

Bharucha, J. J., and Stoeckig, K. (1986). Reaction time and musical expectancy: Priming of chords. *Journal of Experimental Psychology: Human Perception and Performance*, 12:403–410.

Bharucha, J. J., and Stoeckig, K. (1987). Priming of chords: Spreading activation or overlapping harmonic spectra? *Perception & Psychophysics*, 41:519–524.

Cuddy, L. L., Cohen, A. J., and Miller, J. (1979). Melody recognition: The experimental application of musical rules. *Canadian Journal of Psychology*, 28:148–157.

Deutsch, D. (1969). Music recognition. *Psychological Review*, 76:300–307.

Deutsch, D. (1978). Delayed pitch comparisons and the principle of proximity. *Perception & Psychophysics*, 23:227–230.

Dowling, W. J., and Harwood, D. L. (1985). *Music cognition*. New York: Academic Press.

Fukushima, K. (1975). Cognitron: A Self-organizing Multilayered Neural Network. *Biological Cybernetics*, 20:121–136.

Grossberg, S. (1976). Adaptive Pattern Classification and Universal Recoding: Part I. Parallel Development and Coding of Neural Feature Detectors. *Biological Cybernetics*, 23:121–134.

Kohonen, T. (1984). *Self-organization and Associative Memory*. Berlin: Springer-Verlag.

Krumhansl, C. L., Bharucha, J., and Castellano, M. A. (1982). Key distance effects on perceived harmonic structure in music. *Perception & Psychophysics*, 32:96–108.

Krumhansl, C. L., and Kessler, E. J. (1982). Tracing the dynamic changes in perceived tonal organization in a spatial representation of musical keys. *Psychological Review*, 89:334–368.

Krumhansl, C. L., and Schmuckler, M. A. (1986). The *Petroushka* chord: A perceptual investigation. *Music Perception*, 4:153–184.

Mandler, G. (1984). *Mind and body: Psychology of emotion and stress*. New York: Norton.

Meyer, L. (1956). *Emotion and meaning in music*. Chicago: University of Chicago Press.

Rumelhart, D. E., Hinton, G. E., and Williams, R. J. (1986). Learning Internal Representations by Error Propagation. In D. E. Rumelhart and J. L. McClelland, eds. *Parallel Distributed Processing: Explorations in the Microstructure of Cognition. Vol. 1*. Cambridge: MIT Press.

Rumelhart, D. E., and Zipser, D. (1985). Feature Discovery by Competitive Learning. *Cognitive Science*, 9:75–112.

Schenker, H. (1954). *Harmony* (O. Jones, ed., E. M. Borgese, trans.). Cambridge: MIT Press. (Original work published 1906).

Shepard, R. N, & Jordan, D. S. (1984). Auditory illusions demonstrating that tones are assimilated to an internalized musical scale. *Science*, 226:1333–1334.

von der Malsberg, C. (1973). Self-organizing of Orientation Sensitive Cells in the Striate Cortex. *Kybernetic*, 14:85–100.

Schwanauer describes his Music Understanding System Evolver (MUSE), a learning machine for voice-leading rules. As a rule-based system, MUSE evolves for learned contexts by adjusting its rule-agenda priorities or propagating new rules.

MUSE has five a priori stages for learning: (1) completing the inner voices for a given soprano and bass, (2) completing the inner voices for a soprano and bass with figures, (3) harmonizing a figured bass, (4) harmonizing an unfigured bass, and (5) harmonizing a chorale.

Learning in MUSE occurs in two passes: during the composition process and afterwards. The first learning pass, classed as failure-based learning, adjusts rule priorities in agendas to satisfy constraints for local contexts. The second pass, classed as success-based learning, scans the musical output of the first pass for patterns of both notes and rules that occur at least three times and "chunks" the rules themselves or the higher level semantic constructs behind the rules into new rules.

Rules learned by MUSE include traditional leading directives described in tonal harmony textbooks. MUSE occasionally also infers new rules that are irrelevant.

The constrained environment of MUSE's five stages of learning inherently focuses what can be learned to a small set of possibilities. Learning in music, however, occurs well past the rudimentary stages of solving chorale exercises. Further work could concentrate on the distinctions at more advanced levels of compositions between learning voice-leading and decisions about "artistic choice."

23 A Learning Machine for Tonal Composition

Stephan M. Schwanauer

The Music Understanding System Evolver (MUSE) learns and then applies fundamental concepts of common practice harmony. As a rule-based system, MUSE infers simple rules of doubling and of voice leading in general with the reordering of production rule agendas and the "chunking" together of production rules that lead to successful solutions. Success in a solution is defined as satisfying a small set of a priori voice-leading constraints.

MUSE reorders its agendas of production rules to satisfy compositional constraints only during the actual composing process. Since the agenda reorderings occur as MUSE rejects rules until its constraints have been satisfied, this class of learning is *failure-based*. Future occurrences of the same melodic/harmonic contexts index the learned agenda reorderings to circumvent tried-and-false rules.

Once MUSE has satisfied all of its compositional constraints to complete a musical exercise, it scans both the notes of its musical output and the rules of its action histories for patterns that occur three or more times. For each acceptable pattern, MUSE chunks the rules leading to the pattern for future contexts of the same pattern. Since MUSE's learned composite rule for each acceptable pattern results from successful solutions to MUSE's composing pass, this class of learning is *success-based*. Future occurrences of the same pattern contexts index the learned composite rules to apply an immediately acceptable solution.

MUSE sessions explore the possibility of learning an extended set of voice-leading rules and compositional practices from a small set of *first principles*: voice-leading constraints and directives. (See section Learning from Instruction). To the extent that it acquires knowledge from these first principles, machine learning in MUSE shows what may be learned in the inherently controlled environment of chorale composition.

Learning in MUSE can best be described in the context of its learning techniques, a subset of those possible for compositional learning machines.

- learning by rote
- learning from instruction
- learning from failure

MUSE: A Learning System for Tonal Composition (Ph.D. thesis, Yale 1986).

- learning from examples
- learning by analogy
- learning from discovery

Learning in MUSE

Learning by Rote

Learning by rote is the simplest form of learning to represent. Since the human memorizes what has been given to him without questions, MUSE simply represents this form of learning implicitly. All structures to be learned unquestioningly by the student are built into MUSE as assumed information for each of its five, progessively more advanced stages (Schwanauer 1986).

1. completing the inner voices for a soprano and bass in root-position triads;

2. completing the inner voices for a soprano and figured bass;

3. writing a soprano line and completing the inner voices for a figured bass;

4. writing a soprano line and completing the inner voices for an unfigured bass;

5. harmonizing a chorale melody.

The goals for these stages capture the choices required for each stage of composition. MUSE's scheduler remembers the priorities of the goals in a list. When the LHS condition of a goal has been satisfied, the RHS goal fires and starts the inferencing of subgoals; when the LHS has not been satisfied, the scheduler looks for the next appropriate goal. Learning, in the form of rule propagation or reprioritization, occurs at the lower level of subgoals. The scheduler in MUSE, however, reflects rote learning, invariant compositional goals.

First Stage: Completing the Inner Voices of Chords in Root Position
GET-NEW-CHORD directs MUSE to the section of production memory in MUSE's agenda that checks for the position of the soprano. In the first stage, for root position of the triad, the possibilities are the position of the third (POSTHI0), of the fifth (POSFIF0), and of the octave (POSOCT0).

The spacing can be keyboard, for example, posfif*kb-8, or chorale, for example, posfif0*ch-8, where the final '-8' indicates octave doubling.

COMPLETE-INNER-VOICES has the task in production memory of completing the inner voices of the triad for different positions of the soprano. Although it is possible to double the octave for the position of the fifth and the third, for example, it is not acceptable to double the octave for the position of the octave.

TEST-NEW-NOTES applies a list of constraints and directives to the proposed notes. The constraints are (1) to avoid parallel octaves, (2) to avoid parallel fifths, (3) to resolve half steps properly, and (4) to avoid dissonant leaps. Rejected notes are stored together with metalevel descriptions of their contents for future reference. The directives, which merely try better notes if they exist, do not reject notes outright. In descending order of importance they are: (1) to avoid leaps greater than a third, (2) to avoid disjunct motion, and (3) to maintain common tones.

TEST-ALTERNOTES tries alternate notes for the doubling of a chord when a production in TEST-NEW-NOTES rejects the previous solution. Alternatives are chosen on the basis of the position of the soprano and the voice-leading constraints for a note. For example, in the event that TEST-NEW-NOTES rejects a solution for POSOCT0, which always fills in the remaining third and fifth for a triad, TEST-ALTERNOTES also rejects it.

GET-LAST-CHORD is the scheduling goal that activates backtracking to the previous chord or chords whenever all attempts fail to complete the inner voices in the previous goals.

Second Stage: Completing the Inner Voices of Chords with Figured Bass
GET-IMPLIED-BASS-NOTES triggers a list of productions to find the notes implied by the figured bass.

The following goals for the second stage are defined above. Here they are adjusted to include figured bass expressions, for example, if GET-IMPLIED-BASS-NOTES indicates a six- five chord, GET-NEW-CHORD can change the internal state to add-fifth-and-sixth.

GET-NEW-CHORD

COMPLETE-INNER-VOICES

TEST-NEW-NOTES

TEST-ALTERNOTES

GET-LAST-CHORD

Third Stage: Writing a Soprano and Inner Voices for a Figured Bass
FIND-PRIMARY-HARMONIC-GOALS starts a search for the primary
harmonic goals of a phrase. Thus, all bass notes that can be considered
tonic or dominant representatives or cadential parts are labeled accordingly. The productions in this goal assume the ability to be able to identify correctly whether a harmony is primary or secondary. Only after
the underlying root progression to a figured bass is known can MUSE
label tonic/dominant pairs. A later goal, COMPOSE-SOPRANO, checks
whether a tonic/dominant pair occurs at the end of an exercise.

FIND-SECONDARY-HARMONIC-GOALS starts a chain of substitutions for harmonies within the outlines not already defined in FIND-
PRIMARY-HARMONIC-GOALS. Since the cadences define points of
arrival, COMPOSE-SOPRANO has to dovetail the harmonies from the
beginning of a phrase with those from the end. In order to satisfy the
criteria both for a good soprano line and for good voice leading, MUSE
remembers the secondary harmonies implied by the given bass figures.
Using this knowledge, MUSE can determine important constraints for the
composition of a soprano line. For example, if the progression I–IV–V–I
occurs at the end of a phrase, MUSE disallows a doubling of the root of
the first I chord in the soprano to prevent it from upstaging the final I
chord in musical emphasis. The criteria for chord combination possibilities
are stored explicitly in MUSE's knowledge base. If a problem arises of
connecting its secondary harmonies with the harmonies presupposed by a
cadence, MUSE backtracks until it finds an intersection between the harmonies required to lead to the cadence and those allowed by the rules of
substituting secondary harmonies.

COMPOSE-SOPRANO requires the filling-in of a soprano line according to the conditions required for good voice leading, that is, minimal
leaps, and the notes allowed within the harmonic possibilities. It does the
backtracking when all the current harmonic and soprano possibilities have
been exhausted.

The following goals for the third stage are defined above.

GET-IMPLIED-BASS-NOTES

GET-NEW-CHORD

COMPLETE-INNER-VOICES

TEST-NEW-NOTES

TEST-ALTERNOTES

GET-LAST-CHORD

Fourth Stage: Writing a Soprano and Inner Voices for an Unfigured Bass
The following goals for the fourth stage are defined above.

FIND-PRIMARY-HARMONIC-GOALS

FIND-SECONDARY-HARMONIC-GOALS

GET-IMPLIED-BASS-NOTES

COMPOSE-SOPRANO

GET-NEW-CHORD

COMPLETE-INNER-VOICES

TEST-NEW-NOTES

TEST-ALTERNOTES

GET-LAST-CHORD

Fifth Stage: Harmonizing a Chorale   ANALYZE-MELODY starts a set
of productions to find the possible, simple harmonies (root position) implied by a soprano line. MUSE finds the intersection between all of the
primary harmonies (I, IV, and V), which include the soprano among their
notes, and chords considered acceptable in MUSE's chord-progression
arrays.

GET-MINIMAL-HARMONY sets simple harmonies to establish an
initial bass list from which to establish more sophisticated harmonies. Bass
notes are filled in using the chords considered acceptable by ANALYZE-
MELODY.

SUBSTITUTE-SECONDARY-HARMONY replaces secondary harmonies for the primary harmonies given by GET-MINIMAL-HARMONY
when COMPOSE-SOPRANO calls for a change in the harmony and can
no longer find an acceptable primary harmony to satisfy its constraints.

COMPOSE-BASS backtracks to the previous chord when the possibilities for harmonic and bass completion have been exhausted for the
current chord.

The following goals for the fifth stage are defined above.

GET-IMPLIED-BASS-NOTES

GET-NEW-CHORD

TEST-NEW-NOTES

TEST-ALTERNOTES

GET-LAST-CHORD

Observe that the five stages divide into three structurally similar phases of composition: the first two with given soprano and bass lines, the second two with given bass lines, and the last with given soprano line. Obvious intersections exist among the subcomponent goals of the separate stages. Thus, for example, GET-NEW-CHORD, TEST-NEW-NOTES, TEST-ALTERNOTES, and GET-LAST-CHORD GOALS are common to all five stages. To prevent redundancy, production memory of MUSE's scheduler has separate modules of production lists for each of the separate goals. The scheduler directs for each of the five separate stages the flow of control to the proper subcomponents of production memory.

Learning from Instruction

Learning from instruction fits into the same category in MUSE as rote learning. It is assumed that the teacher has already done the ground research or inquiry for the student. The implementation of such learning requires a transformation of the teacher's information into the student's internal representation language. MUSE's internal representation language for instructed information is embodied in its constraints and directives.

For each of MUSE's five stages, constraints and directives filter out undesirable solutions. Constraints are absolute; directives, relative. Thus, where a teacher would instruct a student to avoid a situation absolutely, a constraint in MUSE forbids the situation; where a teacher would instruct a student merely to make certain that there is not a better possibility, a directive makes MUSE determine that it has the best relative solution.

Whenever production rule agenda reorderings result from MUSE's constraints or directives, failure-based learning takes place. This is discussed under the section Learning from Failure.

First Stage: Soprano and Unfigured Bass

Constraints

- Parallel fifths are forbidden.
- Parallel octaves are forbidden.

....getting implied bass notes.....
...........getting new chord..........
......completing inner voices.......
............testing new notes..........

[Learning from the current failure of posminthi-parall8.]
<———————————————————————————>
CLASS II LEARNING: HARMONIC COMPLETION

............testing alternotes..........

[ACTIVE PRODUCTION]
(posthi0*kb-3(state add-third-lower-and-fifth) (weaken posthi0*kb-8))

[WEAKEN PRODUCTION]
(posth0*kb-8(state add-fifth-and-octave) (do fail-check))

............getting last chord..........
......completing inner voices.......
............testing new notes............

[Learning from the current failure of posminthi-dissleap.]
<———————————————————————————>
CLASS II LEARNING: HARMONIC COMPLETION

...........testing alternotes..........
...........getting last chord..........

[EXPANDING LEARNING CONTEXT: (posthi6*kb-8)]

TRACK COUNT: 6

............testing alternotes..........

[ACTIVE PRODUCTION]
(posthi6*kb-3 (state add-third-lower-and-sixth) (weaken posthi6*kb-8))

[WEAKEN PRODUCTION]
(posth6*kb-8 (state add-sixth-and-octave) (do fail-check))

Track Count: 7 ^

Figure 23.1
Example of Class II Learning: Harmonic Completion

- Dissonant leaps are forbidden.
- Resolve the leading tone.

Directives

- Use leaps less than a third.
- Use conjunct motion.
- Maintain common tones.

Second Stage: Soprano and Figured Bass

Directives

- The absence of a figure implies root position.
- Treat accidentals without numbers as references to the third.
- Figure 6 implies third and sixth above the bass.
- Figure 7 implies third and seventh and usually fifth above the bass.
- Figure 6/5 implies third and fifth and sixth above the bass.
- Figure 4/3 implies third and fourth and sixth above the bass.
- Figure 4/2 implies second and fourth and sixth above the bass.
- Alterations of seventh chords are indicated with full interval references, for example, 6♯/5/3.
- Dash (–) indicates unchanged note.
- Suspended notes refer to intervals resolving to those in above chords.

Third Stage: Figured Bass

Constraints

- Determine cadences.
- Avoid repetitions of patterns of two or more voices.
- Avoid root doubling on strong beats.

Directives

- Find the implied notes of bass.
- Select a stepwise progression.
- Choose notes that lead to notes in the next step.
- Use consonant skip to next note when no stepwise solution exists.

Fourth Stage: Unfigured Bass

Constraints

• Triads and Seventh Chords

• Fundamental Triad Inversion

• Seventh Chord Inversions

Directives

• Isolate important harmonic goals.

• Isolate secondary harmonic and melodic possibilities and select appropriate chords.

• Write out full harmony, satisfying the constraints for a good soprano line.

Fifth Stage: Soprano

Directives

• Analyze melody for: (a) degree succession, (b) metrical embellishments, (c) melodic progression types, (d) subgroups in the progression.

• Write minimal harmonization (I, IV, and V).

• Invert harmonies to avoid parallel fifths and octaves.

• Use secondary triads as substitutes for primary.

• Introduce 7 and inverted 7 chords.

• Work out voice-leading details as in stage 2.

Like the directives of the fourth stage, Forte's six directives (Forte 1979) for the harmonization of a given soprano build on the previous stages of learning.

Learning from Failure

Learning from failure occurs constantly in MUSE. At the local level of subgoal rule applications, MUSE prioritizes its production agendas in order to circumvent tried-and-false rules for the recurrences of similar contexts. The principles used to determine the failure of a rule include the previously mentioned constraints and directives for local voice leading, primary harmonic goals, secondary harmonic goals, etc. As failures occur, MUSE uses its RHS strengthen and weaken primitives to increase or decrease rule priorities as necessary. One of the motivating reasons to build MUSE was to determine the extent to which important techniques and procedures for tonal composition could be learned (or derived) from a limited set of first principles (Minsky 1975).

For each of the following stages, refer to the constraints and directives listed in the previous section.

First Stage: Soprano and Unfigured Bass   When MUSE can satisfy the first directive, it falls through to the next directive. If it cannot satisfy the first directive, MUSE first reverses the voices and then chooses alternate doublings. In each case, MUSE checks whether the directive is satisfied. If its condition is met, MUSE drops through to the next directive to find an even better solution; if its condition is not met, MUSE defaults to a satisfactory solution. If MUSE does not find alternative solutions for a given soprano and bass note in the directives, it simply moves on to the subsequent soprano and bass notes with its existing solution; if it does not find a successful solution according to its constraints, MUSE backtracks to alternative solutions for the previous soprano and bass notes.

At this elementary stage, MUSE already demonstrates the power of failure recognition. As it backtracks to the previous soprano and bass notes, MUSE pops its solution-history stack to find already tried solutions to the previous notes. When it finds a solution, MUSE immediately checks whether the solution has been tried. If it has been tried, MUSE discards it as a possibility and looks for another solution. This process continues until MUSE finds an acceptable solution or exhausts the available solutions. In the latter case, MUSE simply moves back one more step in the soprano and bass lists and begins the process again.

MUSE records all current solutions in working memory. As it concludes the search for a successful solution for a given soprano and bass note, MUSE pushes the final, successful solution of this list onto a stack of successful solutions. At the end of an exercise, MUSE also stores its entire solution history, along with mistakes, for reference in backtracking.

Already in the first stage MUSE has the capacity to learn, from its ground rules and its ability to recognize previous failures, the following doubling rules:

Major Triads: I, IV, V in major; V, VI in minor

- It is best to double the root.
- It is second best to double the fifth.

- It is third best to double the third.
- It is best to avoid the doubling of the third of V, i.e., the leading tone.

Minor Triads: II, III, VI in major; I, IV in minor
- It is possible to double any note.

Augmented Triads: III in minor
- It is best to double the third.
- It is second best to double the root.
- It is third best to double the fifth.

Diminished Triads: VII in major; II, VII in minor
- It is best to double the third.
- It is second best to double the fifth.
- It is third best to double the root.
- It is best to avoid doubling the root of VII.

KEYBOARD POSITION

Position of the Octave
- Alto is the fifth of the root; tenor is the third of the root.

Position of the Fifth
- Alto is the third of the root; tenor is the doubled root.
- Alto is the third of the root; tenor is the doubled fifth.

Position of the Third
- Alto is the doubled octave; tenor is the fifth of the root.
- Alto is the fifth of the root; Tenor is the doubled third.

Second Stage: Soprano and Figured Bass   MUSE uses all of the directives as productions subject to the collective constraints of the first and second stages. Thus, MUSE regards the figures given in the bass as situations that fire actions to add the implied notes.

It should be noted that MUSE reverts back to the directives prescribed for the first stage when it encounters root-position triads. Otherwise, MUSE applies the directives of the first and second stages to the figured bass and soprano.

As in the first stage, MUSE does an exhaustive search within the parameters defined by the figured bass before backtracking for another successful solution in the preceding bass and soprano notes. In addition to constraints learned to avoid the doubling of a seventh in a seventh chord or a suspended note in a suspension chord, doubling information learned by MUSE includes the following:

Sixth Chords

• It is best to double the third or the sixth.

• It is second best to double the bass.

• It is best to avoid doubling the bass in III6.

Dissonant Sixth Chords: VII6 in major and minor

• It is best to double the third or the octave.

• It is best to avoid doubling the sixth.

II6 in minor

• It is best to double the bass or the sixth.

• It is best to avoid doubling the third.

Major Sixth and Major Third or Minor Sixth and Minor Third

• Double either sixth or third.

Major Sixth and Minor Third

• Double third.

Third Stage: Figured Bass   To determine cadences, MUSE looks for any occurrences of concluding harmonies, that is, I or V. Since the juxtaposition of V and I determines an authentic cadence, MUSE just assumes such sequences as potential cadences. MUSE then checks whether other characteristics of cadences also apply for the newly noticed pair of primary harmonies. For example, a V-I pair at the end of a phrase is generally a cadence.

As it generates the soprano voice to given, figured bass underpinnings, MUSE builds its associations progressively from its generated two-note chord units. If a failure to satisfy the voice-leading constraints results in having to backtrack, MUSE expands its learning context to avoid any steps that have led to a failure. Since the concept of phrase is built into

MUSE's compositional progress in terms of the melodic satisfaction of constraints in COMPOSE-SOPRANO, MUSE also learns important aspects of voice leading in the event of most harmonic combinations.

Fourth Stage: Unfigured Bass Progressions defined implicitly in the above constraints are used by MUSE to determine the possible direction of a bass line. In the absence of bass figures, MUSE must supply its own; steps to be taken include (1) label some of the possible underlying harmonies for a bass by writing a minimal harmonization, for example, I, IV, or V, (2) label the available, intersecting secondary harmonies, and (3) write out the full harmony.

In the absence of soprano possibilities for a given bass and its underlying figure, MUSE tries all alternative figures to the bass and their soprano possibilities. When all possibilities have been exhausted, MUSE backtracks for a change in the previous notes. The failure context for MUSE's future reference includes as its pre- and postcontext information the bass notes respectively before and after the bass for which the information is learned.

These directives for harmonizing an unfigured bass clearly build on the knowledge of previous stages. MUSE, in fact, uses the voice-leading rules it has learned from the previous stage as part of its set of directives. It also uses the constraints given in the previous stages as part of its set of constraints.

Note that, as it learns progressively new patterns, MUSE develops more flexibility. This structural characteristic is implied by what MUSE assumes.

At the elementary first and second stages, MUSE remembers SITUATION-OUTCOME pairs for directives in relative hierarchies. Thus, when a directive is satisfied, MUSE immediately checks for a more highly ranked directive. Although MUSE incorporates this hierarchy into more advanced stages, the learned patterns of melodic construction in the third and fourth stages are remembered only in terms of their original contexts.

Fifth Stage: Soprano In this final stage, MUSE applies the full power of what it has learned in the previous stages. The learning at this stage, as in the other stages, occurs during the completion of harmonies. What MUSE learns in this stage as voice-leading rules and doubling techniques extends its previous knowledge.

TRACK COUNT: 6

........finding primary harmonic goals........
......finding secondary harmonic goals......
...............composing soprano.................

[Learning from the current failure of add-sop-third.]
<——————————————————————————>
CLASS III LEARNING: SOPRANO COMPLETION

........finding primary harmonic goals........
......finding secondary harmonic goals......

[STRENGTHEN PRODUCTION]
(figbase6-sixth (do add-newint 5) (state add-sop-sixth))

[ORDER NUMBER]
8

[NEW PRODUCTION STRENGTH ORDER]
[8 7 9 10 11 12 13]
[14 15 16 17 18 19 20]
[21 22 23 24 25 26 27]
[28 29 30 31 32 33 34]
[35 36 37 38 39 40 41]
[42 43]

.................composing soprano.................
............getting implied bass notes...........
...................getting new chord..................
.............completing inner voices.............
...................testing new notes.................

The current notes (sop alt ten bas) and track count: ((A4 E4 C4 C2) 6)

Completing Track Count: 6

Track Count: 6 ^

Figure 23.2
Example of Class III Learning: Soprano Completion

.................analyzing melody.................
...........getting minimal harmony............
......substituting secondary harmony......

[STRENGTHEN PRODUCTION]
(supertonic=>mediant (do sub-note 4) (state supertonic-implied-mediant))

[ORDER NUMBER]
11

[NEW PRODUCTION STRENGTH ORDER]
[11 18 15 13 14]

...................composing bass..................

[Learning from the current failure of supertonic-implied-mediant.]
<————————————————————>
CLASS IV LEARNING: BASS COMPLETION

...........getting minimal harmony............
......substituting secondary harmony.......

[STRENGTHEN PRODUCTION]
(exhaust-potential (state exhaust-present))

[ORDER NUMBER]
18

[NEW PRODUCTION STRENGTH ORDER]
[18 11 15 13 14]

...................composing bass..................

[EXPANDING LEARNING CONTEXT: (posthi0*kb-8 posoct0*kb-8)]

TRACK COUNT: 14

.................analyzing melody..................
............getting minimal harmony............
.......substituting secondary harmony.......

[STRENGTHEN PRODUCTION]
(exhaust-potential (state exhaust-present))

[ORDER NUMBER]
18

[NEW PRODUCTION STRENGTH ORDER]
[18 11 15 13 14]

...................composing bass..................

[EXPANDING LEARNING CONTEXT: (posoct0*kb-8)]

Track Count: 13^ 14^ 15^

TRACK COUNT: 13

...............analyzing melody................
.........getting minimal harmony...........

[STRENGTHEN PRODUCTION]
(dominant=>subdominant (do sub-note 5) (state dominant-implied-subdominant))

[ORDER NUMBER]
5

[NEW PRODUCTION STRENGTH ORDER]
[5 18 11 15 13 14]

.....substituting secondary harmony.....

[STRENGTHEN PRODUCTION]
(dominant=>submediant (do sub-note 9) (state dominant-implied-submediant))

[ORDER NUMBER]
4

[NEW PRODUCTION STRENGTH ORDER]
[4 5 18 11 15 13 14]

................composing bass.................
.........getting implied bass notes.........
...............getting new chord.................
............completing inner voices...:........
................testing new notes...............

The current notes (sop alt ten bas) and track count: ((G3 E3 B2 E2) 13)

Completing Track Count: 13

Figure 23.3
Example of Class IV Learning: Bass Completion

In all, there are three classes of failure-based learning in MUSE: (1) harmonic completion, (2) soprano completion, and (3) bass completion.

The context in memory for what is learned in each class derives from expandable pre- and postcontext blocks of a priori notes around the failure itself. Thus, for example, whereas the context for harmonic completion in MUSE includes both soprano and bass note lists, the context for bass completion in the fifth stage of chorale harmonization includes only soprano lists.

Learning from Examples

Learning from examples occurs in MUSE as it reviews an exercise that has satisfied the constraints and directives for one of MUSE's five levels. From patterns that have occurred at least three times in its note, action (subgoal), and high-level knowledge construct (goal), (e.g., FIND-SECONDARY-HARMONIC-GOALS) histories, MUSE propagates new rules by chunking, for each of the relevant patterns, a premise taken from the highest level antecedent for the consequent of the pattern with its conclusion. Thus, for instance, it generates a rule that for a bass descent of a third from chord A to chord B, one voice ascends by step from chord A to chord B and two voices maintain common tones from chord A to chord B, although MUSE also remembers the specific notes in the pattern; rather than generating the above rule for the specific notes of the pattern, say, a third descent from C3 to A2, however, MUSE creates it with the most general constructs available.

This represents MUSE's ability to generalize procedures. An example of a more general rule learned by MUSE than the above is that for a bass ascent by step from chord A to chord B in root position, all other voices descend; as MUSE learns from patterns in successful exercises, it expands its pre- and postcontext for new patterns.

Because many more surface patterns than deep, underlying compositional structures exist in tonal music (Lerdahl and Jackendoff 1983), hierarchies exist among musical procedures. Success-based learning in music must consider more than the voice-leading phenomena in MUSE's generalization of procedures.

Nevertheless, success-based learning for voice leading, MUSE's fourth class of learning (see three failure-based classes), represents an important, if small, component of what must be inferred in tonal composition. Success-based rules for voice-leading learned by MUSE include the following:

ROOT-POSITION TRIADS

Bass Ascent or Descent of a Major Second

- All voices move in contrary motion to the bass.

Bass Descent of a Third or Ascent of a Sixth

- Two voices maintain common tones.
- The bass of the second chord is doubled.

Bass Ascent of a Third or Descent of a Sixth

- Two voices maintain common tones.
- The fifth of the second chord is doubled.

Would you like to see the inferred interval pair (y or n)?   y

.........getting inferred rule............

[Learning from inference]
(fourth*ascent (ascend 1 2) (ascend 0 1))
(fifth*descent (ascend 1 2) (ascend 0 1))

<————————————————————>
CLASS I LEARNING: INFERENCE

INFERRED RULE:
If the bass ascends by a fourth from chord A to chord B:

* Two voices ascend by step from chord A to chord B.

* One voice maintains common tones from chord A to chord B.

[ABOVE RULE WAS INFERRED IN PREVIOUS EXERCISE]

INFERRED RULE:
If the bass descends by a fifth from chord A to chord B:

* Two voices ascend by step from chord A to chord B.

* One voice maintains common tones from chord A to chord B.

Figure 23.4
Example of Class I Learning: Rule Inference

Bass Ascent of a Fourth or Descent of a Fifth
- Two voices ascend a step to the second chord.
- One voice maintains common tones.

SIXTH CHORDS

Ascent of a Third or Descent of a Sixth from Root Position to Sixth Chord
- Two voices maintain common tones.
- Other voice leaps up a third.

Descent of a Third or Descent of a Sixth from Root Position to Sixth Chord
- One voice maintains common tones.
- The other two voices resolve outward by step.

SEVENTH CHORDS

- Resolve augmented intervals outward by step.
- Resolved diminished intervals inwards by step.
- Do not double the dissonant note.
- Resolve dissonant note by step.

Learning by Analogy

Learning by analogy occurs when the range of new information can amplify or extend older information. For any given domain of learning, analogy implies the transformation of old rules into new rules. Learning by analogy presupposes the ability to recognize similar situations.

Motivic development and the structural importance of variation in music make learning by analogy an obvious area for further study. While MUSE stores its goals, plans, and expectations in state histories and remembers structurally similar events in its solutions to chorale-harmonization exercises, it does NOT learn, in the strict sense of the term, by analogy. Such learning presupposes cross-contextual reference.

The domain of analogy in tonal composition extends from simple to complex, local to global—fugal retrograde to cadenza, balancing phrase to variation on a theme. A sample list would include the following:

Prime, retrograde, inversion, retrograde inversion

Theme and variation

Motive and diminution

Cross-composer/composition musical references

These and the myriad other possibilities for this list all represent areas for models for learning by analogy. It is perhaps not surprising that composing, which has its roots in extemporizing, should depend to such a great extent on analogy; one of the most famous vestiges of tonal spontaneity, the cadenza, has its thematic origin in its immediate environment; analogy plays a crucial role in other musical idioms as well-jazz, for instance.

Learning by Discovery

Learning by discovery, like learning by analogy, does not occur in MUSE. This form of learning requires the ability to generate completely new knowledge paradigms and to recognize important events. MUSE's learning, by combining separate actions into a single procedure for the context of a rule, remains within the purview of extensions of its original paradigms (Knuth 1973).

This area of learning remains one of the most mysterious, most elusive in tonal composition. How does a composer suddenly come up with a new idea? Does his idea merely pattern itself after another idea, by analogy, or does he actually discover something new?

Learning by discovery, of course, implies a set of criteria by which something discovered may be valued. A useful corollary of the above definition of discovery is island driving. The usual example is that you go to the grocery store for cereal and then "discover" that you also need milk. The musical parallels for discovery in machine models probably include random or quasi- random thematic generation to duplicate the apparently nondeterministic outside influence in human discovery.

Summary

In its five stages of composition, MUSE assimilates some of the standard rules of voice leading included in traditional pedagogies for tonal music, for example, that of C. P. E. Bach (Bach 1949). After it has learned a new rule, MUSE remembers the premise for the rule; by applying rules when their premises recur, MUSE displays procedure generalization. Failure-based learning, also known as learning by skill refinement (Riesbeck 1981), occurs, of course, as agenda reprioritization for production firing. By integrating analysis into its process of composing elementary tonal music through its learning from both successful and unsuccessful solutions, MUSE combines analysis with composition. Its architecture, that of a typical production rule system, allows MUSE to add information in a modular way, as either new or reordered production rules.

It seems that models for learning by analogy and learning by discovery could improve upon the perfomance of MUSE. Clear and useful parallels exist, for example, to narrative models of analogy (Dyer 1983). It became increasingly clear throughout the experience of finding musical solutions with MUSE that the degree to which the environment of chorale exercises is inherently controlled. For the harmony exercises done by MUSE, there was often a "best" answer based on a hierarchy of priorities: (1) for the alto and tenor, to make the voice leading as smooth as possible, that is, to use the smallest possible interval between notes in the same voice and to maintain common tones whenever possible; (2) for the soprano, to use stepwise motion when possible, to avoid repeating a note more than twice, to maintain one high point, and so on; (3) for the bass, to use primary harmonies at the cadences and to subsitute secondary harmonies in between.

Although the solutions to such controlled exercises undoubtedly give a good framework from which to learn inferentially the traditional rules of voice leading, the artistry of music, that is, the choosing among equally acceptable solutions for a given affect or a desired result, depends on information external to voice-leading information learned by MUSE. Why, for instance, do multiple harmonizations usually exist for any chorale?

References

Bach, C. P. E. 1949. *Essay on the True Art of Playing Keyboard Instruments*. Trans. by William J. Mitchell. New York: Norton.

Dyer, Michael. 1983. *In-Depth Understanding*. Cambridge, Mass.: The MIT Press.

Forte, Allen. 1979. *Tonal Harmony in Concept and Practise*. New York: Holt, Rinehart, and Winston.

Knuth, Donald E. 1973. *The art of computer programming vol. 3: Sorting and Searching*. Reading, Mass.: Addison-Wesley.

Lerdahl, Fred, and Jackendoff, Ray. 1983. *A Generative Theory of Tonal Music*. Cambridge, Mass.: The MIT Press.

Minsky, Marvin. 1975. "A Framework for Representing Knowledge." in The *Psychology of Computer Vision*, ed. Patrick Winston. New York: McGraw-Hill.

Riesbeck, Christopher K. 1981. "Failure-Driven Reminding for Incremental Learning." *Proceedings of the Seventh International Joint Conference on Artificial Intelligence*, Vancouver.

Schwanauer, Stephan. 1986. *MUSE: A Learning System for Tonal Composition*. Ph.D. diss. Yale University.

Acknowledgment

The understanding and support of both Yale's Music and Computer Science departments were indispensable for the completion of this interdisciplinary Ph.D.

Appendix   Musical Dice Game

Wolfgang Amadeus Mozart

An Introduction to Composing Waltzes with Two Dice

Game Introduction

The game requires the following:

- two dice
- the number tablets
- the note section, in which you see the individual measures with numbers
- a notebook

The roman numerals over the eight columns of both number tables give the eight measures of both waltz sections; the arabic numbers in the individual columns (the cell numbers), the numbers of the measures of the note section; and the numbers 2–12 before the two tables (the row numbers), the possible outcomes with two dice.

The game begins. If, for example, the first toss yields a 10, then you search in the first column next to the 10 for the number of the measure—in this case 98. Then you toss for the second measure; if you obtain, for example, a 6, then you find the measure number 74 in the second column, and so on. The eighth measure pertains equally for the repetition: you write the given notes under |1| and for the repetition |2|. Toss in a similar manner for the measure sections of the second part of the waltz. If you want a longer waltz, start again from the beginning.

Copyright, 1956, B. Schott's Sohne, Mainz, and reproduced by permission.

Zahlentafel

1. Walzerteil

	I	II	III	IV	V	VI	VII	VIII
2	96	22	141	41	105	122	11	30
3	32	6	128	63	146	46	134	81
4	69	95	158	13	158	55	110	24
5	40	17	113	85	161	2	159	100
6	148	74	163	45	80	97	36	107
7	104	157	27	167	154	68	118	91
8	152	60	171	53	99	133	21	127
9	119	84	114	50	140	86	169	94
10	98	142	42	156	75	129	62	123
11	3	87	165	61	135	47	147	33
12	54	130	10	103	28	37	106	5

2. Walzerteil

	I	II	III	IV	V	VI	VII	VIII
2	70	121	26	9	112	49	109	14
3	117	39	126	56	174	18	116	83
4	66	139	15	132	73	58	145	79
5	90	176	7	34	67	160	52	170
6	25	143	64	125	76	136	1	93
7	138	71	150	29	101	162	23	151
8	16	155	57	175	43	168	89	172
9	120	88	48	166	51	115	72	111
10	65	77	19	82	137	38	149	8
11	102	4	31	164	144	59	173	78
12	35	20	108	92	12	124	44	131

Figure A.1

Notentafel

Figure A.2

Figure A.3
Copyright 1957 by New Music Edition, and reproduced by permission.

Figure A.4

Figure A.5

Index